MORE THAN JUST GAMES

Canada and the 1936 Olympics

D1507613

Held in Germany, the 1936 Olympic Games sparked international controversy. Should athletes and nations boycott the games to protest the Nazi regime? *More than Just Games* is the story of the Canadian Olympic officials and promoters who were convinced that national unity and pride demanded that Canadian athletes compete in the Olympics without regard for politics. It is the story of those Canadian athletes, mostly young and far more focused on sport than politics, who were eager to make family, friends, and country proud of their efforts on Canada's behalf. And, finally, it is the story of those Canadians who led an unsuccessful campaign to boycott the Olympics and deny Nazi Germany the propaganda coup of serving as an Olympic host.

Written by two noted historians of Canadian Jewish history, Richard Menkis and Harold Troper, *More than Just Games* brings to life the collision of politics, patriotism, and the passion of sport on the eve of the Second World War.

RICHARD MENKIS is an associate professor in the Departments of History and Classical, Near Eastern, and Religious Studies at the University of British Columbia. He is co-editor with Norman Ravvin of the *Canadian Jewish Studies Reader*.

HAROLD TROPER is professor at the Ontario Institute for Studies in Education at the University of Toronto. The co-author of *None Is Too Many: Canada and the Jews* (with Irving Abella), his most recent book is *The Defining Decade: Identity, Politics, and the Canadian Jewish Community in the 1960s*.

More than Just Games

Canada and the 1936 Olympics

RICHARD MENKIS AND HAROLD TROPER

UNIVERSITY OF TORONTO PRESS
Toronto Buffalo London

© University of Toronto Press 2015
Toronto Buffalo London
www.utppublishing.com
Printed in the U.S.A.

ISBN 978-1-4426-4954-5 (cloth)
ISBN 978-1-4426-2690-4 (paper)

∞

Printed on acid-free paper

Library and Archives Canada Cataloguing in Publication

Menkis, Richard, author
More than just games : Canada and the 1936 Olympics /
Richard Menkis and Harold Troper.

Includes bibliographical references and index.
ISBN 978-1-4426-4954-5 (bound)   ISBN 978-1-4426-2690-4 (pbk.)

1. Olympic Games (11th : 1936 : Berlin, Germany).   2. Olympics –
Participation, Canadian.   3. Olympics – Political aspects – Canada.
4. Olympics – Social aspects – Canada.   5. Olympic athletes – Canada.
I. Troper, Harold, 1942–, author   II. Title.

GV722.1936M45 2015   796.4'8   C2015-900633-3

University of Toronto Press acknowledges the financial assistance to its
publishing program of the Canada Council for the Arts and the Ontario
Arts Council, an agency of the Government of Ontario.

 Canada Council **Conseil des Arts**
for the Arts **du Canada**

ONTARIO ARTS COUNCIL
CONSEIL DES ARTS DE L'ONTARIO
an Ontario government agency
un organisme du gouvernement de l'Ontario

University of Toronto Press acknowledges the financial support of the
Government of Canada through the Canada Book Fund for its publishing
activities.

Contents

Illustrations follow page 124

Preface

Another Olympiad and more controversy. As we write this preface to a book about Canadian participation in the notorious 1936 German Olympics Games, the Sochi Winter Olympics of 2014 are just over, and it is almost certain that Sochi will join the German Olympics as among the most discussed Olympic Games of the modern era. And with good reason: even before the Games in Sochi began, Western media was spilling huge quantities of ink reporting on the estimated $51-billion price tag for the Sochi Olympics, by far the most expensive Olympics in history. Security was also an issue. Knowing that the eyes of the world were on Russia, one month before the opening ceremonies, a jihadist group in Dagestan – the epicentre of an Islamic insurgence against Russian rule that has enflamed the Caucasus – claimed responsibility for an attack by suicide bombers in Volgograd. They killed thirty-four people, and promised to attack Sochi during the Games.

But what most soured enthusiasm for the coming Games in the months leading up to the opening of the Winter Olympics was controversy about the human rights record of the Olympic host country. Even as Russia was preparing to welcome the world to Sochi, the Russian legislature passed several anti-gay laws. On 11 June 2013, President Putin signed a bill that imposed fines or even prison terms on Russian residents who provide information to minors concerning the lesbian, gay, bisexual, and transgender (LBGT) community, in effect, many argued, criminalizing homosexuality in Russia without explicitly saying so. With street assaults of gays common, Russia also enacted another law that expressly prohibited same-sex couples, including same-sex couples abroad, from adopting Russian children. Gay and human rights advocates denounced these Russian laws as no less than state licensing of homophobia.

Russian homophobia also cast a shadow across planning for the athletes' village in Sochi. Unlike the Olympic Games in Vancouver and London, Russian officials rejected the inclusion of any kind of Olympic Pride House in Sochi, a gay-friendly site where gay Olympic athletes and their supporters might gather during the Games. Against this homophobic backdrop, some questioned whether gay athletes, officials, and Olympic visitors would be safe in Sochi. Human rights and LGBT activists protested that, by allowing a country that so openly and brazenly stigmatized homosexuality to stage the Olympic Games, the International Olympic Committee (IOC) and its member countries were, in effect, condoning Russian homophobia. LGBT activists and their supporters thus called on IOC member countries to boycott the Sochi Games. Failing that, they urged individual Olympic athletes, gay and straight alike, to stand up and be counted in the struggle against anti-gay discrimination in Russia by refusing to attend the Olympics in Sochi.

For its part, the IOC, convinced that the boycott campaign had no traction among IOC member countries, was still concerned the boycott campaign might cut into public enthusiasm for the Games, especially in Western countries, and cause Olympic corporate sponsors to reconsider their support. If the IOC was not prepared to publicly address the issue of gay rights in the Olympic host country, regarded by Russia as a domestic matter, the IOC reassured Olympic athletes and visitors, gay and straight, that they had nothing to fear by coming to Sochi. Typical was an IOC spokesperson who, skirting any direct reference to Russian homophobia, insisted that the Olympic Charter clearly states that "any form of discrimination with regard to a country or a person on grounds of race, religion, politics, gender or otherwise is incompatible with belonging to the Olympic Movement."[1] The Games, she promised, would be free of discrimination, presumably including discrimination against gays. But, some warned, it was Russian law not the Olympic Charter that would apply in Sochi.

In fairness, it should also be noted that the LGBT community did not stand united behind the call for a Russian Olympic boycott. While there were those who regarded it unacceptable that athletes, gay or straight, should participate in any Olympics in a country where homophobia is public policy, there were also those who spoke out in favour of participation in the Sochi Games and decried the boycott campaign as wrong-minded. Boycott Russia? Yes. Refuse to purchase Russian goods and services? Yes. But it was also important to support the Olympics as a gay-friendly international event in a sadly not yet gay-friendly world. And what about those athletes, gay and straight, who had invested time, energy, and resources in preparing for the Games? How would the rights of gays in Russia, or anywhere else for that matter, be advanced by denying gay athletes the opportunity to compete in Sochi? They would not. On the other hand, would not successfully competing and even winning medals in Sochi as hundreds of millions of viewers around the world watched on television be a far more appropriate and in-your-face rebuttal of Russian homophobia than any Olympic boycott? In the end, some world leaders refused to attend, but not one IOC member country supported the boycott. And although a handful of athletes from around the world refused to compete in Sochi, an overwhelming majority of athletes, gay and straight, elected to compete in Sochi.

But the events in Russia still beg the question: What exactly is the relationship of the Olympics to questions of human rights and dignity? Scholar and IOC critic John Hoberman argues that it is a mistake to assume the IOC harbours a human rights agenda. The IOC is not a human rights organization; it is an international athletic and sporting enterprise and, as such, one of its overarching priorities is to ensure as much as possible that all countries of the world gather to compete under the five rings of the Olympic flag. By wedding itself to international inclusiveness, Hoberman argues, the IOC embraces what he terms "amoral universalism." According to Hoberman, ensuring that all countries are equally welcome to send athletes to compete in the Olympic Games means the IOC avoids making moral judgments about the human rights record of IOC member countries. Claiming that sport and athleticism must be kept separate from politics and independent of internal affairs of member countries, the IOC is able to accommodate reprehensible political regimes, and their policies and practices. "What this has meant in practice," according to Hoberman, "is that the IOC has turned a blind eye to any sort of political crime committed by a member of the Olympic movement."[2]

In Nazi Germany in 1936, it meant turning a blind eye to state-imposed racism and antisemitism. With Sochi, it was Russian homophobia. Thus, in spite of an Olympic Charter that speaks to fellowship through friendly competition on the sport field, in practice, the IOC maintains a low human rights bar, low enough for all countries to qualify. To do otherwise, to make strict adherence to the Olympic Charter a yardstick for Olympic participation, would force many countries to either bring their domestic human rights policies into conformity with principle 6 of the Olympic Charter, banning discrimination on "grounds of race, religion, politics, gender or otherwise," or withdraw from Olympic competition. Forced to make that choice, there can be little doubt but that many countries would withdraw from Olympic competition, cutting the legs out from under the IOC's claim to be internationally inclusive. Thus, so long as ensuring that all countries feel comfortable competing in the Olympic Games remains an IOC priority, Hoberman contends, human rights concerns will take second place.

In retrospect, it should also come as no surprise that calls for a boycott of the Sochi Olympic Games fell on deaf ears, as the IOC was sure they would. No Olympic boycott campaign – and there have been a number of them – succeeded unless the boycott call was initiated or acceded to by the government of an IOC Olympic member country. But that does not mean that Olympic Games have not been the focus of political protest. In 1968, protests broke out in Mexico City in part to protest corruption and spending overruns in building the Olympic infrastructure that many felt came at the expense of Mexico's poor. A few weeks before the Olympic opening, thousands gathered in Mexico City's Plaza de las Tres Culturas demanding civil and democratic reform, not Games. One of the protest banners proclaimed, "We don't want Olympics, we want revolution!" Determined that the Mexico City Olympics not be marred by street-level protest, the Mexican government ordered the Plaza de las Tres Culturas cleared. The Mexican army surrounded the plaza and, without warning, opened fire into the crowd. It is estimated that 267 were killed and more than 1,000 were wounded. Many more were arrested. The Games went on.

The Mexico City Olympics were preceded by death; four years later, in 1972, death stalked the Munich Olympic village when eleven Israeli athletes were taken hostage by Palestinian "Black September" terrorists. The terrorists murdered two of their captives; then, in a failed rescue attempt, the remaining nine Israeli captives were killed alongside three of their captors. Controversy surrounding the Munich murders flared again at the 2012 London Olympics, the fortieth anniversary of the Munich slayings, when the IOC denied a request from the Israeli Olympic Committee, supported by a number of IOC member countries, including Canada, that a minute of silence in memory of the eleven slain Israeli team members be observed as part of the London Olympic opening ceremony. Some speculate the IOC refused the Israeli request for fear of antagonizing Arab Olympic member countries. Angered by the IOC's rebuff, the Israeli Olympic Committee, the Israeli Embassy, and the London Jewish community organized a memorial event at London's medieval Guildhall, attended by the British prime minister and sympathetic world dignitaries.

Olympic Games have also proven occasion for head-on collisions over race. In 1962, after a coalition of African countries stated they would refuse to participate in the Olympics Games if South Africa was invited to send a team, the apartheid regime was banished. The ban was only lifted in 1992 after apartheid was officially ended. Just as race has pitted country against country, race has also been divisive of Olympic team unity. At the 1968 Mexico City Olympics, two medal-winning Black athletes were expelled from the American team after raising their fists in a "Black Power" salute during the playing of the American national anthem.

While the IOC claims to hold itself out to be above and outside the many international disputes that engage its member countries, the Olympics has not been immune from these disputes. As in the case of South Africa, IOC member countries have forfeited medal opportunities, or even withdrawn from Olympic competition, because they refused to compete against the country with which they were in dispute. During some Olympic Games, different countries have withdrawn from competition for different reasons. Lichtenstein, the Netherlands, Spain, and Sweden stayed away from the 1956 Melbourne Olympics in protest of the Soviet invasion of Hungary. Egypt, Lebanon, and Iraq withdrew teams from the same Games to protest the Suez War, while the People's Republic of China refused to participate so long as the IOC allowed the Republic of China (Taiwan) to compete. During 1976, a New Zealand rugby team staged a three-month tour of apartheid South Africa, much to the displeasure of the African states. As a show of disapproval at the inclusion of New Zealand in the Montreal Olympic Games later that year, twenty-six mostly African countries refused to participate. Egypt at first sent a team to Montreal but, after competing for three days, the team packed its bags and withdrew in solidarity with the African protest. At the same Games, Canadian immigration officials stirred up controversy of their own. The team from the Republic of China (Taiwan), with which Canada had no diplomatic relations, was at first refused entry into Canada. The team was then given permission to enter Canada if it agreed to compete not as "the Republic of China" but as "Taiwan" instead. The Taiwanese declared the proposed compromise unacceptable and withdrew.

Arguably the most damaging tit-for-tat Olympic boycott exchange pitted the West against the Soviet Bloc. In 1980, in the wake of the 1979 Soviet invasion of Afghanistan, American president Jimmy Carter called upon the American Olympic Committee to deny Moscow the prestige that comes from being an Olympic host and boycott the 1980 Olympic Games in Moscow. Although the Olympic Charter calls upon all national Olympic Committees to "resist all pressures of any kind whatsoever, whether of a political, religious or economic nature," there was no saying "no" to the American president. The American Olympic Committee announced it would not attend the Games in Moscow. Another sixty-two national Olympic teams, including West Germany, Japan, and Canada – but oddly, not the British team – joined the boycott. In the end, eighty nations, mostly the Soviet Bloc and non-aligned nations, assembled in Moscow for the Games. Without a much-anticipated American-Soviet medal race, the Moscow Games lacked drama.

As a consolation prize to those athletes denied the opportunity to compete in Moscow, the Americans hurriedly organized an alternative athletic competition staged at the University of Pennsylvania in Philadelphia. The event was officially titled the Liberty Bell Classic and unofficially the Olympic Boycott Games. The Liberty Bell Classic opened three days before the opening of the Moscow Games. Canada was among the twenty-nine countries that participated in the event and, like the Moscow Games, it generated little excitement.

The next Summer Olympics were scheduled for Los Angeles in 1984. Unwilling to forgive or forget the American-initiated boycott of the Moscow Olympic Games four years earlier, the Soviet Union and fourteen Soviet Bloc allies boycotted the Los Angeles Olympics. While few doubted that the Soviet move was simple payback for the American-led boycott of Moscow, the official Soviet reason given for absenting themselves from Los Angeles was that the United States was incapable of providing Soviet team members adequate security. (Surprisingly, the People's Republic of China was not among the boycotters. In 1984, China returned to the Olympic fold after a thirty-two year absence.) Reminiscent of the Liberty Bell Classic of four years earlier, the Soviet Union staged its own counter-Olympics, the Friendship Games, for those athletes and teams absenting themselves from the Los Angeles Olympics. Sympathetic athletes from around the world were also invited to participate. The Soviet Union unsurprisingly dominated the winners' podium.

The Moscow and Los Angeles Olympics boycotts can be said to be the exceptions. As a general rule, boycott campaign or no boycott campaign, IOC member countries participate in an Olympics unless instructed not to do so by government. Knowing this, why do stakeholder groups organize Olympic boycott campaigns? In part, because they feel they cannot do less. And even if their campaign will not prevent the Olympics from going ahead, does that mean their boycott campaign is a failure? Not necessarily. Even if they do not succeed in derailing the Games, they afford an opportunity to expose a wrong, focus media attention on their cause, embarrass the offender, and perhaps – just perhaps – force a change in national policy or behaviour. The LGBT call for a boycott of the 2014 Sochi Winter Olympics can be said to fall into that category. So too an abortive campaign for an international boycott of the 2008 Summer Olympics in Beijing allowed proponents of an independent Tibet to ally with others intent on drawing world attention to ongoing human rights abuses in post-Tiananmen-Square China. If the call for an international boycott of Beijing did not succeed, boycott proponents could take satisfaction at having drawn world attention to their cause, even if only momentarily.

Looking back, however, the grandfather of all international Olympic boycott campaigns, and among the most viscerally charged of all boycott Olympic campaigns, targeted the 1936 Winter and Summer Olympic Games, both held in Nazi Germany. *More than Just Games* is a history of Canadian preparations for, and participation in, the 1936 Olympics. It is the story of Canadian Olympic officials and promoters who were convinced that national unity and pride demanded that the best of Canadian athletes compete in the Olympics. It is the story of those Canadian athletes, mostly young and far more focused on sport than politics, who wanted nothing so much as to make family, friends, and country proud of their efforts on Canada's behalf. And finally, it is the story of those Canadians so horror-driven by naked Nazi racism, barbarism, and raw brutality that they felt compelled to deny Hitler the propaganda bonanza they feared would flow from Nazi Germany serving as the Olympic host. In the end, no argument could shake the determination of supporters of the Olympics from ensuring that young Canadians, decked out in crimson blazers and carrying the Canadian ensign flag, would march into the Winter Olympic Stadium in Garmisch-Partenkirchen in February 1936, and into the Summer Olympic Stadium in Berlin six months later.

Acknowledgments

There are two names on the cover of this book, but we know full well that this book would not have come into being without the support of many others. Principal among them are the former director of the Vancouver Holocaust Education Centre (VHEC), Frieda Miller, and current director Nina Krieger. With the 2010 the Winter Olympic Games planned for Vancouver, they sensed a unique teaching moment and approached us about mounting a public exhibition exploring Canadian participation in the notorious 1936 Olympic Games held in Nazi Germany. What the Centre needed to know was whether there was a Canadian story to be told and whether there were enough accessible photographs and artefacts to mount an exhibition. The answer to both questions was 'yes.' And, enthusiastic about the topic, we agreed to work pro bono piecing together the relatively unknown story of Canadian involvement in the Nazi Olympics and helping gather documentary and other materials with which to mount an exhibition. The exhibition opened several months in advance of the Vancouver Games. During the better part of a year it was viewed by thousands of visitors, including many school groups, and received much media attention.

After the exhibition closed we decided the story of Canadian participation in the Nazi Olympics was both important enough and thought provoking enough to merit a book. Independent of the Centre, we spent much of the next two years conducting in-depth research into previously unknown details of Canadian involvement with the 1936 Games and, in the process, unearthed a treasure trove of manuscript and other material revealing of our topic. Now that our book is finally complete, we wish to acknowledge a debt of gratitude to the VHEC for inspiring our effort and for graciously permitting us access to the documentary materials gathered for the Centre's exhibition. We also honour the support by titling our book *More than Just Games*, the same title given the VHEC's exhibition. The title for the Centre's exhibition was originally suggested by Jonathan Friedrichs and Shannon Moore, and we are beholden to them for allowing us to reuse this title for our book. We would like to thank the other staff at the VHEC, especially Alia Dharssi, Rome Fox, and Kazuko Kusumoto. The support of the VHEC has continued to the final stages of this project, with the generous support of a publication grant from the Morris & Yosef Wosk Family Publishing Fund of the Vancouver Holocaust Education Centre.

Historical research can be a long, lonely, and tedious enterprise. Our labours were made less so thanks to the encouragement and assistance we received from many along the way. We are especially grateful to all those guardians of the historical record who facilitated our collection of documentary material. They include: Ava Block-Super and Stan Carbone (Jewish Historical Society of Western Canada, Winnipeg); Amy Bowring and Cindy Brett (Dance Collection Danse Archives, Toronto); Michael Cole, Howard Roger, and Sheila Smalkin, (Holy Blossom Archives, Toronto); Dana Herman, Kevin Proffitt, and Gary Zola (American Jewish Archives, Cincinnati); Shannon Hodge and Eiran Harris (Archives of the Jewish Public Library, Montreal); Tim Hutchinson (University of Saskatchewan Archives, Saskatoon); Gail Malmgreen and Erika D. Gottfried, (Tamiment Library/Robert F. Wagner Labor Archives, New York University); Myron Momryk (Library and Archives Canada, emeritus); Eddie Paul (Jewish Public Library, Montreal); Janice Rosen and Hélène Vallée (Canadian Jewish Congress Charities Committee National Archives, Montreal); Noah Shenker (McMaster University Library, Hamilton); Ellen Scheinberg and George Whartan, (Ontario Jewish Archives, Toronto); and Jennifer Yuhasz and Marcy Babins (Jewish Museum and Archives of British Columbia, Vancouver). Our data gathering was also facilitated by hands-on research assistance from Hanno Balz, Elizabeth Bennett, Dana Lori Chalmers, Jeffrey Kamara, Steven Lapidus, Birga U Meyer, Carlos Parra, Melanie Pothier and John Henry Geoghegan, Eniko Pittner, Manori Ravindran, and Robin Studniberg. Some people kindly shared their own research into the Olympics, including Maynard Kirkpatrick, who also drew our attention to some remarkable film footage at the Provincial Archives of British Columbia, and Allana Lindgren, who is working on the history of dance in Canada, including the performances at the Berlin Olympics.

We were only able to interview two people with lived experience of the Nazi Olympic era – John Derry and Lukin Robinson. Sadly, Eva Dawes, 1932 Olympic bronze medal winner for Canada and principled boycotter of the 1936 Games, died in an English nursing home just few days before we were scheduled to interview her. But we learned much from family members who offered us stories as well as personal documents and photos related to the Nazi Olympics, including Marg Archibald, David Halton, Warren Meretsky, Stuart Mulqueen, Arlene Pearly Rae, Louis Royle, Sid Tafler, Anna Yanovksy, and Belle Weisman. David Halton's biography of his remarkable father, Matthew, appeared in print well after this manuscript was submitted, but we greatly appreciated David's wholehearted support of this book. We also value the insight and guidance into the Nazi era and the place of the 1936 Olympics in Canadian history offered us by Doris Bergen, Chris Friedrichs, Faith Jones, Bruce Kidd, David Levine, Cyril Levitt, Ian McKay, Paula Draper, Barb Schober. Hermann Simon, and Jerry Tulchinsky.

Our research agenda demanded we spend time, often more time than we wanted, away from home. We are grateful to those whose cordial hospitality made our time on the road pass more enjoyably. Our thanks go to Pierre Anctil and Chantal Ringuet, Benjamin M. Baader, Gail and Jeremy Cohen, Adina and Yaacov Dayan, Rabbi Steven Garten and Lisa Hans, Norma and Howard Joseph; Barbara and Eric Menkis, Karen and Alan Menkis, Naomi and Eli Nahmias, Norm Ravvin and Shelley Butler, Ira and Sandy Robinson, Judy Young and Arthur Drache, Rachelle and the late Willy Moll, Miriam and Ralph Troper, Phyllis Zelkowitz and Morton Weinfeld, Jane Davidson, and Adele Reinhartz and Barry Walfish.

While we were still drafting our manuscript, we had occasion to address a number of groups about Canadian involvement in the Nazi Olympics. Not only were we encouraged by the interest shown in our topic but we were also pleased by the constructive feedback we received. In this regard appreciate the lecture opportunities afforded by the Association for Canadian Jewish Studies, the Association for Jewish Studies, Rabbi Eddie Goldfarb of Holy Blossom Temple, Ira Schweitzer of Temple Sinai, Mira Goldfarb of Holocaust Education Week in Toronto, Ruth Klein and Tema Smith of the National Taskforce on Holocaust Education, Remembrance and Research, The Emily Carr University of Art and Design, Elisabeth Duckworth and Dennis Oomen of the Kamloops Museum and Archives, and Avia Moore of Klezkanada.

We are also grateful to colleagues in our home departments at the University of British Columbia (Richard is cross-appointed to the

Department of Classical, Near Eastern and Religious Studies and the Department of History) and the University of Toronto (where Harold is in the Department of Curriculum, Teaching and Learning) for nurturing an environment so conducive to scholarly research. We are also indebted to the computer *mavens* in the OISE Education Commons who were considerate enough not to laugh aloud when time and again confronted by our techno-ignorance. And our special thanks goes to Danny Cavanagh, Cheryl Clarke, Christine Dawson, Andra McKay, and the late Janice McPherson for good-naturedly sharing their mastery of the photocopier, scanner and fax machine. Where would our work be without them? Probably jammed in a machine somewhere.

We are equally beholden to go the staff of the University of Toronto Press, especially Len Husband, who encouraged this book from its earliest beginnings, and Frances Mundy who steered our volume through to publication. And our thanks go to Beth McAuley and Melissa MacAulay for their careful copy editing of the manuscript and to our good friend, Andrea Knight, for preparing the index for this volume – a task the authors were only too happy to avoid. Thanks also to our literary agent, Bev Slopen, who negotiated our contract.

This list of acknowledgements would be nowhere near complete without acknowledging the support received from Cathy Lace, the late Ron Silvers, Lawrence and Trudy Chernin, Joan and Hy Eiley, Jerry and Millie Lev, Jerry and Linda Silver, Sharon Harris and Jay Rahn and the Tuesday Lunch Gang, Richard's *chavuraniks*, and many more.

No words can adequately express our appreciation of our families – the Menkis /Best clan – Cathie, Aviva, and Lavi— and the Troper gang – Eydie, Sarah, Lucy, Simon, and Maude and Carla, Kevin, Jonah, Ella. Their love, understanding and emotional support remain a constant comfort.

Abbreviations

Organizations

AAU	[American] Amateur Athletic Union
AAUC	Amateur Athletic Union of Canada
AO	Auslandsorganisation der NSDAP
AOC	American Olympic Committee
CAHA	Canadian Amateur Hockey Association
CASA	Canadian Amateur Ski Association
CASwA	Canadian Amateur Swim Association
CCF	Co-operative Commonwealth Federation
CDLC	Canadian Labour Defence League
CJC	Canadian Jewish Congress
CLAWF	Canadian League against War and Fascism
COC	Canadian Olympic Committee
CPC	Communist Party of Canada
ILP	Independent Labour Party
IOC	International Olympic Committee
JLC	Jewish Labor Committee
JWB	Jewish Welfare Board
LIHG	Ligue Internationale de Hockey sur Glace
OAAU	Ontario Branch, Amateur Athletic Union
RCMP	Royal Canadian Mounted Police
TLCC	Trades and Labour Congress of Canada
WSA	Workers' Sports Association
YMHA	Young Men's Hebrew Association

Archives

AJA	American Jewish Archives (Cincinnati)
BA	Bundesarchiv (Berlin)
CJCNA	Canadian Jewish Congress Charities Committee National Archives (Montreal)
CVA	City of Vancouver Archives
DCDA	Dance Collection Danse Archives (Toronto)
JPLA	Jewish Public Library Archives (Montreal)
LAC	Library and Archives Canada (Ottawa)
McMU	McMaster University Library (Hamilton)
OJA	Ontario Jewish Archives (Toronto)
USaskA	University of Saskatchewan Archives (Saskatoon)
UWOA	University of Western Ontario Archives (London, Ontario)

MORE THAN JUST GAMES

Canada and the 1936 Olympics

Chapter One

Sport, Society, and Politics

Spring weather in Barcelona is often unpredictable. One day can be cool and wet, the next day sunny and warm, encouraging locals to fill the cafés or stroll along the city's beachfront promenade. Late April 1931 was no exception. Those arriving for the annual meeting of the International Olympic Committee (IOC) would have done well to pack judiciously. No telling what one might be called upon to wear. But James Merrick and Sir George McLaren Brown, the two Canadian members of the IOC, were likely less concerned with the unpredictability of the local weather than with the unpredictability of the local political situation. During the year preceding the long-planned IOC meeting in Barcelona, Spain lurched from one crisis to another. As the Great Depression of the 1930s took hold, General Primo de Rivera's authoritarian but moderately reform-minded national government appeared paralysed. Supported by Spanish King Alfonso XIII, but increasingly pressured by the left to reign in the power of the economically privileged, the government vacillated, fearful of a backlash from the entrenched Spanish military elite, Church leadership, and members of the conservative landed aristocracy. As popular street-level support for the government crumbled, a disenchanted middle class, together with more progressive elements within the Spanish nobility and dissidents among middle-ranking military officers, joined the chorus of those denouncing the de Rivera regime for standing in the way of essential and overdue reform. As the call for change grew louder, Barcelona – Spain's second largest city and a Catalan nationalist hotbed – emerged as a centre of anti-de Rivera agitation.[1]

No longer able to govern, de Rivera stepped down. The king asked General Damaso Berenguer, a de Rivera opponent, to form a new government, but it was too late. As Spain's economic woes worsened,

Berenguer failed to win popular support for his promised program of gradual fiscal and democratic reform. Just two weeks before the IOC's Barcelona meetings were scheduled to begin, hotly contested municipal elections were held across Spain. Almost everywhere, anti-royalist and anti-clerical republican candidates swept to power. This republican victory was widely seen as a stinging rebuke of both the national government in Madrid and the Spanish monarchy, and a harbinger of more to come. Fearing an imminent anti-royalist uprising and accepting that the Spanish military could not be counted on to defend his throne, the king, isolated and vulnerable, packed his bags and fled into exile.

Many were convinced the Spanish military, abhorring a political vacuum, would seize power. They were wrong. As the military stood by, a loose coalition of former opposition groups organized a fragile provisional government and, on 14 April 1931, proclaimed the Second Spanish Republic. The new government pledged to build a modern and secular Spain. A constitutional congress was convened with the mandate of drafting a new democratic constitution for Spain.

But not everyone, including some who opposed the previous government, lined up in support of the new government in Madrid. Across Spain, dissidents of every stripe took to the streets to press their own particularist agenda. Clashes between rival political factions, or with the police, were common. Adding to the political unrest, a group of Catalan nationalists in Barcelona, sensing their moment, challenged the fledging Spanish central government in Madrid by declaring an independent republic. Spain appeared to be on the verge of pulling itself apart.

The IOC Decides on the 1936 Olympics

The Spanish political dust was nowhere near settled when, barely two weeks into the new government, members of the IOC gathered in the palatial Barcelona Town Hall in Plaça Sant Jaume on the morning of 25 April 1931 to begin their annual meeting. Certainly the IOC was not immune to the politics of the time. Whatever its lofty ideals, the IOC's working agenda demanded the organization engage with a world not always of its liking. The IOC, the governing body of the modern Olympic Games, was founded in 1894 by Pierre de Coubertin. Officially a non-governmental organization, the IOC's assigned duties include making or revising the rules under which Olympic Games are organized and run, promoting the "Olympic Ideal" as laid out in the

Olympic Charter, and selecting future Olympic venues from among those cities making a bid for the Games. IOC members who gathered in Barcelona in 1931 would be asked to weigh the merits of the several cities which had submitted bids to host the 1936 Olympics. One of these cities was the politically volatile Barcelona.

The IOC might pretend to be above politics but its members were certainly not. Just the opposite; many IOC members were politically connected and may even have been invited to join the IOC because of their political connections. Once on the IOC, they were expected to use their political skills and connections to further the interests of the Olympic Movement, and the interests of the Olympic Movement were not necessarily the interests of the countries from which IOC members came. It is important to understand that in the 1930s, as today, members of the IOC were not officially nominated or appointed by Olympic member countries. Rather, they were co-opted by the IOC itself. Once appointed, and appointed for life, IOC members, even today, are expected to "consider themselves as delegates of the International Olympic Committee to the Federations and Sports Associations of their respective countries" and not vice versa.[2] Irrespective of national origin, each member's first loyalty must be to the IOC.

And who are the IOC anointed? If the Olympic Games are the crown jewel of international sporting events, IOC members are Olympic royalty. In fact, over the years, it has not been unusual for some IOC members to be royalty, and others socially privileged, economically self-sufficient, and politically conservative. As sports historian William Murray notes, "By the 1930s the membership of the IOC was composed of two distinct groups: men with a title to nobility or who at least considered themselves to be 'gentlemen,' and others who shared their passion for sport but whose titles to nobility were more through money than blood and who took part in the world's elite amateur body as representatives of their own national federation in particular sport, often as participants before becoming administrators."[3] If, by virtue of their elevated social and economic station, members of the IOC added lustre to the Olympic enterprise, the reverse was equally true. The IOC offered its members status and confirmation in being members of one of the world's most select clubs, a club that "owned" the Olympic brand.

Countries which had previously hosted an Olympic Games were accorded two and sometimes three member spots on the IOC. The number of IOC members from other countries varied. Some had none; others, one or two. Then, as now, the president of the IOC was chosen from within the IOC's own ranks. Small wonder that IOC members – totally self-selecting and unchallenged in their governance of the Olympic enterprise – have been dubbed the "Cardinals of sport."[4] Like the College of Cardinals, however, the IOC was not without its troublesome internal spats. Even Canadian IOC membership proved subject to dispute. In the late 1920s, Canada, which had yet to host the Olympic Games, had one member on the IOC. The sole Canadian IOC member was James Merrick, a lawyer, amateur sports enthusiast, and administrator. Described as having a prickly disposition with a penchant for "directness and intractable stance on some issues," Merrick assumed the presidency of the Amateur Athletic Union of Canada (AAUC) in 1911. His passion was organizing and regulating amateur sport in Canada and, in particular, ensuring that athletes who participated in AAUC-sanctioned events were true amateurs. Two years later, in 1913, Merrick also became chairman of the Canadian Olympic Committee (COC). He wore both hats until he was welcomed into the club-like IOC in 1921.

Even as Merrick continued to fill Canada's seat on the IOC, some members grumbled that he was not giving the IOC the time or attention it merited. There were also outspoken Canadian amateur sports officials who felt that, because Merrick's business commitments required he spend long periods outside of Canada, he had grown increasingly out of touch with the Canadian amateur sports community. Complaining of Merrick's "ineffective" performance, the COC petitioned the IOC to remove Merrick and replace him with someone else, someone agreeable, even if not someone selected by the COC.[5]

The IOC, jealously guarding its closed-shop status, was not about to allow any national affiliate a veto over who could or could not be a member of that shop. Nor was the IOC about to let member countries nominate its members. To the IOC, that would be allowing the tail to wag the dog. The selection of IOC members was the prerogative of existing IOC members and, in defence of that prerogative, the Canadian petition was rejected. Nevertheless, the IOC could not afford to slight a national Olympic organization, especially if there was more than a little merit to the Canadian protest. Accordingly, rather than alienate an Olympic member state or expel one of its own, in a Solomon-like move in 1928, the IOC allotted Canada a second member. Merrick stayed but Canada got its new member.[6]

The new appointee was Sir George McLaren Brown, a socially prominent sixty-year-old executive with Canadian Pacific Railway who,

before the First World War, relocated from Canada to London to over-
see Canadian Pacific's European operations, including the company's
extensive fleet of ocean-going vessels. A well-placed amateur sports
enthusiast, Brown, like Merrick, had a long history of involvement
with Canadian amateur sport and, even though he lived in London,
kept in touch with the Canadian sports scene. From his home base in
London, he could also be counted on to use his Canadian Pacific connections to arrange discount travel fares for amateur Canadian athletes
and officials.

As far as the IOC was concerned, Brown had another important advantage over Merrick. Brown was a respected member of the
social elite, if not titled by birth then by royal designation. During the
Great War, Brown had been seconded to the British War Office where,
assigned the rank of lieutenant colonel, he was charged with logistical
responsibility for the transport of men and supplies to British combat
fronts. Following Germany's defeat, Brown stayed on at the War Office
coordinating transportation for a military then in the process of demo-
bilization. In gratitude for his national service, Brown was appointed
Knight Commander of the British Empire, a rare honour which hugely
boosted the Canadian's status among London's elite social set. It also
made Brown – an amateur sports enthusiast and successful corporate
executive in favour with all the right people – an obvious choice to be
Canada's second IOC member. The IOC, very much an exclusive club,
top-heavy with men of social and economic standing, welcomed only
the most deserving into membership, by which they meant others like
themselves. Brown fit the bill.[7]

In late April 1931, both Merrick and Brown arrived in Barcelona to
attend the IOC's annual meeting. Most IOC members did not. This was
unprecedented; the annual three-day meeting of the Olympic ruling
body was invariably very well attended. Absenteeism was frowned
upon as showing a lack of commitment to the Committee. An IOC member who repeatedly missed meetings could be asked to withdraw.[8] But
at the 1931 meeting in Barcelona, only nineteen of sixty-four IOC members showed up. Even the IOC's two Spanish members were no-shows.
And there was no need to ask why; it was assumed that all those who
sent their regrets were fearful about attending meetings in a city where
political tensions might at any moment explode into street violence.[9]

Saturday morning at 10:30, Committee members assembled in a
stately room in Barcelona Town Hall across from the Plaça Sant Jaume
public square, often the site of loud political demonstrations. The great

public square in front of the Town Hall was uncharacteristically quiet as IOC president Count de Baillet-Latour, seemingly unperturbed by the poor turnout, called the meeting to order. First on the agenda, the mayor of Barcelona, accompanied by local civil, military, and academic dignitaries, officially welcomed the IOC delegates to his city and wished them a productive meeting. Several other local dignitaries added their own words of welcome before the municipal functionaries left the room and the delegates got down to business. High on the their agenda was a review of preparations for the upcoming 1932 Olympic Games – Summer Games in Los Angeles and Winter Games in Lake Placid, New York. During the several days of meetings the delegates also approved a proposal to increase the number of Olympic women's events at the 1932 Games and another proposal to authorize an international competition to compose an Olympic hymn. They also discussed ways to encourage greater Olympic participation from Latin America.

Once these and several lesser matters were dispensed with, the IOC delegates turned to the all-important final agenda item – selecting the host city for the 1936 Olympic Summer Games. Rome, Barcelona, and Berlin had each previously submitted a bid to host the Games. No sooner did the chair open this item for discussion than the IOC's Italian delegate, knowing Rome had no chance of being selected, advised the meeting that the Italians "waived their claim for the 1936 Contest at Rome, but at the same time begged to be given the Olympic Games later." After a brief in-camera discussion of the two remaining bids, the delegates proceeded to vote. A majority of the votes cast were for Berlin. However, the IOC members present in Barcelona, not even one-third of the Committee's total membership, agreed that the choice of the 1936 Olympic venue was too important to be left to so small a minority. Accordingly, it was resolved that final selection of the 1936 Summer Games location should be postponed for three weeks so as to allow time to solicit mail-in votes from absent members. It was further resolved that the formal announcement of the 1936 Olympic venue would be made at the Olympic Movement headquarters in Lausanne, Switzerland, once the absentee votes were tallied into the total. Before closing off discussion on the issue of Olympic venues, Merrick and Brown served notice that Canada – buoyed at its success in hosting the first ever Empire Games in Hamilton, Ontario in 1930 – intended to submit a bid to host the 1940 Olympic Summer Games.[10]

No sooner did the Barcelona meeting adjourn than IOC staff in Lausanne started polling absent IOC members about their preferred venue for the 1936 Olympics. The two Canadians had already voted. Several Canadian newspapers reported that the Canadians had both opted for Berlin.[11] If correct, the Canadians voted with the majority. On 13 May 1931, it was announced that Berlin was awarded the 1936 Olympic Summer Games.

Berlin, Before and After

From the vantage point of 1931, Berlin seemed a far more reliable bet to successfully host the 1936 Olympics than Barcelona. Spain, mired in crisis, and Barcelona, home to frequent strikes and political demonstrations, was regarded as so threatening that most IOC members did not turn up for the 1931 IOC meetings. And if most IOC members regarded Barcelona as dangerous, why would they agree to send the cream of world amateur athletes to Barcelona? In the end they didn't. Some voiced surprise that Barcelona even received sixteen of the fifty-nine IOC votes cast.

In contrast to Spain and Barcelona, the German Weimar Republic and Berlin, if hardly rock stable, seemed to IOC members a far safer bet to be able to mount a credible Olympic Games. What is more, after the carnage of the First World War, Weimar Germany, anxious to win reinstatement into the community of nations and, most immediately, back into the international sporting community, lobbied hard to get the Games. This is not to imply that IOC members were oblivious or indifferent to problems in Germany – that would be wrong. But with the Great Depression tightening its grip everywhere, what country could claim to be problem-free? And to IOC members, intent on protecting the Olympics' good name, Germany, and especially Berlin, had much to offer. Compared to the daily political uncertainty of Barcelona, Berlin in 1931 appeared calm and orderly. What is more, Berlin, in the hub of Europe, was easily accessible to the world. Reassuringly, all levels of German government were on side with the Olympic bid and the German Olympic Committee promised to give the world not one but two good shows. According to Olympic rules in place in 1931, the country selected to host the Summer Olympics was also given the option of hosting the Winter Games that same year. Germany, with its own Alpine regions, made it clear it would welcome the opportunity to host the Winter Olympic Games at an appropriate site yet to be selected.

If Berlin was the obvious choice, was it the right choice? Just below a thin veneer of surface calm, a toxic political cauldron was bubbling away. Berlin and Germany were staggering through a prolonged period of political uncertainty that many regarded a lingering legacy of the Great War. With the German defeat in the First World War, the German monarchy collapsed. A republic was proclaimed and a national constitution agreed to. The constitution provided for an elected president with broad political and military powers, who was, at least on paper, responsible to a democratically elected national assembly, the Reichstag. A democratic national election was held to elect deputies to the Reichstag and centrist parties swept to victory. The resulting government became known as the Weimar Republic.

But if a democratic governing structure was in place in the Weimar Republic, the conditions under which the fledgling government assumed office were hardly conducive to stability. Shortly after taking their seats, the Reichstag members had no option but to ratify the Treaty of Versailles imposed on Germany by the victorious powers. The Treaty's terms were punitive: Germany was forced to assume full blame for the war and, in consequence, compelled to pay reparations for all civilian damages caused by the war. In addition to the severe economic burden this imposed, Germany also forfeited its overseas colonies and large wedges of former German territory to its neighbours. The Rhineland, a thirty-mile-wide German strip on the east bank of the Rhine, bordering France, Belgium, Luxembourg, and the Netherlands, was demilitarized. Limits were also imposed on German armaments and future military strength. The Treaty, intended by the victorious powers to prevent Germany from ever again emerging a military power strong enough to threaten its neighbours, turned out to have the opposite effect. The hated Treaty proved so economically onerous to Germany that it hobbled the country's post-war recovery and weakened public confidence in the ability of the government to protect the national interest. As a result, rather than contain Germany, the Treaty became a lightning rod for German nationalist anger and helped pave the way for Hitler's rise to power and the building of a German military machine, the likes of which Europe had never before known.

Any hope that Germany might be able to shoulder its financial obligations under the Treaty while also building a stable, democratic state were dealt a crippling blow when the economic collapse of 1929 sent money markets into a tailspin. The German economy was particularly vulnerable to the crash since it was dependent on borrowed capital and foreign trade. Just as Germany's loan and reparation payments came due, world markets for German exports shrivelled. The German industrial machine ground to a halt. Workers were laid off. Banks failed. Family savings were wiped out. As it became increasingly difficult for German families to purchase basic necessities, the standard of living plummeted. Many Germans, convinced the existing political structure was incapable of coping with the crisis, were ready to listen to anyone who promised to deliver them out of the chaos.

Enter Hitler and the Nazis. While hardly a widespread movement during the 1920s, Nazi fortunes changed as the Great Depression took hold across Germany. Hitler and his Nazi Party, previously dismissed by many as crude, disgruntled, and simple-minded nationalist street thugs, gradually emerged as a tightly controlled and highly disciplined organization, increasingly attractive not just to many of the dispossessed, but also to hard-pressed German industrialists and upper-middle-class professionals and entrepreneurs. Disenchanted with a dispirited and ineffectual democratic government – which, if not yet dead, than was certainly on life support – they were taken with the Nazi promise to restore national pride, order, and discipline, to repudiate the Treaty of Versailles, and to punish those internal enemies guilty of driving Germany to its knees. For Hitler, those most culpable were the Jews.

Even as Hitler began to roll up support, fractious Weimar legislators continued to bicker among themselves. Efforts to piece together a coherent policy to deal with the faltering economy eluded legislators. A year before Germany was awarded the Olympics, a desperate German chancellor, unable to muster Reichstag support behind his economic action plan, appealed to President Hindenburg to invoke emergency powers under the German constitution to allow the president to rule by decree. Doing so provoked such an opposition outcry in the Reichstag that Hindenburg rescinded the emergency powers but, hoping a new Reichstag would be able to offer Germany more decisive national leadership, in July 1930 he dissolved the Reichstag and called new elections for 14 September.

Hitler and his Nazi Party entered the election fray appealing to voters with a charismatic campaign unlike anything ever previously seen in Germany. Hitler played the crowd. Uncharacteristic of mainstream German political leaders, Hitler travelled the country delivering dozens of speeches, attending meetings, shaking hands, kissing babies, posing for pictures, and signing autographs. And what of his message? The German people, Hitler urged, were weary of the political stalemate in Berlin. They were tired of disorder, tired of misery, tired of weakness, tired of the unjust terms of the Treaty of Versailles, and tired of the erosion of traditional family values – all inflicted on Germany by Jews, who, Hitler insisted, were at the root of all the nation's problems. In their search for order, increasing numbers of Germans, especially in rural and small-town Germany, were attracted by Hitler's pledge to restore stability, prosperity, and national pride. Hitler's grab bag of promises contained something for everyone: work for the unemployed, prosperity for failed business people, profits for industry, revitalization for the military, social harmony and an end to class barriers for idealistic young people, a pledge to honour traditional German values and restore German glory for nationalists, and a promise to exorcise those, especially Jews and Bolsheviks – often lumped together as one – who thrived on German distress.

An American political scientist who observed the election was outspoken in his disgust at the Nazi tactics: "Its campaign talk was the sheerest drivel. Never – even at home – have I heard such blithering nonsense." But when the final voter tally was announced, the Nazis won just over 18 per cent of the national vote – and 18 per cent of the seats in the German Reichstag. It was a stunning achievement for Hitler – a 664 per cent increase in the Nazi Party vote. Overnight, the democratic process had catapulted the Nazi Party into the second largest political party in Germany's multi-party Reichstag. One month following the vote, newly elected Nazi deputies, dressed in brown shirts and with right arms extended in the Nazi salute, marched in unison into the Reichstag and took their seats. When the roll call was taken, each one responded, "Present! Heil Hitler!"[12]

Six months later, when IOC members had the choice of Barcelona or Berlin to host the 1936 summer Olympic Games, they chose Berlin. For Germany's Olympic proponents, the prospect of the Games coming to Germany was a point of national pride. This was in spite of lingering distrust of Germany among its former enemies in the Great War, in spite of German resentment at the one-sided terms imposed by the Treaty of Versailles, and in spite of the emergence of the Nazis as a political force to be reckoned with. Here was a positive sign that Germany was being welcomed back into the family of nations. Here was recognition by the IOC, the world's pre-eminent sporting organization, that Germany was not only worthy of participating in the Olympics as one among equals, but worthy of hosting the world in 1936. With five years lead time before the Olympic Winter and Summer Games were to begin, the German Olympic Committee knew it had its work cut out for it, but it was also convinced that the Olympic prize won in 1931, a prize Germany would unwrap before the world in 1936, would be worth the effort.

Even as the German Olympic Committee celebrated its successful bid, the German economic and political situation continued to unravel. A multi-party Reichstag coalition, formed in the wake of the 1930 election, gradually fell apart as opposition Nazi members of the Reichstag joined their communist arch-enemies in undermining constructive governance. In another attempt to create a workable Reichstag, yet another election was called in 1932. This time Hitler emerged with approximately 42 per cent of the popular vote. While not a majority, the Nazis were now the largest party in the Reichstag. Sensing his moment, in January 1933 Hitler negotiated Nazi Party entry into a minority governing coalition with himself as chancellor. Just as the Nazis dominated the Reichstag, they also sought to command the streets. Emboldened by their party's electoral success, vicious brown-shirted Nazi thugs followed their own law, especially when it came to escalating violence against Jews, defacing Jewish property, and intimidating those who patronized Jewish shops, restaurants, and department stores.

Nor was it just the Jews who suffered the Nazi heel. So too did the Reichstag. German president Hindenburg, again hoping to find a more workable majority government, called yet another Reichstag election for early March 1933. On 27 February, just days before the vote, the Reichstag building was partially consumed by fire. While the Nazis are assumed to have secretly set the blaze, Hitler immediately accused the communists of burning the building as part of a plot to seize power. In order to crush the alleged communist coup, Hitler convinced the aging president to suspend freedom of speech, freedom of the press, and other civil liberties. The ongoing election campaign now proceeded under a cloud of repression and Nazi intimidation. When the vote was counted, the Nazis polled 44 per cent of the votes, still short of a majority, but with the support of smaller right-wing and nationalist factions in the Reichstag, and with elected communist members denied permission to take their seats, the Nazis controlled the Reichstag. With virtually no discussion, on 23 March 1933, the Reichstag passed the Enabling Act, a measure that granted Hitler dictatorial authority. In a stroke, German democracy was gone. Hitler quickly crushed any and all opposition to his rule and moved to subordinate German institutions to Nazi Party authority. What had previously seemed impossible suddenly was inevitable. The Nazis were in control of Germany.

As the world looked on, Hitler pressed forward his policy of *Gleichschaltung* (coordination), by which the Nazi Party solidified its control over all aspects of German society and ensured all German institutions functioned tongue-in-groove with the Nazi world view. Key to that world view was antisemitism. With Hitler solidifying his grip on the state, antisemitism increasingly shifted from Nazi sloganeering and sporadic street-level intimidation of Jews to legally enforced public policy. Jews, less than 1 per cent of Germany's population, found themselves increasingly frozen out of any and all interaction with non-Jews, a process of extrusion historian Marion Kaplan has termed the "social death" of German Jews.[13] And this was not simply a matter of public shunning; the pruning of Jews out of German society was given legal sanction. A "Law for the Restoration of the Professional Civil Service" was proclaimed in April 1933, less than a month after Hitler was proclaimed chancellor. This law dictated the removal of all Jewish and "politically unreliable" public servants from state employ – including employ in the public school system. That same month, another German law imposed crippling quotas on the number of Jewish students allowed to attend German schools and universities and severely limited Jewish participation in the medical and legal professions. Local municipalities, doing their part to further the national antisemitic agenda, restricted the ability of Jewish professionals to practice their crafts. Jewish lawyers were refused leave to interact with public institutions – even to do a title search – and Jewish doctors were cut off from treating non-Jews.[14] Dr. Ernst Hanfstaengl, chief of the German foreign press section, justified the expulsion of Jews from the public sphere by explaining that "the Jews who already have been ousted were put out because they were morally and politically unfit to safeguard German interests."[15]

There was nowhere for German Jews to turn for relief from the Nazi program of state-mandated antisemitism. The police, the courts, and the institutions that mediated the relationship between citizen and citizen, and citizen and state, were made off-limits to Jews.[16] The dejudaization of German society even extended to sport. Under the Nazis, all sports federations, organizations, and clubs were declared agents for the betterment of the Aryan race. Since Jews by definition were non-Aryans, it was directed that all Jews and other non-Aryans be expelled from membership in German sporting federations and clubs. The German Boxing Federation was among the first, if not the first, to eject Jews. On 4 April 1933, Toronto's *Der yiddisher zhurnal* reported that the German Federation of Amateur Boxing had banished Jews from participating in amateur bouts.[17] Two weeks later, the *Toronto Daily Star* detailed the justifications offered for this expulsion. According to the

Federation, German boxers put in all the effort only to be ruthlessly exploited by Jewish managers, trainers, doctors, and lawyers who "got all the gravy." The organization overseeing boxing in Germany offered one sure and just solution:

> All Jews, including those baptized, are ruled off the lists of [boxing club] members; all honorary members of Jewish blood are asked to hand in their cards; every German boxer is ordered to tear up any contract with a Jewish manager; Jews are barred from the club rooms; Jewish capital is barred from the financing of Jewish boxing shows; [boxing] union members are forbidden to engage Jewish doctors, dentists or lawyers; foreigners are hereby suspended until further notice; all club officials, not in harmony with the New Germany, should resign; all members not in harmony with the new movement [Nazism] should also quit; men in the confidence of the government are to sit in on all meetings.[18]

What was true of boxing soon became true of other German athletic and sporting organizations. Jews were expelled both from membership in sports clubs and from participating in athletic competition against non-Jews. The German Tennis Federation was no exception. Daniel Prenn, a Jew ranked Germany's best tennis player, was expelled from the German Davis Cup team as the Tennis Federation declared, "No Jew may be selected for a national team or the Davis Cup; no Jewish or Marxist club or association may be affiliated with the German Tennis Federation; no Jew may hold an official position in the Federation."[19]

The extrusion of Jews from German sport extended to children. In June 1933, the Ministry of Education ordered Jewish children expelled from all youth, welfare, and gymnastic organizations and the facilities of all athletic clubs so as to guarantee those spaces would be free of Jews. An editorial in *Der Stürmer*, a widely read and rabidly antisemitic weekly, applauded the move: "We need waste no words here. Jews are Jews and there is no place for them in German sport. Germany is the Fatherland of Germans and not Jews, and the Germans have the right to do what they want in their own country."[20]

The Nazis and the Olympics

Given the speed with which the Nazis moved to Aryanize German sport by purging sporting organizations and competition of any "corrupting" non-Aryan influence, German Olympic officials were confronted with a problem. The Nazi ethnic cleansing of German sport obviously did not comport with the Olympic ideal of open athletic competition free from racial or religious discrimination. This being the case, would the IOC allow the Olympic Games, awarded to Germany not quite two years before Hitler took power, to proceed as originally planned? And, equally important, would the rulers of the new Germany permit German athletes and officials to participate in, let alone host, an Olympic Games that would have athletes of different races and religions compete as equals? Some had their doubts on both counts. What is more, much as the Nazis might wax lyrical about the mythically idealized male Aryan body type and trumpet the virtues of personal fitness, muscular training, and more "manly" martial arts – especially as they promoted a military elan[21] – Hitler was said to be personally indifferent to athletics and team sports. But, measured by his comments before assuming power, he was not indifferent to the Olympic Games – he was hostile. The Olympics seemed antithetical to all that the Nazis stood for. The Olympic Charter proclaimed the power of athletic and sporting competition as a tool for the promotion of peace and unity between people and nations. Fundamental to this Olympic vision of peace and harmony through sporting excellence was the expectation that the Olympic Games must take place in an atmosphere of mutual respect and without the burden of political, religious, or racial prejudice. In the Olympic arena, all are equal.

If Hitler had little use for sport for sport's sake, he had even less use for the notion of sport as a path to international fellowship. For the Nazis, the notion of international harmony, let alone racial and religious equality – even in sport – was not only wrong-minded, it was dangerous. During the 1920s, the Nazis, still a decade short of power, heaped scorn on the Olympic Games and Olympic supporters, dismissing the latter as a bunch of cosmopolitans and internationalists who tolerate, if not celebrate, the mixing of whites with inferior and "degenerate" races – Jews, Gypsies, Blacks – in the name of sport. Not only were inferiors allowed to compete as equals, but they were honoured with medals as well. To the Nazis, humankind was not a fraternity of equals; it was a hierarchy of competing races in which Aryans had an obligation to defend their dominance over lesser peoples, not mix with them.

If the races of humankind were not meant to mix as equals, what did the Nazis make of an international event, the Olympic Games, open to the entire family of humankind on an equal basis? According to the Nazis, it ran against nature and certainly against the interests of the Aryan race. This being the case, whose manipulative hand or pocket did the Nazis understand to benefit from all this racial degeneracy? Before the Nazis assumed power, Julius Streicher, publisher of *Der Stürmer*, contemptuously dismissed the Olympic Games as an "infamous" spectacle dominated by Jews.[22] Hitler was no less hostile. Referring to the 1932 Olympic Games in Los Angeles, he contemptuously dismissed the event as a nefarious exercise in race degradation and "an invention of Jews and Freemasons."[23]

Given the Nazi record of antagonism to the vaunted Olympic ideal of international cooperation and fraternity though competition in sport without regard to racial and religious distinction, the German Olympic Committee had reason to worry that the Nazis, now in power, would withdraw the German invitation to host the 1936 Olympics.[24] They need not have worried. Shortly after the Nazis assumed power, senior members of the German Olympic Committee approached Joseph Goebbels, newly minted Nazi minister of propaganda. It took little to convince him that the 1936 Olympic Games, organized by Germans and staged by Germans, were more than just games – far more than just games. The Olympics afforded Germany and the Nazi Party a potential propaganda bonanza, an arena in which to showcase the new Germany. Goebbels, in turn, convinced Hitler that the German Olympic Committee might seem to the world to be a free-standing organization but, like all institutions in the new Germany, it was now subservient to the interests of the German state and, therefore, of the Nazi Party. German Games organizers might have to pay lip service to the Olympic ideal but, Hitler was given to understand, all the talk about international fraternity and equality was just that – talk. In actuality, a German Olympiad would showcase to the German people and the world a reborn "German vitality and organizational experience," even as it affirmed the superiority of the Aryan race.

Convinced, Hitler surprised many by publicly embracing the German Olympic Games and putting the full weight of his office behind the German Olympic planning effort. Whatever it took to produce an Olympic Games worthy of the new Germany would be made available. As if to affix Hitler's personal seal of approval on the German Olympic Games, Germany's invitation to the youth of the world to assemble in Germany for the 1936 Olympic Games was officially issued not in the name of the German Olympic Committee but in Hitler's name.[25]

No doubt the potential propaganda windfall that had fallen into his lap excited Hitler, who was never much interested in sport or athletics for its own sake. But historian James Pitsula argues there was more to it

than that. Certainly Hitler and his inner circle dismissed the internation-
alist ideal that many regard as intrinsic to the modern Olympic movement, and, yes, Hitler and his inner circle relished the opportunity of
boosting domestic Nazi stock by putting on a show in which Germans
could take just pride. But, Pitsula argues, Hitler was also convinced that
the Olympics held great symbolic meaning for Germans. To Hitler's
mind, there was a straight-line connection between the ancient Greeks
and modern-day Germans, an unbroken blood bond. Ancient Greeks
and modern-day Germans were one people. The Olympic Games,
then, should be seen as a Greek bequest to the German people, to the
Nazis, and, accordingly, Germany had as much, if not more, proprie-
tary right to the Games than did the International Olympic Committee.
Thus Hitler looked with favour at the notion that the Olympic Games
might someday find a permanent home in Germany. This eventuality,
in Hitler's view, would allow for a reinstatement of storied elements
of the ancient Greek Olympics that resonated well with Nazism: the
cult of the male body, the ennobling and purifying power of struggle,
gladiator-like pageantry, a to-the-winner-go-the-spoils ethos, and the
ancient Greek practice of excluding all those held to be unworthy of
competing as equals. Thus Pitsula concludes that "for western democratic nations, the games were meant to promote liberal ideals and
world peace; for the Nazis they heralded revitalized paganism and the
beginning of a new world order."[26]

Whether, as Pitsula argues, the Olympic Games represented for Hitler
a modern-day manifestation of a timeless German link with a mytholo-
gized and heroic Greek past, or an opportunity to charge nationalist
batteries at home while parading the new Germany before the community of nations, Hitler relished the notion that the 1936 Olympic Games,
Winter and Summer, would be the Nazi Games. And more than simply
offering his pro forma endorsement of the event in officially affirming
Germany's willingness to host the Olympic Games, Hitler was making it abundantly clear the 1936 Olympics would be a German state
enterprise. Although, for all the world to see, the German Olympic
Committee continued as the official 1936 Olympic organizing agency,
the German Olympic Committee was no more than a servant of state.
Everything it did or said was cleared by the state.

Not only was the German Olympic Committee a Nazi tool, but Hitler, excited by the idea of hosting the Olympic Games, also assumed a
hands-on role in making certain that the Games would be a celebration
worthy of the Nazi state, his state. To ensure that the public face of his

Olympics would stand testament to the greatness of the new Germany, he took a personal interest in Olympic preparations, going so far as to reject a preliminary architectural rendering for a purpose-built Olympic stadium planned for Berlin. It was not monumental enough. The plans were redrafted so as to be a more fitting monument to the Nazi state.

But what of the Olympic creed as set out by the founder of the modern Olympics, Pierre de Coubertin, and repeated during every Olympic opening ceremony? "The most important thing in the Olympic Games is not to win but to take part, just as the most important thing in life is not the triumph, but the struggle. The essential thing is not to have conquered but to have fought well." To Hitler these words were laughably empty of meaning, except to the weak. To fight, to conquer, to stand triumphant – these were life imperatives. There was no glory in playing well if you don't win. As in war, so in sport. Second place is defeat. With the Olympics coming to Germany, Hitler insisted German athletes not just do their best; he insisted they win, both as individual athletes and as ambassadors of the new Germany. And for Hitler, winning meant amassing a greater number of gold medals than any other country. Hitler may have had little if any personal interest in competitive sport, but he ordered that nothing should stand in the way of Germany mounting the best trained and most highly motivated team possible. Technical niceties about ensuring the amateur status of German athletes were not even observed in the breach. Other nations might blur the line between amateur and professional – the Nazis erased the line. German athletes became "state amateurs." The state made available and picked up all costs for the best in athlete medical support, travel, coaching, equipment, facilities, and even extra food rations in a country suffering food shortages. Under the table, the Nazis also provided athletes "compensation for lost wages," which was tantamount to making Olympic trainees state employees, a blatant violation of Olympic amateur rules. Whatever the cost, whatever Olympic rules needed to be trampled, the Nazis were determined their athletes were going to win.[27]

Given the obvious disconnect between the Olympic credo, with its commitment to international amateur athletic excellence and fair play free from the burden of religious or racial discrimination, and the bedrock racist and antisemitic agenda of the Nazi regime, what of the Olympic dictum that the Olympic Games must be open to all who qualify? As host of the Games, German Olympic authorities certainly had to pay lip service to the Olympic Charter with regard to visiting athletes and so they did at the 1933 annual meeting of the IOC held in Vienna. But even as they pledged there would be no discrimination in the treatment of visiting teams, the German Olympic Committee danced around the issue of whether Olympic-quality German-Jewish athletes would be allowed onto the German Olympic team. The IOC president sidestepped the issue. He allowed that he had assurance at the highest level that Germany would adhere to all the Olympic rules with regard to eligibility of visiting athletes, even if "certain limitations of our International Rules should seem to be inconsistent with recent orders laid down in Germany." On the matter of the make-up of the German team, a German member of the IOC dared only say, "As a principle German Jews shall not be excluded from German Teams at the Games of the XIth Olympiad."[28] Principle, as it turned out, was one thing; practice was another.

If the IOC accepted Germany's pledge to adhere to the Olympic Charter at face value, at least publicly, only the most self-deluded of Olympic observers would deny the obvious. Olympic Charter or no Olympic Charter, the Nazi pledge to free Germany from the rapacious grip of conspiratorial Jews was politics and not about to be set aside in the name of Olympic sportsmanship. Accordingly, no matter how much or how often the Nazis paid lip service to the Olympic Charter, on no account were the Nazis prepared to leave the politics of race in the Olympic Stadium parking lot. Both the glorification of Aryan superiority and the exclusion of non-Aryans from the German Olympic team were a given. One would have to be wilfully blind not to see that a racialized state would field a racialized Olympic team. And so it would be. German Jews, already stripped of membership in German sporting clubs and federations, a prerequisite for participation in German Olympic trials, were regarded prima facie ineligible from membership on the German Olympic team.

Canada, Amateur Sports, and the Olympics

Through 1933 and into 1934, as the Germans broke ground on the Winter and Summer Olympic sites, and initiated both a promotional campaign to encourage domestic interest in the Olympic Games and training programs for would-be German Olympic competitors, across the ocean the Canadian Olympic Committee had barely begun preparing for the 1936 Olympics. But though the COC was slow off the mark, no one doubted Canada would eventually mount an Olympic team. Canada had participated in every Olympic Games since 1908. Certainly, Canadians proudly sporting the maple leaf on their uniforms would participate in both the 1936 winter and summer competitions. Of course, Canadian Olympic organization had changed markedly since the 1908 Olympic Games in London and the Stockholm Games in 1912. Preparation for these pre-First World War Games had been very much a seat-of-the-pants affair run by an ad hoc Olympic committee cobbled together a few months before the Games and dissolved just as quickly once the Games were over. Under pressure from the IOC to organize a permanent Canadian Olympic support structure similar to that of other Olympic member countries, in 1913 a formal committee – the COC – was set up. It was quickly constituted as a standing committee of the Amateur Athletic Union of Canada (AAUC), founded in 1909 as an umbrella organization overseeing amateur sports in Canada. In addition to serving as Canadian liaison with the IOC, the COC assumed oversight responsibility for overseeing Canadian Olympic trials, validating the amateur status of Olympic team members, and, together with various amateur sport federations across Canada, securing funds to meet the costs associated with putting a worthy Canadian Olympic team in the field.[29] According to sports historian Bruce Kidd, after a somewhat unsteady beginning, the COC gradually assumed "greater control of the increasingly prestigious Olympic project."[30]

Since the COC suit was fashioned out of AAUC cloth, it is no surprise that many of the issues that engaged the AAUC also wove their way into COC deliberations. For example, both the AAUC and the COC wrestled with how and where to draw the line between amateur and professional athletes. Unlike the German Olympic Committee's preparations for the 1936 Olympics, for the most part AAUC and COC officials held fast to a narrow definition of amateurism: no pay for play. Any violation of the so-called Amateur Code could lead to an athlete being barred from amateur competition and, of course, barred from trying out for the Canadian Olympic team.[31] But, inasmuch as the COC defended amateur sport and athletics, its primary concern was still to ensure that Canada would be represented in Olympic competition. Simply stated, there was no point in having a Canadian Olympic Committee if Canada did not mount a Canadian Olympic team. Accordingly, the COC was not just concerned with oversight of Canadian Olympic participation; it was, above all, concerned that there should *be* Canadian Olympic participation. And what about the quality of that participation? What was the appropriate balance between waving the flag and winning medals, between encouraging a large Canadian participation and sending an elite contingent to the Games? This was sometimes a difficult question. The two might not be mutually exclusive, but prioritizing one over the other could determine how limited resources were assigned. For the COC executive, the stakes were high. As Kidd argues, public support for the COC and Canadian Olympic participation was dependent on acceptance of the notion that mounting a team contributed "significantly to Canadian unity through the elite of Olympic sports," and a shared vision of a Canada infused with a "spirit of public-mindedness and 'fair play'... inseparable from responsible citizenship."[32]

But as much as the COC claimed to be promoting the Canadian Olympic enterprise in order to build the Canadian national spirit, Canadian amateur sport fell short of being inclusive of all Canadians. Rather than sport and athleticism drawing Canadians together as one, the Canadian playing field remained through the 1930s fractured by class, regional, ethnic, racial, linguistic, religious, and gender cleavages. As Kidd notes, if the Canadian amateur sports establishment "managed to add significantly to the framework for pan-Canadian sport," in the interwar years, their "'nation building' suffered from the familiar myopia of English-Canadian nationalism. Few French-Canadians. Few [Native], immigrant, and working-class sports groups were included." The involvement of women in amateur sport was growing but very much circumscribed by what was then regarded as appropriate and feminine.[33]

Much though the mainstream amateur sports establishment might wish to claim an inclusive tent, membership on the COC suffered from that same "myopia." Those appointed to the COC, like most administrators who oversaw Canadian amateur sport during the Depression, were a select group. All were either AAUC appointees or representatives of Canadian sporting federations that participated in Olympic medal events. But there was something else that characterized COC members. While tens of thousands of depression-ravaged Canadians struggled to put food on the table, the COC remained the preserve of men with the luxury of leisure time, social status, and the means necessary to attend annual COC meetings, which were held in conjunction with the AAUC plenary that convened each year in a different Canadian city. And while the Canadian Olympic effort might be considered a pan-Canadian undertaking, the Maritime Provinces and French Canada were under-represented on the COC, partly because of the costs of travel and, in the case of French Canadians, because of the Anglocentric bias that so dominated mainstream amateur Canadian sport of the day.

Since the COC met as a committee of the whole only once a year, a small COC executive committee managed the COC's day-to-day operations, especially as an Olympic Games drew near. The COC inner circle was centred in or close to Toronto, as was the AAUC headquarters. But Toronto was more than just the administrative nexus of amateur sport in Canada; it was in the interwar years a city suspended between two worlds. One was the North American world that hailed individualism and honoured up-by-the-bootstraps success. The other world was more conservative and bound to notions of civil order and social conformity predicated on loyalty to the British Crown and the guarded optimism about sharing in the glory of British imperial greatness. In this latter regard, 1930s Toronto publicly prided itself on being a staid and white-bread municipal bulwark (some might say backwash) of Anglo-conformity, in which sobriety and social reserve were professed civic virtues. This did not mean that "Toronto the Good" was really that good but, at least in polite society, what went on behind closed doors was expected to stay behind closed doors. What was good for Toronto was assumed to be good for the rest of Canada as well; as the COC executives would have it, those Canadian athletes privileged to wear the maple leaf should be both a source of national pride and ambassadors of courtesy, sportsmanship, and fair play to the world. Canadians should be the embodiment of the Olympic Charter.

Did this also apply to those who actually organized and managed the Olympic brand in Canada? Not really. Perhaps because COC executive members felt proprietorial ownership of the Canadian Olympic enterprise, and because of their self-important vision of themselves as engaged in nation building through sport, they tended to regard the Olympic Games as their personal fiefdom. And in many ways it was. Except for annually reporting to the AAUC on the previous year's activities, the COC executive remained largely untrammelled by interference from the AAUC, its constituent amateur sports federations, or, least of all, government at any level. Unlike the hands-on role the Nazi state took in preparation of the 1936 Olympics, federal, provincial, and municipal governments in Canadian took a hands-off attitude towards the Olympic process. Federal government involvement, for example, was largely confined to making a financial contribution to help defray Olympic-related costs and to providing necessary diplomatic liaisons, as required, with the German Olympic Committee and the representatives of the government of Germany.

If the COC executive functioned as the executive board of a business enterprise, then P.J. Mulqueen was its CEO. Mulqueen was appointed chair of the COC in 1922. At first glance, he might seem an odd choice. Born in Toronto in 1867, just a month shy of Confederation, Mulqueen was raised in Toronto's gritty Catholic-Irish Cabbagetown neighbour-hood at a time when Protestant churches and the Orange Lodge domi-nated City Hall; Catholics were expected to know their place, and that rarely included high-profile community positions. But Mulqueen was an exception. A graduate of St. Michael's College in Toronto, a mem-ber of the Toronto Council of the Knights of Columbus, and a business success, Mulqueen was also a generous supporter of amateur sport. Mulqueen's start in business was with a grocery store and bakery in the city's east end. He later bought the Tremont Hotel at the corner of Yonge and Queen in the heart of downtown Toronto. The Tremont was a popular watering hole for many of Toronto's sport, theatre, press, and political movers and shakers. It also proved a very good investment, allowing Mulqueen to ride out the Depression without a great deal of pain. Mulqueen may have been one of his own best customers. It was no secret among COC insiders, and Mulqueen himself even admitted, that he drank, sometime to excess. In one case he was said to be too intoxicated to chair a COC meeting.[34]

Mulqueen had also been an accomplished athlete in his youth. He had been an oarsman with the Don Rowing Club and the Toronto Rowing Club, and a member of several local rowing teams that won the North American championship, the National championship at Saratoga, New York, and the prestigious Northwestern Regatta. But his enthusiasm for sport extended well beyond rowing. Mulqueen was a familiar presence at all kinds of local sporting events and he became a stalwart of the AAUC. In spite of Mulqueen's reputation as a tippler, in 1920 Ontario premier Ernest Drury appointed him chairman of the Ontario Athletic Commission, responsible for regulating professional boxing and wres-tling in Ontario. Mulqueen's great love, however, remained amateur sport, and in 1922 he became chairman of the COC.[35]

In 1920s Toronto, where the Orange Lodge was a major political force, Roman Catholic Mulqueen becoming head of the COC was a social feather in his cap. It was a point of pride to have successfully over-come social, political, and economic barriers that commonly restricted the upward mobility of Catholics and others regarded as religious and racial outsiders by Toronto's and Canada's Anglo-Protestant power brokers. It was not that Mulqueen was suddenly welcomed into the parlours of the private clubs that were the home away from home of Toronto's Anglo-Protestant elite; rather, it was that in amateur sport, unlike many other areas of social interaction, performance generally counts more than pedigree. Thus, even in Anglocentric Toronto it was possible for someone at the social margins to excel and be celebrated.

This was also true for the members of other minorities. Fanny Rosenfeld, nicknamed "Bobbie" for the bobbed hair that was very much part of her signature look, was born into a Jewish family in Dnipropetrovsk, Russia, in 1903. She immigrated with her family to Barrie, Ontario. While still in high school, Rosenfeld showed a remarkable aptitude for athletics of all kinds. In 1922, she moved to Toronto, where she was soon a dominant figure on the women's amateur athletic scene. She was so proficient in so many different sports that it was claimed that "the most efficient way to summarize Bobbie Rosenfeld's career is to say that she was not good in swimming." In 1928, the first year that women's track and field events were included in the Olympic Games, Rosenfeld was one of the "matchless six" Canadian women's contingent in Amsterdam. She took a gold and then a silver medal, the latter for a hotly contested event which many believed Rosenfeld actually won and for which, according to her believers, she should have been awarded a second Olympic gold.[36]

Although Rosenfeld, like Mulqueen, exemplified the status opportunities sport offered to those outside the ethnic or religious mainstream, there is no denying that through the 1930s amateur sport in Canada was nevertheless siloed by language, ethnicity, and even politics. As Kidd notes, French Canadians were under-represented within the AAUC and, not surprisingly, conspicuous by their general absence from Canadian Olympic teams. This may, in part, be put down to Anglo indifference to the participation of French Canada. Certainly there was little by way of AAUC outreach to French Canada, and Quebec largely rejected the Anglo-controlled operation. As a result, even in 1930s Montreal, the notion of two solitudes in education, culture, and sport was a fact of life and bifurcated English and French or Catholic and Protestant relations.[37]

When it came to Canadian Aboriginal athletes, they too were under-represented in amateur sport on Olympic teams. Tom Longboat continues to stand out as the exception that proves the rule. A distance runner born in 1887 on the Six Nations of the Grand River First Nation Indian Reserve near Brantford, Ontario, Longboat dominated international long-distance running competitions in his day. He won the Boston Marathon in 1907 and represented Canada at the 1908 London Olympic Games. During the London Olympic marathon, Longboat collapsed at about the twenty-mile mark, as did several other leading runners. Interest in what went wrong during the London marathon was so great that a "rematch" was organized in New York's Madison Square Gardens. Longboat won and promptly turned professional. Otherwise, Aboriginal athletes, like French Canadians, remained conspicuous by their absence from the Canadian amateur athletic ranks, including during the 1930s.[38]

Canadian sport was not divided just along religious, ethnic, and linguistic lines; it was also divided along ideological lines. The AAUC, together with public school athletic organizations, the YMCA, and organized municipal playground athletic programs, officially served the broader community and claimed to be above partisan politics. However, just below a sports veneer of political neutrality there was, even in the AAUC, a world of political allegiances reinforced by shared social class and business connections. AAUC and COC leadership was often well connected to one or the other mainstream political parties. For example, Mulqueen, like many Canadian Catholics during the 1930s, was a strong supporter of the Liberal Party, and he was not above using what political leverage his Liberal connections provided him to score the cooperation of municipal, provincial, and federal support for amateur athletics. Mulqueen was not alone. Planning for a British Empire Games in Hamilton, Ontario was much facilitated by the ability of Games organizers to reach and enlist government support, financial and otherwise, particularly at the municipal level. Even though Hamilton was suffering a severe economic downturn, the city came through with money for venue construction, athlete travel, and accommodation. Because of the infusion of municipal money, the British Empire Games in Hamilton proved so successful that participants agreed to turn the British Empire Games into a once-every-four-years event. Canadian members of the IOC were so buoyed by the success of the Hamilton event, and so convinced that further government financial support was there for the asking, that at the IOC meeting in Barcelona they announced that Canada hoped to submit a bid to host the 1940 Olympic Games.[39]

Publicly, the AAUC and COC claimed to be above politics, just as they demanded all amateur sports and athletics should be. But, on examination, this claim rang hollow, and certainly there were elements of the Canadian amateur sports world in which politics was a raison d'être. Workers' Sports Associations (WSA) stand out in this regard. Modelled on European labour union and socialist sporting associations, Workers'

Sports Associations were imported into Canada by sometimes competing groups on the political left to counterbalance the appeal of "bourgeois" middle-class athletic outreach to the "working class" and help coalesce youthful support for leftist political activism. When a non-WSA group invited WSA athletes to participate in one of its events in 1928, the National Executive Committee of the WSA explained that it "did not accept the invitation to participate in sports organized for the purpose of befogging the minds of working-class youth ... [It] is necessary to build a strong and virile workers' sport movement and break down the influence of the capitalist-controlled Amateur Athletic Association [sic] of Canada."[40] But sport and athletics in the context of the political left were no less fractious than the left itself. Like the left elsewhere, the Canadian left was highly divided into factions often as hostile to one another as they were to free-market capitalism. Through the 1920s and early 1930s the ideological divide between the communist and non-communist left, and even different subsets of the non-communist left, often made it difficult for observers to keep track of who was accusing who of "false consciousness" in betraying the interests of the working class. Labour union turf wars that spilled over into violent confrontation created a weakened political left and cut into the left's ability to act as one in pushing back against the rising tide of fascism at home and abroad.

Canadian Jewry

The other leading Canadian opponent of Nazism, the Canadian Jewish community, was also weak.[41] The year that Germany was awarded the Olympics was a census year in Canada. According to the 1931 census, Jews constituted approximately 1.5 per cent of the Canadian population – almost twice the percentage of Jews in Germany, although at 155,000, the number of Canadian Jewish was much smaller than Germany's more than 500,000 Jews. Also by way of contrast, the proportion of Jews in the Canadian population was much smaller than that in the United States. The American Jewish community stood at 3.5 per cent of the American population, or approximately 4,300,000 individuals.[42] But American and Canadian Jewish communities of the 1930s differed not just in numbers, but also in context. The Canadian Jewish community was then still far more an immigrant and first-generation community than that of the American Jews. Without an appreciable immigration of German Jews in the 1840s and 1850s, Canadian Jews were mostly of eastern European origin, largely Yiddish speaking and Orthodox by tradition and ritual if not always in observance. They were also, even in the first generation, overwhelmingly urban-based wage earners, tradesmen, or small shopkeepers. The fact that Canadian Jews, unlike American Jews, were so predominantly urban was a burr under the saddle of Canada, which had long assigned policy priority to the settlement of agricultural immigrants and those willing to take jobs working on Canada's lumbering and mining frontier. Jews, the most urban of all immigrant groups to Canada, stood out like a sore thumb. In 1930, 80 per cent of Jews in Canada lived in either Montreal or Toronto, while fewer than 4 per cent of Jews lived in rural Canada. By contrast, more than 80 per cent of Ukrainian immigrants, almost 70 per cent of Scandinavians, and 70 per cent of Dutch and German immigrants and their children were rural. Indeed, no group had a lower rural residency rate than Jews.[43]

In a post–First World War Canada, where guardians of the immigration gate demonstrated little sympathy for urban-bound settlers, Jews were regarded among the most problematic of immigrant groups and, as a result, were in the sights of those gunning for immigration restriction. Regarded by many, including key immigration officials, as unwanted cast-offs of the Russian and Austro-Hungarian empires, Jews were also widely held to be clannish, aggressively competitive with "real" Canadians, and given to alien ideologies such as anarchism, socialism, and communism. Wasn't Marx a Jew? Emma Goldman, Leon Trotsky, and Rosa Luxemburg? And by hiving themselves off into their own urban neighbourhoods – the Main in Montreal, the legendary North End of Winnipeg, and first St. John's Ward and then Kensington in Toronto – Jews were said to have barricaded themselves against Canadianization.[44] With the flow of immigration out of Europe beginning again after the end of the Great War, agents of the Canadian way, including educational authorities, public health officers, police, and immigration officials, joined in demanding hard-nosed immigration restrictions. And topping their list of those who many felt should be excluded from easy Canadian entry were Jews.[45]

Of course, throughout the interwar period, Canadian politicians and immigration officials had more to contend with than Jews. In the aftermath of war, servicemen and servicewomen were being demobilized into a Canada suffering a sharp economic downturn. Jobs were scarce and social tensions, aggravated by wartime-inspired xenophobia and eugenicist arguments, spilled out into the open in the wake of the 1919

Winnipeg General Strike.[46] With the anti-labour press filled with talk of foreign Bolshevik and Anarchist agitators, and anti-immigrant spokespersons decrying the degenerative impact of open immigration, the government responded with a series of draconian immigration restrictions that severely cut the number of immigrants allowed Canadian entry. Between 1919 and 1923, immigration officials restricted the entry of both skilled and unskilled labour, raised monetary requirements for admission, instituted new passport and visa control barriers, narrowed the definition of those eligible for reunification with family in Canada, and moved immigration inspections from port of admission in Canada to port of exit in Europe. The door of open immigration was slamming shut.

In 1923 the government introduced restrictive immigration regulations that hit Jewish immigration particularly hard. Without changing the Immigration Act, the government instituted several far-reaching administrative refinements designed to dead-end remaining avenues to Jewish admission. First, the government closed the door to all unsponsored immigrants except bona fide agriculturalists and British and American citizens.[47] The government then moved to control those described as belonging "to races that cannot be assimilated without social or economic loss to Canada."[48] The mechanics of restriction were as artfully simple as they were transparent in intent. The government instituted a hierarchical ranking of all other would-be settlers by their degree of similar "racial characteristics" to the Anglo-Canadian majority. Prospective European immigrants were separated into three groups: the Preferred Group, the Non-Preferred Group, and a Special Permit Group. The Preferred Group administratively clumped together those from countries of northern and western Europe, including Germany. Immigrant applicants from these countries were exempted from nearly all restrictive provisions of the regulations except some general visa, health, and fiscal formalities. The Non-Preferred Group included those from Austria, Hungary, Czechoslovakia, Russia, Yugoslavia, Poland, Rumania, and the Baltic states – areas of Europe with the heaviest Jewish populations. Emigrants from these countries were permitted into Canada only so long as they were going to settle the land and could show sufficient money to ensure they would not become a public charge.

The immigration officials, however, were not about to let Jewish immigration continue even under the restrictive provisions of the Non-Preferred category. All Jews, irrespective of citizenship or place of birth (excepting those born British subjects or in the United States or those sponsored by immediate family in Canada), were streamed into the Special Permit Group together with those from Italy, Greece, Bulgaria, Syria, and Turkey. Would-be immigrants in the Special Permit Group were effectively removed from the regular immigration process. Under the new regulations, Jews and southern Europeans could only be admitted to Canada if issued a special entry permit. Issuing this permit was not in the power of immigration officials. Rather, it was the sole prerogative of Cabinet, most often as an act of patronage. This meant that immigration of those in the Special Permit Group was relegated from the regular administrative process to the political arena. For would-be Jewish and southern European immigrants, entering Canada was no longer a matter of satisfying specific criteria. It was a matter of political influence, and this was a commodity in very short supply.

The Special Permit Group included both Jews and southern Europeans, but Jews were the most directly and immediately impacted. Because the new fascist government of Italy moved to restrict emigration except to Italian colonial holdings, and because the number of immigrants from other special permit countries was never great, the Special Permit Group was primarily designed to restrict the immigration of Jews. In effect, the Canadian government adjusted immigration regulations to ensure that Canadian entry for Jews was more difficult than for others holding the same citizenship. In distinguishing Jews from non-Jews of the same citizenship, Canada predated Nazi regulations denying Jews and non-Jews equal status under the law by more than ten years.[49]

In the end, the 1923 immigration regulations turned the immigration law on its head. Rather than permit immigration of everyone except specifically prohibited groups, the regulations now prohibited everyone except specifically permitted groups. Aside from those few Jews able to squeeze into Canada under the restrictionist regulations as first-degree relatives of those already in Canada, Canada's door slammed shut on Jews.[50] By 1926, when the immigration changes came into full effect, the filing of applications by individual Jewish would-be immigrants was increasingly replaced by organized Jewish community lobbying for a withdrawal of the special permit regulations. It failed. "Between the upper and the nether millstone," commented one Toronto rabbi, "the Jew as usual will be crushed."[51]

The 1923 regulations bespeak, at least in part, how Canadian Jews of that era were regarded by many of their non-Jewish neighbours and, more importantly, by the Anglo-Canadian elite. Put simply, Jews might have been in Canada, but they were not regarded as part of Canada. And as outsiders, while they might have legally become Canadian citizens, they were still expected to act like guests in Canada, by sufferance, not right. But in the lee of the First World War, the spectre of antisemitism, immigration restriction, and the desperate plight of many overseas Jews hung like a dark cloud over the Canadian Jewish community. Moved to create an organized response, Jewish delegates from across Canada gathered in Montreal in 1919. As immigration restriction moved onto the government's front burner, the assembled delegates founded the Canadian Jewish Congress (CJC), an umbrella organization intended to speak out on the interests of Canadian Jews while coordinating humanitarian efforts on behalf of distressed Jews overseas. To deal with looming Jewish immigration concerns, the gathering founded the Jewish Immigrant Aid Society (JIAS), assigned to tackle problems of Jewish immigrant settlement in the urban context. JIAS, headquartered in Montreal with sister offices in Toronto and Winnipeg, assisted individuals negotiating Canadian immigration procedures and then helped smooth their settlement process. JIAS would soon find itself in a losing battle against the onslaught of immigration restrictions.[52]

The establishment of JIAS was a singular accomplishment of the Canadian Jewish Congress. It would be a long time before it had another. By 1921, the CJC imploded, hobbled by a lack of money and weak leadership. The organization became an organization in name only.[53] A decade later, with Hitler now in control of Germany and antisemitism on the rise both at home and abroad, the need for a strong Jewish voice was never more important and never more elusive. CJC reinvented itself in 1933, and hoped to meet the challenges. One of the many issues the rebuilt CJC faced was how to react to Canadian participation in the 1936 Olympics.

Chapter Two

Press, Preparations, and Protests:
January 1933–August 1935

In January 1934 the German general consul for Canada, Dr. Ludwig Kempff, forwarded to Canada an invitation, over Hitler's signature, that it send a large contingent of athletes to the 1936 Olympics. Kempff added that the German government was deeply moved by the Olympic spirit and regarded the Olympic Games as "one of the most important institutions for creating in the youth of all countries mutual understanding and a feeling of respect."[1]

In truth, the Nazis had no interest in the Olympic Games as a vehicle for enhancing "mutual understanding." For the Nazis the Olympics represented cosmopolitanism, redolent of the ideals of the hated Weimar Republic and the antithesis of the Nazi ideal of Aryan superiority and exclusivist nationalism. Even though Hitler became open to the Olympics in the first months of his regime, the two prime movers behind the games, Theodor Lewald and Carl Diem, were still concerned Hitler would pull the rug out from under their Olympic plans.[2] On 16 March 1933 Lewald met with Hitler, propaganda minister Josef Goebbels, and interior minister Wilhelm Frick. Lewald knew what to say to his new bosses. He confidently promised that "no other event can even remotely match [the Olympics] in terms of propaganda value."[3] Hitler, taken with the idea of showcasing his new Germany, confirmed his support for the Olympics, and Goebbels set up a special Olympic committee within the Propaganda Ministry.[4]

But there could be no "propaganda value" if countries refused to come to Nazi Germany to attend the Olympics, and the Nazis made enemies abroad almost as quickly as they implemented repressive measures at home. As early as April 1933, Avery Brundage, the president of the American Olympic Committee (AOC), had to answer American questions about holding the Games in a land riddled with racial and religious prejudice. That month, *Newsweek* had reported that "anti-Jewish feeling [had] spread through German sport."[5] And how could there be a successful Olympic Games without the Americans? After all, in the 1932 Olympics in Los Angeles, American athletes had taken forty-one gold medals. Their closest competitor was Italy, with twelve.[6]

As the Americans contemplated their options, the organizers of the Olympic Games offered reassurances, first that there would be no restrictions on Jewish athletes from abroad, and then that the German team would not exclude Jews. Many Americans, however, remained sceptical. In November the powerful Amateur Athletic Union (AAU) issued a sharp warning that it would not certify American athletes for the Olympics if the German Olympic Committee did not offer reassurances – "in fact as well as in theory" – that Jews would be eligible for the German team.[7]

Although Brundage and his AOC tried to lessen the impact of the AAU's threat, Olympic officials in other countries, including Canada, took note of the American protests. In early November 1933, P.J. Mulqueen, president of the Canadian Olympic Committee (COC), told the *Toronto Daily Star* that he would not be surprised if the Amateur Athletic Union of Canada (AAUC) decided at its December meeting in Winnipeg that it was not going participate in the Games in Nazi Germany. Mulqueen insisted that Canada would take the high moral road, even if it led away from Germany. Alluding to two prominent Canadian Jewish athletes, track star Bobbie Rosenfeld and world-class speed walker Harry Cieman, Mulqueen told the press, "Think how difficult it would be for us to place into competition in Berlin in 1936, the 1936 edition of Bobbie Rosenfeld, or a Harry Clemans [*sic*]."[8]

The responses by Canadian Olympic officials set up a pattern of behaviour that would become all too familiar: make some sympathetic noises about ensuring the Olympic Charter is respected, and proceed privately as if nothing was wrong. As historian Bruce Kidd has pointed out, the minutes of the Winnipeg meeting made no mention of the discrimination issue.[9] Only weeks after that meeting, John Howard Crocker, secretary of the COC, made it clear that there was little doubt about Canada's participation. Ottawa had forwarded the German invitation to Mulqueen but, because Mulqueen was away, Crocker answered that the final decision on attending had yet to be made, but that, "as Canada has been represented at the Olympic Games wherever held, I have no doubt that the reply will be favorable."[10] Crocker's confidence was justified. Once Mulqueen returned from his travels, the executive of the COC met and affirmed its desire to send a Canadian team. Crocker proudly conveyed the information to the German Olympic Committee, and promised that "Canada will do her part in presenting a good team for participation in the 11th Olympiad in 1936."[11]

The official decision to participate in the Olympics ultimately would rest with delegates to the AAUC's 1935 annual meeting. However, Canadian opponents of the Nazis, especially the organized Jewish community and those on the political left, were not about to let the final decision be made without a fight. For many of them, derailing the Olympics was a battle, and an important one, in the larger struggle against Nazi Germany. The weapons in the battle were public education, organized protests, and political pressure. But to prepare for battle, Canadian opponents of Hitler's regime had to organize themselves and court allies.

Press and Protests: Background

The Anglo-Canadian press gave full coverage to Hitler's assumption of power in 1933, but there was little press consensus on Hitler's significance to Germany or to the world. Two liberal newspapers, the *Winnipeg Free Press* and the *Toronto Daily Star*, repeatedly pointed to the brutality of Hitler's regime. Within days of Hitler's Enabling Act, the reporters and editorialists of John W. Dafoe's *Free Press* began railing against the Nazis' suppression of free speech. In late March 1933, Dafoe denounced the regime's antisemitism and the contemptible attempts to hide it: "There is no mania quite so revealing as that of Jew baiting ... The nation that indulges in it 'places' and 'dates' itself far beyond the power of the most skillful casuists to enter apology or defence."[12] In the summer and fall of 1933, the *Free Press* also expressed alarm at the wholesale expulsion of Jews from the German universities and justice system as part of a policy of "Nazification."[13]

The *Toronto Daily Star* shared many of the anti-Nazi positions of the *Winnipeg Free Press*. This was no surprise. After the First World War, the owner of the *Star*, Joseph E. Atkinson, turned his paper into a voice for progressive reform in domestic matters. Soon it was the most read newspaper in Canada. While some of its more conservative rivals denounced it as communist, the *Star* most often supported the federal Liberal Party, but freely turned on them when it felt the Liberals were not supporting progressive causes.[14] The *Star* was equally outspoken on international affairs and maintained its own small stable of foreign-based journalists. Atkinson's correspondents in Europe, mostly notably Matthew Halton, Pierre van Paassen, and Coralie van Paassen, wrote harrowing accounts of the Nazification of German society.

The most remarkable of them – and a figure of great significance in the Olympics story because he would attend both the Winter and the Summer Games in Germany – was Halton. Born in Pincher Creek, Alberta, in 1904, Halton studied at the University of Alberta and then the London School of Economics before he began working at the *Star* in 1931. Atkinson astutely identified the young Halton as a rising star, one who possessed a sharp critical sense and an intelligently belligerent style. One year after Halton started, at the age of twenty-seven, Atkinson posted him to London, from where Halton reported on events unfolding in Europe.

Halton travelled twice to Germany in 1933. In March, he sent back reports on how the Nazis were teaching hatred, including a chilling description of "a parade of hundreds of children, between the ages of seven and sixteen, carrying the swastika and shouting at intervals, 'The Jews must be destroyed.'"[15] Halton had no patience for the optimists who saw Hitler's regime as a nightmarish passing interlude that would end once Germans came to their senses. With eerie foresight, Halton predicted "that Hitler has come to stay until he is displaced by assassination, civil war or a disastrous foreign war."[16] Later that year, Halton returned to Germany for a month and the *Star* published twenty-seven articles further detailing the Nazification of Germany. Even using the correct German term – *Gleichschaltung* – Halton explained how the regime was coordinating all aspects of society.[17] He made it clear that political dissidents, especially the communists, had been stripped of their rights, and he worried for the future of the Jews: "The least that a Jew in Germany can suffer to-day for the crime of being a Jew is the loss of ordinary rights of citizenship. What else is in store for them, apart from what the history of this year has already recorded, will soon be known."[18]

The more conservative Canadian newspapers also covered German developments, but with a generally less accusing tone. In the summer of 1933, the *Toronto Globe* and the *Montreal Gazette* published thirteen articles by Erland Echlin, whom the *Globe* portrayed as a "young Toronto newspaperman posted in Germany to supply authoritative information."[19] Echlin portrayed Hitler as commanding the total support, even adulation, of Germans of all ages. After an exclusive interview with

Hitler, Echlin described the Führer as "moderate" and "kindly," a man who "stands for peace."[20] The *Globe* and the *Montreal Gazette*, joined by the *Toronto Evening Telegram*, dismissed the *Toronto Daily Star*'s anti-Nazi reporting as gross exaggeration. The *Evening Telegram* made a point to praise Hitler's anti-Bolshevism.[21]

The mainstream Canadian daily press may have been politically partisan but it was rarely monochromatic. On one occasion the *Star* ran a story that laid part of the blame for Nazi antisemitism on the behaviour of the Jews.[22] The same *Toronto Evening Telegram* that had reacted scornfully to the *Star*'s descriptions of the horrific brutality of the Nazi regime included in its 29 July 1933 issue a careful refutation of outlandish German denials that Jews were being persecuted.[23] Other Canadian newspapers also issued mixed messages. In Vancouver, the *Sun* and the *Province* oscillated between mocking Hitler as a political clown and expressing horror at his untrammelled power. These newspapers also condemned Nazi antisemitism, but their coverage was generally short on specific examples.[24]

In the midst of this back and forth in the press were those intent on swaying Canadian public opinion. German consular officials actively courted positive German coverage in the Canadian press. Among their other responsibilities, Ludwig Kempff in Montreal and Heinrich Seelheim in Winnipeg reported on what was being said about Germany, and by whom, and sought ways to ensure the regime was seen in the best possible light. Because of their official status, they had ease of access to a press interested in events unfolding in Germany. In September 1933, the *Montreal Gazette* printed Kempff's denial of systematic Nazi mistreatment of German Jews during the first month of Nazi power. Jews were not targeted, the consul insisted; Germany was only intent on defending itself against those Jews with communist tendencies. Besides, if Anglo-Saxon countries were so sympathetic to the Jews, he demanded, why was immigration of Jews to those countries virtually impossible?[25]

The consuls also worked behind the scenes to shape the news. The German consuls in Canada were thrilled to see Erland Echlin's sympathetic articles on the front pages of the *Globe*, especially as compared to the negative reporting by Halton. After eight of Echlin's articles were published, the journalist, reputed to be low on funds, was quietly granted funding by Goebbels's Ministry of Propaganda, likely on the advice of the German consuls in Canada.[26]

Fascism was not just an overseas phenomenon. Adrien Arcand in Quebec, as well as various "swastika clubs" and the Canadian Union of Fascists in Anglo-Canada, sought to create a "made in Canada" Nazism, but they were more noisy than influential.[27] Several groups of German speakers also tried to set up pro-Nazi movements, the most prominent being the Deutscher Bund of Canada. Although its membership never surpassed 2,000, with most of them in Western Canada, the *Bund* exerted some influence on German Canadians through the German-language newspaper *Deutsche Zeitung für Kanada*, established in June 1935.[28] Pro-Nazi forces were also successful in turning some of the festive *Tage* or German Days into occasions where German Canadians could lift up their voices in rousing choruses of the Horst Wessel song and hear Nazi propaganda as the swastika flag flew overhead.[29]

The Canadian left and the Jews worked hard to counter the message being put out by the German consuls and Nazi sympathizers in Canada. First, they spoke to their respective constituencies. Canadian communists had their own English-language newspaper that cautioned about the influence of Nazi propaganda in Canada. German-speaking communists in Canada also had their own newspaper that carefully monitored the actions of the consuls and their German-Canadian sympathizers. When one German fascist organization tried to represent itself as a cultural organization, the German communists were quick to expose the organization as a Nazi front.[30]

The Canadian Jewish press also wasted no time in negating the pro-Nazi propaganda and attacking the brutality of Hitler's regime. Toronto Yiddish newspaper *Der yidisher zhurnal* offered its readers disturbingly detailed reports on events following Hitler's assumption of power, especially the enlarging circle of Jewish repression in Germany.[31] By the end of March 1933 the Montreal-based *Canadian Jewish Chronicle* was taking the non-Jewish press to task for minimizing threats facing the Jewish community of Germany.[32] In Vancouver, the *Jewish Western Bulletin* initially hoped that the ostracization of German Jews in the early months of Hitler's regime would be no more than a short-lived chapter in the long history of antisemitism. By the summer of 1933, the paper's diagnosis and prognosis became bleaker: "As the Nazis tighten their strangle-hold on the Jewish people in Germany, the more evident does it become that this nightmare is going to last for some time to come."[33] On the first anniversary of Hitler's regime, the *Jewish Western Bulletin* sadly proclaimed that the "Nazi regime celebrated its first anniversary

... with nothing to indicate that the storm of international protests against its cruelties has had the slightest effect."[34]

Talking to the converted, however, was not enough. How could the opponents of the Nazi regime counter the "expert" and "insider" knowledge of German consuls, and get the attention of the Canadian public? One of the most effective strategies for the opponents of fascism was to offer alternative eyewitness accounts of events unfolding in Germany. Few visitors to Germany commanded more Anglo-Canadian press attention than Rabbi Maurice Eisendrath. Eisendrath was an American-born Reform rabbi proud of his German-Jewish ancestry and of the cultured, cosmopolitan Germany that had produced Beethoven, Brahms, Goethe, Schiller, and Kant.[35] He was hired in 1929 to serve as spiritual leader of Holy Blossom Temple, the congregation of Toronto's Jewish elite. He was not, at first, a favourite of working-class and Yiddish-speaking Jewish Toronto. Within weeks of his arrival in Canada, he became embroiled in a confrontation with the strongly Zionist and working-class Eastern European Jews of Toronto. Over time the tension abated somewhat, but the road to understanding between the Reform rabbi of Toronto's wealthy Jews and the more downtown-based immigrant Jews was, in fact, a rough one.[36]

If downtown Jews regarded Eisendrath as an outsider to the experience of immigrant Jews, his education, eloquence, high profile in the media, and previous experience in Jewish-Christian dialogue made him an obvious choice to lead the Jewish community's anti-defamation work.[37] He also had an established reputation among both Jews and non-Jews as an excellent orator. Posters announcing his lectures before non-Jewish audiences painted him as a "Brilliant Hebrew Scholar Preacher and writer," and as "The Silver Tongued Orator." Eisendrath reached many with his preaching, both directly and indirectly. On Sunday mornings he delivered well-attended weekly sermons, which were frequently announced on the church page of the Saturday *Toronto Daily Star*, always concluding with, "The public is Cordially Invited." Many of these addresses were later printed and circulated as separate issues of a publication titled *Holy Blossom Pulpit*. Summaries of his sermons regularly appeared in the *Toronto Daily Star* and in the Jewish press. Through the 1930s, Eisendrath even had a popular prime-time weekly radio show, *Forum of the Air*, making him the first rabbi to host a national radio program. His broadcasts, either Sunday afternoon or Sunday evening, earned him a wide audience and, as his reputation grew, he was frequently invited to address Jewish and non-Jewish gatherings.[38]

Eisendrath was deeply committed to Jewish-Christian relations before the Nazis came to power. Thus there was no hint that the bridges between him and the non-Jewish community were artificial or crudely opportunistic when the Jewish situation deteriorated in Germany. From the time of the rabbi's arrival in Toronto, he followed in the footsteps of his predecessor Ferdinand Isserman, exchanging pulpits with Protestant ministers and participating in the massively successful interfaith York Bible Class. Eisendrath's passion for the ethical implications of the prophetic teachings brought him in close contact with leading liberal Protestant ministers imbued with the Social Gospel. He was soon invited to join committees dealing with social issues and he became active in the Toronto chapter of the pacifist Fellowship of Reconciliation.[39] Eisendrath also met regularly with a small group of ministers, including his friend and fellow pacifist United Church minister, G. Stanley Russell. Once the Nazis came to power, Russell immediately expressed his solidarity with Eisendrath and promised to help lead the fight against the Nazis: "I have written [to another member of the group] and told him that I am rather ashamed that nothing has been done by the Christian churches of the city to protest against the mediaeval happenings in Germany. I have told him that I hope the Group will act ... I need hardly say that I have spoken freely in my own church already."[40] For Eisendrath, who was comfortable speaking to Christian groups and lecturing about Christianity, it was a relatively smooth transition from delivering a pre-1933 talk he called "The Relationship of the *Sword* with the Cross" to one entitled "The Relationship of the *Swastika* to the Cross."[41]

In order to deepen his understanding of the events in Nazi Germany, Eisendrath visited twice, first in the summer of 1933 and then again two years later, in the summer of 1935. His reputation as an anti-Nazi activist preceded him. In June 1933, the German general consul in Montreal, Kempff, wrote to his superiors in Berlin informing them of the rabbi's arrival and describing him as "one of the main instigators against Germans."[42] Eisendrath lived up to his reputation. Soon after leaving Germany in 1933, Eisendrath met Halton in Paris, and the resulting interview made it to the front page of the *Star*. Eisendrath was, in Halton's words, "[a] young man, well known in Canada as a liberal and human thinker whose beliefs know no barrier of creed." And what did he see? Eisendrath insisted that the reports of brutality against Jews and Hitler's political rivals were all too true. The rabbi described to Halton how the Jews in Germany were "rapidly being reduced to the condition of pariah dogs," and how he saw teachers separating Jewish children from their classmates. He spoke of the Nazi distortions of Christianity to serve their militaristic aims: "I saw armies of little children marching ... they are being taught that to die on the battlefield is glorious, and that in eternal peace mankind is ruined."[43]

Eisendrath complemented his observations with research. He worked hard, as he would tell one audience, to understand Nazi antisemitism: "While in Germany I took great pains to read tomes of [the] venomous propaganda, which one can procure in any book stall or official Nazi store."[44] He also consulted with foreign consuls based in Berlin to find out if they thought the reports of the foreign press were exaggerated. The consuls insisted they were not. What about those reporters who quoted leaders of the German Jewish community who said that things were not so bad? Eisendrath tried to convey, from his experience, why these statements were not to be believed: "I know how these denials are procured ... Perhaps a band of Nazis come to your house at dead of night [sic], bearing a carefully prepared statement. You are asked to sign. No? Well, by your side a babe is sleeping. They say to you 'Maybe a careless kick of the boot will kill the child.'"[45]

But as Eisendrath discovered, there were others who also claimed the status of witness – others who also travelled to Germany and drew very different conclusions about what was taking place in the new Germany. Victor Lange, a native of Germany and professor of German at the University of Toronto, frequently returned to visit his homeland. In November 1933, after a four-month stay in Germany, Lange was interviewed by *Canadian Comment* magazine. He claimed the persona of the impartial but informed witness, able to grasp and explain essentials while eschewing sensationalism. According to Lange, the Third Reich was born of spiritual conviction, drawing on what was best in both Christian and Germanic cultures. He dismissed Weimar as having produced no real German culture; in contrast, the new Germany would produce an "authentic" German culture, one mindful of its Christian roots and duties. What of book burnings? According to Lange, the banned books that the Nazis gleefully torched were works of "colorless intellectualism" rampant in Weimar and better gone. The German government was not malevolent, he continued, but was pursuing legitimate political goals. The widely misunderstood concentration camps were there not to punish, but to protect state goals. He even suggested Nazi policies then being implemented had much in common with Roosevelt's New Deal. As to the Jews, there were obvious adjustments needed, as they were over-represented in certain segments of German society – including the Communist Party. And, he explained, the Reich was getting a lot of bad press because "international public opinion is moulded by a Press which is in no instance independent."[46] All this was too much for Eisendrath. The Toronto rabbi wrote a stinging response, calling into question Lange's statistics, innuendos, and false analogies. Where in the United States, for example, are "camps being filled with people who have never seen the inside of a courtroom?"[47]

A year later, Eisendrath took on another traveller who had returned from Berlin with positive views of the regime. On 9 October 1934 the *Toronto Daily Star* reported on an "illustrated lecture" that Rev. Dr. Bingham of Toronto's Temple Baptist Church delivered, entitled "From Toronto to Berlin." Bingham was one of the forty Canadians who travelled to Berlin in August for the World Assembly of Baptists. According to historian Robert Wright, the Canadian Baptists were proud that the Nazis did not hijack their conference; however, "not a few of them" left with views more favourable to the Nazis than when they arrived.[48] One of these, unnamed by Wright, was Bingham, who attended as a representative of Quebec and Ontario. As reported in the *Star*, Bingham portrayed Hitler as an "idealist" whose ideals may not be to everybody's liking but were valid. Bingham, like Lange, also said that Jews were over-represented in Germany as doctors and lawyers. Bingham's effort to be even-handed could offer no comfort to the Jewish community. According to the *Star*, "Declining to offer any opinion as to the justness of Hitler's action, Dr. Bingham acknowledged the great hardship it had brought upon the Jewish population."[49]

In a letter to the *Star* written two days later, Eisendrath breathed fire. He was astonished that a Christian minister could not understand that Hitler was "making a mockery of his own Christian religion." That, according to Eisendrath, was Bingham's prerogative, but Eisendrath could not stand by quietly when Bingham came back to Canada looking to spread distorted views "fed by Nazi propagandists." Eisendrath insisted that there are those who travel to Germany and see through the regime, and those who become the dupes of the regime. He had no doubt that Bingham fell into the latter camp: "Having been to Germany myself and having listened to the self-same speakers, I have little difficulty in recognizing the superficial source of the so-called facts and figures which he has been presenting as authoritative."[50]

By the spring of 1935 Eisendrath felt he was losing ground as an authoritative commentator on what was going on in Germany. It was

two years since he had visited Germany and, without first-hand experience of a quickly changing Germany, Eisendrath worried he could no
longer command media the way he did following his 1933 visit. His
name was more likely to appear on the social pages than in hard news
stories. As a result, although he had not planned on going to Germany
again, when he set out on a trip to Palestine with his wife in the summer of 1935, he decided that he had to add Germany to their itinerary:
"I owed it to my fellow Jews both in Germany and at home, to find out
the truth, the unadulterated and naked truth. I owed it likewise to my
fellow citizens ... to become one more eyewitness of these events which
are so seriously and perhaps irreparably challenging all the values of
our respective religions and our common civilization."[51]

Anti-Fascism and the Left

Few other anti-Nazi activists in Canada equalled Eisendrath's high profile, but even the most well-known crusader could not do battle alone.
There were just too many challenges: the rise of fascism overseas, the
emergence of home-grown fascism, and biting antisemitism at home.
In response to these developments, opponents of the Nazis – especially
the political left and the Jews – fumbled their way towards organizing
an anti-fascist campaign.

Socialists and communists around the world did not have to wait
long to see the horrific implications of Hitler's appointment as chancellor in January 1933. The day after the Reichstag fire of 27 February
1933, an act the Nazis blamed on the communists, the elderly president
von Hindenburg signed the "Decree for the Protection of the People
and the State." With one stroke, the Nazis ended various rights, including freedom of assembly, freedom of speech, and freedom of the press.
And with dizzying speed, the Nazis began to arrest political opponents and throw them into hastily arranged concentration camps (also
known as "wild camps"). Goebbels' *Der Angriff* proudly announced
the arrest of 130 Communists in Berlin and 140 in Hanover. It is estimated that the Nazis imprisoned 50,000 so-called political opponents
by April.[52] Among the most famous of the prisoners was Ernst Thäl-
mann, the communist leader who had on various occasions run for the
German presidency. In early May the authorities occupied union offices
across Germany, arresting labour leaders and seizing union assets. By
the middle of the month all unions were forcibly incorporated into the
German Labour Front, an organization run by the Nazi Party. In June

the Social Democratic Party was outlawed, and in mid-July a law was enacted outlawing all new political parties.[53]

While the Nazis may have decided that there was no difference between red and pink, left-wing politicians of different hues did not join forces easily. How could they? In the five years before the rise of the Nazis, in what would become known as the Third Period in communism, the communists made a virtue out of sowing disunity. In 1928 the Comintern abandoned its previous orthodoxy – that it was necessary to work within the existing trade unions – and moved to a policy demanding that communists set up their own radical unions and political parties. The diagnosis from Moscow was that the capitalist order was on its deathbed and the time was ripe to build a new order. The social democrats were attacked as enemies and their unions and political ideals dismissed as tools of the existing political order that stalled the inevitable victory of communism. The social democrats were, in fact, "social fascists," and must be viewed as adversaries in the class struggle.[54]

The new directive had significant results. In the summer of 1928, the Communist Party of Canada (CPC) formed two "red" unions, the Auto Workers Industrial Union and the Industrial Union of Needle Trade Workers, to challenge for membership. In late 1929 the Party created its newest variant of a central union, the Workers' Unity League. Each of these creations led to deep rifts within the Canadian labour movement. Among garment workers, for example, there were vicious fights over membership and tactics between communist and non-communist unions.[55] The Workers' Unity League took up the struggle of the Communist Party against the umbrella organization of craft unions, the Trades and Labour Congress of Canada (TLCC). Although labour had made few inroads in Canadian electoral politics, communists took aim at J.S. Woodsworth, the most prominent of the social democrats in Ottawa.[56] At the local level, at least in Winnipeg in the late 1920s and early 1930s, communist aldermen drew heavily on the party vocabulary to call their rivals in the Independent Labour Party (ILP) "social fascists"; in riposte, the ILP counterparts accused the communists of promoting dictatorship.[57]

As communists attacked others on the left, they also had to be wary of the authorities. The communists lived in the shadow of section 98 of the Criminal Code that threatened and inflicted harsh penalties on associations charged and found guilty of planning or promoting the overthrow of the government. Although this could limit the appeal of the CPC during the "Third Period," with the onset of the Depression and the increased labour vulnerability, many workers supported the militant unions set up by the communists.[58] The popularity of the CPC surged even more when, in 1931, the RCMP charged eight members of the CPC with seditious conspiracy under section 98 of the Criminal Code. The Canadian Labour Defence League (CLDL), an organization established in 1925 and much in sympathy with the communists, took up their cause. The CLDL had previously made a name for itself by defending workers, including the foreign-born radicals who were subject to deportation. The defence of the eight arrested became the organization's most publicized campaign. Still more support fell their way when prominent communist Tim Buck was arrested for fomenting a riot while in prison, and the general secretary of the League, the Reverend A.E. Smith, was charged in 1934 with sedition for claiming that the prime minister was responsible for an order to shoot Buck in prison. With all this publicity, the CLDL grew; with Smith's acquittal, however, membership dropped precipitously.[59]

Officially, the "Third Period" and its confrontational approach to others on the left ended at the Seventh Comintern held in Moscow in the summer of 1935. In the new diagnosis of the world scene, fascism represented, in the words of one communist official, "the open terrorist dictatorship of the most reactionary, most chauvinistic, and most imperialist elements of finance capital."[60] Events in Italy and even more so in Germany demonstrated that the old tactics of confrontation with social democrats had not halted the spread of fascism, and needed to be replaced by "united fronts" of labour and "popular fronts" or political alliances between communists, social democrats, and other antifascists. Unofficially, advocates for concerted action against fascism had begun reaching out to others several years earlier. In 1932 the French communist Henri Barbusse organized the Amsterdam World Congress against (Imperialist) War, and in 1933 a Workers' Anti-fascist Congress was one of the organizers of the World Youth Congress against War and Fascism that convened in Paris. Although still communist-driven, a number of preparatory conferences brought together communists and socialists. With this pressure coming from below, Stalin endorsed "bourgeois coalitions" in 1934.[61]

These initial efforts at international anti-fascist cooperation were complemented by changes, also before the seventh Comintern, at local and national levels. The mushrooming of anti-fascist groups in

Canada – well documented in RCMP reports – suggests Canada experienced much the same as what historian Nigel Copsey describes was also taking place in Great Britain, namely a "grassroots involvement in the loose patchwork of local anti-fascist committees that was already beginning to emerge ... in 1933."[62] Events in Verdun, Quebec, during the fall of 1933 clearly demonstrate that some communists were ready to embrace the new form, while others remained antagonistic to their old enemies. The Verdun Workingmen's Association called a meeting that included a number of churches and athletic bodies in hope of organizing a "United Front Anti-Fascist Conference." Two hundred people heard several speakers discuss the threat of fascism and the need to press for popular action. Some of the unreconstructed communist participants, however, retained their "third-period" thinking and insisted that only workers should be involved in the fight – that there was no reason to trust let alone unite with the "petty bourgeois" and intellectuals.[63]

Youth organizations appeared much more ready to embrace the popular-front idea. Peter Hunter was ten when he moved to Hamilton with his family in 1922. He joined a Marxist youth group a decade later. The group, he said, had grave concerns about the rise of fascism and made anti-fascism a priority. It also reached out to all those opposed to fascism. As a result, the doctrinaire communists taunted the group for being "social fascists," but the youth's call for inclusive activism gathered momentum. Hunter was not himself initially a member of the Party or of the Young Communist League, but his popular-front committee raised enough to send a delegate to the 1933 World Youth Congress against War and Fascism in Paris, and Hunter was the group's choice.[64]

Several months after his return, Hunter was busy promoting a Canada-wide youth organization and planning for a National Youth Congress against War and Fascism to be held in August 1934. Local anti-fascist groups also sought to build broad-based support with mixed results. In Winnipeg, for example, the local anti-fascist committee invited twenty-seven churches to join a local youth congress against war and fascism. In the end, the local congress consisted almost entirely of organizations affiliated with the Communist Party.[65] The National Youth Congress took place in Toronto with over 200 delegates joining together from across Canada. For the most part, the leadership and the membership were communists, although one of the lead speakers was a municipal politician from Ontario from the socialist Independent

Labour Party.[66] The Youth Congress also attracted some support from liberal clergy, such as the well-known advocate of the Social Gospel, Salem Bland, and the ubiquitous Rabbi Eisendrath.[67]

One of the results of the Youth Congress was another call for a "United Front" in the struggle against fascism. The delegates of the Youth Congress moved for the creation of a provisional committee to plan a conference that would spur organization of a national league against war and fascism. The provisional committee, concerned to bring together all those opposed to fascism, reached out to trade union organizations, cultural groups, fraternal organizations, and the various clubs of the recently established Co-operative Commonwealth Federation (CCF).[68] The base support for anti-fascist activity was widening elsewhere as well. In late September, twenty-six organizations came together in Edmonton, including a Reverend Black of the Central United Church in Edmonton, who stated, according to the RCMP report of the meeting, that "the United Church in Canada is heartily supporting the anti-war and anti-fascist movement."[69]

The culmination of the anti-fascist initiative was the First Canadian Congress against War and Fascism held in Toronto on the 6th and 7th of October 1934. As its communist initiators hoped, the gathering endorsed and promoted the establishment of an expansive anti-fascist coalition. Supportive telegrams came from socialist leaders such as Otto Bauer of Austria, and from the well-known journalist Pierre van Paassen of the *Toronto Daily Star*, who explicitly called for "the widest possible front. From this moment onward let there be no enemies on the left."[70] The chairman of the American League against War and Fascism, Methodist minister Henry F. Ward, gave one of the opening addresses, and his presence was said to have "effectively dispelled the Communist plot myth."[71] But old habits die hard. Some of the communist delegates could not get their minds around cooperation with non-communists and dismissed social democrats as "petty reformers," while a spokesman for "Rationalists" delivered a withering attack on those attracted to anti-fascist activity out of religious conviction.[72] Despite these tensions, even the RCMP informant monitoring the gathering admitted that "the Communists have cause to be well satisfied with the result of this congress. It is indeed one of the outstanding achievements in the history of the Communist Party of Canada."[73] The organizers of the Congress against War and Fascism announced that it had set into motion a wide movement against war and fascism with the title "Canadian League against War and Fascism."[74]

Anti-Fascism and the Jewish Community

The rise of Nazism abroad and antisemitism at home also created demand for an organized response from Canadian Jews. Hitler's assumption of power in the spring of 1933 brought representatives from more than 100 Toronto Jewish organizations together in mid-March to plan a mass anti-Nazi rally. On 2 April Toronto's Massey Hall filled quickly, and according to the local Yiddish press, many thousands had to be turned away.[75] On that same day, Winnipeggers gathered in the Winnipeg Auditorium for an anti-Nazi protest rally organized by sixty local Jewish organizations that came together in a "Temporary Winnipeg Committee."[76] In Montreal, a People's Committee to Protest against Anti-Semitism in Germany organized a rally for April 6, and invited prominent politicians and clergymen to speak. According to the press reports, over 10,000 people filled the Mount Royal Arena.[77]

However successful these and other rallies turned out to be, they were one-shot events. What was needed was a sustained anti-Nazi campaign, and for that organizers realized that they needed a national organizational structure dedicated to the cause and which could command respect from politicians and the media. This was not the first call for such an organization. In 1919, a number of Canadian Jewish groups, with the Labour Zionists at the forefront, joined in establishing the CJC, to serve as the "parliament of Canadian Jews." After some initial enthusiasm, the organization became, for the most part, moribund.[78] H.M. Caiserman, an immigrant journalist and Montreal Labour Zionist committed to strengthening the Jewish community and deepening Jewish identity, kept the weakened CJC on life support. Until the early 1930s he remained the lone voice of a hollow organization.

In the wake of both Hitler's rise to power and heightened concern about home-grown antisemitism, there was increasing support for the idea of a national Jewish umbrella organization that could serve as a voice of the Canadian Jewish community.[79] Less than two weeks after the anti-Nazi rallies, leaders of the Winnipeg protest wrote to Caiserman, suggesting that the time was right for a re-energized national organization. The drive to organize quickly gathered momentum. In early May 1933 a group of prominent Jews from Montreal, Toronto, and Winnipeg met in Montreal to discuss a renewed CJC and proposed a national organizing conference in Toronto for early June. Not surprisingly, there was some disagreement on the organization's proposed mandate. Some felt that the organization should concern itself exclusively with the immediate situation facing Jews in Germany. Others pressed for a broader organizational mandate, including Jewish relations with government and the non-Jewish community, especially with regard to combatting antisemitism in Canada. The June meeting eventually concluded that a large tent vision was best,[80] but the struggle against Nazism remained a priority.[81] On a practical level, however, what could Canadian Jews and their revitalized Canadian Jewish Congress do? Toronto Jews proposed organizing an economic boycott of German goods and services. But, much to the chagrin of one correspondent from Toronto's Yiddish newspaper, representatives from Montreal and Western Canada rejected that strategy as too confrontational, preferring instead to fight a war of words – educate the public, woo press sympathy, and lobby government for support of the German Jewish cause.[82]

It was one thing for delegates to the May meeting to agree on an organizational agenda; it was another thing to deliver. The fledgling CJC would have to draw in various constituencies of the Jewish community before it could even claim to speak for the mainstream Jewish community. Eastern-European Jews dominated the original Canadian Jewish Congress organized in 1919, and the Labour Zionists who remained at the heart of the movement had little patience or, for that matter, contact with, the more established and wealthy Canadian Jews – the so-called "uptown" Jews. For their part, these more established Jews who, in the main, belonged to Reform synagogues, displayed limited concern for the immigrant Yiddish community. But Caiserman and others knew that Congress would need to draw uptown Montreal and Toronto Jews into the organization. This was less a problem in Western Canada where, according to Caiserman, Winnipeg and the other Western communities had a "more intense Judaism and national consciousness," and more natural commitment to unity.[83] In the cities with the two largest Jewish communities, however, the Jews of the West End of Montreal and the Jews of the "Bond St. Synagogue" (Eisendrath's Holy Blossom Temple in Toronto), as well as the "elements that follow them in various cities in Canada," had historically kept themselves apart, and that risked undermining any national organization.[84]

Caiserman worked hard to bring uptown Jews into the CJC organizational fold. It was not easy, Caiserman explained to a colleague, but he was ultimately able to convince the "West End" Jews of Montreal to set aside their often class-biased reservations and join the CJC movement.[85] On another occasion Caiserman explained that earlier experiences – especially issues to do with the placement of Jewish children in a Montreal educational system bifurcated along Catholic and Protestant religious lines – had convinced him of the value of bringing immigrant and established Jews together under one organizational roof. Besides, without the financial support of the wealthier part of the community, there could be no CJC, or no CJC with muscle.[86] To shore establishment support for the CJC in Toronto, Caiserman approached Rabbi Eisendrath after the latter returned from his summer 1933 trip to Nazi Germany. Eisendrath, quickly recognizing that a single united Jewish organizational platform was essential to establishing a Jewish community anti-Nazi campaign, was quickly onside provided, of course, that downtown Jews were indeed prepared to share organizational power. Eisendrath had felt slighted by the Toronto organizers of the earlier Jewish anti-fascist protests who, he believed, had deliberately excluded his participation.[87]

Even with Eisendrath on side, tensions between different Toronto Jewish community factions could not be completely papered over. This was hardly surprising given the basic differences in world views. When Egmont Frankel, a wealthy Toronto scrap dealer and one of Eisendrath's "group," showed up in Montreal in late 1933, Caiserman and several others met with him to discuss the workings of the CJC. Frankel, it seems, could not fathom the notion of an organization that not only spoke in the name of the Jewish community, but also acted with the consent of the Jewish grassroots. Caiserman asked his colleague in Toronto, A.B. Bennett, to please make Frankel understand that *noblesse oblige* was no longer enough. "The masses behind a movement also means [sic] something."[88] At the same time, the *Canadian Jewish Chronicle* warned against any backsliding from organizational democracy: "We have had enough of the *shtadlans*[89] and self-appointed spokesmen. Canadian Jewry has been woefully remiss in the establishment of an organization that actually represents the unanimous voice of the people throughout the land."[90]

But who would control the new organization: the Labour-Zionist-dominated downtown Jews, or the more affluent uptown Jews? The tension between the two camps threatened to derail the January 1934 plenary, which, for all intents and purposes, was the true founding moment of the new CJC. The Labour Zionist group moved that the new organization "support the Jewish Agency in the development and upbuilding of the national homeland in Palestine." Eisendrath, who was wary of all nationalisms, including Zionism, wanted the wording "national homeland" removed so that the resolution would call for the support "of the Jewish Agency in the upbuilding of Palestine." Delegates voted in the first wording, but when Eisendrath left with a threat to abandon the CJC and take his "group" with him, the matter was discussed again and Eisendrath's wording accepted. Incensed at the reversal, two prominent Zionist leaders, convinced that the plenary had been hijacked by patricians, promptly resigned.[91] They left, but Eisendrath returned and was put in charge of the fledgling organization's anti-defamation work for Ontario, an obvious appointment given his public profile and his connections with leading progressive churchmen.

Although Eisendrath rendered, by all accounts, yeoman's service in the CJC, there remained a chill between him and many in the Yiddish-speaking and working-class Jewish majority. On at least one occasion, the Yiddish press of Winnipeg sang secular hosannas in praise of the rabbi's speech on the fate of German Jewry, which would seem to indicate a rapprochement.[92] But in the eyes of many he remained an elitist patrician. In an editorial in early 1937, Moses Frank, editor of Toronto's *Jewish Standard*, took note of Eisendrath's increased warmth towards Zionism following his visit to the Jewish settlement in Palestine in the summer of 1935. He also acknowledged the great strides that had been made by Canadian Jewish Congress to bring together the disparate elements of the Jewish community. As far as Frank was concerned, Eisendrath remained distantly aloof and needed to learn more about the Toronto Jewish masses: "[Eisendrath] showed a most remarkable aptitude in that direction in the six weeks he spent in Palestine. He might do well to take off six weeks for an intensive study of the College and Spadina district."[93]

Divisions among the Anti-Fascists

While both Canadian Communists and Canadian Jews responded to the frightful realities of the early 1930s by establishing organizational structures they hoped would be effective in confronting the fascist threat, old antagonisms did not evaporate. The older "third-period" communists distrusted the advocates of the united front, and in the Jewish community the gulf between older established Jews and the more recent Eastern-European Jewish immigrants was not easily bridged. If some understood the necessity of unity, others rejected invitations to work together.

The most significant socialist organization in Canada to reject the call for a united front was the social democratic Co-operative Commonwealth Federation (CCF). Established in 1932 as the political amalgam of existing democratic socialist and labour groups, the CCF ratified its manifesto in Regina in 1933, and looked with optimism towards its political future. And the optimism seemed justified; in the Toronto municipal election of 1934, James Simpson was elected mayor on the CCF ticket.[94] The communists wasted no time trying to join forces with the CCF. The Canadian Labour Defence League (CLDL) also made overtures to the CCF at its Regina convention, calling for a "united front" to free Tim Buck and to repeal section 98. The CLDL proposed that the respective national executives of the CCF and the CLDL meet to organize "joint mass meetings, delegations and demonstrations on this burning issue." CCF leaders responded that they wanted a repeal of section 98 and the release of Buck and the other prisoners, but they would not work in union with the communists. The CCF leadership argued that as a democratic movement dedicated to using constitutional methods to achieve its goal, they did not regard "civil strife" as either inevitable or desirable. Formal collaboration with the communists was not an option.[95]

When the CCF first rejected the overture, it was rejecting the partisans of an organization that had its roots in the "third period" of confrontation. When the organizers of the First Canadian Congress against War and Fascism approached the CCF, however, it was ostensibly a different group with a different approach,[96] and it seemed that there were some signals on both sides that collaboration was possible. *The New Commonwealth*, the CCF weekly, publicized an anti-fascist rally in Toronto in August 1934 that was sponsored by the newly formed Canadian League against War and Fascism (CLAWF) and subsequently printed a full report on the event. The report noted the enthusiasm of the crowd, concluding with an appeal from the secretary of CLAWF "to support the October Congress and specifically for broad united campaigns in Toronto."[97] From RCMP reports on CLAWF meetings across the country, and from CLAWF itself, there can be little doubt but that many members of the CCF were attracted to the notion of a united front.

The central leadership of the CCF, however, was determined to hold firm against any formal ties with the communists or any of their front organizations. The editor of the *New Commonwealth*, Graham Spry, was all the more convinced of the correctness of that policy after he read a harsh condemnation of the CCF's decision to keep at arm's length from the communists penned by his communist counterpart, Leslie Morris, the editor of *The Worker*. Morris denounced the CCF for not joining in this new anti-fascist movement. CLAWF, Spry responded, is a communist-inspired and communist-led organization, and as democratic socialists the world over know, the communists have "sought not to co-operate but to destroy."[98] Two weeks after CLAWF's formation, the *New Commonwealth* reminded its readers of the official policy of the party, that the "units in the C.C.F. are expressly and definitely prevented from cooperation with any other political movement by the provincial and national constitutions. The Communist party, under whatever guise, is another political front with any Communist unit." The separation message was important because communists all over Canada – and all over the world – were looking to build alliances. More specifically, "unit after unit of the C.C.F. has been approached in Ontario, and invariably the proposal of a united front has been rejected."[99] But the official CCF stand against common action with the communists did not eradicate the members' enthusiasm for united front-like action, even among CCF stalwarts. In March 1935, the Toronto and District Conference against War and Fascism had as one of its speakers Frank Underhill, a leader of the League for Social Reconstruction, the inspiration and brain trust of the CCF.[100] Moreover, the CCF's *New Commonwealth* frequently publicized CLAWF publications.[101]

Some members of the Jewish community were also partisans of united front cooperation, including cooperation with CLAWF. Eisendrath, for one, eagerly embraced the possibility of a broad-based coalition. He attended the first CLAWF organizational meeting in October 1934 and became convinced of its historic importance. With unabashed enthusiasm, he proclaimed that this meeting was "one of the most thrilling events in the history of Toronto." He admitted that he had come to the gathering with "misgivings," probably because of the widespread suspicion that it was going to be a propaganda ploy by the communists. His concerns, however, were "banished by the splendid spirit shown throughout." After visiting Germany in 1933, he welcomed every effort to muster support for the crusade against war and fascism. According to the published report of the gathering: "Rabbi Eisendrath finished [his talk] by making a stirring and dramatic plea for a united front as the only means of stemming the tide of fascism in Canada and of beating back the plans of the war mongers."[102] Eisendrath also agreed to serve on the new group's Program Committee, and subsequently sat on the body's National Council.[103] Eisendrath was not the only prominent Canadian Jew at the Toronto meeting. Ida Siegel, whose credentials as an activist in Jewish communal affairs were impeccable, also participated. She was at the time an elected school trustee for the Toronto Board of Education, and she wanted to see school children brought into the anti-fascist struggle.[104]

Eisendrath hoped in vain that the newly revived Canadian Jewish Congress would share his enthusiasm. It was not to be. Caiserman wrote Eisendrath that he had read in the press about Eisendrath's participation at CLAWF's foundational meeting and wondered what the Toronto rabbi was doing at a communist gathering. Eisendrath tried to deflect the implied criticism by informing Caiserman that the group was honestly dedicated to working with non-communists, even including them in the leadership.[105] And, not to be forgotten, CLAWF was ready to combat the fascists even as most "middle class and right-wing groups have stood idly by."[106] Caiserman would have none of it. He wrote Eisendrath a long and hard-hitting reply warning that Jews could well end up further marginalized by this kind of alliance. One of the Nazis' core antisemitic canards, one that had some purchase with wider audiences, was that the Jews were subversive radicals ready to overturn the established order for their benefit. Caiserman worried that the closer Jews were seen to get to communists and communist front organizations, the more the Nazi claim would ring true in the popular mind. Caiserman suggested Eisendrath look critically at CLAWF. Did not the Trades and Labour Congress of Canada, the leading organization of craft unions, refuse to have anything to do with CLAWF? The same was also true of the CCF and most churches. With scarcely contained contempt, Caiserman challenged "anyone to show me one constructive piece of work done by the Communist parties of Canada, either in their own name or otherwise, during the last fifteen years of their existence." Rather than jeopardize the good name of the Jewish community by allowing Eisendrath to associate his name with a communist front organization, Caiserman cautioned the rabbi that he would do better to forge alliances with religious denominations, or with the League of Nations society, "or any other one which can command the confidence of every group."[107]

Eisendrath disagreed with Caiserman and continued to work with CLAWF, even as he pressed on with his responsibilities to the CJC. Eisendrath contributed to the newly established journal of CLAWF, *Action against War and Fascism,* in its first issue of May 1935.[108] Caiserman had little choice but to acquiesce. Eisendrath was so important to CJC activities in Toronto that it was unthinkable that he should be forced out. But Caiserman remained concerned about the danger of close contact between Jews and communists, an argument he made to other Jews attracted to CLAWF, and again without much success. In February 1935 he wrote to J.A. Cherniack of Winnipeg, repeating his fears about the dangers of consorting with a communist organization.[109] Cherniack, however, was willing to work with communists and, years later, remembered how active the local chapter was in its anti-fascist activities, how popular it was on the Jewish street, and how it "aroused the anger of certain Congress people, especially my friends Keller, Sheps, Steinberg and Rabbi Solomon Frank, President of the Congress. We had bitter encounters."[110] In early 1935, Caiserman and the members of the Hamilton Branch of the *Arbeter Ring* (Workman's Circle) exchanged harsh words on the same issue. The *Arbeter Ring* mocked the CJC's role in the anti-fascist struggle and disdained the CJC's anti-communism. As a result the group resigned from the CJC in favour of working with CLAWF. After a few attempts to resolve the dispute, Caiserman basically said good riddance.[111] Clearly the CJC – like the CCF – would have liked to have more control over its anti-fascist campaign. Just as clearly, many anti-fascists believed they would be most effective in forging alliances that were as broad as possible.

Anti-Fascist Campaigns

While some were debating the proper organization of anti-fascist elements in meeting halls, others were taking the anti-fascist campaign into the streets. In March 1935, for example, the German light cruiser *Karlsruhe* arrived in the port of Vancouver. The visit was marked by protests against both the presence of the ship and the cordial welcome from the local German community and Canadian naval establishment.[112] Fourteen months later, the German training cruiser *Emden* sailed into Montreal over the protest in Parliament by CJC president and long-standing Liberal, S.W. Jacobs, with equally harsh condemnation from CLAWF and the Trades and Labour Council.[113] Words, however, did not satisfy an ad hoc group made up of Young Communist League members and boys from the Young Men's Hebrew Association (YMHA) who marched down to the port of Montreal to protest.[114]

But rallies and street protests were one-of-a-kind events. Both the CJC and CLAWF wanted to organize sustained and ongoing anti-fascist activities. The CJC and various groups on the left, for instance, advocated for a boycott of German goods and services. At the CJC's plenary meeting in 1933, while some delegates called for such a boycott, the idea was set aside. However, the 1934 General Session of Canadian Jewish Congress, now well aware of the organized Nazi boycott of German Jewish businesses, joined Jewish organizations around the world in endorsing a boycott of German goods.[115] A resolution called on the CJC national executive to "take steps to co-ordinate and support all existing efforts in Canada ... as long as present persecutions in Germany prevail."[116] The CJC struck an economic boycott committee. Among its first moves, the committee petitioned the government to limit trade with Germany and reached out to Jewish and non-Jewish businesspeople in hope of convincing them to boycott German goods or sales to Germany.

According to a mid-1935 boycott committee report, the CJC was successful – more or less – in bringing many Jewish-owned businesses in line with the boycott, even suggesting alternative sources for the purchase of goods previously secured from Germany. The CJC's overall success, however, was far more limited. This is not altogether surprising. How could pro-boycott advocates convince a Depression-era government and business community, desperate to find markets for Canadian exports, to close its doors to a growing German market? Politicians and businesspeople, after all, could argue that would mean sacrificing the national economic good to benefit parochial Jewish interests. Accordingly, CJC insiders agreed: "What must be accomplished is the divorce of 'boycott' and 'Jewish.'" In an effort to ensure the CJC would "not be the public face," or the only face, of the boycott campaign, efforts were made to find liberal and labour organizations that would front the CJC's boycott campaign while allowing the CJC to continue to plan, research, and finance the effort.[117] Throughout 1934 and 1935 the non-communist Trades and Labour Council was helpful in this regard, passing resolutions endorsing the boycott at several of its meetings. But the economic boycott's exact impact is hard to gauge. One thing is certain: the Canadian government was unmoved. As of the fall of 1936, the government was not debating the ethics of trading with Germany but rather how to increase bilateral trade between Germany and Canada.[118] And even as it pressed on with its economic boycott campaign, the organized Jewish community was very much involved in a parallel boycott campaign – a campaign to have Canada boycott the 1936 Nazi Olympics.

Turning to the Olympic Campaign

The year 1934 seemed to start off well for organizers and supporters of the German Olympics. Early in January, a short item in the *Toronto Globe* announced that with "political and racial prejudices apparently forgotten, German sports officials have commenced preparations for the 1936 Olympic Games."[119] Canadian game advocates had every hope that rumblings of an international Olympic boycott would come to nothing, and that the Nazis and the national teams could go about the business of preparing for the Winter and Summer Olympics. The plot, however, unfolded somewhat differently.

In March 1934, as Olympic preparations were building up a head of steam in Germany, a variety of American labour groups sponsored a mass anti-Nazi rally in New York City's Madison Square Gardens. As part of an anti-Nazi platform, several speakers proposed a boycott of the German Olympic Games. Several weeks later, the American Jewish Congress publicly demanded that the American Olympic Committee (AOC) study the situation in Germany to determine how holding the Olympics in Germany would impact Jewish athletes who might wish to compete. As a result of this challenge, Brundage, who was warned that the Amateur Athletic Union (which was a completely separate body from the AOC, unlike in Canada) might not allow athletes to compete in Germany if there was any discrimination against Jewish or other athletes, agreed to embark on a fact-finding mission to Germany in the summer of 1934. He returned from his trip, which was carefully orchestrated by the Nazis, insisting that the Germans would show no prejudice against Jewish athletes.

In Great Britain, anti-Olympic pressure was also building. In 1933 labour groups and the Jewish community raised concerns about Nazi racism and antisemitism prompting the head of the British Olympic Committee, Lord Aberdare, to write to Theodor Lewald, chair of the German Olympic Committee, in early 1934. Lewald reassured Lord Aberdare that the Germans would abide by Olympic rules. And if some particular Jewish tennis stars or boxers were being excluded, what of it? Restrictions on Jewish participation in German sports clubs had been in existence for years, and it was also well known that Jews were excluded from various clubs in Great Britain. Lord Aberdare may have been satisfied with the response he got, but the Jewish community was not. It worked to mobilize opinion at home, and started to reach out to Jewish communities abroad asking them to join an Olympic boycott campaign. On 3 July 1934, the London Jewish Council wrote to the CJC in Montreal, warning that the Olympics in Nazi Germany would be more than just games – they would be a showcase of Nazi racism and antisemitism. Jews worldwide were implored to bring pressure to bear on their respective national Olympic organizations to deny Germany Olympic glory and to join the boycott campaign against the Berlin Olympics.[120]

Less than two weeks later, Canadian Jewish Congress responded with the promise that it would indeed pick up on the issue.[121] However, the CJC was hardly in a position to mount any concerted anti-Olympic campaign. Newly revived, understaffed, and underfunded, the CJC was focusing its limited resources on the economic boycott and anti-defamation work in Canada. It also was trying to keep a lid on those in the Jewish community who favoured the kind of public protests that the CJC leaders feared would alienate the larger public and frighten off some in the Jewish establishment still unsure about working with the CJC's largely immigrant and pro-Zionist rank and file. Thus, despite their reassurances to London, the CJC did not act on the Olympic boycott file in any systematic fashion for another year. Nor did the other anti-fascist groups; while 1934 witnessed a growing number of anti-fascist activities, most notably with the creation of the Canadian League against War and Fascism, the issue of the Olympic boycott was not yet on the radar in Canada.[122]

Others, meanwhile, were busily engaged with planning for the Nazi Olympics. The German consuls in Canada fulfilled their brief by monitoring negative press coverage and responding when necessary. In one mind-boggling case, the German consul in Winnipeg, Heinrich Seelheim, marched into the offices of the local Yiddish newspaper, *Dos yidishe vort*, in order to correct what he held to be misconceptions about what was taking place in Nazi Germany. What about Nazi racism? Jaws must have dropped when Seelheim explained that National Socialism does not teach that Jews are inferior; rather, that they are a race apart. And mass arrests? Prisoners in concentration camps are treated humanely, he continued, and are there in order to decrease racial hatred. And what about rumours that the Olympics would not be open to all peoples? Seelheim proclaimed that all foreign athletes, regardless of race or religion, would be treated with fairness. Whether Jews would be permitted on the German team was quite another matter. Consistent with his other remarks, Seelheim made the case that any absence of Jews from the German team should not be regarded as racism but as in line with German policy of keeping the races apart and, as such, might be regarded as a German version of the American court-endorsed doctrine of "separate but equal." As a parting gift, Seelheim left the Yiddish newspaper a pamphlet by the Reich minister of the interior, Wilhelm Frick, on the race question. Who could have been a better expert on race than Frick, one of the architects of the "social death" of German Jews?[123]

Although there was little organized anti-Olympic activity in Canada in 1934, Canadians who read the mainstream press would be well aware of Games preparations in Germany. The *Toronto Globe*, for example, reported on the lavish construction plans for the Olympics and associated cultural events.[124] Another article conveyed admiration for the athletic training of youth in Germany: "They take instruction very seriously and follow what the coach tells them. I'd like to take a group of young Germans and work with them. They are fine physical specimens and anxious to learn."[125]

The readers of the *Globe* were also exposed to mounting anti-Olympic protests, particularly in the United States. The newspaper reported on both protests lodged by the Jewish community and the counter assurances by Avery Brundage, head of the American Olympic Committee, that there would be no discrimination against Jewish athletes.[126] There were no editorials on the Olympics in the *Globe* in 1934, although the battle over the Olympics did encourage one *Globe* reporter to mock the much-heralded unifying power of international sports. The writer quipped: "Those loudly ballyhooed international events, known as the Olympic Games, have proved on the whole no less prolific of international irritations than disarmament conferences."[127]

Given the increasingly fractious debate over American Olympic participation, it is remarkable how little "irritation" was played out in Canada throughout most of 1934. That would change in November when the AAUC held its annual meeting in Toronto. Much to the shock of the Canadian Olympic Committee executive, the Alberta chapter presented a direct and uncompromising proposal to the Resolution Committee. Why Alberta? Although documentation from the meeting is scarce, one of the leading members of the Alberta delegation, W.G. Hardy, a classicist at the University of Alberta who was also a central figure in the Alberta amateur hockey establishment, reported his own experience to a colleague. Hardy explained that in late 1933 he had been "on the borders of Germany ... and saw quite enough then to convince me the Nazi regime is one of force violence and repression."[128]

The Alberta resolution made explicit and powerful reference to the persecution of Jews:

Whereas, the Olympic games are scheduled to be held in Germany, in 1936, and whereas many of the outstanding athletes of the world are of Jewish descent; and whereas a definite policy of discrimination and repression has been pursued by the German government against the Jewish population of that country; and whereas the policy of discrimination has surely not tended to produce an atmosphere of good fellowship and will surely not produce international comradeship among the representatives of all the competing nations, which we believe essential to Olympic games; Be it therefore resolved that through the proper channel, we ask for the assurance from the Committee in charge of the 1936 Games that no discrimination will be shown any athlete whatever his or her race or creed, and in the event that such assurance cannot be given that this branch favour a change of location for the 1936 Olympic Games.[129]

According to a report of the Resolution Committee, the issues caused "considerable" discussion. Opponents of the resolution claimed that there was no need for the resolution as the American Olympic Committee headed by Brundage had already decided there would be no discrimination. In order to salvage the resolution, committee member J. Hornstein, a Jew who sat on the board of the Quebec branch of the AAUC, countered that the resolution should be brought to the floor, but without the demand for a change of Olympic venue. He was convinced that "it was quite in order that Canada should officially express herself on the matter."[130]

A majority of the Resolution Committee agreed with Hornstein, and the resolution was forwarded to the general meeting of the AAUC. But then the chair of the Canadian Olympic Committee, Mulqueen, stepped in. Hoping to avoid fueling discussion of a possible Olympic boycott, he argued there was no need for the AAUC to make a public statement. He told the meeting that his Olympic Committee only agreed that Canada should send athletes to the Olympics after it he had been satisfied by a "direct report" from the Americans that the 1936 Olympic would be free of discrimination.[131] Taking a further cue from the Americans, Mulqueen pledged that Canada would withdraw from the Olympics if Germany did not live up to its obligations. Mulqueen's arguments convinced the delegates, and Alberta withdrew its resolution and left the matter up to Mulqueen's COC.[132]

Discussions in the Press

Mulqueen had dodged a bullet and, as far as he was concerned, the matter was closed. The matter did not appear on the agenda when the COC executive met the next day, nor did the press pick up on it.[133] The *Toronto Daily Star*, which followed the Olympic scene more closely than any other major newspaper in Canada, gave a single-paragraph mention to the Alberta resolution in the middle of a catch-all article on the AAUC annual meeting. The item ended parroting the official line coming out of Germany: "Several delegates said sufficient assurance had been received from German officials to discard the fear that discrimination would be shown."[134]

Although the COC executive did not deem it necessary to discuss the likelihood of German Olympic racism, it did discuss kick-starting serious preparations for the 1936 Games. The committee's major concern was with financing the Canadian team in the midst of a biting economic depression. Mulqueen informed the group that he did not expect the federal government to offer as large a subsidy as it had on previous occasions. To underscore the committee's precarious financial situation, the COC treasurer reported that the committee had a grand total of $400 in the bank. With funding tight, the COC would have to mount fundraising campaigns, but even at that, Mulqueen warned that athletic clubs and sporting federations that wanted to send their athletes to the Olympics would have to come up with the lion's share of the cost.[135]

However, Mulqueen remained confident that sufficient means would be found to send a strong Canadian team to the 1936 Olympics and called on the COC to start publicizing the upcoming Games. By the time the November meeting took place, the COC was already in receipt of promotional photos, mats and printed materials from the German Olympic Committee and German tourism authorities. The COC's Secretary declared the time was now appropriate to release them to the media.[136] Several months later, the Secretary sent a letter "To the editors of the Canadian newspapers," informing them that the Winter Olympics were only a year away and that Canada planned to send a good-sized team." The Secretary also told the press that the German Olympic Committee had opened ticket sales on 1 January 1935 and that in short order more than 1,000 tickets were sold. The implications were clear. The Olympics was going to happen. They would be big. Canada would be there and a Canadian cheering section should be there too. The COC promised to supply the press with materials from the German Olympic

Committee as they became available and the newspapers gave assurances they would do their part in publicizing the world's premier sporting event.[137]

The press did help. The newspapers' sports pages reported tidbits on Olympics preparations both in Germany and Canada, and the COC also had some personal press connections it could call on to wave the Olympic flag. Influential sports columnist Lou Marsh of the *Toronto Daily Star*, for example, was a very close friend of Mulqueen and an Olympic advocate.[138] But the COC also had to fend off press allegations that the COC members were elitist fat-cats unable to relate to the common people and less caring of athletes than of inflating their own self-importance. The Vancouver papers hardly ever bothered to refer to the Canadian Olympic Committee by name, instead preferring to talk about the "Old Boys."

If the COC had an image problem, it also had the problem of dealing with the endless stream of ugly news coming out of Germany. In February 1935 Canadian newspapers reported on an upsurge in antisemitic violence in Germany that escalated yet again between June and August. According to the press, this violence was not spontaneous. It was well organized. Looking to incite hatred of the Jews "from below," the Nazi Party orchestrated physical and economic attacks against Jews across Germany. The implications were obvious. In September 1935 Vernon McKenzie of the *Toronto Globe* reported: "Striking indications have been observed during the past two months to show that the Nazi hatred and harassing of Jews is not going to abate." In the face of this stark reality, McKenzie was disheartened that there were still some in Canada who fooled themselves into believing that Nazi antisemitism was exaggerated or somehow the fault of Jews. According to McKenzie anyone who still adhered to these views in the fall of 1935 was captive to wilful blindness. Moreover, McKenzie admitted that he too had previously underestimated the depth of antisemitism in Germany: "Two years ago I believed sadistic anti-Semitism to be a temporary Nazi policy, practiced by Nazis not yet fully under central party discipline. I fear that I was wrong."[139]

With the increase in anti-Jewish violence, and with the Olympics on the horizon, the Canadian press increased coverage of the international demand for an Olympic boycott. On 6 August 1935 the *Vancouver Sun* printed a lengthy front page article from the Associated Press claiming that the Nazis were harassing foreign journalists reporting on the anti-Jewish and anti-Catholic violence.[140] In an editorial on the same day, the *Vancouver Sun* pointed out that the pro-boycott movement was getting stronger and if a boycott did indeed come to pass, "the Germans will have only their own government to blame." And what about the claim that the Olympics was supposed to be above politics and free from manipulation of government power? Could the Nazis be trusted to treat all athletes with equal respect? Certainly there was cause for concern. The editorial noted that Jews and Catholics would be on teams from around the world, and "these young men [*sic*] can hardly be blamed for being reluctant to accept hospitality from a government which is persecuting their fellows." And what of the call for a boycott? The editorial allowed that it was worth considering. It would demonstrate to the Nazis the degree to which their actions stirred international revulsion and might just "lead to a modification of the policy and a curbing of some of the more empty-headed Nazi fire-eaters."[141]

In the wake of the anti-Jewish riots in Germany, the American Jewish Congress and the newly established Jewish Labor Committee joined in demanding an American boycott of the Olympics. More dramatically, the head of the AAU, judge Jeremiah Mahoney, at odds with Brundage, became an advocate for the boycott.[142] Some Canadians latched onto the rising tide of anti-Olympic sentiment in the United States as inspiration for an Olympic boycott campaign north of the border. In early August, Marsh published in his *Star* column a letter written by a Canadian boycott supporter who claimed that any "fair-minded" person would have to acknowledge the increase in Nazi persecution. Citing the progressive *Christian Century* out of Chicago, the letter writer demanded that "the world must show that they can't play with a people who have lost all sense of a civilized people." According to the letter writer, "just as the Americans were taking the idea of a boycott seriously, so must the Canadians."[143] The Jewish press also found hope in developments to the south. *The Canadian Jewish Chronicle* informed its readers that one of the most influential editors of the day, Arthur Brisbane, of the Hearst press empire, called for the removal of the Games from Berlin because of religious persecution – and when the Hearst Empire spoke, those in power listened.[144] Vancouver's *Jewish Western Bulletin* reported that donations to the AOC were down because Catholics and Jews opposed its decision to participate in the Berlin Games.[145]

But Olympic proponents refused to yield, even in the face of the news coming out of Germany, and the press acknowledged the pro-Olympic arguments as well. The same *Vancouver Sun* that had come out for serious consideration of a boycott also reported Brundage's oft-repeated endorsement of Germany's pledge of fair play.[146] The *Toronto Globe* gave full coverage to the views of a sports writer from Los Angeles who told Americans that they should behave like other nations that "recognize that the political and racial questions do not belong in a discussion involving the Olympics." The only result of a boycott, he argued, would be the "loss of United States athletic prestige."[147]

The sports editor of the *Globe*, M.J. Rodden, personally shared these views. Rodden endorsed Brundage's claim that Germany would not discriminate at the Olympics, and, if he were wrong, any show of discrimination would surely result in a change of venue. Rodden then expressed his hope that "common-sense ideas will prevail, and that the games will go on as scheduled." While it was important, he felt, to send Hitler a message that there should be no religious prejudice, he also claimed that "those who fear the worst should at least be charitable and not jump at hasty conclusions."[148] By implication, Rodden was saying that the riots of the summer of 1935 did not constitute enough evidence to "fear the worst."

The Protests Take Shape

Although the press response to the call for a boycott was mixed, the left and Jews around the world became increasingly forceful during the summer of 1935 in demanding that the Games be removed from Germany. But getting organized over the issue of sports was no easier than getting organized over other issues. Through much of the interwar period, the world of sports reproduced the political animosities that had riven the left. The socialists had their own organization (best known as the Lucerne Sport International, established in 1920) and their Workers' Olympics. The latter attracted huge numbers: in 1931 over 76,000 athletes from twenty-three countries gathered in Vienna.[149] In response, the Comintern announced the Red Sport International in 1921, and introduced its own international competition, the Spartakiads. In Canada, the Young Communist League took on the task of creating party-led sports organizations for the workers. The resulting Workers' Sports Associations, with branches across the country, treated with disdain the "bosses' sports organizations" – the YMCA, YMHA, and the Amateur Athletic Union of Canada and its branches – and looked to destroy them, especially with the introduction of "third period" tactics in 1928.[150]

But then these "third period" tactics fell out of favour. In 1935 Canadian communists and their supporters began organizing popular fronts even before the official Soviet approval of the popular front idea. The meeting establishing the Canadian League against War and Fascism, the group with the highest profile of all Canadian anti-fascist organizations, was, according to RCMP reports, a success. But the meeting made no mention of an Olympic boycott, and discussion of an Olympic boycott did not figure prominently in communist publications in the first half of 1935, even though the pro-boycott arguments were then gaining traction in the United States.

In June, however, the anti-Olympic campaign gathered momentum. The Workers' Sports Association made plans for Canadian athletes to visit the USSR to tour Soviet health and fitness programs and compete with Soviet athletes. The tour was presented as preferable to attending the Olympics in Berlin.[151] Also in June, Moscow breathed new life into the boycott campaign. The Canadian communist member attached to the executive of the Comintern wrote back to Canada that the Red Sport International had decided that its sections should start working with "reformist" sports groups to create a united workers' sports movement or, in other words, a popular front. On the international sports scene, the communist Red Sport International decided to begin discussions with the socialist Lucerne Sport International. Moscow wanted more organizations in each nation to press for the boycott of the Berlin Olympics. In Canada, the CPC and Young Communist League used the Workers' Sports Association to bring the issue to Canada and to create a popular movement against the participation in the "Hitler Olympic Games." To achieve their goal, Moscow informed them, they needed to reach out beyond the "revolutionary sportsmen." It was time to drop the old taunts of "bosses sports" and work with "factory sports leagues, ... local and national amateur organizations, [and] church and fraternal sports clubs and teams..." Moscow, for its part, would start to produce boycott materials to be used in the campaign. With so many workers involved in sports," the directive continued, the "possibilities of such an anti-fascist movement among sportsmen are tremendous." Party members should not just look to sports groups; they were specifically encouraged to draw the League against War and Fascism into the campaign. The correspondence concluded by reiterating both the importance of the work and that the CPC and YCL should adapt the campaign to the Canadian situation. The Party and the press had to focus on the sports movement, "and in particular, at the moment, to the anti-Olympiad agitation. At the present time, this is not done."[152]

The Communist Party's new marching orders were clear and, by the end of the summer, party stalwarts were lining up to take the lead in anti-Olympic activism. The party newspaper devoted to youth issues took up the boycott cause. The linkage between the delegation of Canadian athletes to the Soviet Union and the anti-Olympic cause was made even more explicit than before. In the words of Jim Turner, national secretary of the Workers' Sports Association, "the Canadian delegation leaving for the Soviet Union is the first successful step in the Anti-Olympic campaign."[153] Several weeks later, Turner again put pen to paper in a more detailed article on the Olympics and the boycott campaign, documenting the exclusion of non-Aryan athletes by the Nazi sport. He ended the article with a call to action: "Build up the anti-Olympic committees in your organizations and protest to the International and Canadian Olympic Committees."[154]

During the summer of 1935, party members were also actively working to reach Canadian youth with the boycott message. The most prominent of Canadian youth organizations at the time was the Canadian Youth Congress, with local councils across the country. It was formed in Toronto in August 1935 with an explicit anti-fascist mandate. At its initial meeting in Toronto, the Canadian Youth Council – which regarded itself as the "continuation committee" of the Congress against War and Fascism – was addressed by long-standing Communist Party organizer William Kashtan, who pressed the importance of an Olympic boycott. He called on the Canadian Youth Council to immediately set up a committee to "initiate action" against the persecution of Catholics and Jews, and called on the Council to "work out measures to develop feeling amongst the sportsmen against the Olympics being held in Germany next year." In the discussion that followed, some felt the Council could do little more than "register a direct protest," while others pressed the Council to act as catalyst to the formation of a Council of Sports Organizations that could lead the campaign against Canadian participation in the Nazi Olympics. There were also calls for further research on what was taking place on the ground in Nazi Germany. One of the names offered as a knowledgeable resource on the situation in Germany was Rabbi Eisendrath, who was then in Germany but would be returning soon. In the end, the Council decided to charge one of its members of the Council, Clare Claus, with the responsibility of "looking into all sides of the [Olympic] question."[155]

In his capacity as "Director of Research, Canadian Youth Council," Claus moved quickly to fulfil his mandate. Two weeks after the meeting, he sent letters to the editor of the *Toronto Star* and at least one other paper.[156] His "research bureau," he claimed, sought to ascertain the truth about allegations of religious and racial prejudice in Germany and by German Olympic organizers in particular. If allegations of racial prejudice proved as horrific as reported, the Council was ready to lobby the Canadian government to lodge an official protest with the Germans and, at the same time, implore individual Canadians to support the economic boycott of German goods and services and join in the protest against holding the Olympic Games in Nazi Germany.

At the same time, the organized Jewish community was also moving on the Olympic boycott issue. As the situation of German Jews continued to deteriorate, the Canadian Jewish street increasingly demanded action. On 25 July, the Dominion executive and the executive of Canadian Jewish Congress' Eastern Division met in Montreal to map out a plan of action. Once again, a key question was whether the CJC should support mass public protest. Some of the uptown community's "older guard" argued that very little could be achieved by a mass protest. They wanted a more temperate and diplomatic approach. Hirsh Wolofsky, editor of the *Keneder Adler* and a man with a finger on the pulse of the Jewish street, countered that the anti-Nazi rallies of 1933 were quite successful, obviously not in toppling the Nazis, but in unifying the Jewish community while alerting the larger society to the threat of Nazism and antisemitism at home. Opponents pointed out that those rallies predated the re-establishment of the CJC. Now the community would be better served by letting the CJC "direct the policies of the Dominion Jewry" in a less militant fashion. Another discussant insisted that mass protests in Montreal could not bring the Montreal Roman Catholic majority on side; that could only be done through the outreach of quiet diplomacy. In the end, the majority opted for quiet diplomacy. The meeting penned a resolution protesting German treatment of Jews to be sent to Ottawa, the British government and the League of Nations. When a member proposed an amendment that the resolution be submitted to a mass community meeting for its approval, the amendment was defeated.[157]

This Montreal meeting made no direct reference to the Olympics. The Olympics was put forcefully on the CJC's agenda in Toronto, home base of the COC "Old Boys." Five days after the Montreal meeting, the Executive Committee of the Central Region of the CJC held an emergency meeting in Toronto. They too were worried that pent-up anti-Nazi sentiment would spill out into street-level protest. The *Arbeter Ring*, which remained outside the CJC tent, had been calling on union and labour groups to join a mass anti-Nazi protest the following day. The Toronto CJC, minutes of the Montreal meeting in hand, feared this kind of protest could get out of hand and undermine CJC efforts to win government and press support for the economic boycott of Germany. The executive chairman of the CJC's Central Division, A.B. Bennett, pressed for a strategy – "in view of the present great interest" – to boycott the 1936 Games. He proposed that the CJC should publicly and loudly advocate "among Canadian sports circles" for a boycott of the Games, and that sports writers be specifically lobbied to support a boycott. He also called on the CJC to find sympathetic "leaders of public opinion" who could be quoted in the press. In short, he proposed a diplomatic campaign on an issue that he thought could win support in the non-Jewish community and convince Jewish community activists that Jewish community leaders were determinedly working on the Nazi file.[158]

Several concrete proposals emerged from the Toronto meeting. Members decided to attend the *Arbeter Ring* event the next day in order to propose joint action but, following the Montreal lead, eschewed mass public protest. They affirmed their support for lodging a protest with Ottawa although, rather than dispatch a telegram to Ottawa, they wanted the resolution delivered in person. They also agreed to set up a special committee to explore the issue of the Olympic boycott or, more specifically, to consult with "a few of the more important Jewish athletes" on how to get a sympathetic hearing "for our proposal of Canadian abstention from the Olympics if the latter is held in Germany."[159]

The Central Division knew that by refocusing on the Olympic boycott, it was taking the CJC's anti-Nazi work in a new direction. The next day Bennett forwarded to Caiserman minutes of the meeting along with a plea that any protest to Ottawa be delivered in person, as it would be less cold than simply forwarding a telegram. A meeting with ranking officials in Ottawa might, he pleaded, also go a long way to satisfy the community "hotheads" who were clamouring for street-level protest. He also asked Caiserman's opinion of the Toronto plan to prioritize the Olympics boycott.[160]

Caiserman's initial reply was approving but not particularly helpful. He suggested that any Olympic boycott committee should involve the "best men in the community," code for finding CJC sympathizers and not community hotheads and, perhaps, for searching out non-Jews. In addition, Caiserman allowed that, as far as he was concerned, an Olympic boycott campaign might help educate the Canadian public to the dangers of Nazism, but the chances of actually dealing a decisive blow to Canadian participation in the Nazi Olympics were at best unlikely. Nevertheless, it was important to try. As he put it, "I do not know where it will be possible to influence the Olympic committees in the various countries to change the meet from Germany to another country, but anything that we can do to bring this about as far as Canada is concerned, is in my sincere opinion, of the greatest importance."[161]

In short order Caiserman also put the Olympic boycott on the CJC agenda. In order to find out what other organizations close to the Olympic issue were doing, he got in touch with AAUC insider Hyman Ernest Herschorn and asked him to feel out the president of the AAUC on the Olympic issue. Herschorn was certainly plugged into the Canadian Olympic world. Born in the last decade of the nineteenth century, he received his law degree in 1914 and was a member of a prominent Montreal firm for nearly fifty years. Despite a crippling disease that affected him shortly after his legal career began, Herschorn had seemingly unbounded energy to dedicate to amateur sports. By 1935 he had served as the president of the Canadian Amateur Swim Association (CASwA) for more than a decade, and had coached the swimming teams at the 1928 Amsterdam and 1932 Los Angeles Olympics. He had a vote at the meetings of the AAUC and at the Amateur Athletic Union (AAU) in the United States.[162]

Herschorn was also the president of Montreal's YMHA. The "Y" was, in effect, a Jewish community centre with a wide range of educational and athletic activities, modelling itself on the famous 92nd Street Y in New York City. The organization opened an excellent new sport and cultural facility in 1929; one year later, a prominent official of the Jewish Welfare Board (JWB), the parent organization of YMHAs in North America, told senior members of Montreal's "Y" that "your own beautiful home typifies in its plan and design the more recent Y.M.H.A. and Jewish Centre buildings that may be found throughout the United States."[163] In 1934, Montreal's "Y" registered 1,200 participants in its various education classes, and 2,000 in the Department of Physical Education. There was no other organization like it in Canada, and it is with justice that one reviewer of the various YMHAs in Canada could call Montreal "the seat of the premier Y.M.H.A. in the country," and the "Y" "one of the primary Jewish forces in the city."[164] In June 1935, Herschorn was elected to a second term as president of the organization.

Herschorn was especially valuable to Caiserman for the former's strong connection to the world of amateur sport. Perhaps unknown to

Caiserman, Herschorn and Mulqueen had a running feud going back to the 1928 Olympics, when Herschorn refused to authorize the entries to the Canadian team of several swimmers who were already in Amsterdam. But, according to Marsh, *Toronto Star* sports writer, the two had "buried the hatchet" in April 1935.[165] When Caiserman and Herschorn met in August, Herschorn, who had already raised the Olympic issue with the AAUC's resolution committee, shared a file of correspondence on the question of Canadian participation in the Olympics dating back to 1933. Herschorn agreed to press Jewish community concerns with the AAUC, and asked Caiserman to prepare a document on the Nazi persecution of Jewish athletes. Caiserman was convinced that he had found a solid ally in the Canadian sporting establishment: "I have the feeling," Caiserman wrote, "that anything that can be done is being done by him."[166] Indeed, Herschorn would figure largely, if not always effectively, in the subsequent campaign to boycott the Games.

By the spring of 1935, the call for a Canadian boycott of the Nazi Olympics was a priority agenda item of both the popular front left and the organized Jewish community. But while they shared the common goal of derailing the Nazi Olympics, they would not share a common platform. Even as they worked separately to prevent Canada sending Olympic athletes to Nazi Germany, the Nazis and the organizers of the Games were moving ahead with their plans to showcase the new Germany. As readers of the German-Canadian press would discover, ethnic Germans around the world were offered a special tax break if they visited Germany during the year of the Olympics.[167] The expatriate Germans did not have to actually attend the Games. Rather, German tourist authorities believed their visits would enhance the aura surrounding the games and solidify their lasting bond with the *Vaterland*. The German Olympic Committee also started publicizing a series of planned educational and cultural events complementary to the Games. If some Canadians were repelled by the thought of holding the Olympic Games in a militant and aggressively racist Germany, others, and certainly the COC, embraced the Games as their own. The tensions between these two camps escalated dramatically in the fall of 1935.

Chapter Three

"Moving Heaven and Earth"

It might be said that Rabbi Maurice Eisendrath never met a lectern he didn't like. And with reason; Eisendrath was a dynamic public speaker, so much so that the pews in Toronto's Holy Blossom Temple were often filled to overflowing when Eisendrath delivered his weekly Sunday morning sermon. Many of those who packed the Temple sanctuary were not even his congregants. Jew and non-Jew, they came because of Eisendrath's well-earned reputation as a spellbinding and often fiery public speaker. If his style was sometimes theatrical, his audience always left with something to think about.

In late 1935 Eisendrath turned the full force of his rhetorical power against Hitler and the new Germany. Only a few months earlier, the rabbi had returned to Canada from his second visit to Hitler's Germany. Eisendrath's voice pulsed with anger as he spoke of the evil he encountered in an emotion-charged sermon entitled "I Re-Visit Nazi Germany." The rabbi took special aim at brutal Nazi repression of racial and religious minorities and that of Jews in particular. Of course, Eisendrath did not need to revisit Germany to know that the Nazis were persecuting German Jews. Eisendrath went, he said, because he felt compelled to go. He needed to have his own personal encounter with the inhumanity of the Nazi oppression. "I would return to Germany," he explained to his audience, "to ascertain for myself just what internal difficulties were causing this new wave of barbarism and brutality which was sweeping over the land."[1]

But Eisendrath also knew that his going to Germany was not without danger. There was certainly no love lost between the Nazis and this prominent American-born Reform rabbi and outspoken critic of Hitler and the Nazi regime. He was apprehensive as the train he and his wife were travelling on crossed the border into Germany. But for all his concern, Eisendrath's entry into Nazi Germany was uneventful and, once in Germany, he was not personally harassed. Although he knew the Nazis to be viciously antisemitic, Eisendrath sensed that they were trying to avoid unflattering press coverage in advance of the Olympic Games. He was convinced, however, that Nazi authorities would closely monitor his movements and, as a result, he was circumspect about where he went and, more importantly, with whom he spoke, lest he inadvertently put innocent people at risk.

As Eisendrath later explained to his Toronto audience, a critical part of the Nazis' Olympic preparations was projecting an atmosphere of welcome for Olympic visitors. To do this the Nazis were forced to put a temporary lid on coarse public displays of antisemitism that might upset international visitors, at least in those locations where Olympic athletes, tourists, and other international guests were likely to gather. The heavy in-your-face brown-shirted Nazi presence in the streets that Eisendrath encountered two years earlier was not nearly so evident, in an effort to airbrush away anything that might offend. And with only five months to go before the Winter Olympics, and a little more than a year before the Olympic village in Berlin would be alive with Olympic athletes, judges, and officials from around the world, Nazi officials seemed determined to keep it that way.

Though the Nazis might have temporarily hid their mailed fist in a velvet glove of Olympic civility, Eisendrath warned it was all for show. The reality of Nazi antisemitism, even in heavy-traffic tourist areas, was not hard to find if one would but look. But, Eisendrath sadly observed, most tourists and even some journalists preferred not to look. Like Hitler and the International Olympic Committee (IOC), most visitors to Germany were invested in the success of the Olympics and willed themselves into believing Nazi talk of sportsmanship and international goodwill, and accepted the Olympic Potemkin village the Nazis constructed as real. Just as international Olympic officials were only too happy to be deceived, Eisendrath claimed, many visitors to Germany were programmed to sing the praises of the new Germany and its Olympic preparations. Seeing only what the Nazis wanted them to see, they expressed awe at Nazi German energy, industry, order, and efficiency, and dismissed reports of repression and antisemitism in Germany as just talk – maliciously exaggerated talk – spread by those who would do Germany and the Olympics harm.

Eisendrath cautioned his Toronto audience not to be taken in. The reported absence of brown shirts in the streets did not signal any softening of iron-fisted Nazi control. Storm troopers, he insisted, still stalked the German street: "They are there by the millions, only one can no longer detect them by their uniforms. Consequently, the atmosphere of terror has only increased for no one knows whether the person next to him in the omnibus or in the subway or looking into the store window is a spying storm trooper or not." Behind painted smiles, the local population still cowered in fear. Nobody felt safe. Compared to his German visit of two years earlier, "the terror has abated not the slightest, but that whispering, for example, [is] still the principal medium of speech and the furtive glance behind one's shoulders [is] still the prelude to every conversation."[2]

What of German Jews? Eisendrath allowed that Jews were certainly not the only ones being ground under the Nazi heel. Many Catholics, liberals, labour leaders, and members of other "minorities" were also subject to Nazis barbarism. But unlike these other Germans, every German Jew, without reference to age or gender or station in society, was consigned to the earthly hell the Nazis reserved for those defined as enemies of the state. In the two years since Eisendrath's previous German visit, those German Jews who had not somehow managed to emigrate or had not, as in the cases of several individuals he knew personally, taken their own lives, had come to know that "the terror still walks abroad by day and the pestilence rages still by night." German Jews, Eisendrath lamented, were "like helpless sheep in the slaughter house, plunging piteously forward toward the axe."[3]

Eisendrath warned that the axe, sharp as it was, was unlikely to fall full force until after the 1936 Olympic Games. But it *would* fall – of this Eisendrath had no doubt. Much though the Nazis and Olympic officials might speak of fellowship through sport and athleticism, and though storm troopers remained on their best behaviour, Eisendrath cautioned that "the Olympic Games will come and go, and the Nazis, relieved of the restraint this year is imposing on them in order not to jeopardize their chance to hold these contests, may break forth in the Fall of 1936 into a wholesale massacre even more bloody and brutal than Kishinev or St. Bartholomew's Eve."[4]

Eisendrath Turns to the Canadian Jewish Congress

As his 1935 visit to Nazi Germany left him feeling disheartened, Eisendrath admonished his listeners that humanity demanded all people of conscience speak out in opposition to Hitler and the Nazis. And the Nazis had given those of goodwill a tool to use against them. Eisendrath came away from Germany sensing that the very Olympic Games that the Nazis so prized as a propaganda tool was also the Nazis' Achilles' heel. Germany, he pointed out, was heavily invested in the Olympic Games; Eisendrath was witness to the fact that the Nazis spared no expense in preparation for the Games. But the Nazi commitment to the Games was not just financial. More importantly, the Nazis were investing German national prestige in the Games, for domestic and international consumption.

Eisendrath was convinced the undoing of Hitler might well begin if the world would but deny him his Olympic triumph. Others had come to the same conclusion, including George S. Messersmith, American consul in Vienna. He reported to Washington that, "should the Games not be held in Berlin, it would be one of the most serious blows which National Socialist prestige could suffer within an awakening Germany and one of the most effective ways the world outside has of showing to the youth of Germany its opinion of national socialist doctrine."[5] In Britain, the United States, and other democratic countries, Olympic boycott campaigns were gearing up to deliver that blow.

Returning to Toronto from Nazi Germany in early September 1935, Eisendrath was determined to do all that one person could do to toss a spanner into the Nazi Olympic machine. He wrote CJC leader Caiserman on the Olympic issue. Eisendrath did not mince words: "One of the main messages with which I have come back from my unexpected but necessary visit to Germany is the absolute necessity of moving heaven and earth to keep Canada and America out of the Olympics. This is far more crucial that those of us on this side [of the Atlantic] can even imagine." Eisendrath, already active with the Canadian Jewish Congress in Toronto, served notice he was ready to roll up his sleeves and take a lead role in furthering the Olympic boycott campaign. Eisendrath requested Caiserman immediately provide him an update on CJC boycott efforts and any future plans.[6]

Caiserman was excited by Eisendrath's offer to take a hands-on role in the Olympic boycott campaign. He was, however, taken aback at what he regarded as Eisendrath's bold if somewhat foolhardy sojourn to Nazi Germany. Caiserman confessed to Eisendrath, "Your information to the effect that you have visited Germany, terrified me. How did you dare take such a chance? I thank the Gods that they have protected you and brought you back safely. My dear friend, there should be a limit to taking chances for me no matter what important causes or service." Grateful for Eisendrath's safe return, Caiserman welcomed

Eisendrath's eagerness to take on a leadership role in the boycott campaign as a godsend. Eisendrath would almost certainly give the CJC's Olympic boycott campaign a much-needed boost in Toronto, national head office of both the Amateur Athletic Union of Canada and its Canadian Olympic Committee. His was also a name to be reckoned with. He was media savvy and reputed to have access to many in the non-Jewish power elite. And, very important to Caiserman, who was an Eastern-European immigrant to Canada, when the American-born Eisendrath spoke, it was without a Yiddish accent.

Caiserman immediately put Congress's limited resources at Eisendrath's disposal. Caiserman also confided to Eisendrath that Congress's Olympic boycott campaign had what he hoped would be an ace-in-the-hole Jewish insider on the Canadian Olympic Committee, H.E. Herschorn – someone, according to Caiserman, who was "persona grata with the sport organizations of the Dominion." Herschorn, Caiserman explained, had agreed to personally put the Jewish case against Canadian participation in the Nazi Olympics before the Canadian Olympic Committee at its next meeting. In the meantime, Caiserman hoped Herschorn could assist Congress by providing useful advice on the ins and outs of dealing with the Amateur Athletic Union of Canada (AAUC) and its Canadian Olympic Committee (COC).[7]

In an effort to soften the ground for Herschorn's intervention, Caiserman requested Eisendrath intercede with P.J. Mulqueen, chairman of the Canadian Olympic Committee, who, according to Herschorn, was both "a Roman Catholic and a great admirer of yours [Eisendrath's]. He is a man to be seen by you." The fact that Mulqueen was a Roman Catholic, Caiserman hoped, might incline Mulqueen to the pro-boycott side. In the United States, prominent Catholics were taking a lead role in the anti-Olympic movement. Judge Jeremiah Mahoney, president of the Amateur Athletic Union, was but one of a number of Catholic leaders supporting a boycott. Others included Al Smith, governor of New York, and James Curley, governor of Massachusetts. The influential liberal American Catholic magazine *The Commonweal* put its editorial weight behind the campaign against American participation in the Nazi Olympics.[8] George N. Shuster, managing editor of *The Commonweal*, was scathing in his assault on those who endorsed sending an American Olympic team to Germany. In November 1935 he sent a reminder to his Catholic readers:

It is true that the coming Olympics are designed to be a glorification of the Nazi doctrine of youth, and therewith necessarily a repudiation of the

Catholic faith and the Catholic heritage. Little stress need be laid upon the fact that American Catholics ought to oppose participation. I know perfectly well that a young man or woman finds it hard to renounce a chance for fame and fortune. It is certainly not I who will pooh-pooh the laurels won by the modern athlete. Just because the honor and the sacrifice are alike great, the chance to make a choice is of such critical importance.

In a life replete with chance and debate, few things are certain. But on the issue under consideration, no doubt exists. It seems to me quite incredible that the Catholic clergy of the United States will not raise their voices against this new temptation to offer incense at the altar of Baal, provided they realize in time what issues are at stake. Those of us who love Germany will hope that the truth is known before it is too late. And those of us who love the Church will remember the steadfast sons of Caesar's Rome who did not offer sacrifice.[9]

Might Mulqueen also be persuaded to join fellow Catholics in favouring a boycott? Caiserman hoped so. And, if he did, it would certainly serve to reinforce Herschorn's expected intervention on behalf of the boycott. In approaching Mulqueen, Caiserman assured Eisendrath, he would not be alone in reaching out to top-level Canadian amateur sports officials. Local Jewish leaders across Canada were being asked to meet with AAUC and COC members in their particular communities in the hope of winning their support for the Olympic boycott. But if Caiserman hoped for the best out of these meetings, he was also prudent enough to plan for the worst. With no guarantee even the key meeting between Mulqueen and Eisendrath would prove productive, Caiserman suggested boycott advocates be ready with a backup plan. As Caiserman explained to Eisendrath, "If your conversations with him [Mulqueen] bring results it will be marvelous, but in case they do not, please inform me immediately so that we do not fire our entire ammunition at one time. In other words, on the basis of your report the next step from here will be decided. It is the opinion of the sport group here [at Congress], that for the time being diplomatic action be pursued."[10]

Eisendrath agreed to meet with Mulqueen but begged for a little time to get up to speed on the Canadian Olympic boycott campaign. Time would also allow Eisendrath to clear the High Holy Days that consumed so much of a congregational rabbi's time each autumn. But he pledged that once the High Holy Days cycle was over, the Olympic boycott campaign would be his number one priority. In the meantime he contacted Mulqueen requesting a meeting and, "because of the close connection between himself [Mulqueen] and the present [Liberal] Government of

Ontario," Eisendrath also invited David Croll, Ontario's first Jewish cabinet minister, to be present at the meeting. Croll agreed.[11]

Another Line of Attack on the Olympics

Just as Eisendrath was returning from his European tour, several Canadian athletes were on their much-hyped tour to the Soviet Union, sponsored by the Workers' Sports Association (WSA).[12] The communist press had kept up the pro-boycott momentum; Jim Turner, for his part, kept up the campaign he had started in August and, in September, came out with yet another *Young Worker* article – "Force the Olympics Off Nazi Soil!" – in support of a boycott. With the return of the athletes from the Soviet Union, however, the party had a fresh line of attack on the Berlin games with support from several prominent mainstream sports figures.

Although the AAUC had originally permitted amateur athletes to participate in the trip, the organization reversed its decision and insisted that no athlete should go, or risk suspension.[13] One of the athletes who nevertheless decided to go on the tour was the high jumper Eva Dawes. Born in Toronto in 1912, she was one of six children. When Dawes showed early promise as a high jumper, her father dug a landing pit and trained her hard. By age fourteen she was outperforming her age category but she could not compete in official amateur events until she was eighteen. This meant she was not eligible for the 1928 Olympics. She earned a bronze medal at the 1932 Los Angeles Olympics, and two years later she took second place in the British Empire Games. At the invitation of the WSA, she set sail from Montreal in August 1935 with eight other athletes and sports officials to compete in Moscow, as was duly noted by the RCMP in its monitoring of the left.[14]

On her return to Canada, Dawes offered words of praise for what was happening in the Soviet Union, especially contrasting her positive experiences there to the negative depiction of events in the press which seek to "discredit in every way the great and marvelous work that has been accomplished in a country owned and built by workers." She also had harsh words of condemnation for the planned Olympics in Berlin: "I'll hang up my spikes rather than take part in an amateur meet, where discrimination is keeping many fine sportsmen from taking part."[15] The response of Dawes seemed to vindicate the strategy of reaching beyond the party to build anti-fascist alliances in general, and a pro-boycott mentality more specifically.

Events in Germany: The Nuremberg Laws

As Eisendrath prepared to take on Mulqueen, the Nazis were taking on issues of a different sort – issues that would further erode the position of German Jews. While Germany's preparations for the Olympic Games were moving ahead, state-imposed antisemitism, or rather its administration, was proving more cumbersome than the Nazis might have hoped. Simply stated, no matter how many punitive anti-Jewish regulations were proclaimed or how iron-fisted their application, the Nazi effort to exorcise German Jews from German society and, in the process, eliminate root and branch any and all Jewish influence in German society, was being undermined by a lack of definitive agreement on who was and was not a Jew. This was no simple matter. Unlike the crude visual representation of Jews in Nazi propaganda and the Nazi-controlled media, not all Jews had Jewish-sounding names, hooked noses, beards, fat lips, and rounded shoulders. Not all Jews even acknowledged their Jewishness. It was unclear to many whether someone had to "behave" like a Jew, "look" like a Jew, or somehow publicly self-identify as a Jew to be a Jew. For that matter, was being a Jew a fact of biology, a matter of lineage? And, if being a Jew was a biological inheritance, what was the status of non-Jews who converted to Judaism, or Jews who converted to Christianity, or those Christians who married Jews or were born of mixed ancestry? And, if they were not Jews, were they Germans? Or might there be some middle ground between Jew and German? If so, should these partial Jews or partial Germans be subject to the same constraints as full-blooded Jews? Clearly, for the Nazis state intent on exorcizing Jews and all traces of Jewish corruption, a precise and workable definition of who is a Jew was a necessity.[16]

The need for a precise definition was all the more acute if Germany was going to root out closet Jews – Jews who, Nazis were convinced, secretly passed as Germans so they might worm their way into German society. These dissemblers needed to be identified, exposed, and contained. What is more, having a clear-cut definition of who is a Jew would not only enable the state to ferret out Jewish dissemblers, but it would also serve to protect those real Germans who might inadvertently be mistaken for Jews. And this did happen, sometimes with regrettable results. In mid-July 1935, fashionable downtown Berlin was the scene of the "Kurfuerstendamm riots when hundreds of Nazi storm-troopers raided theaters and restaurants, assaulting men and women who looked Jewish, smashed windows and left a trail of bleeding victims on the streets, and continuous detention and torture of Christian church leaders."[17] The riot in the German capital, home base to the international press corps, a riot in which non-Jews and well as Jews were assaulted and property was destroyed, made headlines and sparked editorial condemnation around the world, much to the chagrin of German Olympic organizers guarding against accusations of antisemitism in advance of the Olympics.[18]

In the lead-up to the Olympic Games, German Olympic officials were not the only ones concerned by the attacks on Jews and Jewish property. Behind the scenes, others in Nazi leadership positions were worried that overt anti-Jewish violence – at least of the kind that attracted foreign press comment – was having a detrimental impact, not on Jews but on the German economy, an impact Germany could ill afford. German economic growth began to falter. There were growing shortages of foodstuffs and consumer goods. Making matters worse, there was also a decline in public confidence in the ability or even willingness of state authorities to maintain order, including order on German streets. In the wake of a series of violent incidents in which non-Jews were set upon and non-Jewish property destroyed, culminating in the all-too-public July Berlin riot, there was widespread grumbling that the police and other authorities were permitting undisciplined Nazi Party rowdies to place themselves above the law and freely intimidate anyone they wished. Of course, if they confined their actions to Jews and Jewish property, that would be one thing; the problem was the disorderly and seemingly random nature of this violence that too often also swept up non-Jews mistaken for Jews. This undermined public confidence in the authorities and threatened the public's sense of order and security essential to economic stability and growth. It even made foreign money markets skittish about investing money in a Germany that tolerated, if it did not actually incite, violence in the streets.

Ensuring the security of the streets for non-Jews was one problem; riotous anti-Jewish violence that too often led to wanton destruction of Jewish property or damage to Jewish-owned and Jewish-operated enterprises essential to local, regional, and sometimes even national economic growth, was quite another. Economic self-interest and job stability dictated that extruding Jews from the national economy had to be done in an orderly and efficient fashion. In no small part this required not just dampening the exuberance of the mob but, as suggested, establishing a definition of who was or was not a Jew so as to ensure an orderly process for shearing Jews of their assets and Germany of its Jews.

Key to accomplishing this was the September 1935 passage of the Nuremberg Laws announced by Hitler in his speech before the most celebratory of yearly Nazi events, the annual Nuremberg Nazi Party Congress, better known as the Nuremberg Rally. Historian Karl Schleunes explains that these multi-day events, first begun in 1927, six years before the Nazis assumed power in Germany, "were calculated to renew the spirit and enthusiasm of the [Nazi] movement through a meticulously planned pageantry, unmatched in the twentieth century."[19] The 1935 Nuremberg Rally was no exception. Like its predecessors, the 1935 Rally was assigned a special theme: "freedom." In Nazi doubletalk, "freedom" was interpreted to mean the freedom to serve Hitler and to re-arm the fatherland by the 1935 implementation of compulsory military service in Germany, an act in blatant violation of the Treaty of Versailles that severely restricted German rearmament. With choreographed passion, the 1935 Rally exhorted the German martial spirit even as it proclaimed Hitler, the heroic saviour of the German nation, a man anointed by divine providence to lead his people reborn out of the humiliation of defeat in the First World War towards a triumphant destiny.

All this was carefully packaged in an emotionally charged spectacle. Historian Klaus Fischer notes these annual Nuremberg Rallies "evolved in time into gigantic rituals of mass intoxication, featuring blood rituals, funereal orations, marches, torchlight parades, and sacred chants of victory ('Sieg Heil') or to the Führer (Heil Hitler)."[20] In September 1935, two years after the Nazis assumed power and less than two weeks after Eisendrath's return from Germany, thousands of uniformed Nazi faithful stood in rigid military formation and swore a collective oath of loyalty to the Nazi Party and its leader. Several prominent Nazi leaders then addressed the Nuremberg gathering. The *Toronto Daily Star* and the *Calgary Daily Herald* took special note of Goebbels's ferociously anti-semitic speech in which he railed against the threat posed to the German people by Jewish-controlled Soviet communism.[21] Finally came the rally's emotional climax. Hitler mounted the podium in full military uniform. On cue, the assembly erupted in an explosion of "Heil Hitler" salutes. The Führer, standing triumphant, acknowledged the cult-like adulation until, with a raise of his hand, the thunderous salute came to a halt and Hitler began his speech.

The Nuremberg Rallies, for all their fiery theatre and raw appeal to the emotions, were seldom occasion for formal policy announcements, let alone discussion of important policy initiatives. But the 1935 Rally was something of an exception. As the thunderous salute to Hitler died down, Hitler addressed the Nazi faithful on a matter he identified as one of great urgency. The assembly broke into thunderous cheers as Hitler announced a major legislative initiative – the Nuremberg Laws, laws that Hitler promised would deny Jews any and all protections of the German state, including citizenship, and gave legal sanction to the total excision of Jews from German society. While the Nazis began erecting legal barriers to Jewish participation in the German mainstream the moment Hitler assumed power, the Nuremberg Laws and accompanying edicts would provide legally binding racial markers separating Jew from German and, in so doing, pave the way to the final delegitimization and legal denaturalization of those defined as Jews. To the delight of those assembled at Nuremberg, German Jews would henceforth be rendered legally stateless in the country of their birth and thereby outside the protection of the law. But the Nuremberg Laws would do more than that. By denaturalizing German Jews, the new legislation paved the way to the orderly appropriation of German-Jewish assets by the state, and promised to do so without frightening international money markets at a time when Germany was in need of their cooperation.[22]

Accordingly, if Hitler approved a pause in "individual actions" against Jews in the lead-up to the Olympic Games, there was no stay in "state actions" against Jews. With the Nuremberg Laws, the state became the exclusive arbiter of who was and was not a Jew, and the guardian of the German people against the Jewish scourge. The state also promised to retrieve Jewish assets declared rightfully the property of the German people. To these ends, it was important that the content of the Nuremberg Laws be as transparent as their intent. True to Hitler's word, the day following his Rally speech, the Reichstag, meeting not in Berlin but in Nuremberg for the first time since 1534, enacted the Nuremberg Laws without debate and certainly without dissent.

The Nuremberg Laws and their supplementary edicts had an immediate impact on German society and, crushingly, on those legally designated as Jews. And who was a Jew? Simply stated, a Jew was now legally defined as someone who had one or more Jewish grandparents. Those who fell on the wrong side of this German-Jewish divide were no longer held to be German citizens. The social death of German Jews was final. Panic gripped those who suspected a Jewish skeleton might be discovered rattling around in the family closet. And if there were no Jewish taint in the family bloodline, one would be well advised to ensure against even the hint of contaminating contact with Jews. What was the best way to protect one's family and assets from malicious accusations of Jewish contamination? Churches became important guarantors of racial purity. A grandmother's baptismal certificate was suddenly not just a family heirloom; it was the gold standard of proof that one was a true German free of Jewish corruption. But even if one's immediate family was *judenrein*, what about one's friends, business partners, or clients? Best to be cautious; best to check out one's family doctor, fellow workers, the children's teachers and classmates, and even old friends, to be sure they too were without Jewish stain.[23]

Among those in Nuremberg who heard Hitler's announcement of the new race laws were prominent dignitaries, including members of the International Olympic Committee. American Charles Hitchcock Sherrill was among them. In an effort to defuse Olympic boycott campaigns in Western democratic countries, and particularly in his own United States, Sherrill, a Hitler admirer, was dispatched to Germany in September 1935 in hopes of convincing the German Olympic Committee to add a token Jewish athlete to the German Olympic team. He met with Hitler, who invited Sherrill to be his guest at the Nuremberg event. Sherrill was flattered by the invitation and was in the stands when Hitler announced the Nuremberg Laws. What Sherrill personally thought of the Führer's blistering antisemitic tirade and proud announcement of the Nuremberg Laws is not recorded. What is known is that Sherrill was impressed, as he was meant to be, by the enthusiastic crowds, the stirring parades, and the triumphalist celebration of *Volksgemeinschaft*, a vision of a nation united by mythic bonds of racial purity. The sight of thousands of uniformed Nazis spilling out of the Rally grounds to command the larger city stirred Sherrill. Locked arm in arm, the Nazi faithful paraded through the streets of Nuremberg to the cheers of enthusiastic onlookers. They eventually regrouped en masse in the torch-lit Nuremberg town square where they were again received by Hitler and were entertained by a public performance of Richard Wagner's opera, *Die Meistersinger von Nürnberg*. If the Nazis could mount a spectacle like this for the Party faithful, Sherrill might well have imagined the kind of spectacle the world could expect when the 1936 Games opened – the Olympic Winter Games scheduled to begin only a few months after the 1935 Nuremberg Rally and the Summer Games just six months later. In his autobiography, Sherrill recalled with great pleasure his attendance at Nuremberg and the thrill of witnessing the military precision with which the rally was executed. "I was," he boasted, "Hitler's personal guest for four days in mid-September 1935 ... It was beautiful! You could almost hear the [Nazi] units click, as each fitted into place, exactly on time." Sherrill left Nuremberg convinced the coming Nazi Olympic Games would be an event to remember. He was right.[24]

The Canadian Press Reacts to the Nuremberg Laws

The American Sherrill was obviously caught up by the spirit of Nuremberg, but what about Canadians? What did they learn from the mainstream press on the Nuremberg Rally and, more particularly, the promulgation of the Nuremberg Laws even as preparations for the Olympic Games continued?[25] There was no shortage of coverage. In the several months before the 1935 Nuremberg Rally, and especially after the anti-Jewish Berlin riot in July, the news pages of most Canadian newspapers, even those that might previously have drawn a distinction between repulsive antisemitic acts of hotheads and the actions of the Nazi state, increasingly accepted as a given that the Nazi state was now a racist state. Rather than back-pedal on antisemitism and racism, as some in the press had originally predicted, the Nazi state was reportedly intent on implementing a racist agenda. But the Nuremberg Laws – laws that both clarified and codified the legal demarcation line between German and non-German – were not just more of the same. The press suggested that by stripping German Jews of their citizenship and relegating them to the outer reaches of society, the state was not simply sanctioning the antisemitism of the mob – it was superseding the mob as the chief threat to German Jews.[26]

Within hours of the Reichstag vote enacting the Nuremberg Laws, Canadian papers, like their American counterparts, began to speculate on how the Nuremberg Laws would further reshape Germany. The *Calgary Daily Herald* published as a front-page headline, "Nazis Bar Jews from Citizenship,"[27] while the *Toronto Globe*, also concerned a remilitarized Germany would threaten its neighbours, proclaimed, "Nazis Outlaw Jews and Lash Lithuanians."[28] The *Winnipeg Free Press* informed its readers that German Jews were now officially excluded from citizenship in the new Germany. As such, they were now rendered stateless, aliens in the country of their birth. As a step towards drawing a rigid line of separation of German from Jew, the Nazis designated all sexual relations between Jew and non-Jews – even within marriage – a threat to German "blood and honour" and a punishable offence.[29]

The Canadian press also reported on the Nazi supplementary decrees necessary to implement the Nuremberg Laws. There were also reports on how the loss of German citizenship was impacting Jews. There were articles on who could and could not attend public schools, who could or could not sit in a park bench, who could and could not marry a German and who was and was not subject to violence. On 18 October, several weeks after the 1935 Nuremberg Rally, Corallie van Paassen reported to the *Star* that, during a scrum with reporters, Goebbels publicly dismissed incidents of anti-Jewish violence in Berlin. What the international press reported as antisemitic incidents, Goebbels insisted, were no more than a temperate and legitimate citizen response to recalcitrant Jews, defiant of the German state, who needed to be kept in place.[30] That place was certainly far removed from the German body politic. As if the right to vote still mattered in Germany, a front page *Calgary Daily Herald* headline read, "Jews in Germany Lose all Political Rights by Government Decree,"[31] and a day later the *Globe* published a second-page story under the headline "German Jews Lose Franchise."[32]

A few days later, a toughly worded editorial in the *Globe* took to task the German ambassador to the United States, Hans Luther, for claiming, in spite of all the evidence to the contrary, that "there is no persecution of any kind in Germany." The *Globe* editorial dismissed the ambassador's denial as a fantasy. If the Nuremberg Laws were not state-mandated persecution, what word was appropriate to describe the enactment of laws "to segregate a million German-born inhabitants, deny them the right of citizenship and place them socially in a class with criminals and imbeciles?" The racist intent of this legislation was plain for all to see, and the editorial concluded with a note of sarcasm: "It might have resolved a seeming paradox if Dr. Luther could have been persuaded to give ... an ambassadorial definition of what Nazi Germany calls persecution."[33]

The newspapers reported on the heightened vulnerability of Germany's Jews. The *Toronto Star* published a series of articles by van Paassen exploring how difficult day-to-day life had become for Jews in Germany. On 28 September, immediately following the enactment of the Nuremberg Laws that smoothed the way for the Nazi seizure of assets from those legally defined as Jews, van Paassen reported on how Jewish-owned stores and commercial establishments were being starved of clients. The article was accompanied by images of two "tickets" that all Jewish-owned businesses were legally required to post in public view. One berated Aryans who dared frequent Jewish-owned businesses branding them traitors to Germany and the German people. The other proclaimed the Jew to be a "bloodsucking enemy."[34]

The parade of Canadian press articles dealing with the Nazi persecution of Jews continued. On 12 October, the *Star* ran the story of a German-produced ballet that was forced to open in London rather than Berlin because the pianist-composer was a Jew "with whom the company refused to part."[35] That same day, van Paassen reported that *Die jüdische Rundschau*, the last independent Jewish newspaper in Germany, had been forced to close.[36] On 5 November van Paassen pointed out that the number of regulations and decrees restricting Jewish life in Germany were now so voluminous that "the anti-Jewish laws in various parts of the Reich could fill a book."[37] By way of example, van Paassen noted one German town in which municipal ordinances prohibited Jews from entering the town museum or hiking trails in the nearby Bavarian mountains, and even prohibited Jewish butchers from shipping cattle for slaughter in the same trucks used by non-Jews to transport cattle for slaughter.[38]

Although not all mainstream Canadian newspapers offered their readers as much detailed information on the plight of German Jews as did the *Toronto Daily Star*, there was no shortage of stories on the crisis of Jews in Germany. On 1 October 1935, the *Calgary Daily Herald* picked up on an Associated Press story about Jewish notaries who had previously been allowed to continue serving the public if they had served in the German military in the Great War. As a result of the Nuremberg Laws, those previously exempted were forced to close their offices. The article also accused the German press of routinely blaming Jews for each and every woe affecting Germany, no matter how outlandish the charge. By way of example, the article noted that the German press held Berlin's Jews collectively responsible for a local subway construction mishap in which several workers died. Since Jews were collectively responsible, the German press demanded that Jews be forced to pay for all construction repairs and compensate the families of those who died.[39]

The Canadian Press and the Olympics

With the Canadian press in agreement that the oppression of Jews was not only rampant in Nazi Germany but also in state policy, one might wonder why the press did not come down hard against Canada dispatching a team to the Nazi Olympics. Certainly, boycott advocates tried, with limited success, to convince the press that the rising tide of antisemitism in Germany should be answered with a ringing Canadian rejection of Hitler's invitation to participate in the Olympic Games. And the press acknowledged that there was no line of separation between the German government and the Olympics. There were published press reports about Olympic-quality Jewish and other athletes, declared "enemies of the state," being systematically denied the opportunity to train or compete for a place on the German Olympic team. But with few exceptions, the Canadian press, in spite of reporting on the rising tide of antisemitism in Nazi Germany, did not join in calling for an Olympic boycott. Persecuting Jews was one thing – the Olympic Games was another.

In the wake of the Nuremberg Laws, the Canadian Jewish Congress and its Unity and Goodwill Association revved up their pro-boycott campaign, although always carefully trying to keep their efforts discretely separate from those of Canadian communists and the communist-dominated League against War and Fascism, lest the Jewish community effort be tarred with a pro-communist brush. And it was with anti-communist labour unions and other sympathetic and progressive organizations that the Jewish boycott campaign had its easiest success. The CJC approached the non-communist Trades and Labour Congress of Canada along with its many affiliate unions to endorse both the Olympic boycott and a more general Canadian boycott of all imported German goods and services. The Trades and Labour Congress meeting in Halifax in September 1935 endorsed a resolution calling on all its affiliate unions, their members, and all those of goodwill

> to influence the non-participation of Canadian sportsmen [sic] in the contemplated World Olympic games to be held in Germany in 1936. The failure of the participation of the Canadian sportsmen in the Olympic games will serve as an indication to the Nazi government that Canadian sportsmen are opposed to the brutalities and oppression the Nazi government exercises with full vigor.

Across Canada, local Canadian Trades and Labour Congress affiliates pledged to boycott the Nazi Games, including the withholding of financial contributions to the COC or Olympic-bound athletes.[40]

But sports journalists remained a much harder group to convince. Efforts to encourage sports writers for major newspapers to come onside with the Olympic boycott campaign were largely unsuccess-ful.[41] Most sports writers dismissed any one-on-one links between the Olympic Games and Nazi antisemitism and, as a result, sloughed off the call for a boycott even as editorial pages in the same newspapers decried Nazi antisemitism. There were exceptions. One of those was Elmer Ferguson, lead sports writer for the *Montreal Herald* and among the most respected Canadian sports columnists. Ferguson was quoted in *Sports Magazine* as arguing, "Better the collapse of the Olympic idea than the [Canadian] endorsation through association, of a government perpetrating the present atrocities and association utterly foreign to the real Olympic tradition."[42]

Much as Ferguson's comment was appreciated, the majority of sports journalists proved of a different mind. Reporting to Caiserman on a conversation he had with widely syndicated Toronto sports writer Lou Marsh, Eisendrath noted that although the editorial policy of the *Toronto Daily Star* might be strongly anti-Nazi, the sports pages did not tow the editorial line. In the case of the Nazi Olympics, the sports writer denied a connection between Nazism and the Olympics, or at least denied enough of a connection to warrant an Olympic boycott. Eisendrath and Marsh had a heated exchange, as the rabbi reported to Caiserman:

Following a conference with Mr. Lou Marsh, sporting editor of "The To-ronto Daily Star" I realized that our task with regard to arousing public opinion against Canada's participation [in the Nazi Olympics] is a for-midable one. The sporting editor, and the [Canadian] sporting world as a whole, takes the position that the whole matter [of German racism] is an internal problem that concerns Germany and not ourselves. I had quite a verbal tussle with Mr. Marsh, but left in the very best of spirits, and with the request from him that I contribute an article on the subject for his sporting page. I shall endeavour to do this in the near future.

Eisendrath pressed Marsh, who opposed a boycott, for a suggestion as to what more Jewish boycott advocates might do to convince the Canadian sports writing fraternity and, through them, the larger Cana-dian public, that Canadian participation in the Nazi Olympics was antithetical to the ideals for which the Olympic movement stood and that participation would bring shame to the Canadian amateur athletic movement. Eisendrath was taken aback by Marsh's reply. Much of the material that Congress and its Unity and Goodwill Association distrib-uted to the Canadian Olympic Committee and athletic associations, to politicians, the press, and other opinion makers, was gleaned from pro-boycott material supplied by the American boycott movement, including articles culled from the American press. Marsh, who had served in the Canadian military in the First World War, cautioned Eisendrath that "Canadians will not be influenced by American opinion." Reporting to Caiserman on his meeting with Marsh, Eisendrath explained that "the host of [American] names I marshaled before him was of little avail. They [Canadian sporting officials and journalists] will be influenced by British opinion. Therefore, it is imperative that you secure and send me at your earliest convenience whatever material you may have that comes out of England or other places in the Empire."[43]

Canadian Jewish Congress and the Olympic Boycott

This Anglophilia should have come as no surprise to Eisendrath. He shared it. Since coming to Canada the American-born rabbi had come to appreciate Canada's British connection and publicly praised its virtues.[44] But little did Eisendrath imagine that Canada's British connection would interject itself into his much-anticipated meeting with Mulqueen. With the fall Jewish High Holy Days cycle finally over, the meeting, "a lengthy and detailed discussion of the entire situation related to Canada's participation in the forthcoming Olympic Games to be held in Berlin," took place in the rabbi's book-lined study at Holy Blossom Temple on 16 October, without David Croll. If Eisendrath played the Catholic card, pointing to a shared Catholic-Jewish interest in opposing Hitler and the Nazis, it is not recorded. Instead, in a "Confidential Report" on his meeting, Eisendrath described Mulqueen as "diplomatically non-committal" with regard to a Canadian Olympic boycott, although he also judged Mulqueen to be personally "cordial and sympathetic" to the notion of an Olympic boycott. This did not mean that Mulqueen was about to come out publicly in favour of the boycott, but Eisendrath reported that Mulqueen did assure him "in strictest confidence that his personal sympathies were with our cause, but as one of the leaders of the entire Canadian athletic group, he felt it necessary to refrain from giving definite expression to his opinions until the group itself meet in Halifax on November 21st [to formally respond to the German Olympic invitation]." Did this mean that the COC or the AAUC might yet refuse the German invitation? Yes, according to Eisendrath. Mulqueen "instimated [sic] that because this meeting would be held in so remote a city as Halifax, there would be a very

small representation [from across Canada] and agreed with my suggestion that his own feelings might be able to influence the body."

Mulqueen left Eisendrath with the impression that, in spite of Mulqueen's public pronouncements on the subject, if the boycott campaign
could but win over several other influential members of the COC executive, he, as chairman of the Canadian Olympic Committee, would then
feel free to also come out at the Halifax meeting in support of an Olympic boycott. But Mulqueen warned that Olympic boycott campaigners
would not necessarily have an easy time of it. They were up against the
inclination of many on the COC to take their cue from the British Olympic Committee. As Eisendrath explained to Caiserman, "the Canadian
[Olympic] organization is in constant touch with the English organization, and I assume, from reading between the lines [of what Mulqueen
said], that even though not admitting the fact, Canada would be largely
guided by British policy."

The thought that the Canadian Olympic Committee executive and
the AAUC would simply play follow-the-British-leader and, in the
name of imperial unity, blindly accept Hitler's invitation to participate
in the Olympics if the British Olympic Committee signalled it intended
to participate, was disheartening. But Eisendrath was buoyed by Mulqueen's implied promise to speak out in favour of the boycott at the
Halifax meetings if convinced he would not be alone in taking that
stand. With this in mind, Eisendrath advised that Congress pull out
every stop to ensure that Mulqueen had allies in Halifax ready to vote
with him. Eisendrath wrote Caiserman that "an effective, though not
too flamboyant publicity campaign between now and November 21
might be helpful. The time is very short but the persons to be influenced in a country such as Canada are so very few that I believe we
might be successful, if immediate and strategic action is taken."[45]

Caiserman promptly wrote a number of senior Canadian Jewish Congress leaders across Canada imploring them to redouble efforts to reach
AAUC and COC officials in their respective communities and deliver
the Olympic boycott message. It was critical, Caiserman explained, if
not to convince them to support the Olympic boycott then at least to
keep an open mind on the issue. Each of the Congress leaders was also
sent a package of pro-boycott material put together by the Unity and
Good Will Association for all those who would be making the trip to
Halifax.[46]

Some of the feedback Caiserman received was encouraging. M.I.
Lieberman, a prominent Edmonton Jewish lawyer, arranged to meet

with sergeant John Leslie, secretary of the AAUC, second vice-president of the Canadian Amateur Hockey Association, and, by chance, Lieberman's close friend. Lieberman was pleased with the exchange. "For your private and confidential information," Lieberman shared with Caiserman, "I have Sergeant Leslie's word and assurance that he will vote against sending any Canadian athletes to the Olympic games in Germany." Leslie also volunteered to lobby other delegates planning to attend the Halifax meeting in the hope of perhaps bringing them onside in support of an Olympic boycott. But Leslie cautioned Lieberman that some AAUC delegates might resist any rejection of the Nazi invitation for fear the move would alienate the Canadian government. Ottawa, he explained, had promised a financial grant to help subsidize the travel costs of Olympic-bound athletes. Some amateur athletic officials might worry that the refusal to send a Canadian team could sour the Canadian government on any subsequent Olympic grants and maybe grants for other amateur athletic undertakings as well. To preclude this eventuality, Lieberman suggested asking S.W. Jacobs, the lone Jewish member of Parliament for the Liberal Party, "to take up this matter immediately" so as to reassure amateur athletic officials that "any action of theirs as regards the Olympic games at Berlin would not prejudice their position in securing a grant in the future."[47]

Caiserman acted quickly. He dispatched a letter to Jacobs, but not the letter that Lieberman had requested. Rather than solicit promises of ongoing support for the amateur athletic community, Caiserman asked Jacobs to do all he could to "prevent Canada from granting any funds to the Canadian teams for the Olympics." Caiserman included a copy of a resolution recently submitted to the American House of Representatives by Emanuel Celler, representative for the heavily Jewish New York tenth congressional district. Celler, who was already on record opposing the United States sending athletes to the 1936 Olympic Games, called on the House to

discourage American participation in the Olympic Games to be held in Germany, and in a protest against the unsportsmanlike attitude of the Reich, no public or semipublic finds ... shall be allotted, or sued to defray expenses of any American athletes to participate in the Olympic Winter Games to be held in Garmisch-Partenkirchen, Germany, February 6 to 16, 1936, or in the games of the Eleventh Olympiad, to be held in Berlin Germany, August 1 to 16, 1936.

Jacobs forwarded Caiserman's letter and supporting material to the undersecretary of state for external affairs with a request that appropriate action be taken. It would seem that external affairs concluded that the best action was no action – it sat on Jacob's letter. The federal grant of $10,000 to the Canadian Olympic Committee went unchallenged.[48]

Like Lieberman, M.J. Finkelstein, president of the CJC in Winnipeg and chairman of the local CJC Anti-Defamation Committee, was asked by Caiserman to meet with the regional head of the AAUC. Finkelstein informed Caiserman he had contacted newly appointed G. Sydney Halter, a young Jewish lawyer and amateur sports enthusiast. If Caiserman thought that discovering a Jew as the AAUC regional head was a lucky break, he was soon disabused of that notion. Finkelstein met with Halter and found him surprisingly "not very familiar with the situation nor with the very cogent arguments against Canada participating in the Olympics." Finkelstein reported that Halter, once apprised of the facts, "was quite sympathetic." But sympathy would not translate into action. Halter begged off becoming involved. He pleaded he was the wrong person to lead the charge against Canadian participation in the Nazi Olympic. Halter felt that because he was a Jew, other AAUC officials would discount any special pleading he would do on behalf of the Olympic boycott. What is more, if he went out on a limb and came out publicly in favour of the boycott, he could be accused of putting his Jewishness before the good of amateur sport and athletics in Canada. This, Halter argued, would jeopardize his place on the AAUC executive and set back Jewish entrée into sports administration in Canada. Showing sympathy for Halter's position, Finkelstein explained to Caiserman that since Halter did not intend to go to the Halifax meeting, and because Halter is Jewish, "it would be very difficult for him to take the initiative and he thought that it should come from some other direction."[49] With time growing short before the Halifax meeting, Halter was let of the hook.

Finkelstein hoped that he might find a more agreeable pro-boycott partner in J.I. Morkin, a local Winnipeg lawyer, vice-president of the Canadian Olympic Committee, and, like Mulqueen, a Catholic prominent in local amateur athletic circles. Like Mulqueen, Morkin, in confidence, shared that he was personally sympathetic to the boycott campaign. But that was as far as he went. He was not ready to speak out in favour of an Olympic boycott and, what is more, like Halter, Morkin was not going to Halifax. He was also unsure of who, if anyone, would represent Winnipeg at the Halifax meeting or what position that person might take with respect to an Olympic boycott.[50]

If Caiserman was disappointed by the news from Winnipeg, he was likely even more disappointed by the news he received about two influential London, Ontario, delegates who were planning to attend the Halifax meetings – the honorary secretary of the COC, J. Howard Crocker, and COC member Professor N. C. Hart. Neither, Caiserman was told, was "ready to vote against Canada's participation" and nothing was going to change their minds.[51]

If Caiserman was keeping a running tally of the Halifax votes for and against the boycott, he certainly had reason to feel discouraged. Mulqueen had intimated that he might be ready to support an Olympic boycott if other ranking COC or AAUC delegates at the Halifax meeting could be induced to come out in support of a boycott first. Congress's attempt to find delegates who were ready to endorse a boycott had come up short. But Caiserman still hoped for the best. He knew from the beginning of the CJC boycott campaign that there would be Olympic supporters so fixed in their views that there would be no way they could be moved. On the other hand, there were also those AAUC members who had expressed sympathy for the boycott, although, had Caiserman looked more closely, he would have noticed that the more AAUC members were ready to indicate personal sympathy for the boycott campaign, the less likely they were to be going to Halifax. With the much-anticipated Halifax meeting only a month away, Caiserman, like Eisendrath, still hoped against hope that Mulqueen's private expression of sympathy for the Olympic boycott would turn into public action. After all, Mulqueen was president of the Canadian Olympic Committee. If he were moved by conscience to come out in favour of a boycott, would not others follow?

The COC Meets in Montreal

With so much riding on Mulqueen's private expression of sympathy for the Olympic boycott campaign and less than a month before the expected Halifax debate on Canadian Olympic participation, the COC executive committee met in Montreal together with local COC members. Preceding the meeting, Mulqueen answered reporters' questions about Canadian Olympic participation. In response to a question about protest against Canadian participation in the Games, Mulqueen shocked CJC officials by denying first-hand knowledge of any pro-boycott campaign and claiming that, to the best of his knowledge, the COC had received not one single protest against Canadian participation in the either the Winter or Summer Games.[52]

The actual Montreal meeting proved no more promising for boycott advocates. Minutes of the meeting, presumably made available to the CJC by Herschorn, reveal that, as promised, Herschorn broached the issue of Canadian participation in the Nazi Olympics, but before he could speak on the issue, the group decided to put off all consideration of Canadian participation until after the AAUC's Halifax meeting at the end of the month. Equally important, they agreed "no expression of opinion should be made until that time." Optimists might imagine this silence was imposed so that a full airing of whether or not Canada should participate in the Nazi Olympics would be left to an open discussion by delegates at the Halifax meeting rather than have that debate coloured by pre-emptive musings of COC executive members in the few weeks before the meeting. But optimists would be wrong. As far as the COC executive was concerned, muzzling Herschorn and putting a moratorium on public comment on the question of Canadian acceptance of the German invitation were not designed to facilitate a full and open airing of the boycott issue in Halifax; it was rather a first step to squelching discussion. For the COC executive, there was no good that could come from discussion of the boycott issue. If the COC were called upon to defend Canadian participation, the organization would lend credence to the notion that there was something that had to be defended – that there were arguments, legitimate arguments, for why Canada should not attend. To avoid that debate and allow ongoing preparations for sending Canadian teams to both the Winter and Summer Olympic Games to proceed uninterrupted, it was felt best to ignore – even stonewall – the pro-boycott clamour.[53]

Whatever impression Mulqueen left with Eisendrath, the truth was that the COC was completely committed to going to Germany. Barring a miracle, nothing was going to change that. And the press was not fooled. The *Vancouver Sun* headlined an article on the COC Montreal meeting: "Old Boys All for Olympics: Mulqueen and Co. Make Plans for the Winter Games."[54] The *Montreal Gazette* declared that the COC executive was working under the ironclad assumption that Canada was going to attend the Olympic Games and nothing was going to change that. Nor was there anything new in that; the *Gazette* claimed the COC executive had long since decided to attend and, as far as the COC executive was concerned, nothing protesters said or did was going to alter that decision. The obvious implication was that the upcoming vote in Halifax was no more than a formality and it had never been otherwise. The only possible thing that might have derailed Canadian participation in the Olympics would have been a decision by the British Olympic Committee to boycott the Games – but Britain was going. And if Britain was going, the *Gazette* concluded, Canada was going, even if nobody at the Montreal meeting would go on record stating this was the case. Thus, the fiction remained that the final decision on Canadian Olympic participation would be made in Halifax.[55]

If anyone required further proof that the COC was intent on sending athletes to the Winter and Summer Olympics, they needed look no further than the decision by the Montreal meeting to accept a German invitation that Canada send a group of thirty school boys and a separate group of thirty physical fitness instructors to participate in conclaves to be held in conjunction with the Summer Olympic Games. Herschorn, the man in the middle, at once president of the Montreal YMHA and head of the Canadian Amateur Swim Association, reportedly dissented "because of the present conditions in Germany" and the propaganda prize that Canadian participation in these gatherings would offer the Nazis. According to the *Gazette*, J. Howard Crocker, COC secretary and director of physical education at the University of Western Ontario, brushed Herschorn's concerns aside. Crocker, who "saw no reason for refusing the invitation," carried the majority with him and was immediately authorized to form a subcommittee to look into the logistics of sending the groups to Germany. It was suggested that if he felt the idea had merit, he might consider engaging the services of someone experienced in school group travel or, perhaps, contracting out the planning and execution of the visits to a third party.[56]

The major agenda item facing the Montreal COC meeting was receipt of reports from a number of athletic and sporting associations on their preparations for the Olympics. One of those to report was Herschorn, wearing his cap as head of the Canadian Amateur Swim Association. He reported that the Canadian team was prepared to hold Olympic trials and he was confident the Canadian swim team would be ready to compete against the world's best.[57]

But Herschorn was also dispirited. He had been outgunned by the majority and not permitted to make the Jewish community's case for a boycott. He now felt certain the Halifax meeting would endorse Canada going to the Nazi Olympics. In hopes of softening the blow to the organized Jewish community, and perhaps to guard against accusations that he had stood by spinelessly while the COC endorsed participation, Herschorn pleaded a deal with Arthur S. Lamb, a powerful member of the COC's inner circle and director of the Department of

Physical Education at McGill University. Herschorn implored Lamb to ensure that any final motion put before AAUC delegates in Halifax confirming Canadian participation would include a statement abhorring racism and discrimination in sport. Lamb agreed to try but, in the end, Herschorn would be denied even this small concession.[58]

Caiserman may not have been aware of the agreement Herschorn made with Lamb, but he was aware of and shocked by Mulqueen's denial of any knowledge of protest against Canadian participation in the Nazi Olympics. Caiserman allowed that Mulqueen might be technically correct. The COC might not have received any formal protests because the protests would likely have been addressed to the AAUC, the COC's parent organization. But if Mulqueen ever had any interest in voicing sympathy for the boycott campaign, he not only missed his chance in Montreal, but he also closed the door on others doing so. In a note to Eisendrath, Caiserman's choice of words was restrained but his anger showed through. According to Caiserman, Mulqueen's claim "that he had knowledge of no protest whatsoever may be technically correct, but it is, nevertheless, a dishonest statement."[59] Whether the protests went to the AAUC or the COC was beside the point. Mulqueen knew full well the extent of anti-Olympic sentiment in Canada. If nothing else, he and Eisendrath had talked about it. Mulqueen might pretend his meeting with Eisendrath was a simple exchange of views, but Eisendrath and Caiserman regarded it integral to the CJC boycott campaign and Mulqueen knew it. As far as Caiserman and Eisendrath were concerned, Mulqueen had played them. He had deliberately misled them as to his sentiment on the Olympic boycott and lied when he told the press he was unaware of any anti-Olympic protests.

For CJC boycott advocates, assured by Mulqueen that the final discussion on whether or not to send Canadian athletes to the Nazi Olympics would be made only in Halifax and not before, press reports out of Montreal were discouraging. But rather than concede defeat until the Halifax meeting made its decision official, efforts to move the delegates in favour of the boycott would continue. But, recognizing that the chances of an anti-Olympic vote in Halifax were almost nil, it was also critical for the CJC to think beyond Halifax and consider other ways it might derail Canadian Olympic participation.[60]

But what was the CJC to make of Mulqueen? Following Eisendrath's meeting with Mulqueen, much of the CJC's boycott strategy was predicated on Mulqueen's suggestion that he would come out in favour of the boycott if he were assured that he would not be alone in doing so. By the date of the COC executive's Montreal meeting, not only did Mulqueen indicate no sympathy for the boycott cause, but he also dismissed the anti-Olympic protest as inconsequential. It was, he said, as if the Olympic boycott campaign did not exist. Why did Mulqueen change his tune? Whatever his private views of Hitler and the Nazis, Mulqueen left his meeting with Eisendrath with the uneasy impression that the boycott campaign could build a head of steam. But by the time of the Montreal meeting in early November 1935, Mulqueen was convinced that the campaign had no appreciable traction among AAUC delegates, athletes, or the larger Canadian sporting establishment, including sports journalists. Yes, arguments in favour of an Olympic boycott had won over a politician or two, a few clergymen, a sports writer here or there, and perhaps even the odd delegate to the AAUC meeting in Halifax – but what did this really amount to? Not much. In the Canada of the day, any protest movement that was largely identified with Jews on the one hand and leftists on the other, was easily dismissed at source or brushed aside as undeserving of consideration by those, like the COC executive, for whom Canadian participation in the Olympics was held out as an exercise in nation building. As a result, as far as Mulqueen was concerned, the boycott was a dead issue. The Halifax meeting was going to affirm Canadian participation in the 1936 Olympics and that was that.

To Eisendrath and Caiserman, however, Mulqueen's public dismissal of the anti-Olympic protest was more than a duplicitous betrayal; it smacked of personal insult. If Mulqueen thought he was going to be able to stand up in Halifax and again deny any knowledge of an Olympic protest, as far as Eisendrath and Caiserman were concerned, Mulqueen had another thing coming. Confident that the Olympic issue was going to be on the agenda at the Halifax meetings, and with only three weeks before those meetings were to begin, Caiserman and Eisendrath were determined to prevent Mulqueen from again playing blind man's bluff with anti-Olympic protest. They wanted the CJC's pro-boycott arguments forcefully put forward when the AAUC agenda turned to the issue of Canada's Olympic participation. If Canada in the end did accept Hitler's invitation to participate in the Nazi Olympics, which Eisendrath and Caiserman were increasingly convinced was going to happen, it was not going to be because the organized Jewish community did nothing to protest it.[61]

The Last Campaigns before Halifax

In one last anti-Olympic push before the Halifax meeting, the organized Jewish community played to its strengths. Using it connections
with organized labour, especially through the needle trades, the CJC
reached out to sympathetic unions and labour organizations, inviting them to publicly endorse an Olympic boycott, discourage their
membership from supporting Olympic-bound athletes, and refuse to
otherwise support the Olympic enterprise. Trades and Labour Council-
affiliated unions needed little encouragement. In Toronto an anti-Nazi
labour rally called on unions across Canada to bombard the AAUC
meeting in Halifax with pro-boycott telegrams.[62] In Vancouver the
local district Trades and Labour Council called for a boycott of German
goods and "specifically a boycott of the Olympics." Also in Vancouver, after much organized lobbying by pro-boycott activists, the British
Columbia Amateur Athletic Union, which decided not to send a delegate to Halifax, pledged its nine votes to a proxy representative who
would vote against sending Canadian athletes to Germany unless the
German Olympic Committee "very definitely and concretely denies the
discrimination against Jews competing for the Olympics."[63]

Several municipal councils also approved the boycott. The Winnipeg
city council voted to withhold financial support for Olympic-bound
athletes.[64] Similarly, the long-time trade union activist and left-leaning
mayor of Toronto, Jimmy Simpson, came out in favour of a municipal boycott on the purchase of German goods and services and voiced
his opposition to the city contributing any money in support of the
Canadian participation in the Nazi Olympics. "Not sending a team,"
the Mayor claimed, "would show the attitude of mind of the Canadian
people as to undemocratic procedure in [Germany] dealing with their
citizens. I believe a protest of this kind will be very effective."[65]

Boycott advocates also found support on campuses. Of course, the
Canadian amateur athletic community was heavily comprised of university students, but it was also true that the campus was home to many
who were sympathetic to the anti-Olympic campaign. On 7 November,
a day after the COC executive's Montreal meeting and two weeks before
the scheduled AAUC meetings in Halifax, a public debate was held at
the University of Manitoba on Canadian participation in the Olympics
in Germany. A student speaking in favour of Canadian participation
cautioned that any boycott of the Nazi Olympics would only serve to
antagonize Germany and thereby make the situation worse for those,

presumably Jews and leftists, who pro-boycott advocates claimed they
wanted to shelter from persecution. What is more, he argued, there was
no reason to punish Canadian Olympic athletes for the actions, no matter how reprehensible, of the German government. Nazi Germany was
only the host venue for the Olympics, not its moving spirit. "Political
discrimination of the German government does not come into the question because the games will be under the direction of the International
Olympic Committee."

Also speaking in favour of Canadian participation was C.C. Robinson, honorary treasurer of the AAUC. Pointing an accusing finger at
pro-boycott advocates, he derided them for deliberately undermining
the separation of sport from politics. He demanded the Olympic ideal
be protected from the pro-boycott movement intent on sacrificing sport
on the altar of political gain. He concluded with an appeal to Canadians, whatever their personal view, to unite in supporting the final decision of the AAUC and its COC as regards to sending Canadian athletes
to compete in Germany.

Speakers who advocated for a Canadian boycott argued it was
wrong-minded to imagine there was any sport in Nazi Germany independent of the state. Nazi ideology, they claimed, informs every aspect
of German life, and Olympic sport was no exception. "Under such circumstances," lamented a student speaker from the Catholic Newman
Club, "the ideals of sportsmanship are impossible" in Nazi Germany.
A Jewish student, wrapping himself in the Union Jack, proclaimed a
Canadian boycott of the Nazi Olympics was a matter of "British fair
play and common decency." Those attending the debate agreed. A
front-page story in the *Winnipeg Free Press* reported that by a vote of 90
to 20 the gathering endorsed a Canadian Olympic boycott.[66]

Several days before the University of Manitoba debate, an ad hoc
committee of student and youth representatives from communist and
non-communist left-wing organizations convened in a private home
in the fashionable Rosedale neighbourhood of Toronto. Their self-
declared goal was to help build support for the anti-Olympic cause.
There were clearly problems in raising the profile of the protest. One of
those attending the meeting, labour representative J.W. Buckley, secretary of the Toronto District Labour Council, was surprised to discover
that those most vocal had little or no awareness of the CJC campaign
against Canadian participation in the Nazi Games.[67]

Among those who attended were representatives of the Canadian
League against War and Fascism and members of the Canada Youth

Council. Also attending were several labour union officials and several athletes who supported the boycott campaign including high jumper Eva Dawes, recently returned from the Soviet Union where she participated in sporting events. The AAUC, which claimed the right to pre-approve all participation by Canadian amateur athletes in foreign competition, declared Dawes's Soviet trip, undertaken without authorization, a violation of its rules. As punishment the AAUC suspended Dawes's AAUC membership and, thereby, her Olympic eligibility. Dawes told the meeting it would be counterproductive for her to take a public stand against Canadian participation. Rather than benefit the cause, Dawes feared it would permit the AAUC to claim she was acting not out of conviction but out of animus at the AAUC's disciplinary action.[68]

Although Dawes dared not speak out, others were ready to do so. The Canadian Youth Council members sought and won meeting consent for a follow-up event, an information meeting to be held one week later, at which some fifty invited participants would "discuss the advisability of boycotting the Games in view of the fact that the German authorities who are the hosts of the games, have carried on a prolonged persecution of Protestants, Catholics and Jews and their persecution greatly affected the selection of the German Olympic Team."[69]

As if to demonstrate a concern to hear all sides in the Olympic debate, the Canadian Youth Council extended an invitation to the German consul general in Montreal to attend and speak for the Reich. The consul responded that he could not attend. Instead he suggested the meeting organizers invite Werner Haag, German State Railway representative in Toronto and representative in Canada of the German Olympic Organizing Committee. "I am sure he will be glad to present to the assembled youth the position of the Reich as a 'host nation' on the question of Canada's participation in the Olympic Games."[70]

Haag, who had arrived in Canada in the summer of 1935, was then busy setting up a Toronto office for the German State Railway.[71] It was the only office in Canada, one of nineteen "overseas" offices, all tasked to promote Olympic tourism. The consuls clearly understood Haag as their partner in protecting Germany's image, with Haag's responsibilities including counteracting pro-boycott advocacy in Canada. More directly, Haag offered his full cooperation to the AAUC and COC's Olympic organization efforts. He was active in pushing back against pro-boycott protest with his own well-funded barrage of slick, multicoloured Olympic magazines, leaflets, posters, and other pro-Olympic materials, much of it directed at the press. With an almost daily stream of leaflets and press releases, for and against the Olympics, flowing into press rooms across Canada, a sports columnist at the *Vancouver Sun*, Hal Straight – unusual among sports writers for his sympathy for the boycott movement – complained to his readers that he was being "swamped" with paper.

Straight was also convinced that Canada's official acceptance of Hitler's invitation was a foregone conclusion. Once the "Old Boys" of Canadian Olympic establishment announced in Halifax that Canada would attend Hitler's games, Straight concluded, the only remaining way that pro-boycott advocates might still derail the Olympics was to somehow choke off the flow of funds necessary to send Canadian Winter and Summer Olympic teams to Germany. If Canadians could be made to care about the daily horrors taking place in Nazi Germany, Straight argued, then "by the time athletic organizations go panhandling for money the public will be lukewarm and won't dig very deep … The result will be most likely a small entry at the games which would no doubt bother Herr Hitler. I hope so." Barring a funding shortfall, like it or not, Straight warned, Canada was going to send a full team to the Olympics.[72]

This message was no surprise to Jewish boycott advocates. But so long as the German Olympic invitation had yet to be officially accepted – so long as there was even a tiny chance that delegates to the Halifax meeting could still be moved to reject the German invitation – the organized Jewish community was determined to press on. An appeal over the banner of the Unity and Goodwill Association and marked *"URGENT IMPORTANT CONFIDENTIAL"* went out to Canadian Jewish Congress supporters across Canada. Each was exhorted to "act TODAY, not TOMORROW" in gathering personal statements of support for an Olympic boycott from "leading Canadians in your community." But in soliciting support from non-Jews, canvassers were cautioned, "Do not *over-emphasize* the 'Jewish' element of the Nazi persecutions, but acquaint [those approached] with the Nazi terrorism in general." With the Halifax meeting drawing near, the stakes were high.[73]

And they grew higher. The same day Straight's article appeared in the *Vancouver Sun*, the Reich Ministry of the Interior in Berlin, responsible for implementing the Nuremberg Laws, issued its First Executive Order specifying the citizenship provisions of the Nuremberg Laws. Article 4/1 of the Order proclaimed, "A Jew cannot be a citizen of the Reich. He cannot exercise the right to vote; he cannot hold public office."

In that instant every German Jew officially became a non-person. And who was a Jew? Article 4 of the Order went on to delineate that, for legal purposes, a Jew was determined as such by the number of his or her Jewish grandparents. Those with one or two Jewish grandparents were declared partial Jews and subject to lesser restrictions than full Jews. Those with three or four Jewish grandparents were designated full Jews and subject to the full weight of the law which, in effect, meant that they were afforded no protection of the law. Their social death was complete.[74]

The organized Jewish community was quick to point out the obvious implications the Nazi action had for the inclusion of Jewish athletes on the German Olympic team. In a joint letter to the president of the AAUC that was sent to the meeting headquarters in Halifax, Caiserman and Sam Jacobs, Liberal Member of Parliament and president of the Canadian Jewish Congress, argued that the First Executive Order to the Nuremberg Laws put the lie to any claim that an 1936 Olympics held in Germany could possibly honour the Olympic ideal of openness to all.

> The latest enactments in Germany, only a few days ago, have deprived our [Jewish] brethren of the right of citizenship, which is a definite denial of the public statements made by the German Olympic Committee, to the effect that the Jewish athletes shall be given the opportunity to represent Germany in the Olympic Games.
>
> SINCE CITIZENSHIP IS AN ESSENTIAL REQUIREMENT FOR REPRESENTATION OF ANY COUNTRY, AND SUCH CITIZENSHIP IS DENIED TO JEWISH ATHLETES, HOW AMAZING THEN IS THE PUBLICIZED STATEMENT BY GERMAN OLYMPIC AUTHORITIES THAT REPRESENTATION BE GIVEN TO ALL ATHLETES WITHOUT DISCRIMINATION![75]

With only two days to go before the Halifax meeting was to convene, and after the Canadian Jewish Congress had warned the AUCC of the implications of the First Executive Order for the Olympics, an overflow crowd of more than 100 gathered in Toronto for the forum called only a week earlier by the Canadian Youth Council. The single topic for discussion was whether Canada should participate in the upcoming Olympic Games. As the room filled, it was announced that the German consul had been invited to address the meeting, as had been a representative of the Catholic Church. Both invitations were declined. Rather than portray this as a slight, the crowd was advised that while the "open character of the meeting was agreeable to these latter, it was impossible on the notice given for them to supply a speaker." The explanation was greeted with muted laughter. But the pro-Olympic side did not go unrepresented, as forum organizers welcomed James Merrick, Canadian member of the International Olympic Committee, to speak against an Olympic boycott. The Reverend R.J. Irwin, of the United Church of Canada, and Rabbi Eisendrath argued against Canadian Olympic participation. If many in the CJC were uneasy at Eisendrath's public involvement with what they regarded as a communist-front organization, even to further the Olympic boycott, they kept their concerns in-house.

After what was described as a "full discussion" of the issue during which Merrick defended Germany as an appropriate host for the Olympics, a contention vehemently rejected by Eisendrath, the forum unanimously adopted a resolution to be forwarded to the Canadian Olympic Committee in Halifax. The resolution called on Canada to refuse to participate in the Olympic Games if the Games were held in Germany. Instead, Canada should insist on a change of Olympic venue. The gathering also demanded that the Canadian Olympic Committee "investigate all circumstances surrounding the Olympic Games in light of religious, racial, and political prejudice apparent in German sports in violation of the Olympic Code." The resolution also called on the Canadian Olympic Committee to regard the matter of Canadian participation in the Olympics "as a purely moral issue affecting all creeds." Finally, the motion invited all Canadian youth to weigh in on Olympic issues and make their views known to both the Canadian Youth Council and the Amateur Athletic Union of Canada, the parent body of the Canadian Olympic Committee.[76]

As delegates began gathering in Halifax, the pace of the protest picked up. Some regarded this as a hopeful sign. The executive secretary of the Canadian Jewish Congress in Toronto, P. Stuchen, reported that a last-minute surge in non-Jewish activism in favour of the boycott was taking place in Toronto and that "further protests are being recorded by other local organizations, and will be forwarded to the Halifax meeting next week."[77] Rabbi Eisendrath had reason to take some pride in the behaviour of the interfaith "Jewish-Gentile Continuation Committee." Made up of prominent clergymen, including Eisendrath, Salem Bland, and the Quaker G. Raymond Booth, the group passed a resolution in favour of a boycott of the games because "we gravely doubt ... the

Olympic Games could be carried on in an atmosphere of complete international and interracial camaraderie and good will as is the basis of Olympic competitions." They sent the decision to other clergy and figures prominent in the world of Canadian amateur sport.[78] In Vancouver, Rabbi Samuel Cass, who was active in CJC's campaigns, was the newly appointed chairman of a fledgling anti-defamation group associated with B'nai Brith. Cass reported to B'nai Brith that the CJC was taking action on the Olympic file and that the provincial branch of the AAUC had "forwarded a resolution to the meeting of the National Body in Halifax demanding an investigation by the Dominion council of conditions in Germany specifically with regards to anti-Jewish discriminations." Cass was under the impression that "other Canadian divisions had adopted a similar point of view."[79]

Jewish leaders might have taken heart from anti-Olympic statements coming from labour organizations, progressive religious leaders, students groups, and even municipal officials. But there were also glaring failures. One influential figure they did not convince was Ernest Best, general secretary of the National Council of the YMCAs of Canada. Rev. G. Raymond Booth – a friend of Eisendrath's, a Quaker and a member of the Jewish-Gentile Continuation Committee[80] – had forwarded his committee's resolution, asking for Best's support. What Booth got in return was an earful. Best was not only unwilling to endorse the declaration, but he had already voiced support for the National Council of the YMCA's encouragement of the AAUC "to continue in their preparation for participation in the Olympic Games in Berlin." In contrast to the boycott advocates, Best believed that the purpose of the Games, "both in ancient times and during the last forty years," was to foster goodwill and that one had to respect the guarantee of Olympics organizers that their Games would be held "without regards to the political, racial and religious conflicts which are around us." Besides, what good are sanctions if they are too feeble to change the behaviour of the offending party? The only effect of sanctions, Best held, would be to make matters worse for those said to be under threat: "I believe that protests of this kind only tend to aggravate the situation in Germany and to intensify the persecution." Best called on Booth and his friends to re-evaluate their opposition to the Berlin Olympics.[81]

There were other failures. In the same letter to Caiserman that pointed to an upswing in non-Jewish support for the boycott, Stuchen admitted that in several critical areas – among athletes, sports journalists, and, most importantly, among those who would attend the meeting in Halifax – efforts to win support had fallen short. He confessed to Caiserman that Eisendrath had "personally called on most of the leading sport writers and has found them non-cooperative in this matter." Equally disappointing, Congress had "not had any success in contacting non-Jewish sportsmen who are opposed to Olympic participation. Those athletes whom we have contacted are willing, if chosen, to go to Germany."[82]

Bracing for Bad News

For the organized Jewish community there could be no backtracking on the call for a boycott. In the last weeks leading up to the Halifax meetings, boycott supporters continued to press their case even though CJC insiders regarded success as but a faint hope. Eisendrath was no exception. On Friday evening, 17 November, just four days before the AAUC was scheduled to respond to Hitler's summon to the youth of the world to gather in Germany for the Olympics, Eisendrath delivered a disheartening sermon entitled "Hitler Invites the Youth of the World. Shall Canada Accept? Fictions and Facts Concerning the Olympics." It was a sad and sometimes bitter concession of defeat for the pro-boycott side. Labelling Hitler a lying tyrant and a cold-blooded murderer who has "hounded every truly noble and chivalrous German from his borders" and for whom no deed is too dastardly if it furthers his "ends and aims," Eisendrath asked, "shall Canada accept the invitation of such a man?" The answer, he lamented, was yes.

"By all means," say a multitude of Canadians who, although the citizenry of most other countries have been veritably seething with controversy over this problem, are much too apathetic and indifferent even to have given a scintilla of their attention or thought to this vital matter. Such apathy I for one cannot comprehend. Opposition of the intensest and most virulent kind I could well understand and with the arguments, some of them valid, many of them spurious and bitter I shall deal in but a moment; but this deadening indifference of the Canadian public opinion in the presence of so burning an issue is disillusioning and depressing indeed. Except for certain labor groups, themselves vitally affected by what is happening in Germany, except for a few idealistic young men and women ... except for [some in the press] and the occasional utterance of a few isolated individuals, the large mass of Canadians and the majority of its so-called leaders have remained shamefully silent on this subject which is being so feverishly debated in every other land.

Eisendrath again laid out the "veritable avalanche of so-called 'practical' objections" to rejecting Hitler's invitation: think of the athletes, who have trained so long and hard; it is wrong to mix sport and politics when the Olympic is above politics; Canada has no right to interfere in the internal affairs of another country; Germany is a major power that Canada would do best not to alienate; the Olympics can usher in a new and positive appreciation for tolerance in Germany; why single out German for its discriminatory racial laws when so many other countries, including the United States, also practice racial discrimination; an Olympic boycott would only exacerbate Nazi antipathy to its Jews, making things worse for those for which boycott advocates claim to be concerned; Canada should follow the lead of the mother country; why so much fuss over a few Jews?

A Jewish question, forsooth! It is every bit as much a Christian question, a moral question, a Canadian question, if you will. Yes a Canadian question for if ever there was a Canadian issue it is here and now, for the Nazi regime has not so much insulted and offended and humiliated a few Jews or Catholics or Protestants as it has derided and scorned and violated everything Canadians and Britishers are supposed to hold dear and instead of waiting cautiously to see what other nations, what Great Britain especially will do first, as most sports writers and sport leaders have assured me we shall do, I should covet for Canada the dignity and the loyalty to Canadian ideals of democracy and tolerance and brotherhood; [instead] of waiting ignominiously for the counsel of the motherland, spontaneously and of her own accord to stand upon her own feet and courageously to declare that she will not compete in games of sport with those who have given all the abundant evidence that they recognize not the first principles of fair play and sportsmanship ... Of course, our cause may be lost. Apathy and ignorance are against us. The moral lassitude of the majority may conquer our utmost zeal. But is that any cause for capitulation? Should we who love peace surrender to the warmongers because it seems certain that the dogs of war will be let loose again? Should we ourselves favor the trafficking with moral lepers merely because the official action of some sports organizations is predicated on "practical" rather than ethical grounds?

Eisendrath's answer was "no." He called on his congregants and all Canadians of good will, even with only four days left before the Halifax meeting, to register their opposition to Canada's participation in the Nazi Olympics. To do anything less was to be complicit in what he sensed was coming on 21 November – AAUC acceptance of Hitler's invitation. Eisendrath also reminded his listeners that failure in Halifax by Olympic opponents, while a blow to the boycott cause, was not the end of the campaign. Just because the AAUC and its COC approve Canada going to the Olympics, "our task is not yet done. By similar and incessant action we can place every moral obstacle possible in the path of those who would raise funds to send our athletes into this inferno of burning hatreds which would reduce all Europe into a shambles."[83]

The Halifax Meetings

As it turns out, 21 November 1935 was a "slow news day." Among the few newsworthy events press wire services could come up with was the departure of the first commercial trans-Pacific flight of Pan American Airway's now legendary China Clipper – San Francisco to Honolulu, to Midway Island, to Wake Island, to Guam, and finally to Manila in the Philippines. The event was hailed as opening a new era in international aviation. Far less media attention, even in Canada, was accorded the AAUC decision to officially accept Nazi Germany's invitation to participate in the upcoming 1936 Winter and Summer Olympic Games. Months of campaigning by pro-boycott supporters turned up sum zero. The organized Jewish community and the left did not even have the satisfaction of seeing the Olympics issue debated by AAUC delegates. Instead, the only recognition of the hard work done by boycott advocates was a reference in the minutes of the 1935 AAUC meeting to the fact that "this Union is in receipt of a large number of communications from various parts of the country expressing opinions concerning the participation of Canada in the Olympic Games." There was no detail offered as to what these "opinions" were, let alone that any of the "communications" opposed Canadian participation in the Nazi Olympics.

Rather than an open discussion as to the morality of attending the Nazi Olympics, AAUC delegates were simply presented with a motion drawn up by the COC executive stating that "after careful consideration of all communication addressed to it," the organization recommends simply following Great Britain's lead. Since Great Britain had already accepted the German invitation, Canada should do likewise. The motion was carried without discussion or opposition. Canada would send teams to both the 1936 Winter and Summer Olympic Games in Nazi Germany.[84]

In approving a motion to simply follow the British lead and to do so without dissent, delegates to the Halifax meeting demonstrated unanimity of purpose rarely achieved on other issues. For example, the AAUC Executive Committee requested that delegates approve a motion easing stringent prohibitions against the mixed participation of professional and amateur athletes at AAUC-sanctioned sporting events. The subject sparked an acrimonious three-hour debate that ended in a negative vote. A lengthy *Winnipeg Free Press* article devoted to this and several other contentious issues occupying delegates at the Halifax meetings noted in passing, "There was no discussion about whether or not Canada would participate in the Olympics. The resolution committee said the Union had given careful consideration to communication on the subject and its recommendation that 'Canada follow the action of Great Britain' passed without question."[85]

Unbeknownst to the press and pro-boycott advocates, discussion among members of the COC executive did not include any serious consideration of arguments made by pro-boycott advocates; rather, they turned on whether or not to make any kind of motherhood statement rejecting racial or religious discrimination in sport and athletics. In a note to Herschorn, who did not attend the Halifax meeting, Lamb advised that there had been a resolution approving Canadian participation in the 1936 Olympics but including an affirmation that "this Union deplores racial distinction and persecutions." According to Lamb, "after much discussion" the motion was amended so as to "make no mention of persecutions." The revised resolution passed unanimously. Herschorn, who hoped the Halifax meeting would at least issue a statement decrying discrimination in sport – a crumb of a victory, if not for boycott supporters then for human dignity – got nothing.[86]

The pro-boycott campaign, for all the effort of its proponents, was crushed in Halifax. Canada accepted Hitler's invitation to the Olympics. For the Jewish community, however, and for left-wing parties and organized labour, the defeat in Halifax could not be the end of the road for the anti-Olympic campaign. The horror that had become Jewish life in Germany, and the political repression there more generally, precluded giving up on somehow blocking Canadian participation in the Olympics to be held in Hitler's Germany.

Chapter Four

"How Lonesome Our Position Is Becoming"

For Lou Marsh, sports editor of the *Toronto Star*, the Halifax decision was both a foregone conclusion and the right one. In an article of twenty-seven short paragraphs on the meeting highlights, Marsh made passing reference to the boycott question in the twenty-fifth paragraph and endorsed the colonial mentality that the AAUC took in justifying its decision to accept Hitler's invitation. As Marsh put it, "Canada has no real reason for dropping out of the Olympics unless Great Britain decides to withdraw her team."[1] Another Toronto journalist, J.V. McAree of the *Mail and Empire*, also offered an endorsement of the AAUC decision to participate in the Nazi Olympics, although he did acknowledge that "we have been deluged with protests."[2]

The supporters of a boycott may not have been surprised by the AAUC's decision to send a Canadian team to the Olympics, but many were outraged that the decision was made without any effort to address their concerns. The Unity and Goodwill Association, handmaiden of the CJC, published an editorial on the "moral tragedy" of Halifax. The editorial decried the callous self-absorption it regarded as behind the Halifax decision to turn a blind eye to evil, asserting that the AAUC position was, "We do not want to know! We do not want to hear! We do not want to be disturbed! Let Christianity be annihilated! Let barbarism prevail! It is not our concern as sportsmen! We want to go to the Olympics! We will go!"[3] The Yiddish-language newspaper of the Communist Party of Canada protested the decision as "an insult and challenge to all workers, anti-fascists and freedom-loving people," and "a boon to fascism and Hitler's regime."[4] The editorial cartoon of the English-language communist daily, *The Worker,* showed Hitler wearing hockey gear, but his stick is replaced by a blood-stained axe.[5] In December,

Gerhard Seeger, a former social democratic member of the Reichstag then visiting Montreal, expressed public dismay that Canada would allow Hitler to "misuse the Olympics for propaganda purposes" rather than call for a change in Olympic venue. Seeger delivered two seething anti-Nazi talks in Montreal, one covered in the *Montreal Gazette* and both monitored by the German consul general in Montreal and duly reported to Berlin.[6]

Others were furious that the AAUC and Canadian Olympic Committee did not even acknowledge receiving their protests. COC President P.J. Mulqueen's earlier comments in Montreal that the COC knew of no pro-boycott protests elicited scorn from *The Worker*. The paper cited letters of protest from two Canadian Legion branches, including the Jewish Branch (No. 256).[7] Two weeks later, the *Toronto Daily Star* published a letter to the editor in which the writer claimed he knew of four Legion chapters that had sent protests to the AAUC, complete with resolutions opposing Canadian Olympic participation.[8] The YMHA of Montreal complained that a protest petition it sent to the AAUC ended up in some sort of administrative black hole where all anti-Olympic protest magically disappeared. The president of the AAUC tried to respond, but was hardly convincing. The YMHA petition, he said, was referred to the resolutions committee, and it got no further.[9]

Canadian boycott advocates became even more frustrated with the Halifax decision when they compared it to the lively and open debate south of the border. The AAU held its 1935 annual meeting in New York in early December and Judge J. Mahoney, who had embraced the cause of an Olympic boycott the previous summer, locked horns with his nemesis, Avery Brundage, head of the AOC. Stories of these two butting heads were well covered in the Canadian press. Ironically, the news item next to Marsh's column that there was no "real reason" for a Canadian boycott dealt with the Americans who had indeed found a "real reason" for dropping out, and had ratcheted up their protests, beginning with a parade of 10,000 in New York City.[10] The final vote of a much-divided AAU was close: by a vote of 58.25 to 55.75 Brundage and the supporters of the German Olympics carried the day. Two votes going the other way and the United States would not have sent a team to Nazi Germany.

Unnoticed by most Canadians, three of their countrymen had played a role in the events unfolding at the AAU. H.E. Herschorn, P.J. Mulqueen, and J. Merrick (one of the two Canadian members on the

International Olympic Committee) attended the convention and all had votes. The three Canadians, however, chose not to cast their ballots. With every vote counting, why did they abstain? And, more specifically, why did Herschorn not cast a negative vote after he had come out so strongly against holding the Games in Germany? Herschorn must have fielded some heated questions at home with regards to his abstention. Two months after the AAU meeting, he placed a confidential and self-justifying memorandum "for record purposes" in the files of the YMHA. In it Herschorn explained that by not voting he had, in fact, strengthened the side of Judge Mahoney and the pro-boycott forces. It was "common knowledge" that Mulqueen and Merrick would vote for American participation.[11] Herschorn claimed to have suggested to his two fellow Canadian voters that the proposed American boycott was an internal American matter, so it would be "an act of courtesy on the part of the Canadians not to cast his vote." As a result, Herschorn argued, he sacrificed his one Canadian vote for a boycott in order to cancel out two Canadian votes for participation.[12]

While the role of these Canadians may not have attracted much press attention at home, other aspects of the debate in the United States did. As reported in the *Canadian Jewish Review*, Harvey Golden, the executive director of the Montreal YMHA, was particularly struck by the differences in Canadian and American decision-making. Like Canada, the Amateur Athletic Union in the United States did not vote for a boycott; unlike Canada, at least the topic was raised and publicly discussed. And again unlike Canada, he noted, the final AAU resolution approving American participation called for ongoing vigilance of Nazi racist behaviour in sport, and made it clear that AAU's certification of athletes to compete in the German Olympics should not be read as endorsement of the Nazis:

How different was [the AAU] public discussion from the tranquil deliberations of the Canadian Amateur Athletic Union. Indeed, from what one hears, our Canadian sports leaders hardly deliberated on the matter. One would think that the prospect of sending Canada's finest young men and women involved no breach of Olympic ideology; one would think that the complete domination of the Games by a hate-raising official gang involved no principles of human progress. No wonder many Canadian are ashamed of the hanky-panky method adopted at the Halifax meeting of the A.A.U. of C.[13]

Golden felt that the American advocates for a boycott could at least claim a moral victory, and Brundage and his AOC did not get off scot-free. The Nazis remained under scrutiny, and if the German Olympic enterprise was publicly tarnished as racist, approval of the American team's participation could be revoked. There was no similar consolation prize in Canada, not the way the COC and AAUC had frozen out protest, muzzled debate, and refused to issue in Halifax even the weakest warning against Nazi Germany.

Organizing the Games: Preparations in Germany and Canada

Even as the Nazis monitored with some concern the international reaction to the Games, they continued their preparations with vigour. By December 1935 the Nazis had invested enormously in preparation for the major event, the Summer Games in Berlin. But they were also very concerned about making the Winter Olympics, to be held in February 1936 in Garmisch-Partenkirchen, both a propaganda boost at home and a successful dry run for Berlin.

But to achieve their goals, the organizers had to overcome a number of logistical problems, some of them man-made. Before welcoming the world to Garmisch-Partenkirchen in Bavaria (or "Gapa," as it was sometimes shortened), the authorities had infrastructure work to do. The Nazis broadened and straightened the mountainous ninety-kilometre road between Munich and Garmisch-Partenkirchen. By August 1935 it was ready, although the celebratory opening for the "Olympic Road" would have to wait until January. The railway track was also upgraded in the expectation that trains would run between Munich and Garmisch-Partenkirchen every seven to ten minutes. The Germans estimated that during the Games there would be as many as 20,000 daily trips to "Gapa" by car, and 50,000 trips every day by rail. German authorities were confident that housing for athletes would not be much of a problem as many locals were volunteered to billet competitors. The hotels in Munich were also judged ready to accommodate most of the guests and host even the most lavish of the Olympic parties and receptions.[14]

But German authorities had their work cut out for them to ensure that the sporting venues were to be world class. In 1931 when Germany agreed to host the Winter Games, the local bobsled run and ski jumps fell short of Olympic standards. They were upgraded quickly and declared ready in early 1934. The organizers had more trouble with the arena for hockey and figure skating. The official story was that in an outpouring of local pride, the indoor rink was built during 1934 with civic cooperation, efficiency, and skill in only 104 working days.[15] Actually, the towns of Garmisch and Partenkirchen, which were officially merged on 1 January 1935, fought one another for the right to have the arena built in their respective towns. Much to Partenkirchen's resentment, Garmisch won out, and the modern rink, with room for 10,000 fans and the press, was built close to the regional train station in Garmisch.[16]

While German Olympic organizers could rest easy regarding the sporting venues and accompanying infrastructure, they remained uneasy at how the local population would respond to visitors from abroad. Bavaria was a heartland of Nazi support and fully embraced the antisemitism the Party espoused. The nearby town of Oberammergau was – depending on one's perspective – famous or infamous as the site, since 1634, of a passion play that maximized Jewish responsibility and guilt for the crucifixion of Christ. Hitler attended the play's tercentenary and proclaimed it excellently edifying. When Garmisch and Partenkirchen merged in early 1935, the Nazi members of the city council immediately called on "Gapa" to expel all its Jews. The motion passed, but implementation was put on hold until after the Olympics.[17]

But antisemitism was still a fact of local life. Visitors to the area in 1934 and 1935 could not miss the anti-Jewish signage that blanketed the region. In May 1935, the president of the organizing committee for the Winter Olympic Games, Karl Ritter von Halt, wrote to the undersecretary in the Interior Ministry responsible for the Games pleading something had to be done, and fast. The good citizens of Gapa were so whipped up in an antisemitic frenzy, Ritter warned, it would not surprise him if during the Games they attacked anybody who even looked Jewish. The results would be disastrous not only for the Winter Games, but would lead to a boycott of Berlin. Ritter made it clear that his concern was not the reality of the antisemitism. That was understandable and justified. But in the context of the Olympics, Ritter assured the undersecretary, it was an inconvenience: "Mr. Undersecretary, please be convinced that I am not expressing my concern in order to help the Jews, but only in the interest of the Olympic idea and the Olympic Games for which I have volunteered all of my free time for many years."[18]

But local supporters of Nazi racial policy were not ready to set their antisemitism aside, even for the Olympic moment. In late 1935, Count

Henri de Baillet-Latour drove through the region, and was stunned by the number of blatant antisemitic road signs he encountered. One of them warned drivers approaching a curve to slow down – except for Jews; they were welcome to crash. After some give-and-take with Hitler himself, the IOC secured the promise that the signs would be removed. The resulting order by the Interior Ministry demanded the removal of all signs and posters hostile to the Jews in the region of Garmisch-Partenkirchen. The rationale was included in the order: "so as not to endanger the 1936 Olympics Games in Berlin." Antisemitic signage in areas less likely to see Olympic visitors was left in place.[19]

One sign proved particularly embarrassing to the Olympic organizers. In late 1935, a picture of a sign, ostensibly posted at the entrance to an official Olympic site office that read "Olympic Tourism Office/ Ski Club Partenkirchen/Jews-No Entry" appeared in both a Dutch pro-boycott pamphlet and the *Manchester Guardian*. For the opponents of the Games, here was proof positive, just weeks before the beginning of the Winter Games, that antisemitism was both open and condoned by the authorities. The German Ministry of Propaganda turned to the press officer for the Games for an answer, thinking the photograph must be a fake. But it wasn't a fake – just an embarrassment. The Officer explained that the Olympic Tourism Office had moved out of that location, and its name should have been removed before the "No Jews Allowed" poster appeared. The Office, he explained, had nothing to do with the sign; he did not, however, indicate that it protested the message.[20]

The sign fiasco was disconcerting to German officials because they wanted a positive propaganda bump from Olympic tourism and, above all, international tourism. The authorities had established a tourism arm within the German State Railway (Reichsbahnzentrale für den Deutschen Reiseverkehr, or RDV) to promote the Games internationally, and antisemitic imagery was hardly helpful. The RDV opened up offices across Germany, the rest of Europe, and overseas. These offices were tasked with both publicizing the Games and countering negative press about holding the Games in Nazi Germany. The RDV provided its offices with prodigious amounts of literature, including fifty-eight different brochures and pamphlets in fourteen languages, thirteen different large posters in thirteen languages, postcards in three languages, and poster stamps in German and English. All told, the RDV printed about three and a half million items, distributed in forty countries.[21] The volume of literature certainly staggered one Canadian, the sports writer of the *Calgary Daily Herald*, Ralph Wilson. He was convinced, on the evidence of the "formidable bundles" of pamphlets arriving at his office, that the Germans "are turning out more publicity on the 1936 athletic classic than any country in the history of the event."[22]

Canada would get more than just pamphlets. In the summer of 1935, the RDV assigned Werner Haag as its local representative in Canada.[23] His office was the only RDV office in Canada, and was almost certainly located in Toronto rather than Montreal because the COC was headquartered in Toronto. By November, the German consul general in Montreal was referring all inquiries about the Olympics to Haag.[24] However, while Haag's office was open to the public, he held back an official opening until 5 December 1935, when he planned an elegant event at Toronto's upscale Royal York Hotel to draw maximum publicity.

But although Haag waited a few weeks to officially open his office doors, his arrival in Canada did not go unnoticed. Towards the end of November, Colin Gravenor, a non-Jewish sports writer who was working with Canadian Jewish Congress as the head of the "Canadian non-sectarian anti-Nazi League," visited Haag's office to collect official Olympic literature. Gravenor also managed to secure an invitation to Haag's opening bash at the Royal York; Gravenor, however, wrote to Caiserman stating he was planning to picket the event, not attend it.[25] Caiserman thought it was an excellent idea, but told Gravenor that he should be in touch with CJC people in Toronto.[26] In early December, Maurice Eisendrath dropped his own bombshell about Werner Haag. The rabbi informed the press that he had evidence that Haag was not only a Nazi, but had been investigated in the United States for his fascist activities.[27]

The opponents of the Games now had a target for their post-Halifax frustrations. The Second Congress against War and Fascism, held in early December, passed a resolution protesting Haag's presence in Canada.[28] Smaller groups also weighed in. The German Work and Farm Association, Regina local, sent a letter of protest to Ottawa complaining about Haag.[29] The Canadian Jewish Congress was quite content to let Gravenor front the Royal York protest and take credit in the press. The more than 100 guests arriving at the Royal York – "including many prominent railwaymen and leading Canadian sportsmen" – were greeted by a line of placard-waving anti-Nazi protesters.[30]

CJC also worked behind the scenes, setting up a meeting between CJC officials in Toronto and a ranking Canadian immigration official to discuss Haag's status in Canada.[31] S.W. Jacobs, CJC president and a Liberal Member of Parliament, took the case directly to F.C. Blair, director of the Immigration Branch, asking for an inquiry into how Haag got into Canada and whether he ought to be deported. The request to look into Haag also made it to O.D. Skelton, influential Canadian undersecretary of state for foreign affairs, who wrote to the Canadian chargé d'affaires in Washington, H.M. Wrong, requesting background information on Haag.[32]

Haag did not have to worry. Information gathered by Blair and Skelton showed that, whatever his politics, Haag was in Canada to work for the German State Railway and there was no cause to re-evaluate his immigration status. Blair, never shy about sticking it to the Jewish community, mused about what might happen if his officials were to investigate all the cases of people who brought "their Old World politics and quarrels to Canada." Blair specifically addressed the protest outside the Royal York, warning Jacobs that this kind of public display was unseemly. "I think," Blair wrote Jacobs, "it is regrettable that there would have occurred in Toronto on Thursday evening last such a demonstration as reported in the press. Such incidents are not helpful to the cause they are supposed to represent and while not designed to do so, make Governmental action more difficult than it would otherwise be."[33]

All that Canadian Jews got from the Haag affair was Blair's unwanted homily on civics. Haag received a special resolution of thanks for the Royal York event from the COC, and he remained in Canada until the Summer Olympics, developing a close working relationship with the COC and the German consuls.[34]

Boycott Strategies after Halifax

Faced with the finality of the Halifax decision and ongoing Olympic preparations in Germany and Canada, boycott supporters had to rethink their strategies. Some things did not need change. The Canadian Jewish Congress continued to monitor developments overseas and in Canada. Caiserman continued to caution the Jewish community to keep its distance from organizations with strong communist ties. In mid-November, two B'nai Brith members in Port Arthur and Fort William, including Dr. M. Stitt, were invited to attend a district meeting of the CLAWF, held in preparation of the group's National Congress scheduled for early December 1935.[35] The local meeting attracted, according to the RCMP report, about 100 delegates, who ostensibly represented 8,000 local members. Most of the delegates represented "Communist and radical organizations," but the two B'Nai Brith members were not the only non-communists present. Some of the delegates were from church groups, CCF clubs, and non-communist trade unions.[36] The gathering selected three representatives to attend the National Congress, including one of the members of the B'nai Brith.

But Stitt was uneasy. Concerned that the communists were running the meeting, he wanted to be sure that the Jewish community did not put itself in a difficult position. He consulted with both the editor of the local newspaper and the local chief of police. Both offered the same advice: Stay away. The League was indeed a communist front. Stitt was still perplexed. In a letter to Caiserman, he asked why the list of officials of the executive committee of CLAWF included Rabbi Eisendrath and several other Jewish notables.[37] Caiserman wrote back that CJC was deliberately and officially steering clear of the CLAWF because of its domination by communists. As Caiserman put it, "To be identified with the Communists at the present temper of Canadian politics is a vital danger for the Jewish population and plays into the hands of Nazi agents from coast to coast." And what about Eisendrath? When it came to the CLAWF, Caiserman explained, the rabbi was in no way representing the CJC. He was there in a private capacity. Sensing more of an explanation was required, Caiserman continued that Eisendrath's "services to us are too valuable from the point of view of Anti-Defamation work in Canada, that we should interfere with his personal opinions." The implication was clear: if Caiserman had his way, Eisendrath would not be involved with the CLAWF, but that was not going to happen.[38]

Much to Caiserman's regret, Eisendrath was not the only Jew who endorsed the activities of the League or participated in its annual Congress. Several organizations from the non-Zionist left also attended the Congress. Four branches of the *Arbeter Ring* were represented, as well as two branches of IKOR, *Idishe Kolonizatsie Organizatsie in Rusland* (Organization for Jewish Colonization in Russia), which sought support for the autonomous Jewish region set up in the USSR.[39] More surprising was the attendance of delegates from Young Judaea, a mainstream Zionist youth organization.[40] The presence of Young Judaea, in spite of Caiserman's repeated warnings against Jewish involvement with the CLAWF and similar organizations, demonstrates that the popular front had achieved some traction, limited though it might be, in Jewish circles, and not just on the far left. It was hard to argue that Jews should not lend support to those who shared their anti-Nazi and anti-Olympic zeal.[41]

Like the CJC, the CCF also officially rejected involvement in popular front organizations, but it too had some trouble controlling its members. One of the keynote speakers at the second National Congress against War and Fascism was Rev. T.C. Douglas, by then a CCF Member of Parliament. The Congress elected Douglas a vice-president of CLAWF. Representatives from thirteen CCF clubs were also present.[42] When reproached, the participants argued (as Caiserman had for Eisendrath) that they were only attending as individuals, not as representatives of the party. CCF founder J.S. Woodsworth, however, was not impressed. Both his concern to keep the CCF separate from communist front activities, and the pressure from certain CCF quarters for cooperation with all genuine anti-fascist groups would continue.

Worried about ongoing Jewish fraternization with popular front organizations, Caiserman came up with what he thought was an innovative solution – Canadian Jewish Congress should create its own broadly based "popular front." In late November Caiserman wrote with enthusiasm to Eisendrath that, after several abortive attempts, CJC had finally succeeded in getting a non-sectarian anti-Nazi front group up and running under the direction of Colin Gravenor.[43] Gravenor seemed the answer to Caiserman's prayer. Here was a well-connected non-Jewish and non-communist sports writer ready to pull together a like-minded group to take up the battle for both the economic boycott and Olympic boycott.[44]

Banking so much on somebody who was an unknown to the Jewish community was a risk. Less than two weeks after Caiserman's excitement about Gravenor's involvement, the CJC in Toronto started raising concerns about him. Local CJC executive secretary, P. Stuchen, informed Caiserman that Gravenor was trying to accomplish too much and was stepping on toes in the process. He was also looking to create a boycott committee when, according to Stuchen, one already existed. Gravenor, without consultation, planned to invite Judge Mahoney to come to Toronto and speak on the Olympics matter. Stuchen also passed on local scuttlebutt that Gravenor was an opportunist who could easily shift sides and therefore "needs to be watched."[45] Several weeks later Eisendrath reported that he was also privy to information about Gravenor "which constrains me to be most suspicious with regard to his present motives and activities." Eisendrath asked Caiserman to investigate.[46]

Shortly after this exchange, Gravenor was out of the picture. His unexplained departure left the role of non-Jewish spokesperson for the boycott campaign unfilled. While some were no doubt pleased to see

Gravenor gone, others felt the boycott campaign lacked for an articulate non-Jewish voice speaking out in its favour. The Hamilton B'nai Brith chapter thought it found someone who could fill the role, Em Orlick, the outspoken physical education director at the University of Western Ontario and, according to Kidd, "a thorn in the side of 'bourgeois sports organizations.'"[47]

The YMHA

No Jewish organization, with the possible exception of the CJC, was as engaged with the Jewish Olympic boycott campaign after Halifax as Montreal's YMHA. Originally founded in 1910, by the mid-1930s it was a major Montreal Jewish organization that, according to its mission statement, served the "social, cultural, recreational and intellectual needs" of the Montreal Jewish community. The "Y" was also an important Montreal amateur sports venue and, as such, its teams and athletes competed under the AAUC umbrella. But when it came to the Nazi Olympics, the YMHA and the AAUC parted company. The AAUC voted to send Canadian athletes to the Olympics; the YMHA was firmly in support of the boycott. During the lead-up to the Halifax meeting, the YMHA quietly made its opposition known to the AAUC leadership. But, in view of the Halifax decision, the Y decided to take its protest public. Harvey Golden, executive director of the YMHA, had written a strongly worded attack on the Halifax vote published in the *Canadian Jewish Chronicle*. He denounced the AAUC's treatment of the issue as compared to the open debate of the AAU south of the border. But the Y and Golden did not just register complaints: as the premier Jewish athletic organization in Montreal, and the largest in Canada, the Y had to decide what to say to its athletes who could be contenders to go to the Olympics. And what would the Y say to the AAUC (of which the Y was a constituent member) and the COC when it came time for amateur athletic organizations to contribute funds and volunteer time and facilities for the Olympic trials?

Canadian Jewish Congress, for all its commitment to the Olympic boycott, had no real experience dealing with athletes and the amateur sports establishment. For help in answering these questions the Montreal YMHA turned to its sister organizations to the south. Once the AAU had made its decisions to attend the Nazi Olympics, the YMHAs across North America had to confront the reality that both American and Canadian athletes would be going to Germany. But what about athletes and teams associated with YMHA organizations? Golden wrote to Harry Glucksman, executive director of the Jewish Welfare Board, "national organization of the YMHA's, YWHA's, and Jewish Community Centers," to ask about its policy on the matter. Glucksman cautioned that he could not recommend what Canadians should do, but he insisted that in the United States the boycott campaign would continue. Many in the United States objected to the Olympics, and the opponents of participation continued the fight "not on the basis of sabotage but rather from the viewpoint of continuous and sustained public education." As always, Glucksman insisted, the Jewish Welfare Board would work with non-Jewish organizations so that the boycott movement was seen to be non-sectarian.[48]

The Montreal YMHA, hoping to coordinate its response to Canada's Olympic plans with American YMHAs, dispatched Golden to New York to confer with Jewish officials and athletes. His mandate was to determine whether there was value in a common strategy. For four days Golden met with Jewish officials, Jewish athletes, and representatives of various pro-boycott groups. If he expected to find agreement on a plan of action, he was sadly disappointed. What he found instead was a messy hodgepodge of notions on how to proceed and organizations working at cross-purposes. Yes, Jewish organizations were against participating in the Olympics in Germany, and yes, they believed that the deteriorating situation in Germany meant there was need for action. But according to Golden, the concern did not translate into inter-organizational cooperation. There were divisions between the American Jewish Committee and the American Jewish Congress on the handling of the Olympic issue, and the American League against War and Fascism was at odds with the liberal Committee on Fair Play. If there was any agreement at all among the organizations, it was that there should be a complete Jewish refusal to cooperate with any aspect of the Olympics. But, as Golden knew, this blanket rejection did not take into account the needs and hopes of Jewish athletes. Some athletes had stated they would not go to Germany under any circumstances, others would go under certain circumstances, and still others thought they could compete "for the honour of representing the U.S.A." and then turned around and refused to go to the Games. In sum, there was no American model to adopt.

Oddly, Golden was convinced that Canadian Jews had given more thought to the issues than the Americans; in fact, instead of picking up tips from the Americans, Golden was asked to remain in New York to be part of a special inter-organizational meeting of Jewish officials and athletes to discuss the issues that Golden had raised. The result of the meeting – after some "considerable disagreement" – was a middle ground between the pro-boycotters and the desire of athletes to represent their country. The Jewish Welfare Board endorsed a plan whereby athletes would be encouraged to compete for a national title or standing, but not in events specifically designated as Olympic trials. However, Jewish athletes would be asked to pledge in advance that should they win an event, and should those winners be given an automatic spot on an Olympic team, they would not accept. What is more, athletes were asked to only compete in events where no funds were being raised in support of the Olympics.

Golden thought that these were good compromises, but he knew that they would not be easy to implement. He was especially concerned that the American Jewish leaders would have a tough time convincing American athletes not to attend the Olympics. He also wondered whether this compromise would work in Canada, as the distinction between Olympics trials and national trials was clearer in the United States. He also thought that the respective size of the Jewish communities was relevant. His observation on this point is somewhat unclear: "The position of the Canadian community as a tiny minority is more difficult that [sic] that of the United States. Canadian Jewry as such is not committed to a given course of action as is the United States." Presumably, he was saying that the small Canadian Jewish community had less sway on the national stage than he felt was true of its American cousins. If that was his meaning, he was right. He was nevertheless convinced that Canadian Jewry must still let its voice be heard. Any Canadian gesture of cooperation with the Olympics would harm the morale of North American Jewry, and strengthen the position of Brundage, who, Golden was convinced, was determined to see North American youth serve the propaganda ends of Nazi Germany.[49]

Golden's trip to New York not only helped bridge the divide between various American players in the pro-boycott camp, it also helped stiffen the YMHA's resolve to stand bold against any cooperation with the Olympics and its planning. It came at a very important juncture in the run-up to the Olympics, not so much as regards the soon-to-be-held Winter Olympics, but rather because of ongoing preparations for the Summer Games. Montreal managed to outbid Hamilton and other rival cities for the right to host a number of Olympic trials. It was then the responsibility of Montreal organizers to locate appropriate sports venues and qualified officials. In mid-January, McGill's Athletic Board decided to lend a helping hand to the COC, and granted the Quebec Track and Field Association permission to use the university's field for the trials.[50] The Board of the Directors of the YMHA followed a very different course. It affirmed that the YMHA would refuse to participate in the Olympics. Although some members of the Board thought that they could still behave as "good Canadians" and volunteer as referees and timekeepers, the Board concluded that even this lesser level of participation could be misconstrued, and would harm the North American campaign against Olympic participation.[51]

As Golden had discovered in the United States, it was easier to proclaim a blanket policy of non-participation than to implement the policy. To handle this difficult file, the Montreal YMHA struck a Special Committee that included Herschorn as a member. The decisions of the Special Committee reflect some of the casuistry of Golden's meeting in New York, especially·the need to avoid an appearance of support for the Olympics no matter how distant. For example, the Committee ruled that the YMHA should not host an upcoming fencing tournament that would include the YMHA Fencing Club lest the public think it was hosting an Olympic trial. Furthermore, the YMHA's fencers were instructed to inform tournament organizers, no matter where the event was held, that they were entering "from the angle of sport alone" and not as part of any Olympic trial. The Committee was also concerned about ensuring adherence to the Olympic ban among YMHA members and controlling YMHA's message of non-participation. The Committee decided that members of YMHA teams who played in various amateur leagues should not answer Olympic-related questions from the public or press, but should instead refer all questions to the Special Committee.[52]

Unfortunately, aside from the Montreal YMHA, very little is known about how other Jewish sporting organizations in Canada dealt with issues related to Olympic participation. The only other reported pushback from this period comes from Toronto where on New Year's Eve the local YMHA sponsored an amateur boxing card. Jews figured prominently in a variety of amateur sports in Toronto, but it was boxing, above all, that engaged both Jewish and non-Jewish fans. Jewish gamblers and fight fans formed a boxing subculture in the Jewish fight clubs that mushroomed and shrivelled in Toronto's immigrant Jewish neighbourhoods.[53] Marsh, who attended the Toronto YMHA's event on New Year's Eve, wasn't sure what to make of the *gut yontifs* he was hearing.[54] However, to run an amateur match required the sanction of the Ontario branch of the Amateur Athletic Union (OAAU). The YMHA secured that permission, but subsequently, in early December, the OAAU passed a regulation mandating that 5 per cent of all gross gate receipts must be turned over to the OAAU "for Olympic purposes." Several days before the big night, the YMHA announced that it would not turn over the 5 per cent for the Olympics, but would give any earnings to charity. The OAAU dug in its heels and insisted on the money.[55]

According to Marsh, the boxing he saw on 31 December 1935 was spectacular even if attendance was not. And no sooner were the fights in the ring over than the fight over the receipts began. In one corner was the YMHA, which refused to hand over any gate receipts that would go to support the Canadian Olympic team, and in the other corner, the supervisor of boxing for the OAAU who rejected the right of the YMHA to pick and choose what it would or would not support:

> What right have the Y.M.H.A. to tell us where our percentage goes no matter what their feelings are? Now that Canada has determined to send a team to Berlin we are out to get the money to finance the boxing team, and in spite of the objections of the Jewish organization, they will have to fall in line or suffer the consequences.[56]

Several weeks later the OAAU met to decide what to do about the YMHA. Nobody from the YMHA showed up at the meeting, but the organization did send a letter apologizing for not being able to attend. The letter reiterated the YMHA's refusal to hand over the money. Instead, they explained that the money, totalling a staggering $23.87, had been sent to the Hospital for Sick Children. With such a pittance at stake, the conflagration was clearly a conflict over principles and authority. The Ontario branch of the AAUC suspended the YMHA, which meant that henceforth it would not be able to hold any more AAUC events, and the athletes from the YMHA had to be "unattached" or belong to another authorized club in order to compete in AAUC-sanctioned events.[57]

Strategy: Target the Funding

Although the controversy in Toronto was over a paltry sum, money remained the Achilles heel of Canada's Olympic planning. At the COC meeting in 1934, Mulqueen had made it clear that only minimal support would come from Ottawa, and that athletic associations and clubs would have to muster their own funds to get athletes overseas.[58] With the various associations looking for funding, the pro-boycott forces fought hard to ensure that the money would not come from the different levels of government. Just before the Halifax vote, the national office of Canadian Jewish Congress wrote to its branches and contacts across the country and called on them to do all they could to scuttle municipal, provincial, and federal subsidies.[59] The Western Division of the CJC responded with an account of the history of its success with the city of Winnipeg. It had earlier managed to convince the Financial Committee of the City not to offer funding to Olympic trials. In mid-November, the executive of the local Trades and Labour Council met with the CJC in Winnipeg. Together, they decided that the Trades and Labour Council should continue to lobby the city against offering grants to any sporting organizations with Olympic teams.[60] The Council did just that, and with success. The City Committee reiterated its commitment not to offer financial support to Canadian athletes heading to the Olympics.[61]

The supporters of a boycott had also counted on James Simpson, the socialist mayor of Toronto who came out of the Trades and Labour Congress, and who had on several occasions declared himself against Canadian involvement in the Nazi Games. It was a bitter blow when Simpson lost the civic election in early 1936 and his successor, Sam McBride, almost as a first act on assuming office, announced that the city would reconsider supporting the Canadian Olympic team, and the location of those Games would not be a factor.[62] In Montreal, it's not even clear if the local boycotters bothered to approach Mayor Camillien Houde. It would have been to little avail; Houde, one of the few French-Canadian public figures to show an interest in amateur sports, was an enthusiastic supporter of Canada's Olympic teams.[63]

Opponents of the Games also targeted the federal government. Ottawa committed itself to $10,000 and, in late October 1935, handed over to Mulqueen one-half of that amount as its first instalment. In the weeks after the Halifax decision, the pro-boycott forces hoped they could dissuade Ottawa from making the second payment. The National Labour Council wrote to Liberal Prime Minister Mackenzie King requesting that Ottawa deny any further support for the Canadian team to complete in Germany "owing to the attitude of repression of all freedom that is taken by the Dictator Hitler."[64] George Langsner of the Unity and Goodwill Association also wrote to Ottawa asking that the second instalment be withheld. The reason, he said, should be amply clear from the press: "Every item about Germany in the newspapers is an item of degradation, barbarism persecution, militarism and Middle Age ideology."[65]

The COC expected and needed the Ottawa money. A continuing shortfall in revenue would drastically reduce the level of Canadian Olympic participation. In early January, the COC held a meeting focused solely on finances, where acting chair Fred Marples reminded his colleagues that the government's $5,000 was still expected in spite of protests.[66] Still smarting from the behaviour of the COC in Halifax, the organized Jewish community could not bear the thought of the federal government supporting the COC. The editor of the *Canadian Jewish Chronicle* complained that the COC maintained a "conspiracy of silence" on the Olympic file, and with this additional news of the government grant, "we Jews can realize how lonesome our position is becoming." Sure, politicians have come to protests, and spoken with "indignant voices," but then why is there public money to support sports in "Naziland?" Again, the editor wailed out of frustration and helplessness, "Of what avail is the piping voice of an outraged people among devotees of sport?" The editor also wondered aloud whether the government would provide the funding if the Olympics were to be held in the Soviet Union.[67]

Supporters of an Olympic boycott may have been frustrated, even disheartened, but they kept on fighting. They also brought the fight closer to the athletes themselves and targeted the myriad ways that athletes and their organizations were trying to fund their trips to Germany. The problem of finances was an ongoing concern to the COC, and one that divided the amateur athletic community. At the COC's executive meeting in January 1936, two organizations expressed anger with COC fundraising policies. A representative of the Canadian Amateur Ski Association (CASA) was particularly outspoken in his criticism. He explained how CASA managed to raise funds from across Canada, with some additional support specifically from Montreal. But it was still not enough to support all Olympic-eligible skiers. Vancouver Norwegian-born skier Tom (né Tormad) Mobraaten was fortunate that the members of his ski club and other friends helped him raise the $600 to go to Germany. Another British Columbia skier, Hans Gunnarson of Revelstoke, was not so lucky. He could not find the necessary funding, despite being chosen for the team.[68] CASA offered no funding to women, but several Canadians skiers already in Europe were invited to join the Canadian team.

CASA protested that the COC had not made fundraising easy. CASA recommended that in future the COC inform its constituent associations of any shortfall so they could better organize to fill the funding gap.[69] In the end CASA managed to send a team of five men, four women, and one manager, all of them either self-funded or with privately raised support.[70]

The representative for amateur skating, responsible for both figure skating and speed skating, also complained that his organization was not given enough notice of the need to fundraise.[71] The representative for skating could have pointed out to the COC that Canadian speed skaters were especially deserving of consideration, as they had competed very successfully at the 1932 Winter Games in Lake Placid, New York. Canadians won five medals, with the most successful of the Canadians, Alex Hurd of Sudbury, earning a silver in the 1,500 metres and a bronze in the 500 metres. In 1936, the skating representative told the COC that his organization had pulled together enough funding for six figure skaters and two speed skaters, Tom White of Saint John, and Alex Hurd. But the report was premature. Alex Hurd informed the *Toronto Daily Star* three days after the meeting that he was not going with the team. On his own he had managed to raise $362. He needed an additional $300 and could not afford to stake that amount himself. He complained that his skating association was a "cheap bunch" and that he was not given enough time to find the funds.[72] But there was more to that story. Sudbury's mining giant, INCO, had offered to cover some of Hurd's expenses and asked its workers to contribute; the workers, however, supporting the pro-boycott protests of labour and the left, declared, "No money for Hitler," and, as a result, Hurd received no funding from workers or the company.[73]

The Skiers Who Did Not Go

Two Canadians skiers did not compete, but not because of lack of money or talent. On 16 April 1935, seven months before the Halifax meeting would officially decide whether Canada would take part in the Olympics and ten months before the Winter Olympics were scheduled to begin, members of the Canadian Olympic Ski Committee met in Montreal and, "subject to future contingencies and sufficient financial support," announced the names of eight skiers chosen to wear Canada's Olympic colours.[74]

P.J. Mulqueen's identification card for the Summer Games in Berlin.
(Mulqueen Family Collection)

Matthew and Jean Halton, in front of the Brandenburg Gate, Berlin, 1933.
(David Halton family collection)

Rabbi Maurice N. Eisendrath photographed by Violet Keene.
(Canadian Jewish Congress Charities Committee National Archives)

Photograph of H.M. Caiserman taken at Jacobys Studios, Montreal, with handwritten inscription dated 1931. (Canadian Jewish Congress Charities Committee National Archives)

Photograph of the Canadian Jewish Congress's Second Plenary Assembly in 1934, which marked the re-establishment of the organization as a permanent body. This meeting took place in Toronto. (N.C. Hichenson photograph; Canadian Jewish Congress Charities Committee National Archives [PC1–3-40-CJC])

1935 Yiddish poster calling for an Anti-Hitler Mass Meeting. The organizers expressed their frustration with the response of the mainstream Jewish organizations. They were further to the left than even the left-leaning mainstream Jewish community. (Canadian Jewish Congress Charities Committee National Archives; Canadian Jewish Congress organization records collection ZA1935–4-60-A)

Anti-Olympic editorial cartoon, by Joseph Abugov, mocking Hitler's invitation to the world to attend the 1936 Olympics. (*Canadian Jewish Chronicle*, 1 November 1935)

A cartoon by "Avrom" (Avrom Yanovsky) from *The Worker*, newspaper of the Communist Party of Canada, 25 November 1935. (Collection of Anna Yanovsky)

Poster promoting the Summer Olympics in Berlin. The German State Railway
was responsible for promoting the Games, and this poster includes contact
information for the office opened in Toronto in late 1935.
(Mary Wilder Scrapbook, 213.2012-S1–14, Dance Collection Danse)

SHOULD CANADIANS SUPPORT THE NAZI OLYMPIC GAMES?

•SYMPOSIUM•

Friday, Mar. 27, 8.15 P.M.

STRATHCONA HALL

772 Sherbrooke St. W.

ADMISSION FREE

- **NORMAN GILLESPIE**, President, Quebec Football Association.
- **HARVEY GOLDEN**, Executive Director, Young Men's Hebrew Association.
- **MADELEINE SHERIDAN**, Member, Women's Catholic League; Member, Prov. Council, C.C.F.
- **J. B. ST. JOHN**, Member Youth Forum, Emmanuel Church; Member C.C.Y.M.
- **STANLEY RYERSON**, Member, Montreal Council, League Against War and Fascism.

Will each talk for 15 minutes. Discussion from the floor will follow.

Auspices: Canadian League Against War and Fascism.

A Montreal symposium on Canadian participation in the 1936 Olympics. The Canadian League against War and Fascism was an organization largely inspired by the Communist Party of Canada, with the aim of developing an anti-fascist front with non-communist organizations.

(YMHA collection, Jewish Public Library Archives, Montreal)

Eva Dawes, a high jumper who won a medal in the 1932 Olympics, decided to boycott the 1936 Olympics and travelled to attend the alternate games to be held in Barcelona. (Canada's Sports Hall of Fame; sportshall.ca)

Canada's 1936 Winter Olympic team, opening ceremonies. The athletes are extending their arms sideways in the Olympic salute, which was easily confused with the Hitler salute.
(Ullstein Bild/The Granger Collection, New York)

Sammy Luftspring, a Jewish boxer who reluctantly decided to boycott the Berlin Olympics, instead travelled to Europe to attend the Barcelona alternative. (Canada's Sports Hall of Fame; sportshall.ca)

───── The officers of the ─────
CENTRAL DIVISION ... CANADIAN JEWISH CONGRESS
cordially invite you to attend the presentation by this body of a
Canadian and a Jewish flag to be made to
Sammy Luftspring and "Baby" Yack
outstanding Jewish athletes, at
.:: A STAG ::.
in their honor on the occasion of their departure to Barcelona
to compete in the International Games organized in
opposition to the Nazi Olympics.
THURSDAY, JULY 9th, 1936, 7 p.m.
Community Centre   9-13 Brunswick Ave.
───── ADMISSION FREE ─────

Canadian Jewish Congress held a stag to help raise the funds for the two Jewish boxers going to Barcelona, just hours before their departure from Toronto. (Sammy Luftspring, with Brian Swarbrick, *Call Me Sammy*. Scarborough, ON: Prentice Hall of Canada, 1975, p. 89)

Canadian athletes who decided to go to Barcelona and not Berlin. They are carrying the Union Jack, a flag with the Star of David, and a third flag, difficult to identify, but presumably a Canadian flag. (*Toronto Daily Star*, 20 July 1936)

1936 OLYMPIC SILVER MEDALLISTS-BASKETBALL. 1st row: L to R (athletes only) Jimmy Stewart, Gord Aitchison, Don Gray. 2nd row: Tom Pendleburg, Doug Peden, Ian Allison, "Red" Wiseman, Ed Dawson. 3rd row: (coach) Gord Fuller, "Toots" Meretsky, Chuck Chapman, Norm Dawson, "Red" Nantais, Art Chapman

Canada's basketball team, which won a silver medal at the 1936 Olympics. Irving "Toots" Meretsky (top row, second from the left) was the only Canadian-Jewish athlete known to have gone to the 1936 Olympics. (University of Windsor Archives/Accession Number 96–030, Box No. 51/ Series II, Subseries A Gordon Fuller Scrapbook)

Boris Vladimirovich Volkoff dancers in Volkoff's work *Mon-ka-ta*, 1936. (James Pape Portfolio, 223.2012–1-3, Dance Collection Danse)

Berlin youth gathering organized in conjunction with the Summer Olympics.
(John Derry private collection)

Frank Amyot, only winner of a gold medal for Canada at the Berlin Games. (Canada's Sports Hall of Fame; sportshall.ca)

Phil Edwards, track star who won bronze medals in the 1928 Games in
Amsterdam, the Los Angeles Games of 1932, and in Berlin.
(Canada's Sports Hall of Fame; sportshall.ca)

W.L. Mackenzie King at the opening ceremonies of the All-German Sports
Competition, Olympic Stadium, 27 June 1937.
(Prsees-Bild-Zentrale/Library and Archives Canada)

One of those chosen was nineteen-year-old Lukin Robinson. Lukin was a longtime member of the Toronto Ski Club. His father, Christopher, was a successful patent lawyer in Toronto and, according to Lukin, "a good old fashioned liberal." He was also adamant that his sons should appreciate the culture of Europe. Accordingly, Lukin and his brother Peter, one year older, spent four of their elementary school years in Switzerland where they leaned to ski under the watchful eye of an expert instructor. In 1928, Lukin and his brother, not yet in their teens, returned to Toronto where they continued to ski with the Toronto Ski Club. But they would soon be uprooted again. Lukin's father, his law practice hit hard by the Depression, retired and moved his family to Geneva where the Robinson brothers went to school and skied. They even began to compete in amateur ski events – Peter in the ski jump and Lukin in downhill.

All the while Europe was changing. Hitler came to power in 1933 and, according to Lukin, the Führer's every move was fodder for discussion at the Robinson table. His father, a die-hard anti-Nazi and close friend of *Saturday Night* editor B.K. Sandwell, accepted an invitation to write for the magazine, offering a "Canadian's eye view" on European events.[75]

In 1935 the Robinson brothers, both experienced competitors on the European amateur ski circuit, were regarded obvious candidates for inclusion on the Canadian Olympic ski team. Not only were the Robinson brothers fine skiers who had competed against Europe's best, but they were already in Europe – no small advantage for Depression-racked Canadian skiing officials hard pressed to meet the ski team's travel costs. Explaining the inclusion of Lukin on the Canadian team, the 1935 *Canadian Ski Year Book* ranked Lukin "one of the coming younger ski men, and being so well acquainted with European conditions, may be expected to make a good showing." Much the same was said of Lukin's brother Peter, although forewarned that Peter had just begun a program of study in London, the *Year Book* allowed that Peter would "add great strength to the Canadian Team provided his work permits him to join with us." It didn't; Peter declined the invitation.[76]

Lukin, however, was personally excited by the invitation to ski in the Olympics and ski for Canada. Many European skiers he knew well would be competing for their countries. But Lukin's parents would not hear of their son competing in the Nazi Olympics. His parents had enjoyed a bicycle tour through Germany in 1932; but once Hitler took power, Lukin's parents swore they would not again step foot on German soil until Hitler and his Nazis were gone. They kept their word. Lukin's mother, no less anti-Nazi than his father, even burst into tears on hearing about the signing of the Munich Agreement, the only time Lukin ever remembers seeing his mother cry. Bowing to his parent's wishes, Lukin informed Canadian Olympic ski officials he would not be joining the team. If Lukin was disappointed at the time, he later came to regard not participating as a point of personal pride.[77]

Hockey: Pre-Olympic Controversies

Choosing a hockey team to send to the Winter Olympics should have been much easier than piecing together the ski team from across Canada and even Europe. Rather than an all-star team, it was envisioned to be the best of the amateur teams, defined as the winner of the Allan Cup, annually awarded to the best senior hockey team in Canada.[78] In April 1935 the Halifax Wolverines thrilled a hometown audience by winning the Allan Cup, defeating the Port Arthur Bearcats two games to none. As the Allan Cup winner, the Wolverines were tapped to represent Canada at the Winter Games. But there was a glitch. The Wolverines were part of Maritime Canada's Big Four League. The three other league teams had suffered major financial losses in 1934–5, and were reluctant to commit to another costly season. As a result, in the fall of 1935 the Wolverines, no longer part of a league and without that league affiliation, the Canadian Amateur Hockey Association (CAHA) decided that the Allan Cup runners-up, the Bearcats, should go to Garmisch-Partenkirchen. The CAHA did promise, however, that eligible Wolverines would be given special consideration should the Bearcats need strengthening. Haligonians knew that this was, at best, a consolation prize, but at least they would see some members of their team set sail in pursuit of Olympic glory. In the fall of 1935, the CAHA decided that five Bearcats, four Wolverines, and two other players from teams in North Battleford and Montreal would make up the Olympic team, although the Port Arthur Bearcats were still the official designated Olympic team, and the training and exhibition games would be in and around Port Arthur.

The four Wolverines travelled to Port Arthur, and by all accounts, their incorporation into the team was smooth and they felt appreciated by the Port Arthur fans. Local Olympic excitement was palpable. When Dr. Stitt of Port Arthur wrote to Caiserman about the League against War and Fascism and its protests, he passed on that any pro-boycott activity in his city was likely to generate a negative public reaction: "Port Arthur has been chosen to represent Canada in Olympic hockey and public opinion is quite elated on their choice; hence we do not intend concentrated action against their participation, unless things materialise at a later date."[79]

Others, however, were committed to immediate and public protests. Labour groups and the League against War and Fascism called for a boycott of two fundraising exhibition games – one to be held in Winnipeg on 16 December and a second in Montreal on 28 December – between the Bearcats and local teams.[80] Not satisfied with a simple boycott, the protesters set up pickets outside the arena in Winnipeg.[81] For the Montreal game, the plan was to have several women unfurl a large pro-boycott banner in the arena during the game, but they got cold feet and three of the male protesters were assigned to roll out the banner: "Fair Play Demands Removal of Olympics from Fascist Berlin."[82] The protesters also distributed some 5,000 copies of a leaflet printed by the Montreal League against War and Fascism declaring "Sportsmanship is Dead in Nazi Germany" and demanding "Boycott the Olympics." The Montreal protest was not altogether well received. Years later one of participants in the Montreal protest told his son that an angry mob turned on the protesters who barely escaped into the frigid Montreal night.[83]

But these protests proved of little interest to the press, especially once a more sensational story broke. In early January 1936 the CAHA disqualified the four Wolverine members from the Olympic team because, according to the president of the CAHA, E.A. Gilroy, the Maritimers had *asked* for broken-time payments or remuneration for time taken off from work to compete. The CAHA had strict rules against amateurs taking these kinds of payments, rules that teams in Western Canada and the Maritimes tended to oppose. And for struggling athletes, especially during the Depression, to be denied support in place of wages was an inordinate burden. The four protested that they had previously been promised this money by Gilroy, but their protests were in vain. The "Old Boys" would have none of it, as AAUC president William Fry made clear to the press: "In this situation of affirmation and denial on both sides, we have to believe somebody, and if it's a question of veracity I'll pick Gilroy. I have known him for twenty years and ... [it] is absolutely incredible that Gil' could double-cross anybody."[84] At their January meeting, the members of the COC executive heard from Fred Marples, who chaired the meeting in Mulqueen's absence. Marples insisted that the demand for "broken time" had come from the players and, despite the pressure from the press to reinstate the players, "the Canadian Olympic Committee could not and would not accede to such demands."[85]

Hockey fans and the press in Nova Scotia saw the funding incident as an affront to "Maritime Rights." The officials of the Maritime Amateur Hockey Association met with Gilroy, but to no avail. For no intelligible reason, the CAHA also did not allow the Wolverines to play as part of a Nova Scotia all-star team against the Canadian Olympic team, which sparked further howls of outrage.[86] When the local communists protested at an exhibition game in Halifax, they played to the local anger in their leaflets:

> Boycott the team that boycotts the Maritimes for a 100 percent Dominion team in Olympics outside of Fascist Germany. Don't go to the game. Your money will send a non-representative team to a non-representative country. Germany persecutes labour and religion the way Toronto persecutes the Maritimes...[87]

These last-minute desperate protests had no more success than the earlier protests, and the "non-representative" team sailed for Germany several days after the game.

The Winter Olympics

Despite the hockey controversy, Olympic excitement mounted. The mayor of Montreal, Camillien Houde, sponsored two receptions for the departing athletes. At a farewell luncheon for the ski team and fifty well-wishers, Houde made special mention of Montreal's pride that the manager and three of the skiers were from his city.[88] Eleven days later Houde offered a breakfast farewell to the hockey team and its supporters. The German consul also attended, and was pleased at the support, especially after the protests at the hockey game in the Montreal Forum on the previous night.[89]

As the Winter Olympiad drew near, the press also turned its attention to the Games and its Nazi hosts. The press coverage of Germany in the summer and fall of 1935 had been sharply negative, with reports first on the anti-Jewish riots and then the Nuremberg Laws. Even the sports reporters who opposed the boycott did not deny the Nazi hostility to Jews and other so-called enemies of the state. But with the Games looming and Bavaria all primped for the arrival of the "youth of the world" – and with all the antisemitic signage temporarily removed – reporters sent specifically to cover the Games were more often than not more dazzled by the natural splendour of Bavaria and the *Gemüt-lichkeit* of its inhabitants than they were repelled by the Nazi state. In mid-January, the *Montreal Gazette* proclaimed the "Olympic Games at Garmisch to be Contested in Picturesque Setting," and spoke of the "old world" charm of nearby Oberammergau.[90] In late January, Erwin Schwangart concluded the first of a series of articles for the *Toronto Globe* and other Canadian papers by stating that, although some people may have concerns about German policy, "credit must be given to the people for making sacrifice after sacrifice in the spirit of the Olympic Oath."[91]

Not all shared in this enthusiastic lead-up to the Winter Games. With his usual tenacity, not to mention disdain for the Nazis, Matthew Halton of the *Toronto Daily Star* used the occasion of the visit to London of Hans von Tschammer und Osten, the "Sports leader of the Reich," to puncture inflated Nazi platitudes about the games. The Nazi denied flatly that there would be racial discrimination in forming an Olympic team, and professed ignorance when Halton asked him about the notorious "Jews keep out" sign in Garmisch. Tschammer preferred to rhapsodize about the Olympic village, and repeat promises that the Olympics would lead to "international understanding." Halton concluded his article sarcastically, asking why "get hot and bothered about such a bagatelle as the proscription of a race?"[92]

As Halton suspected, few would get "hot and bothered" about Nazi racism, especially once the athletes started arriving in Germany. The *Winnipeg Free Press* and the *Montreal Gazette* reported on how the presence of hundreds of athletes, all wearing the colourful uniforms of their respective countries, had awakened the rather sleepy Garmisch-Partenkirchen.[93] If there was a concern, it was about the weather conditions. Days before the games were to begin the weather turned unseasonably warm and wet. The ski slopes were green and the bobsled course was unusable.[94] Just as there was talk of delaying the February 6 opening date, the organizers and the athletes rejoiced when a blizzard struck the day before the opening.[95]

The snow continued to fall with dramatic effect on opening day. As they lined up at ten in the morning to wait for the opening ceremonies, the thirty-eight Canadian athletes and officials watched their warm Hudson's Bay coats turn to white.[96] It was the beginning of a long but exhilarating day. At eleven, all the nations made their way to the stadium, and then the teams entered in by alphabetical order, with the exception of Greece, which entered first, and the host country, Germany, at the end. With its German spelling, Kanada was centrally positioned, arriving, most notably, after countries such as France (Frankreich) and Great Britain (Grossbritannien) but before the United States (Vereinigte Staaten). Lois Butler, one of Canada's skiers, recalled it as a "wonderfully organized ceremony." She was impressed by the precision of all the flag-bearers and teams marching past Hitler.[97] The manager of the ski team, A.H. Pangman, was also moved by the ceremonies, with their 400-piece marching bands. At the conclusion, with all the athletes turned towards Hitler, the German dictator declared the Games open, guns shot out in salute, and the bands played the Olympic hymn while the church bells of "Gapa" rang loudly.[98]

The opening ceremonies were, however, also marked by confusion and controversy. As the athletes passed Hitler and the various Nazi and Olympic officials, they turned and saluted. Many in the predominantly German crowd burst out in loud applause when they believed visiting athletes offered the straight-armed Nazi salute as they marched past Hitler. However, others thought the athletes were giving the Olympic salute – also straight-armed, but to the side – not the Nazi salute. Even Olympic officials were confused. Canadian athletes gave the Olympic salute, as shown in a photograph included in the COC's 1936 Olympic report, but many mistook it for the Nazi salute. Worse still, when Great Britain entered, the public address system blared, "The British greet the German Führer with the German salute." British Olympic officials were so shocked at the crowd's misinterpretation of the salute that they resolved not to give any salute at the Summer Games. This is a lesson the Canadians did not learn.[99]

"One Wild and Foolish Expedition"

The Winter Olympics started badly for Canadian athletes and grew worse. The skiers seemed to spend as much time in the hospital as on the slopes. Even before reaching Garmisch-Partenkirchen, two of the four Canadian competitors in the women's alpine races (a combined downhill and slalom event) were injured during practice, one with a cracked bone in her foot, the other with two broken bones in her hand. A third developed a serious case of bronchitis. Rather remarkably, all four women managed to complete the difficult downhill race, and three finished the slalom. One Canadian, Diana Gordon-Lennox (née

Kingsmill), may not have won a medal, but her gutsy performance with a broken hand, not to mention the monocle she wore while skiing and her fluency in German, made her a crowd favourite.[100]

The men's ski team also ran into injury troubles. At a preliminary international event in advance of the Olympics, two members injured themselves, one with a sprained wrist and knee. Several days later, another skier twisted his ankle, leg, and wrist. All these injuries happened before the end of January. Nonetheless, most of the men ended up competing, but their results were disappointing. The highest-ranking Canadian in the Alpine competition came in twenty-sixth, in cross-country forty-seventh, in Nordic combined (cross-country and ski-jumping) thirty-first, and in ski-jumping fourteenth.[101] The figure skaters fared somewhat better. Montgomery Wilson ranked fourth in the men's singles and the two Canadian pairs placed sixth and twelfth. The sole speed skater, Tommy White, of New Brunswick, competed in four events, with his best standing in the 10,000-metre race, where he stood twenty-first.

However much Canadians were hoping for medals from these competitors, they felt assured that their athletes would win a gold medal in hockey, as they had in every Winter Olympics since hockey had first been introduced to the Olympics. In 1936, however, even the hockey team disappointed. The pre-departure problems in selecting the team seemed to set the tone. Even on the trip across the Atlantic, players and officials interacted like oil and water. Team members, some of whom "had nothing in their pocket," were upset by what they regarded as lavishly self-indulgent overspending by officials.[102] Officials, who grudgingly doled out a "few dollars" to players, were said to enjoy shipboard cocktail parties, "which antagonized a good portion of the team who naturally believed that the Association's money was being spent in this way while they themselves had nothing."[103] Tensions between the officials and the players left a foul taste in the players' mouths but, with the Games in the offing, the team eventually settled down. To get themselves into shape after a week at sea, the hockey team held practices in London, played an exhibition game in Paris, and then trained for five days in St. Moritz.

While the players readied themselves for competition, Canadian hockey officials had their first (but by no means only) off-ice skirmish with the international hockey establishment. As historian John Wong explains, Canada may have had an excellent reputation for the quality of its playing, but Canadian officials exercised little influence within the governing body of international hockey, the Ligue Internationale de Hockey sur Glace (LIHG).[104] Canadians did not attend the LIHG meetings, which took place almost exclusively in conjunction with European tournaments in which Canadians did not take part, and few Canadians held positions in the organization. The Canadian lack of political muscle became obvious in the debate that erupted over the eligibility of Canadians playing on the team for Great Britain. According to Canadian Amateur Hockey Association regulations, all Canadians needed its sanction before they could play abroad. Great Britain had a number of Canadians on its team, some of whom had received the CAHA permission, but two of them – the goalie, Jimmy Foster, and right-winger Alex Archer – had not.[105] The CAHA suspended the two (as well as twenty other unsanctioned Canadians playing in Great Britain) and the Canadians expected the LIHG to honour the CAHA suspensions and not permit the two to play. In November 1935 the president of the LIHG, Paul Loicq, ruled that the suspended Canadians should not be allowed to participate in the Olympics, but under British pressure he quickly reversed his decision.

At the LIHG meeting immediately before the Winter Games began, the question of the status of Foster and Archer resurfaced and Canada was again outmanoeuvred. Canada wanted the LIHG to recognize the CAHA sanctions; Britain, of course, wanted to retain its Canadian players, especially its excellent goaltender, and argued that one national organization should not have control over another. Canadians won the vote and Foster and Archer were ruled ineligible. Great Britain, unwilling to take no for an answer, mounted a campaign against the decision. According to one chronicler of the Winter Games, the manager of the British team, Bunny Ahearne, spoke to the British ambassador in Berlin who in turn contacted Prime Minister Mackenzie King asking that in the name of imperial unity he intercede on behalf of the "Canadians" on the British team.[106] At the same time the British also threatened to withdraw from the Games if its Canadian "ringers" were disallowed. Under pressure the CAHA relented and temporarily lifted the suspension of the two players, but not without some harsh words about British hockey from Gilroy, who was not only president of the CAHA but also manager of Canada's winter team.[107]

With this matter resolved in favour of the British team, the Canadians focused their efforts on playing and winning. The tournament rules were both unconventional and complicated. To start, competing teams were divided into four groups with four national teams in each group.

Canada was in group A, together with Austria, Poland, and Latvia. Each team played one game with each of the other teams in its group, and the top two teams advanced to the next round. In this first round, Canada had no trouble beating Poland 8–1, then Latvia 11–0, and concluding with a 5–2 win over Austria.

In the second round, in which there were two groups of four, Canada was in group A with Great Britain, Germany, and Hungary. In the first game of this round – Canada against Great Britain – the unimaginable happened. The British team, coached by a Canadian, played a defensive style of hockey relying heavily on their goalie, Jimmy Foster, one of the players Canada had reluctantly allowed to play. The British struck quickly, scoring their first goal just twenty seconds into the game. Canada tied the game before the end of the first period. The game remained a tie until, with less than two minutes left in regulation time, the British scored a second goal. Foster, who faced sixty-five shots as opposed to the nine shots faced by the Canadian goalie, was heralded the British star player. The Canadians won the other two games in that round, embarrassing the Hungarians with a 15–0 win. In the last game, Canada faced Germany and not only did Canadians trounce their hosts 6–2, they played their usual rough style of hockey which the German fans thought was scandalous. The German fans were so disorderly that Goebbels, who attended the game, labelled the audience "undisciplined" in his diary. He and Goering both tried in vain to calm the crowd, and Goering even visited the Canadian locker room to offer apologies.[108]

But Canadian officials soon discovered that they had a bigger problem than unruly German fans. Four teams advanced to the final round: Canada, Czechoslovakia, Great Britain, and the United States. An unusual feature of the tournament rules stipulated that a team that beat an opponent in a previous round did not have to face that team again; in this case, it meant that Great Britain's previous victory over Canada carried over into the final round. Accordingly, in the final standings Great Britain was deemed to win two games (including the one not played against Canada), and with its one tie, it had five points to Canada's four. Great Britain was awarded the Olympic gold.

Canadian officials were livid, telling anybody who would listen that the rules were changed at the Games, and that Canada had expected to meet Great Britain in the finals. Mulqueen, that fierce proponent of the Games who, following the British lead, professed he could find no fault in the Olympics being held in Nazi Germany, called the British victory "one of the worst manipulations in sporting history." Even journalist

Matthew Halton chimed in on the issue: "I personally, though no sports fan and certainly no sports partisan agree with them that our hockey team got one of the rawest deals that ever marred the Olympics." Halton's story rated above-the-fold front page coverage in the *Star*, with the top headline quoting from the team manager: "'Got Raw Deal at Olympics,' Says Gilroy."[109]

The actual story, however, was somewhat different. When the Canadians discovered that they would not be able to play Great Britain in the final round, they called an emergency meeting of the LIHG. At the meeting, Gilroy claimed that he had misunderstood the rules, not that they had been changed. When the question of the format was put to a vote, only Canada and Germany wanted to have a full final round, without carry-over decisions from a previous round.[110] The overwrought posturing by the Canadian officials after the games was another criticism that the players – and others – raised against their managers. Canadian hockey player Ralph St. Germain wrote after the return of the team to Canada that from all he knew it was simply not true that the rules were changed "and that the games were played out as originally intended, although I must agree that the system did not appear exactly logical."[111]

Another observer had even harsher words for the Canadian officials. J. Percy Bond, a Canadian businessman with a great appreciation for amateur sports, together with his wife, accompanied Canada's Winter Olympic team to Germany. In a letter to McGill University's A.S. Lamb, Bond minced no words in describing the "adventures" of the hockey team: "I use the word 'adventures' advisedly, Dr. Lamb, for it really has seemed like one wild and foolish expedition guided (?) by most incompetent officials." Bond, who also attended the LIHG meetings, was so put off by the incompetence of Canadian officials that he advocated a total overhaul of the method for choosing Canadian managers.[112]

According to Bond and the players, the incompetence extended into post-Games social events. St. Germain, who scored six goals in the 1936 Games, claimed that the Germans invited the Canadian team to a dinner for all medal winners, but Canadian team managers forgot to inform the team. It appeared as if the Canadians were being childlike in refusing to attend out of anger at both the LIHG decision and the team's silver rather than gold standing.[113] Bond, for his part, decided to travel with the team to post-Olympic exhibition games in a number of German cities, as well as Paris, Amsterdam, and Vienna. He cringed at the behaviour of the team's coach and claimed it was only the sportsmanlike behaviour of the athletes that preserved Canada's good name.

Bond's criticisms also reflected the snobbishness he felt comfortable sharing with the "Old Boys" at the COC:

> If you could have seen how this official of Canada's Hockey Team sitting behind a plate *piled high* with something of almost everything on the table, his table-napkin hanging from a high point, shoveling "it in like a King Henry VIII" and telling (in a voice that could be heard almost throughout the hall) the local officials government, municipal and otherwise, of how *he* had been sent by Canada *to see what it was all about* etc. and how when *he returned with the Summer Olympic Team what he would do* ... you have some slight idea of what I am trying to convey.[114]

Others in Canada picked up on the criticism of the team. D.A. Macdonald of the *Montreal Gazette* said that a more tactful management needs to be in place for the Summer Games "or failing that have clothes pins firmly attached to official lips before the boat ever sails."[115]

In the end, no issue related to either the 1936 Winter or Summer Olympics aroused more negative emotions among Canadians than the failure of the Canadian hockey team to win its gold. Sports writers feasted on the story well past the end of the Winter Games. The insults hurled against the British meant that the story even made it to the House of Commons. Conservative MP Thomas Church took offence at Gilroy's attack on British hockey as a racket.[116] But while hockey had the power to arouse public ire, Nazi racism did not, and Parliament took no official notice of the racism of the Nazi regime that had invited "the youth of the world."

In the fallout from the hockey fiasco, the CAHA severed ties with the AAUC in anger at the latter's strict definition of amateur rules. The British victory also surprised non-Canadians. In a souvenir photo album published by a German cigarette manufacturer, the hockey section was simply titled "Ice Hockey Tournament: Canada Overthrown." A picture of the Canadian team bore the caption, "The Canadian hockey team, hitherto undisputed world champions, placed only second, contrary to all expectations."[117]

However dramatic, Canada's loss to Great Britain was not the only hockey story covered by journalists. The world press was also drawn to the gripping story of the "half-Jewish" hockey player on the German team, Rudi Ball. One of Germany's best hockey players, he was born to a Jewish father and a Christian mother who, according to one source, had converted to Judaism.[118] Fascinated with hockey from a young age, Ball became a star player on the first team of Berlin SC, and then played a major role on winning teams in St. Moritz and Milan.[119] There are several reasons why the Nazis may have included Ball on the team despite his Jewish designation: he was talented, his friend and line-mate Gustav Jaenecke threatened to leave the German team if Ball was not allowed to play, and the Nazis needed to offer the international sporting community proof that it was not discriminating against Jews. According to some reports, Ball agreed to participate in order to protect his family from threats of Nazi retribution if he refused to play.

Ball's success in the tournament – at least until he was injured or possibly removed by order of the Nazi echelon – became a talking point among foreign journalists.[120] Here was the child of a Jewish father who, arguably, turned out to be Germany's best hockey player. In anticipation of the more famous representation of Jesse Owens as living proof of the hollowness of Nazi racism, some of the press and Olympics apologists celebrated Ball's skill as proof of the value of the Olympics and of the goodwill of the Germans.

But Halton, in an incisive interview with Ball, tried to probe deeper. He met with Ball towards the end of the Olympics as part of a group that included the coach of the German team, Montrealer Bob Bell, and several other players on the German team. Eventually the others drifted off and Halton found himself alone with Ball. Some of the conversation Halton could not repeat, which was certainly a code that Ball feared to say the worst of what was happening. Halton did ask Ball how he "could bear" to play for a nation that persecuted him. Ball chose his words carefully. He did not accept the clichéd notion that the Olympics and other sports can help foster friendly relations, but Ball did think that refusing to play would not do German Jews any good, "and it might have done them harm." Ball was even willing to venture that it would be good for Germans to see a Jew on the team. Halton, however, reminded his readership that Ball's Jewish roots were a taboo topic in the German press. When Halton asked Ball whether he regarded himself as a Jew or a German, Ball's cautious response, even after the Nuremberg Laws stripped Jews of their German citizenship, was the stock answer of the integrated German Jew: he was a German by nationality, and a Jew by faith. Halton did not press Ball any further on this point. Halton did make the telling observation, however, that throughout their conversation Ball never referred to Germans as "we," but always as "they."[121]

Reactions

Matthew Halton's sad depiction of Rudi Ball's dilemma was not the journalist's only attempt to cut through the artificial aura of tranquility and fellowship that the Nazis created for the Games. The day after his interview with Ball was published, the *Toronto Daily Star* published an article by Halton in which he described the overarching fear that prevents Germans from speaking the truth, a fear enforced by the constant presence of the S.A. and S.S. and their informers. He was outright sarcastic when he commented on the cosmetic changes made for the Olympics, how the Nazis so embraced the "Olympic ideal" that they temporarily took down the anti-Jewish signs, and "even clamped down a little on Chief Jew-Baiter, Julius Streicher."[122]

But Halton knew he was fighting a rear-guard battle, that no matter how revealing his articles, most visitors to Germany, including Canadians, were being taken in by the layers of Nazi Olympic deceit. Shortly after learning of a German clergyman who was imprisoned for six months for offering a prayer on behalf of the Jews, Halton recoiled from an encounter with one of Canada's figure skaters. The young man told Halton that he appreciated the journalist's articles, but now that he had witnessed "the good manners" of the Germans, he no longer believed anything Halton wrote. Halton asked whether the athlete expected to see blood on the streets. "No," he answered, "but no people as courteous as these could persecute Jews or militarize a whole country."[123]

The Canadian figure skater was certainly not alone. A chilling photograph of members of Canada's team clamouring for Hitler's autograph is the first picture in a popular souvenir volume of the Winter Olympics.[124] But to conclude that Hitler mesmerized members of the Canadian team might be going too far. What then was the prevailing Canadian response to Nazi Germany? The overall impression was positive. With the exception of Halton, there is little evidence of negative responses to the stay in Nazi Germany. The Canadian hockey players, who had so many complaints about their coaches, did not want anyone to think their dissatisfaction extended to their German hosts:

> We were royally treated everywhere ... and were able to have a wonderful time which will be remembered by all for a lifetime. Also I must say that I believe the Olympic games to be a real aid to international understanding and friendship of which all nations should take advantage.[125]

Several months later, another exuberant account appeared in the magazine printed up for the spectators attending trials for the Summer Olympics. The article reported that the contestants "returned with glowing accounts of their reception in Germany." The only question in their minds was what was most praiseworthy, the natural and built environment, "or the genuine and hearty hospitality with which the inhabitants received their guests."[126]

At least one journalist for Canadian newspapers proved as enthusiastic as the athletes. Erwin Schwangart, who had written positively about Germany just before the Games started, now summarized the Winter Olympic Games by reassuring Canadians heartbroken over the loss of hockey gold that the Germans were the friends of the Canadians. After all, did they not "champion" Canada's cause at the emergency meeting that had discussed the tournament format? Didn't Goering, "the genial Air Force leader of the Germans," visit the Canadian locker room to profess his belief that the Canadians were the "real world champions?"[127]

With articles such as this, it is no wonder that the Nazis were delighted at the responses to the Winter Games. Goebbels recorded the following in his diary on the last day of the games: "All praise our organization ... At the close, a wonderful sight. Surrounded by the eternal mountains. And then the flame was extinguished."[128] In Canada, Werner Haag revelled in the enthusiasm, and looked to mobilize it for the Olympic main event, the Summer Games. Even while the Winter Games were on, he wrote a piece for the *Toronto Mail and Empire* pointing out that "Canadians are much in the limelight at the Winter Olympic Sports in Germany." He insisted, however, that the true excitement would be in the summer. There would be more athletic competitions and exhilarating additional events, such as the special camps for international youth.[129] In short, he was saying that it was time for Canadians to prepare for Berlin.

Chapter Five

Preparations and Protests: March–July 1936

On his return to the United States, Avery Brundage, head of the American Olympic Committee, wasted no time in declaring the Winter Olympics a resounding success. The leading American opponent of an Olympic boycott praised the German government, which "couldn't have played its part more fairly ... [and] lived up to all agreements and every Olympic Regulation." The suggestion that Germans had treated Jews unfairly, he continued, was unfounded. Rudi Ball played and he "received more applause than any other German player."[1]

Although commenting on the Games just over, Brundage was sending a message about Berlin. There had been no discrimination at the Winter Olympics, and there would be none at the Summer Olympics. It did not take very long, however, for the Nazi juggernaut to risk undermining the goodwill created in Bavaria. On 7 March 1936, Hitler ordered his troops to occupy the demilitarized zone of the Rhineland, a defiant violation of the Versailles agreement, but consistent with what historian Wolfgang Benz describes as the regime's "program of ... expansion and hegemony." The military reaction was, as Hitler predicted, minimal. The French did not have the resources to challenge the move, and the British were not concerned enough to intervene.[2]

The invasion led to flutters of public demonstrations. In France, some anti-fascists wanted their government to rebuke the Nazis for their aggression and renewed the call for a boycott of the Berlin Olympics. They protested that the top Nazis who attended the Winter Games – led, of course, by Hitler – were masquerading as peace lovers while coldly plotting their next aggressive military move. One member of the Académie française, Claude Farrère, writing in the journal *L'Intransigeant* less than a week after the occupation of the Rhineland, claimed links between the Nazi Olympics and Nazi military adventurism. A month later he elaborated on his views in a letter to Pierre de Coubertin, founder of the modern Olympic Games. Farrère claimed that in the German victory-is-all-that-matters mindset, weakness in athletics is a sign of weakness in general. The opposite is also true. Thus, if the Germans proved successful at the Olympics, they would be encouraged to believe that they could successfully defeat their enemies on the battlefield. But Farrère's warnings went unheard not just by the founder of the modern Olympics, but also by Léon Blum's "popular front" government that took the reins of office in Paris several months later.[3]

The Canadian press was generally of the view that Hitler's militarization and aggressive move in the Rhineland were disconnected from the Olympics. Less than a week after the invasion of the Rhineland, newspapers gave positive coverage to a statement by the president of the International Olympic Committee (IOC), Count Henri de Baillet-Latour, that the invasion had no bearing on holding the Games in Berlin, and that only a war could lead to a change of venue. P.J. Mulqueen, the president of the Canadian Olympic Committee, insisted that the Olympics would either be in Berlin or they would have to be cancelled entirely.[4]

Opponents of the Nazi regime in Canada should not have been surprised by the weak international response to the events in the Rhineland. They had already seen how the ongoing arrests and persecution of the members of Germany's political left seemed only to matter to socialists and communists, and of course the Nuremberg Laws had no impact on the decision to go to the Olympics. Olympic officials continued to insist that there was a total disconnect between German policies and the athletic field. Those who attempted to forge a connection where there was none were doing a disservice not just to international sport, but also to hopes for fellowship through sport.

Preparing Berlin

Hitler accurately predicted the flabby international response to the occupation of the Rhineland and, as a result, did not worry that public reaction to the invasion would jeopardize support for the Berlin Olympics. Olympic planners, however, were concerned about getting Berlin ready to welcome athletes and visitors from around the world. The monumental Sports Stadium, which Hitler insisted in 1933 be built in a "classically" German style, had to be hurried along in order to finish on time. Already in 1935 the Nazis knew that they could not meet their target dedication date of 1 May 1936; in fact, the stadium would only be dedicated two weeks before the opening of the Berlin Games. And in order to meet that date, builders were forced to conceal construction materials they knew were not to Hitler's liking.[5]

The Nazis were more successful at keeping to their timetable in constructing the impressive Olympic village, soon-to-be home to most of the male athletes at the Olympics. (Rowers and sailors would stay closer to their event venues, and women were housed in a modest Berlin hotel.) Carl Diem of the German Olympic Organizing Committee had checked out the athletes' village built by the Americans in Los Angeles in 1932, and determined that German architects and planners could outdo the Americans. The Berlin Olympic village, located about fifteen kilometres from the heart of city, was meant to both demonstrate German organizational prowess and ooze the warmth of German hospitality. But even as the village was readied for athletes, steps were taken to ensure the village was easily convertible to its post-Olympic purpose, a barracks for the Wehrmacht. Thinking ahead, German planners even designed the massive eating hall so that it could be quickly transformed into a military hospital.[6]

In laying out their Olympic vision, the Nazis underscored the national commitment to militarism and its role in shaping the new Germany. For example, as Farrère argued in *L'Intransigeant* just after the Winter Games, the Nazis publicly and repeatedly associated dedication to sport with perseverance and sacrifice on the battlefield. The most dramatic example was of this was the Langemarckhalle, an imposing memorial hall constructed below the clock tower (Glockenturm) that reached seventy-seven metres above the Olympic Stadium. The Langemarckhalle was dedicated to the honour of the German soldiers who fell in a late 1914 battle in and around Langemarck in Flanders. Although the actual battle ended in German defeat, within a year, German nationalists turned the battlefield defeat into a mythical victory in which the German fighters were students who had put aside their books in defence of the fatherland. The Nazis co-opted the myth before they came to power in 1933 and the Nazi Party and its Hitler Youth took control of all Langemarck-related events.[7] To forge a tangible connection between the fighting youth at Langemarck and the young German athletes who would defend German honour at the Olympics, Carl Diem directed that a Langemarck memorial be integrated into the Olympic site and offered Langemarck soil, soaked with German blood, to be enshrined in the memorial.[8]

As sociologist Daphne Bolz has pointed out, the Nazis were not the first to commemorate their war dead at the Olympics. At the Los Angeles Games in 1932 there was a "Los Angeles War Memorial Coliseum." In Los Angeles, however, the commemoration was for all the war dead; in Berlin, it was specifically for the Germans who died. The walls of the German memorial were engraved with quotes from nationalist poets glorifying military sacrifice with the overall intent of the monument to fuse the German military ethos with competitive imperative of sport. On the battlefield, as on the playing field, German youth fought to win.[9]

The Nazis' zeal for military might was also incorporated into the Olympic village. The Hindenburghaus was the village's social centre and the largest building except for the dining hall. There were special rooms equipped with televisions where athletes could thrill at the marvel of German technological know-how and view live telecasts of Olympic events. But the largest space was given over to a special hall that seated as many as a thousand for nightly entertainment programs. All those entering the hall had to pass through the Hindenburg Hall of Honour with its large and stark bas-relief of soldiers marching in unison with rifles slung over their shoulders. Even if visitors could not read the German inscription which called on the armed forces to walk with pride and power "as guarantors of a strong German future," the images of the marching soldiers left no doubt as to how the Nazis lionized the military's role in their new order.[10]

For those who cared to look, there was also ample evidence to disprove the Nazi claim that their capital city was open and tolerant. True, Julius Streicher's scurrilous *Der Stürmer* had been banished from tourist areas in the weeks before the Games, but a number of antisemitic signs near the sports venues escaped the clean-up.[11] Not so the Roma and Sinti. The Weimar constitution had granted equal rights to "Gypsies"; but even during the Weimar era, laws against vagabonds in Bavaria and then nationally, undermined the status of the Roma and Sinti. Once the Nazis came to power and their notions of a racial hierarchy became law, the Roma and Sinti, like the Jews, were targeted as both "alien races" and as "asocials." In early 1936 the First Implementation Order to the Blood Protection Law invoked in November 1935 was extended beyond Jews to include "gypsies, negroes and their bastards."[12] This extension offered legal cover to several already existing anti-Roma and anti-Sinti actions, including a 1935 order by local authorities in a number of cities and towns to begin round-up and internment of Gypsies in special camps.[13]

Local authorities definitely did not want the Roma and Sinti in Berlin during the Olympics. On 10 July 1936, police headquarters in Berlin sent out a directive to 520 stations, as well as to the Organizing Committee for the Olympics, ordering them to move Roma and Sinti from Berlin and transport them to their "resting place" in Marzahn, outside of the city. The police were cautioned to avoid the main streets when transferring the Roma and Sinti out of the city, and to keep a watchful eye over the Roma and Sinti once in Marzahn. In classic Nazi doublespeak, the "gypsies are free to leave the Marzahn camp [but only] in an easterly direction, and avoiding Berlin city limits." Six days after the order, the Nazis arrested 600 Roma and Sinti and sent them to Marzahn. They were not allowed to bring any of their possessions.[14] Authorities were cautioned that any visitor to Berlin who bothered to ask about the Roma and Sinti was to be told they were in protective custody. But Marzahn was not protective custody, nor was it dismantled after the Games ended. Marzahn, and a rash of similar camps elsewhere in Germany, continued to expand as systematic persecution of the Roma and Sinti intensified and, more and more, the Roma and Sinti were consigned to forced labour, or worse.[15]

German Invitations, Canadian Responses

The German consuls in Canada and Werner Haag, the Canadian agent of the German Railroad in charge of Olympic tourism, were tasked with whitewashing Nazi behaviour, encouraging as many Canadians as possible to attend the Olympics and, thereby, gain an appreciation for the new Germany. In addition to providing general information about the Games, they heavily promoted the many cultural events that Berlin was to host in conjunction with the Games.

Berlin was especially keen on attracting young men and those who worked with youth. In 1935, the "Organizing Committee for the XI Olympiad" sent out circular letters to all the national bodies, including Canada, inviting each to send thirty boys to a youth camp and thirty male sports students to participate in a sport congress. In January 1936 Haag promoted the idea to A.S. Lamb, a member of the COC and director of McGill's Department of Physical Education since 1920. Arguably the most prominent Canadian physical education expert, he was also the most qualified person to lead Canadian youth and educators to the two camps. Haag encouraged him, however, to be in touch with Carl Gerhard then in Montreal, "who is representing the press of the German youth movement."[16]

In Gerhard, Lamb would be dealing with a "true believer" in Nazi racial ideology. Born in Germany in 1907, he joined a right-wing party (later absorbed by the Nazis) at the age of eighteen. In search of employment, he left Germany for Canada in 1930, but directed his energy into ethnic politics more than work. He was a central figure in creating the pro-Nazi Deutscher Bund Canada and travelled widely in Canada promoting the organization among ethnic Germans. He also became head of the Nazi Party in Canada. Gerhard travelled to Germany in 1934 and again in 1935 to attend the programs of the Auslandsorganisation der NSDAP (AO), an organization that, in the words of historian Jonathan Wagner, "was specifically established by National Socialists to carry on National Socialist business."[17] When he returned after his 1935 trip, Gerhard self-importantly declared himself the führer of all Germans in Canada, which brought him into direct conflict with the German consuls. Gerhard's attempted power-grab was undercut by the AO in Germany as well as Canadian agencies.[18] But as the press secretary for German youth he continued to reach out to Canadian youth, albeit indirectly.

In late February, the German consul in Montreal, Kempff, followed up on the invitations from Germany. He reported back to Berlin that he believed that both Mackenzie King and the undersecretary for external affairs, O.D. Skelton, were very interested in sending young Canadians to Berlin.[19] He met with Skelton in Ottawa and provided him with a memorandum on the proposed youth camp and camp for physical fitness professionals. He informed Skelton that fifteen countries were sending delegates to both camps, and that four more were just going to send the youth, not the educators. The plan, as Kempff informed Skelton, was to acquaint teachers "with the latest German methods of physical education" and to exchange views. He also laid out how the groups would be accommodated "in a somewhat military fashion," and would be encouraged to interact with other participants. The Canadians would also be invited to join other national groups in singing their folks songs at an "Olympic Youth" event on the opening day of the Olympics.[20]

At the meeting with Skelton, Kempff also raised the issue of an invitation to Canada to participate in another one of the cultural events, the art competition that encompassed architecture, painting, sculpture, poetry, and music. Germany invited art submissions from all the nations participating in the Olympics and, by the end of February, fourteen countries had accepted, including Great Britain and the United States.

Canada, however, had not yet responded. Kempff reminded Skelton that Canada had participated in a similar competition in Los Angeles and had received a prize in one category. So why not come to Berlin as well? Kempff well understood that Mulqueen and the treasurer of the COC, Fred Marples, had yet to return from the Winter Olympics, and that a decision on Canadian participation in Olympic-related cultural events could only be made after their return. So what did Kempff want from Skelton? He was convinced that the COC decision would be "facilitated if they knew that the Canadian government would, in principle, participate."[21] As Kempff reported back to Berlin, Skelton indicated positive interest in this proposal.[22]

Despite Kempff's belief that Skelton was sympathetic, the civil servant did not go out of his way to encourage the COC to accept the invitations. In fact, Ottawa had already rebuffed another of the German government's attempts to broaden Canadian participation in the Games, when the German minister of war invited Canada to send an equestrian team to Germany.[23] When it came to the proposals on the youth and educators' camps and the art competition, Skelton forwarded Kempff's memoranda to the COC, suggesting that they might be of use to the COC once Mulqueen returned, but that as far as the government was concerned, "there has been no opportunity yet to give full consideration to this question."[24]

Over the next few weeks, a pattern emerged. The COC eagerly embraced every opportunity to participate in Olympic-related events, but Ottawa remained at best guardedly non-committal. By the middle of March, Mulqueen, back from Germany, wrote to the organizing committee in Berlin that the invitations would be accepted.[25] Skelton, however, was still cool to any Canadian government participation in Olympic-related events and was put off when he found out about COC's readiness to participate, not from Mulqueen, but Haag, a German official who wrote to Skelton on German State Railway letterhead. Skelton wrote to the COC asking why Haag, "whose alleged official status has never been notified to this department," would claim to be writing on behalf of Mulqueen to advise the government on COC plans.[26] Skelton was told the relationship between the COC and Haag was very much hand-in-glove. The COC's secretary noted that Haag "has been very helpful and Mr. Mulqueen uses the facilities at his office a good deal for correspondence."[27] If Skelton was concerned that the COC was too much in Haag's German pocket, the undersecretary for external affairs was not about to see the Canadian government get in there too. He cold-shouldered the youth and educators' camps leaving it to the COC to decide if it wanted to participate and, if so, to organize it on its own.

Skelton proved no more sympathetic to the art competition. Once back from the Winter Olympics, Mulqueen wasted no time in contacting the famed Canadian-born sculptor of athletes, R. Tait McKenzie, who had already exhibited at the Amsterdam and Los Angeles Olympic Games. McKenzie agreed to send several works to Berlin.[28] Mulqueen also turned to the director of the National Gallery of Canada, Eric Brown, asking for help in finding other appropriate Canadian works of art.[29] Brown turned to Skelton for advice. Brown, knowing that any art Canada sent would have to be related to sports, noted that the National Gallery had little that fit that description (except the work of McKenzie). He added that the National Gallery was already committed to sending an exhibition of Canadian art to Great Britain and South Africa and its resources were already stretched thin. As far as Brown was concerned, he just hoped that "this Olympic Games exhibition will not materialize."[30] A week later, Brown wrote again to Skelton, reiterating that any art sent to Germany would have to be sports related and, since Canadian artists had not done much work in the area, whatever is available would hardly cast the best light on Canadian art. Brown, intending to sink any scheme to send art from the National Gallery to Germany, also advised Skelton that the trustees of the National Gallery agreed that, "under these circumstances the occasion is not of sufficient importance to warrant the National Gallery to arrange an exhibition."[31]

Brown hoped that the government would endorse the trustees' decision. Before receiving Brown's second letter, Skelton framed a diplomatic response in which he agreed with Brown that it was difficult to see how the National Gallery could participate, and wrote that "it does not appear that Government themselves are committed to any cooperation or assistance." Skelton added that because the COC had accepted, "further consideration might be given to the question of cooperation." But before Skelton's draft was sent, he received Brown's second note. Putting aside his first draft letter, Skelton responded that the decision of the trustees "meets with the views of the Government."[32] The COC would have to manage on its own without the support of the government.

On at least one more occasion the Canadian government entertained and turned down an Olympics-related invitation from the Germans. The Reich minister of defence, acting on the advice of the German

Olympic Committee, invited all Olympic countries participating in the sailing events to send a warship on an "unofficial visit" to the Baltic port of Kiel, the Olympic sailing venue.[33] O.D. Skelton replied that the Canadian Department of National Defence was not going to be able to send a ship, "owing to other commitments."[34]

Preparations in Canada

Although the COC was keen for Canada to participate in Olympic cultural events, its key focus was on preparing Canadian athletes for Berlin and securing resources enough to send a full team. In early 1936 the COC began planning for the Olympic track and field trials. On 11 February the COC announced that it had accepted Montreal's bid to host the trials and that these would be administered by the Province of Quebec Track and Field Association and sponsored by the Lions Club of Montreal. Winning the bid was something of a feat. Hamilton had also put its hat in the ring and was regarded a strong contender because of a history of support for track and field events, including the first British Empire Games in 1930.[35] To prepare for its bid, the Quebec Association had requested use of McGill University's Molson Stadium for the trials. The Athletic Board of McGill agreed, although it capped its own costs at $100, and hoped for a share of the gate receipts.[36]

In supporting the Olympic trials, McGill hoped to avoid debate over the Olympics. At its February meeting, McGill's Athletic Board acknowledged receipt of a letter from the Montreal Council of the Canadian League against War and Fascism. The letter made the case that the Nazis were in complete and brutal control of sports in Germany, and holding the Olympics in Berlin amounted to nothing less than a "world endorsement of a sports polity that has shocked the thinking people of the world."[37] The letter writer requested support for the boycott or, at the very least, a meeting with a representative from McGill to plan a "Montreal Conference against the Nazi Olympics." The letter emphasized that McGill did not have to sanction the conference, just participate in the discussion.[38] Still this was too much for COC executive member A.S. Lamb and other members of the McGill Athletic Board. Led by Lamb, "it was decided to send no representative and take no action."[39]

At its March meeting, the COC executive also confirmed that Montreal would host the trials for the women's track and field events as well as the swimming events. There was some discussion that an

Olympic trial marathon might be held in Hamilton and the basketball trials in either Toronto or Windsor. Executive members made no decision about the fencing or boxing and wrestling trials, although Montreal had requested to host boxing and wrestling. The COC executive also had to decide what to do about sending a baseball team, as baseball was listed as a demonstration sport in 1936. The discussion was not about whether it wanted to send a team – that it did – but rather how to cover the costs of doing so. It was decided to continue the policy of requiring a demonstration sport team to meet its own expenses and, as it would turn out, in the financial crunch of 1936, many Canadian athletes in accredited Olympic medal events would end up having to do just that.[40]

Questions of money remained uppermost in the minds of the COC executive. As had been the case with the Winter Olympics, the financial situation looked bleak and many more athletes were heading to Berlin than had competed in Garmisch-Partenkirchen. Mulqueen estimated that, on average, the cost of sending an athlete to Berlin was $300, including transportation, costs at the athletes' village, the uniform, and other incidentals. Pressure on the athletes and their organizations to come up with their own funding was enormous. The COC ruled that all athletes would have to pay their own way to and from the trials in Montreal. The executive was also faced with how to pay for the managers for the team, and, as a result, was inclined to favour those managers who could pay their own way overseas.

As the Depression continued to bite, innovative funding ideas were few. What worked before was tried again. Mulqueen met with the premier of Ontario in the hope of securing provincial support. He felt he received a "favorable response," but without the promise of a specific amount. The COC executive decided to produce special Olympic buttons for sale with the earnings going into a general fund, and the COC still counted on a second $5,000 promised from Ottawa.[41] But the problem of money persisted. At the beginning of July, the situation looked very bleak. There was little or no money in COC coffers, and many of qualified athletes were told to expect no support from the COC. Some wondered whether the COC was distributing what funds it had fairly, and the concern even reached the deputy minister of finance, who made inquiries as to how federal funds were being disbursed. [42]

The COC hoped that gate receipts from the Montreal Olympic trials would help alleviate the financial situation. They were certainly an occasion to raise the profile of the Olympics, as the newspapers covered the trials closely. The COC also published the *Canadian Olympic Trials Review* (the *Review*), a large-format magazine of over fifty pages, which sought to generate excitement for the Berlin Games, generally, and for the Canadian team, specifically. Serving as a kind of event program, the magazine had a number of articles about athletes from across the country who were training hard to represent Canada. The Olympic establishment got to say their piece, with the first article by Count Baillet-Latour and the second by A.S. Lamb of McGill, who was also a member of the COC. The magazine included stories extolling the Winter Games and waxed rhapsodic about Olympic preparations for Berlin, especially the athletes' village and the "Reich's Sports Field."

Olympic officials were especially keen to justify the decision to hold the Olympics in Germany. Baillet-Latour made his views on the boycott campaign clear: "The political agitation which has taken place in regard to this year's festivities is to be regretted." Why? Because the IOC was careful in making its decision and was convinced that the Games would be held in "a befitting matter." The IOC, he continues, could move from Berlin "even today" if they felt it was necessary, but the IOC had "no intention of being influenced by agitation originating from a political source." Why should they? The Winter Olympic Games were an unmitigated success in terms of numbers of participants, level of the competition, and the "whole-hearted support from the citizens of the host nation." Moreover, contrary to the message put out by the pro-boycott forces, the Summer Games promised to be an exercise in international fellowship because the Olympic Games are not just an athletic festival, but "more important, they are the means of creating through sport, a union of nations."[43]

In his article in the *Review*, Lamb underscored his argument in favour of Canadian Olympic participation by citing the positive impact of previous Canadian Olympic experiences. He called the revival of the Games in 1896 a renewal of a "spirit of almost religious devotion to an ideal that these great sports gatherings would cause the generation of a more friendly feeling between individuals and nations." The ancient games were, in his view, central to the "development of Grecian culture and international amity," and the modern Games have done the same. He repeated the myth of Phidippides and the first marathon, which Lamb called "the prelude to human freedom against the despotism of the East." In a thinly veiled swipe at boycott proponents, Lamb pointed out that "it is not difficult to find trouble if one is looking for it," but that the emphasis should be on the noble ideas of the founders of the modern Olympic movement.[44]

It is impossible to know whether the readers of the Olympic trials program were convinced, or even interested, in the lofty language and high-minded justifications of Baillet-Latour and Lamb. But popular support for the Olympics intensified in a direct relationship to the excitement generated by the trials. Five hundred athletes paid their way to Montreal, and local sports fans turned out to see the Olympic track and field, boxing and wrestling, and swimming hopefuls.[45] Newspapers across the country covered the trials, carefully reporting on how hometown athletes were faring in Montreal. Montreal sports columnist D.A.L. MacDonald underscored the significance and excitement of the trials by reminding his readers that the events in Montreal were happening at the same time as similar events overseas and south of the border.[46] Canadians would hear of athletes who were (or coming close to) breaking records, and who seemed bound for Olympic glory; or, in the words of one headline on the sport pages, "Canada's Olympic Hopes Mount Daily."[47]

Some of the athletes were well known. Phil Edwards had previously won medals in the 1928 and 1932 Olympics in the 400-metre race, and B.C. swimmer Phyllis Dewar was winner of four races in the Empire Games in 1934. Others came to the fore in Montreal, including track athletes Howie McPhee of British Columbia, Johnny Loaring of Ontario, and Aileen Meagher of Nova Scotia. Once the trials were over, they were among those chosen to set sail from Montreal on 17 July 1936.

Protests: Pro-Boycott Propaganda, and Fighting Financial Support

There were, of course, other Canadians who had fought to keep Hitler's Germany in the public eye, and to keep Canadian athletes from going to Hitler's Germany. Just as the COC was turning its attention towards Berlin after the Winter Olympiad in Garmisch-Partenkirchen, the various supporters of a boycott of the Summer Olympiad had their work before them. In Hamilton, the Trades and Labor Council convened a meeting in mid-March to deal specifically with the issue of the Olympics. They invited Erich von Schroetter, a German-born professor of languages at Northwestern University in Chicago, who was also editor of an anti-Nazi newspaper and active in German-language groups opposing Nazi propaganda in America. He told them of anti-Jewish prejudice in German sport, and described the Nazi militarization of

Germany. He insisted that a boycott of the Olympics would hurt the Nazis and, in so doing, help Germans. The other speaker, a prominent United Church minister, Rev. Crossley Hunter, called on the "whole world of sport" to reprimand Hitler and to tell him, "Until you learn to play the game and show a spirit of sportsmanship, we cannot engage in sporting contests in your country." A CCF member of the Ontario legislature for Hamilton East, Samuel Lawrence, rebuked the president of the Toronto Trades and Labour Council who reportedly said the question of the Olympics was not the concern of the Canadian worker. Lawrence could not believe that the statement was "a reflection of the views of Toronto labor."[48] The result of the Hamilton meeting was a resolution against participating in the Olympics, which was forwarded to the Canadian Olympic Committee and to Prime Minister Mackenzie King. The resolution noted that certain British universities were refusing to attend events in Germany, that various countries were expressing concern about sending athletes, and that Hitler had suppressed the trade union movement.[49]

A broad-based pro-boycott event took place in Montreal a week after the meeting in Hamilton. The Canadian League against War and Fascism organized a symposium on the question "Should Canada Support the Nazi Olympic Games?" The speakers included the president of a mainstream sports organization, the Quebec Football Association. Harry Golden, executive director of the YMHA, was the second speaker. He was to be followed by a woman member of both the Women's Catholic League and the Provincial Council of the CCF, then a member of one of the CCF's youth movement. A key speaker was Stanley Ryerson, born into a well-connected Toronto family and an avowed communist. He moved to Montreal in 1934 after earning a postgraduate degree in Paris, where he was, according to historian Gregory Kealey, "deeply influenced by the turn to the Popular front by the Communist Party of France."[50] Just two weeks earlier he had participated in what the RCMP called "the 'first' open meeting of the Communist party held in Verdun."[51] He was also a member of the Central Committee of the Communist Party of Canada (although that would not have been publicly known), and a member of the Montreal Council of the League against War and Fascism.[52]

Bipartisan support for this event begs several questions. What happened to the top-down CCF policy of not getting involved with communist organizations? What happened to the fear in the organized Jewish community of being associated with communists? The Canadian

League against War and Fascism was certainly a popular front with the communists driving the agenda. There were, however a number of members of the CCF who saw the benefits in working within the popular front, and took up that point of view in the public debates in its newspaper, *The New Commonwealth*, although the CCF leadership ultimately decided against participation. In discussions between CCF parliamentarians and the executive of the League for Social Reconstruction (the unofficial CCF "think tank"), there were those who spoke up in favour of working as part of the popular front in the fight against fascism.[53] Similarly, the CJC never gave up trying to distance itself from the communists, but others in the Jewish community continued to find the popular front an effective outlet for their anti-Nazi passion. A week before the symposium, Caiserman himself took part in a meeting with a Montreal member of CLAWF held in Golden's office at the YMHA.[54]

Perhaps Caiserman thought he could advance the boycott cause without being seen to cooperate with the CLAWF. Golden, in contrast, was willing to go public in collaboration with the CLAWF if it furthered the boycott effort. Golden could well have arrived at this decision as a result of his disdain for the organizational divisions he had witnessed in the United States. The notes he made for a speech at the gathering provide a detailed rendition of pro-boycott arguments. He started by declaring the Olympic Games one of the three main planks of German foreign policy, along with dismantling the post-war treaties and preparing for war. As proof, he quoted from a long letter from American pro-boycott advocate Judge Mahoney to the German Olympic Committee's Theodore Lewald, as well as from translations of Nazi policy statements on the importance of sports in promoting the Nazi political and racial agenda. Given the new Germany's determination to subvert the Games to further Nazi ends, Golden wondered how anybody could believe that

> Olympic ideals can for a moment be maintained in the atmosphere of Nazi Germany. Where the Olympic ideal preaches amity and good fellowship, Nazi Germany glorifies race and war; where the Olympic ideal visualizes fair competition among amateur athletes, lovers of sport for sport's sake, Nazi ideology visualizes a marshaled army of athletes dedicated to the ideal of "Deutschland über alles."

Golden accused the IOC and its president, Count Baillet-Latour, of being wilfully blind to Nazi oppression and aggression in hope that

Berlin could be "the meeting place of all nations and the beginning of a friendly alliance, without which neither peace nor happiness can be realized." For Golden, the "hypocritical gesture" of removing anti-Jewish signs did not signal any change of heart among the Nazi leaders. Even without signs, the state-authorized terror being inflicted on Jews and others marked as enemies of the state continued while the Nazis milk the Olympics for all its prestige and propaganda value.

Golden did not want to aid the Nazis in their plans or, as he put it, "I do not want to see our fine Canadian athletes ... used as a catspaw by the Nazi dictatorship ... Indeed, I am not willing to direct a body blow at democracy as it has been developed under the British flag, by putting Canada's best and finest under the cloying, evil influence of Nazi ideology." Golden also had an answer for those Canadians who regarded it an act of patriotism to support Canadian athletes, and that politics should not be allowed to interfere with sport. Golden claimed it an act of patriotism *not* to go Berlin, as a way to protect the Canadian commitment to democracy and, idealistically, the Canadian heritage "where races and religions mingle in friendship and equality."

Golden also dismissed those who thought that Canadian athletes were capable of resisting the lure of any Nazi propaganda they might encounter. He pointed to the propaganda success that the Nazis scored with the Winter Olympics and, by way of illustration, how the members of the American bobsled team who were so taken in by the Nazis that they proclaimed admiration for the new Germany and declared it their duty to serve as torch-bearers for the truth. Golden claimed the American bobsledders were so spellbound by the Nazis that they allowed themselves to be publicly showcased at an event that concluded with "a cheer for the Fuehrer, with the Horst Wessel song, and the American anthem."[55]

Golden turned to his audience and rhetorically asked, "Shall our athletes also go to Germany to learn the words of the barbarous Horst Wessel song?" If the answer was "no," then no good could come out of sending Canadian athletes to fall "under the spell of the tremendous high-pressure propaganda machine of Dr. Goebbels."

Golden explained that as a Jew, as an athlete, as an educator, and as a Canadian, he felt duty-bound to oppose Canadian Olympic participation. As a Jew, he felt the pain of his co-religionists in Germany; as an athlete, he did not rule out participating in events against Germans, "but I absolutely decline to compete with the Nazi Government's propaganda machine, which will prevail over the Olympics Games of

1936." As an educator, he stood against the idea of young Canadians being subjected to polished Nazi methods, propaganda, and pressure; and, finally, as a Canadian, he thought that allowing the fostering of personal relationships between Canadian athletes and Nazis would be "a first step in the direction of a gradual surrender of the British traditions of democracy and liberty."[56]

While Golden and various anti-fascist groups continued their public education campaign against Nazi Germany and the Olympics, Jews and the left separately attempted to cut off funding and kept on trying to convince athletes not to make the trip to Berlin. They had already expressed their displeasure when the Canadian government paid out its first $5,000 to the COC in time for the Winter Games. In May Mackenzie King's government delivered the other $5,000. Again various groups protested and, again, in vain. A.A. McLeod, one of the leaders of the CLAWF, repeated the familiar refrain that the Nazis were using the Olympics as propaganda, so those "who cherish liberty and democratic rights should vigorously protest against a cent going to assist a Nazi festival."[57] Shortly before the federal government made its decision, Carleton Stanley, president of Dalhousie University in Halifax, came out against Canadian participation in the Berlin Olympics. An outspoken anti-fascist who had already taken strong stances against antisemitism, he was also one of only a few Canadian academic leaders publicly open to welcoming refugee scholars to his university.[58] The newspaper of the Communist Party of Canada, the *Daily Clarion*, noted with irony that Stanley's courageous stance came just before the government's approval of the grant, and the newspaper hoped that others would be inspired: "It is high time that hundreds of thousand [*sic*] voices should be added to Mr. Stanley's in protest against this government giving any aid to Hitler in the way of support to the Olympics. As yet these voices are heard too rarely and too weakly."[59]

After failing to staunch the flow of money from the federal government, opponents of the Nazi Olympics fell back on a previous tactic. As was the case with the Winter Games, Canadian athletic organizations were forced to solicit private funds to assist their members to get to Berlin. Or, more often than not, individual athletes were told they would have to scrape together their own financial support – this on top of whatever it already cost athletes to attend the Olympic trials. In the eyes of Olympic opponents, this made the Canadian Olympic enterprise vulnerable. There was no doubt that there were Canadian athletes who had their Olympic aspirations frustrated because of a lack of money. Most of their stories have not been recorded. One known story is that of "Moose" Rogin, a Jewish basketball player in Windsor, who was invited to join the Olympic-bound Windsor Ford V-8s on the condition that he could come up with $500 to cover his own expenses. He very much wanted to go but could not turn to his family for help. His father's business, battered by the Depression, was teetering on bankruptcy. He next turned to the local Jewish community, but, in view of community support for the boycott, as Rogin gently put it, "nothing was done." Rogin did not go to Berlin.[60]

Rogin aside, the overall Jewish community effort to forestall Olympic fundraising proved a failure. According to Harold Minden of the Jewish community of Hamilton, it could not have been otherwise. In early July, Caiserman wrote to Minden asking him to protest the decision by Hamilton's city council to aid the Leander Club, one of the premier rowing organizations in the country. The club was chosen to represent Canada at the Olympics and received funds to purchase a new shell costing $500. Caiserman hoped the decision could be reversed. Minden responded that the decision had been made and that a protest would only garner "abuse." Minden complained that the CJC acted too late. Perhaps, if it had started canvassing municipalities across Canada earlier and had requested that they refuse financial assistance to help athletes, then a city council in a heavily unionized city like Hamilton would have known that they would be the subject of "severe censure" and would have voted otherwise. Minden suggested that the CJC should turn its efforts to an education campaign that would expose the real Germany behind the Olympic facade, but other protests – especially if seen to be anti-sport rather than anti-Nazi – would be futile. According to Minden, it would be a good idea for Jews to be "on the good side of all 'so called sports' than to have them saying that we, as a body, are always objecting to what they do."[61]

Perhaps Minden was right. Perhaps the CJC and other pro-boycott supporters were not getting their messages across effectively. Perhaps they could have shamed potential donors into keeping their wallets closed. But there is no denying the surging and powerful emotions in the last weeks before the games. Regional pride and national pride coincided when G. Sydney Halter, president of the Amateur Athletic Union of Manitoba who previously begged off serving as a Jewish voice inside the AAUC, raised funds to send Manitoba track star Jack Liddle to Berlin. As Halter told the press, he "wanted to make sure Manitoba has a track man on that Olympic team which sails Friday."[62] The CJC might

pause to wonder that if it could not bring Halter onside with the boycott campaign, what chance did it have with those more distant from
the Jewish community?

And, indeed, other sources of revenue surfaced as the Olympics drew
closer. In Vancouver, mayor Gerald "Gerry" McGeer made municipal
support of the athletes a badge of civic pride. Just after the trials were
over, mayor of Montreal Camillien Houde cabled McGeer to congratulate Vancouver and British Columbia on the "remarkable showing"
of its athletes at the Montreal trials.[63] This was also a very broad hint
that Vancouver's athletes deserved funding. A week later Houde sent
another telegram explicitly asking for support for one Vancouverite left
off the team, coach Bob Granger.[64] McGeer embraced the cause enthusiastically, if somewhat belatedly. The city of Vancouver was celebrating
its Diamond Jubilee, and the mayor decided that a fundraising campaign in support of Olympic athletes would enhance the celebration of
the Jubilee. After all, the athletes were "splendid representatives of the
youth of Vancouver," and the Jubilee was dedicated to "the Youth of
our City and to World Peace."[65] Although McGeer sent out this letter on
the letterhead of the Vancouver Jubilee, he did not consult any elected
officials before beginning his campaign. They would not have been
around in the summer and McGeer may simply have felt that it was
within his power as mayor to identify the city with the Olympics cause.

Vancouverites had already raised over $700 to send the track and field
team to Montreal.[66] How would another campaign go over? One member of Vancouver's elite, the controversial figure, Victor W. Odlum, had
already contributed to support the athletes and felt that "these sports
funds are rapidly becoming a racket." Still, Odlum did not want the
mayor's campaign to come up short, and so made another contribution.[67] Many others also decided to support their mayor. Between 14
July and 17 July almost 150 individuals and businesses answered the
call with small donations that totalled $1,435.30. By the end of July the
total raised increased to $1,682.45. By COC calculations, this amount
was more than enough to send five athletes to the Olympics. Vancouver's money went mostly to support the swim team, with some to help
Bob Granger, as requested by Houde.[68]

Canadians elsewhere also opened up their wallets. Ottawa's mayor,
Stanley Lewis, and "a sportsman," guaranteed the expenses of local
athlete Jimmy Courting, who competed in the javelin throw. Jimmy
Bartlett, a member of the marathon team from Oshawa, could only
go to Berlin if he found the funding. Fundraising by his fellow factory

workers and support from his employer solved his problem. Regina's citizens heard that local wrestler George Chiga could go to Berlin only if private interests pay his expenses. They raised the necessary funds within hours. Swimmer Mary McConkey from Edmonton needed $200 to make the trip. The sum was quickly raised by popular subscription.[69]

This fundraising was both haphazard and effective. The press wrote of last-minute funds that "flooded the hotel room of the COC." The president of the COC, Mulqueen, was himself stunned at the response: "Why, I thought there was a depression ... I should have known it would happen, but I never expected that deluge."[70]

In fact, during the week before the team's departure, the COC even felt flush enough to turn back a number of last-minute offers of financial assistance, including one from the Conservative Party leader of the opposition in Ottawa, R.B. Bennett. Just days before the Olympic Games began, Bennett wrote to Mulqueen stating, "I would like to make some contribution to the funds of your Committee and I would be glad if you would advise me in a general way as to the amount of individual subscription so I may govern myself accordingly." Mulqueen responded, "Let me assure you that the Olympic Committee appreciate[s] your kind offer of financial assistance but find, however, that we are in a position to meet our obligations without any further appeal to our friends, your offer to assist, however, is none the less appreciated."[71] The final COC financial statement would show a modest surplus.[72]

With the funding in place, more than 120 athletes were ready to sail from Montreal on 17 July; two months earlier it would have been half that number. Still, more athletes might have gone, but some chose to boycott the Nazi Olympics.

Protests: Boycotting the Olympics and Olympic-Related Events

The Summer Games promised to have a much higher profile than did the winter event in Garmisch-Partenkirchen. As a result any Canadian Olympic athlete or a sports official who spoke out in favour of a Berlin boycott could expect wide media attention. But would any do so? Certainly it would be a sacrifice for an athlete to forego the Olympics. Winning a place on the Olympic team afforded athletes a sense of pride and achievement while a high-ranking finish in his or her event could add lustre to the athlete's profile nationally and internationally. Olympic success could, as in the case of boxing, also serve as a springboard to a successful professional career. Perhaps it was not so obvious, but Jews in the amateur athletic establishment also stood to sacrifice their hard-earned status if they spoke out against the Olympics. Because of their involvement in amateur sport, several Jews, including H.E. Herschorn of Montreal and Halter in Winnipeg, had won the right to rub shoulders with the "Old Boys" Olympic elite. Would they be willing to toss that aside by coming out publicly in favour of a boycott? Herschorn said yes; Halter, no.

And was speaking out enough? Some anti-Olympic campaigners wanted to go beyond circulating pamphlets or attending protest meetings. They insisted on a more hands-on approach to convincing athletes and sports officials that they should have nothing to do with the Berlin Olympiad or any associated events, including the Canadian Olympic trials. It is difficult to know how successful they were. Certainly, in the end, some eligible Canadian athletes did not go to Berlin. But why? It is difficult to know. Some athletes later explained their non-participation as a conscious stand against a brutal enemy. Other athletes may have had personal reasons for taking a pass on the Olympics. Still others may have simply failed to raise the funds necessary to attend the Olympic trials or feared losing their job if they took off for the Olympics. Again, their stories are lost.

While many individual stories may be lost to history, we do have very clear evidence of a number of organizations and individuals who took a public stance against the Berlin Olympics. The YMHA of Montreal translated into action the decisions it had taken early in 1936 to boycott all events, big and small, that promoted the Olympics cause. As noted, in January the YMHA refused to host a fencing tournament for fear it might have given the appearance that the organization was in support of Olympic trials.[73] In early July, when the Lions Club, sponsors of the Montreal Olympic trials, requested the YMHA help in the distribution of passes, the YMHA politely but firmly responded that it "cannot participate" and returned the passes.[74]

When the YMHA decided not to hold the fencing match, it also declared that those members of the Y who stayed in the competition should make it clear that they are not competing in any way for a chance to attend the Olympics, but "from the angle of sport alone."[75] Were there Jewish athletes in fencing and other sports who could have made the team and who, by not going, gave up their dreams? In early July, when Montreal was in an altercation with the Toronto Jewish community, one prominent Jew in sports in Montreal referred to "two or three boys who could also qualify very easily for the Olympic Games but have refused to do so on principle."[76] Unfortunately, we cannot be sure who they were. It is also true that the YMHA had a number of excellent teams, most notably the water polo team that won the Canadian Senior Champions between 1932 and 1939. The talented captain of the team, Abe Tafler, was so identified with athletics and the team that he wore his championship ring for the rest of his life.[77] But did these members of the water polo team sacrifice Olympic dreams because of their individual support of the boycott? Or, was the decision made for them by the YMHA? It is also worth noting that men's water polo became an Olympic sport in 1900, but Canada did not send a water polo team to the Olympics until the Munich Games of 1972.

One popular figure at the YMHA, H.E. Herschorn, was ready to step down from a much-coveted position in amateur sport. In early 1936 Herschorn was put in in charge of the YMHA's Olympic committee, while also continuing to serve after fourteen years as the president of the Canadian Amateur Swim Association (CASwA). At CASwA's annual meeting in late April, Herschorn explained that he was no longer willing to serve as the president because of his objections to the Olympics and announced his resignation. Rather, he *tried* to resign. The delegates could not understand why their long-time leader was resigning. For an hour, Herschorn tried to explain his reasons. He stated that he did not want to be involved in getting a team ready "to compete in an environment electric with racial prejudice." He would not travel to Germany, "where members of his race are treated as pariahs." These views, he said, would "intrude upon the impartiality of judgment required of the President of the Canadian Amateur Swim Association."[78]

The delegates, however, would have none of it. Percy Edwards from Toronto tried to appease Herschorn, but also didn't understand what Herschorn was pleading. "I cannot see," Edwards said from the floor, "why the C.A.S.A. [CASwA] should suffer the loss of such a capable leader as yourself because of an event taking place thousands of miles away." Herschorn refused to budge. Then a delegate from Montreal proposed that one of the vice-presidents be appointed in charge of the Olympics. Herschorn agreed and was elected president for the fifteenth time. When the discussions turned to the Olympic preparations, Herschorn left the room.[79] There is no recorded reaction from Herschorn, but he must have been pleased that he could simultaneously remain a member of the elite in the Canadian amateur sport establishment, while putting his anti-Olympic position on the record. There is also no explicit reaction from the YMHA. Were they

convinced that Herschorn had found the right balance between protest and accommodation, or would they have preferred his outright
resignation? While it may have been hard to believe that Herschorn
found it impossible to resign from CASwA, he did remain the president of the YMHA, so they may have indeed accepted his balancing act
between commitment to Canadian amateur sports and commitment to
the Jewish community.

The left also pressed for a boycott of the games by athletes. In late
January the executive of the CCF's Ontario branch forwarded one of
several resolutions to the AAUC in protest of Canadian participation
in the Nazi Olympics. The CCF urged that the money for supporting
a team should go instead to the unemployed. Why should athletes
go to Germany where the government had exhibited its "brutal, callous and unsportsmanlike attitude and activities against the working
class of Germany and against the Catholic and Jewish minorities in
Germany"?[80] Other branches of the CCF may quietly have adopted a
similar policy. At its provincial convention in early July the CCF in British Columbia took to task its Sports Committee for featuring a marathon race that was "intended to prepare a competitor to enter the Nazi
Olympic Games." The convention passed a resolution disapproving
the action and declaring itself "in favor of a boycott of the said Nazi
Olympic Games."[81]

The Barcelona Alternative

The CCF in British Columbia did not just come out against the Berlin
games, but also threw its support behind the Popular Olympiad "being
held in Barcelona, Spain, to offset the Hitler propaganda games and
the fascist domination of international sports."[82] While the IOC and the
COC had five years to plan their games, the promoters of the Barcelona
Games, something of a last-minute affair, had moved fast to establish
the Barcelona event as an alternative to the Berlin Olympiad. In late
April 1936 the Catalan Committee for Popular Sports, itself a product of
various left-wing organizations in Spain and drawing on the enthusiasm for the Spanish Second Republic, set up an Organizing Committee
for the Popular Olympic Games. The Committee proposed a Popular
Olympiad to be held in Barcelona immediately preceding the Berlin
event, claiming it, rather than the Nazi Olympics, represented the cher-
ished ideals of the Olympic movement. The Popular Olympiad hoped
to deflect attention from the Nazi extravaganza.[83]

Judging by the reaction in the newspaper of Canada's Communist Party, the *Daily Clarion*, the newly announced counter-Olympics re-energized the flagging boycott campaign. The newspaper reported the news of the Barcelona Olympiad on its front page on 19 May 1936.[84] It followed up ten days later with a story announcing that Canadian athletes were invited to participate and one of their own, Victoria's Ronald Stewart, was involved in the planning of these games.[85] What the *Daily Clarion* did not mention – although the RCMP included it in its weekly security summary (distributed to cabinet ministers, senior civil servants and to other members of RCMP) – was that Stewart had previously been convicted of "inciting to mutiny," jailed in British Columbia's Oakalla prison, and then deported.[86] Going out on a limb, the *Daily Clarion* also rhapsodized about the support that these games could expect from Léon Blum in France who, it was said, would work with his popular-front government to divert funds from the Nazi Olympics. The *Daily Clarion* would be disappointed. Trying to appease both the left and the right in France, Blum eventually agreed to subsidize both Barcelona- and Berlin-bound athletes and ended up earning the scorn of both.

In the weeks following the announcement of the Popular Olympiad, the *Daily Clarion* complemented its support for Barcelona with renewed attacks on the Nazi Games. One headline screamed, "Fascist Orgy this Summer," followed by a long article warning against Nazi subversion of sport and offering a Marxist analysis of sport.[87] Anti-Olympic editorial cartoons appeared, including one that depicted Hitler, Goebbels, and Goering standing pathetically in a vast empty Reich Sports Field, wondering why nobody was coming to Berlin.[88]

The Barcelona Olympiad was not the only alternate athletic event in the works. In the United States, Judge Jeremy Mahoney, bitter at losing his Olympic battle to Avery Brundage, and Charles Orenstein of the Jewish Welfare Board, spearheaded the drive for an American alternative to the Nazi Olympics. Orenstein, like Mahoney, was a firm opponent of the Berlin Games, and lost his seat on the American Olympic Committee in April 1936. Fed by their hostility to Nazi Germany and a mutual hatred of Brundage, in late May they announced a partnership with the Jewish Labor Committee (JLC) to organize the World Labor Athletic Carnival to be held in New York City. The JLC, established in 1934 as a socialist and anti-communist alternative to the communist-led popular front, believed that by assuming a leading role organizing the counter-Olympic event, the organization would raise its profile, boost membership, and access financial assistance. Leading progressive politicians and union leaders assumed a number of honorary and working roles in the Carnival. Event organizers took an in-your-face confrontational approach to the Brundage crowd. They sought and received AAU sanction for the Athletic Carnival and secured use of the same stadium on Randall's Island where the American Olympic track and field trials had been held. They were also deliberate in setting the date for their event, 15 and 16 August – the last two days of the Berlin Olympics.[89]

Some Canadians participated in the New York event. On more than one occasion the press suggested that speed walker Henry Cieman would boycott Berlin and go to Barcelona. He did not. Instead, he headed south to participate in the World Labor Carnival. Tom Lord of Montreal, Canada's best half-mile runner, joined him. Lord had contracted the measles just before the Montreal trials and did not compete for a place on Canada's Olympic team.[90] Also competing at the Carnival was Ulster United of Toronto, the dominant team on the soccer scene in Toronto. It was matched up with the New York Americans in what was described as the North American soccer championship.[91]

Cieman and the soccer team left the Carnival victorious. Cieman's event was the two-mile walk and he beat his closest rival by fifty yards in what was described as a relatively slow race. In soccer, the home crowd enjoyed an evenly matched first half which ended in a 1–1 tie, but in the second half the American audience watched in disappointment as the energy of the Americans sagged while the Toronto team continued its tight defensive game. With the offence coming to life, the visitors won the game 3–1. Tom Lord did not fare as well. He did not qualify for the second heat of the half-mile.[92]

Although the size of Canada's contingent was small, for the organizers it was a boon to have the Canadians there. Originally it seemed there would be quite a bit of international representation, especially from Europe. In the end, the only reason the event could be called international was because of the presence of the Canadians. For both the Jewish organizers and the Jewish community, Cieman's presence held extra significance. When the leading American-Yiddish newspaper, the *Jewish Daily Forward,* reported on Cieman's victory, it added that this was a Jewish athlete who was not only a Canadian champion, he was also invited to be part of the tryouts for the team. But he "wanted to have nothing to do with the Nazi Olympics."[93]

In Canada, the New York Athletic Carnival did not attract nearly as much attention as the Barcelona counter-Olympics. On 17 June the high jumper Eva Dawes and runners Bill Christie and Tom Ritchie declared that they intended to head to Barcelona.[94] Three weeks later, two Jewish boxers, Sammy Luftspring and Norman "Baby" Yack, as well as their manager, Harry Sniderman, joined them.[95]

What motivated the athletes who went to Barcelona? Canadian communists declared the team, small as it was, a victory for progressive forces, but their individual decisions to go were as varied as their experiences. In interviews with historian Bruce Kidd, runners Christie and Ritchie – who were both former national champions – confessed that they were worried they were not in good enough shape to compete in the Berlin Olympics, and had little knowledge of the political furor that surrounded the Games.[96] Eva Dawes' story was different. On her return from her 1935 WSA-sponsored tour of the Soviet Union, the central Ontario branch of the Amateur Athletic Union of Canada suspended her because she participated in an international event without its pre-authorization as required by AAUC rules. With the threat of a ratification of the suspension at the annual meeting of the Women's Amateur Athletic Federation Meeting scheduled for Halifax in mid-November 1935, in early November Dawes announced her retirement from competition.[97]

Losing Dawes meant losing an Olympic medal contender, and the same people who had so recently suspended her reversed themselves and invited Dawes to apply to the AAUC for a reinstatement of her athletic status. She rejected the overtures and chose Barcelona. Asked about her Barcelona trip later in life, Dawes explained that Barcelona was, plain and simple, an occasion for travel. But if travel was on Dawes's mind, why not go to Berlin? Dawes most likely minimized her progressive politics later in life, perhaps, as historian M. Ann Hall has argued, in lingering distrust of the RCMP,[98] or simply because her own politics changed later in life. When interviewed in July 1936, however, Dawes stated her anti-fascist sentiments clearly and eloquently: "I will be glad to compete in an Olympiad where the true meaning of sport will exist."[99]

While Dawes seemed to make the decision to go to Barcelona as committedly and elegantly as she jumped, Sammy Luftspring only went to Barcelona after putting up a scrappy fight in favour of going to Berlin. Luftspring, born in Toronto to immigrant parents in 1915, knew life on the back lanes of the Jewish immigrant community and in the gritty boxing clubs. When he was nine years old, Luftspring watched in awe as the boxer Harry Katz beat Goody Rosen in the crowded, smoke-filled Leonard House in Toronto. For his victory, Katz received a silver cup and then was marched by supporters down Spadina Avenue, the heart of Jewish Toronto, in triumph. Katz's win, and the celebration that followed, left a strong impression on young Luftspring. Years later, when he recounted the story in his memoir *Call Me Sammy*, Luftspring recalled the victorious Katz:

> He was a king that's the only way I can describe it ... And I wanted so much to take his place that I could taste it ... I knew that what I had until then was nothing unless I could have what Katz had – a procession of my own, and a great big silver cup of my own, and all those people yelling their heads off.[100]

Luftspring honed his skills as a boxer and in 1934, at the age of seventeen, he was crowned Ontario amateur lightweight champion. Two years later he came second in the Canadian 135-pound amateur championship. In early June 1936 one of the *Toronto Globe*'s sports writers, Gordon Sinclair, described how Luftspring handily defeated the Canadian champion, Maurice Camyree of Winnipeg, in a five-round decision, concluding with the suggestion that "Ontario will make no mistake sending him to the [Olympic] trials, and Canada will search a long while for a more likely prospect to represent her in Germany."[101]

Sinclair pegged Luftspring a likely Olympic medal winner because of his talent and because the boxer made no secret of his desire to win that medal. Luftspring stated categorically that he would go to Germany if successful in the Olympic trials. He also spoke for two other Jewish boxers, Baby Yack and Lennie Stein, who had come to the same decision. This flew in the face of the organized Jewish community's efforts to prevent Jewish athletes from joining the Canadian Olympic team. When Sinclair declared that "any anti-Olympic trouble Canada might be obliged to countenance before the team sailed from Montreal on July 17 will not come from Toronto's Jewish fight fraternity," the Toronto Jewish leaders were none too pleased.[102] While CJC spokespersons were busy trying to convince government, donors, and anybody else who would listen that supporting Nazi Germany in any way was immoral, here were Toronto Jewish boxers saying that they wouldn't consider giving up their Olympic dreams. And one of them was Luftspring, who fought wearing shorts marked with a Star of David. In the words of Harvey Golden of Montreal's YMHA, "the moral front would be dented [if these boxers] flouted the common opinion of the Jewish communities by participating in the Olympics."[103] Besides, the CJC

thought they had a deal with the Jewish boxers. Several months earlier, a CJC official had talked to the boxers. Luftspring and the others
claimed they only intended to go to the Olympic trials, and if selected
for the Canadian Olympic team, they would refuse to go to Berlin. All
they wanted, they said, was to rank as high as possible in the amateur
listings and then go professional.[104]

The CJC learned that the boxers had decided to go to Berlin just
before their early announcement in the press. There was thus not
enough time for Congress officials to challenge their decision.[105] Two
weeks later, the *Toronto Globe* reported that members of the Jewish community of Toronto were rising in protest at the boxers' decision to go
to Berlin. Luftspring and Yack were at first unmoved by the protests
and remained determined to go to the Olympic trials in Montreal and
then to Berlin. When the central Ontario chapter of the Amateur Athletic Union of Canada warned the Jewish boxers that by participating in
the trials they were, in effect, committing to Berlin, Luftspring and Yack
foresaw no problem. Stein did not answer.[106]

Behind the scenes, the Jewish community tried to regroup. O.B.
Roger, president of the central region of CJC, was pessimistic about getting the boxers to change their minds, but given the body blow their
going to Berlin would deliver to the Jewish boycott campaign, he took
control of the situation. But what could Roger do that others had not
tried? Roger was well aware that Congress officials had previously
met with the boxers several times, but as he said to a Jewish official in
Toronto, "it seems almost impossible to get anywhere with some of the
people concerned."[107] Clearly there was more than a little social distance between the staid world of Jewish community officials and the
rough-and-tumble world of the boxers.

The frustration continued into late June and the first days of July.
On more than one occasion officials in Toronto wrote to Golden at the
Montreal YMHA that it was unlikely the boxers would change their
position.[108] But the CJC dared not give up; the credibility of the CJC campaign was at risk. On Sunday 5 July, Congress officials again met with
Luftspring and Yack. This time they got the answer they wanted, albeit
with conditions.[109] Roger, anxious to inform Caiserman that the boxers
had been "prevailed upon to officially renounce the privilege of going
if invited," immediately dispatched a handwritten letter to Montreal
rather than wait for the CJC office in Toronto to open the next morning. But what of the conditions? The boxers were promised they would
get their trip overseas. Roger told Luftspring and Yack that Congress

would somehow find the money to send them to Barcelona instead of Berlin.[110] A day later the movers and shakers in the Jewish community came together with Jewish sports enthusiasts in the social hall of choice of the Jewish community, Chudleigh House, and confirmed that the community would find the money to fund the boxers and their trainer, Henry Sniderman. Those gathered set up an ad hoc committee to try to raise the estimated $750 and issued a call to members of the Jewish community, and especially sports fans, to contribute.[111]

On the day after the Chudleigh House meeting a passionate letter to the editor in support of the boycott appeared over the boxers' names in the *Toronto Globe*. Almost certainly written for Luftspring and Yack's signatures by a CJC official, the letter expressed the boxers' keen disappointment at not being able to represent Canada, but stated that they "have gone into the question very carefully with our families and friends in the community" and knew in good conscience they could not act differently. After all, they might be safe, but their co-religionists were not. Sadly prophetic, the letter continued, "the German Government is treating our brothers and sisters worse than dogs ... We would have been very low to hurt the feelings of our fellow Jews by going to a land that would exterminate them if it could."[112]

Roger was convinced, with good reason, that the CJC in Toronto had averted a political and public relations disaster. Roger also believed that turning Luftspring and Yack around was a matter of national significance, and approached the YMHA and Congress in Montreal for financial assistance in sending the two Jewish athletes to Barcelona. Montreal YMHA officials had a different take on the deal, and were not interested in offering financial support for what they regarded as an unseemly shakedown by the boxers. When Caiserman received Roger's request for aid, he turned to Golden at the YMHA for advice. Golden's first response, according to Caiserman, was that it "was very fine that the young fellows in Toronto have decided not to go to the Olympics, but why should we pay for the trip? This is against all rules of sportsmanship." Caiserman asked Golden to at least consider the proposal because Barcelona was an anti-Nazi event. Golden said he would. But rather than temper his feelings, Golden dug in his heels. Two days later Golden wrote that from afar it appeared the Toronto community had to buy the loyalty of the boxers. He thought that CJC should have exerted "enough moral pressure in the Jewish community to prevail upon the boys not to escape from the Jewish body politic, and refrain from Olympic participation without substituting a reward."[113] Caiserman fared no better with Ross Vineberg, a member of the Amateur Athletic Union of Canada also active in CJC affairs. According to Vineberg, there were athletes in Montreal who could also have qualified for the Olympics, but their principles dictated that they would not participate. If there had been a team from several cities, then Vineberg agreed that each community should contribute, but if Toronto wants to send its athletes to Barcelona, then it should raise its own money.[114]

While this telling of the Luftspring and Yack story emerges from historical documentation, Luftspring later offered a different narrative. As he recalled the chain of events, it was his parents who persuaded him that the correct Jewish thing to do was not to go to Berlin. It may well be that family and friends tried to convince him and Yack not to go to Berlin. With regard to Barcelona, Luftspring claimed he was approached by communists who encouraged him to consider going to Barcelona, and the Jewish community only stepped in with the promise of financial assistance once it was apparent that he might go with funding from the communists. But did CJC step up because of the fear of being associated with the communists? In all the back-and-forth confidential correspondence between Toronto and Montreal, including that which concerned funding Luftspring and Yack, there is no mention of keeping the communists at a distance. More likely, the CJC in Toronto was desperate to avoid a potentially crippling blow to the Jewish anti-Olympic campaign by having two prominent Jewish boxers defy the boycott and go to Berlin. If it meant quietly funding their way to the counter-Olympics in Barcelona, it was a price worth paying.

Whatever the case, and despite the deal leaving a bad taste in the mouths of Montreal Jewish leaders, the Toronto Jewish community was determined to stick to its deal and honour its champions. The day after the boxers' letter appeared in the *Globe*, Toronto's Yiddish newspaper, *Der yidisher zhurnal*, published an editorial entitled "This is the way that proud Jews should behave." The editorial congratulated the two for their "proud and truly Jewish behaviour," and acknowledged the sacrifice that Luftspring and Yack were making by not going to Berlin. To be sure, the editorial also called on Jews to help raise the money to send these two heroes to Barcelona.[115] Three days after the letter to the editor in the *Globe*, a fundraising stag was held for Luftspring and Yack at Toronto's YMHA on Brunswick Avenue at College Street. As the CJC also reached out to several local Jewish philanthropists for support, the stag brought out a crowd of enthusiastic fight fans and members of the gambling fraternity.[116] As if symbolically declaring that there was no conflict between being a good Canadian and a good Jew, the boxers were presented with two flags – the Union Jack and "a Jewish flag."[117] From the YMHA, hundreds of supporters accompanied Luftspring and Yack, their travel costs guaranteed, down Spadina Avenue and on to Union Station where they boarded the 1 a.m. train for Montreal. Sammy Luftspring, age nineteen, got his parade, or as he stated in his first entry in his Barcelona travel diary, "Our party left Toronto Union Station after a wonderful sendoff by our Jewish friends."[118]

The Barcelona-bound athletes did not, however, impress Alexandrine Gibb, sports writer for the *Toronto Daily Star*: "It's a two-string bow this year. If you can't make Germany or think you can't get out of the trials because of lack of ability or willingness, there was still Barcelona in the offing."[119] This was too much for one reader of the *Star*, who wrote a letter to the editor complaining that Gibb was offering a distorted view of athletes and the Popular Olympiad. Why would she cheapen the decision of the athletes? Why did she did not explain the anti-Nazi purpose behind them, and that "there was a widespread progressive movement behind them"[120]? And this was from a so-called progressive newspaper! But the anti-Olympic movement never did get much support from the mainstream press, and its cause would be further obscured once all the Canadian Olympic athletes, resplendent in their red blazers, answered the call to "the youth of the world" emanating from Berlin.

Chapter Six

Crimson Blazers

The Cunard White Star ocean liner *Alaunia* departed Montreal at noon on 10 July 1936 bound for England. A tiny contingent of only five Canadian athletes was onboard heading for the People's Olympiad scheduled for 19–22 July in Barcelona. The group included three track and field athletes: Eva Dawes, winner of an Olympic bronze medal in the high jump at the 1932 Olympic Games in Los Angeles, and sprinters Tom Ritchie and Bill Christie. They were joined by two boxers – nineteen-year-old Toronto Jewish boxer Sammy Luftspring and his close friend, bantamweight Norman "Baby" Yack – and their trainer, Harry Sniderman. After a hero's send-off from fans in Toronto, the three caught the overnight train to Montreal and arrived "tired and dirty having spent a stuffy and sleepless night." Once aboard the *Alaunia*, the boxers unpacked, showered, and joined the other Barcelona-bound athletes to enjoy the scenery as the ship headed up the St. Lawrence River and out into the Atlantic. In his trip diary, Luftspring recorded seeing the *Duchess of Bedford* pass the *Alaunia* en route to Montreal, where, a few days later, it would board most of the Berlin-bound Canadian Olympic team.[1]

The Overseas Voyage

The Canadian Olympic team gathered in Montreal in the few days prior to their departure. On the morning of 17 July 1936, approximately 120 athletes, coaches, judges, Olympic officials, and their luggage boarded Canadian Pacific's *Duchess of Bedford*. Each was presented with the official Canadian team uniform, a uniform that would be proudly worn not just by Canada's Olympic athletes, judges and officials, but also by

other Canadians participating in Olympics-related events: a crimson
blazer with white piping and a maple leaf on the breast pocket. Men
were also supplied white slacks and women white skirts. Once in their
cabins, many slipped into their uniforms for the ship's departure. But
Canadian athletes were not the only ones wearing a Canadian uniform.
The Olympians aboard the *Duchess of Bedford* were greatly outnumbered
by veterans of the Great War, some of whom were in uniform as they
boarded the ship. The veterans, together with accompanying family
members, were part of a 6,000-strong pilgrimage by former Canadian
service personnel to battlefields and Canadian military graveyards in
France. Their visit would culminate at the site of the 1917 Battle of Vimy
Ridge.

For the veterans the trip was bound to stir difficult memories.
Many had served at Vimy, the first battle in which all four divisions
of the Canadian Expeditionary Force in Europe fought side by side
against the Germans. Their victory came at a high price. The Canadians suffered 10,500 casualties including 3,600 dead. In the intervening
decades – almost twenty years – the sacrifice at Vimy had come to be
regarded as a landmark event on the road to Canadian nationhood.
On 26 July 1936, only a few days before the Canadian Olympic team
paraded into the Olympic stadium where Hitler accepted the athletes'
salute, the Canadian veterans marched onto the fields of Vimy. They
stood silent as King Edward VIII formally dedicated the Vimy Memorial, the Canadian National War Memorial honouring the 60,000 Canadians who died fighting Germany in the Great War.[2]

But as the *Duchess of Bedford* departed Montreal, all that was still in
the future. The veterans and the Canadian Olympic team mingled at
the ship's railings and showered colourful streamers onto a crowd of
friends and well-wishers cheering from the pier as the ship slipped its
moorings. Many of the Canadian Olympians, young and going abroad
for the first time, were filled with excitement at the adventure that lay
ahead and, for that matter, the anticipation of a week-long ship's voyage. Almost certainly, in the midst of a crushing economic depression,
few would have previously enjoyed the level of luxury afforded them
on the *Duchess of Bedford*. The Olympic team was booked into "Cabin
Class," the Canadian Pacific's first class. It bore little resemblance to
the more spartan accommodations to which most athletes were accustomed.[3] When first commissioned in 1928, Canadian Pacific bragged
that "the DUCHESS OF BEDFORD took the concept of the 'cabin-class'

ship to its highest point."[4] At a time when many rural Canadian homes were still void of indoor plumbing, a 1939 Canadian Pacific poster promoting transatlantic travel on the *Duchess of Bedford* and her sister ships in the CP's Duchess line promised "deluxe staterooms in Cabin Class, many rooms with private baths." Cabin class passengers also enjoyed "open sports decks ... gymnasiums, glass-enclosed observation rooms, delicious meals." The more than 1,500 passengers on board were serviced by a complement of seventy waiters, eighty stewards, six chefs, and fifty additional kitchen staff. The total crew numbered 510, including deck and engine room staff.[5]

What the ship lacked was athletic training facilities. In spite of Canadian Pacific touting "open sports decks" and "gymnasiums," training facilities were limited at best. According to swimmer Joan McLagan (née Langdon), "To practice in the tiny pool on board the ship, the girls [swim team] tied one end of a piece of rope to one end of the pool and the other around their waist so they could swim against the rope. The pool was actually too small to swim laps."[6] Boxers had a different problem. Although the transatlantic crossing was generally smooth and athletes suffered little by way of seasickness, the *Duchess of Bedford* tended to lurch so much it was nicknamed the "Drunken Duchess." Boxers, who set up a sparring ring on deck, found it difficult to maintain their balance. Punches often went wildly astray. The basketball team fared no better. With almost a week spent onboard the ship, "the team decided to use the time for drills – a good idea that lasted one workout when two of the team's balls danced across the deck and disappeared into the rolling Atlantic."[7]

Although training had to be cut back or adjusted to accommodate onboard conditions, one activity that was in no way restricted was eating, and eating well. With the Depression biting deep for some Canadians Olympic athletes, even those with experience on the amateur athletic circuit were not always able to guarantee themselves the most nutritious of diets. Some likely even experienced hunger. That was not a problem on the ship. Some may never before have encountered anything comparable to the quality or quantity of food served in the ship's dining room. Breakfast on the first morning at sea included a choice of compote of prunes, stewed raisins and apples, or various dry cereals or fried salmon cakes, tomato sauce and "broiled Yarmouth bloaters," or eggs boiled, fried, turned, or scrambled, on toast with broiled breakfast bacon and potatoes. There was also cold roast beef and bologna sausages, rolls, muffins, Vienna bread, various kinds of toast with jam or marmalade, and coffee, tea, cocoa, and milk. The dinner menu – laid out in grandiose style – was no less inviting. As a starter there was *consommé printanière*, a clear chicken soup with tiny slices of vegetables carved into flower shapes. Following this was a choice of poached brett in anchovy sauce, *émincés* of beef chasseur, or roast cushion of veal in lemon sauce with wax beans panache and potatoes, either boiled or rissoles. Pressed spiced beef was a chilled option and vegetarians could choose a large combination salad. For dessert, passengers could select apple or blueberry pie, or ice cream with caramel sauce. To finish, coffee or tea was served. It was not long before athletes discovered they could order not just whatever they wanted, but also as much as they wanted.[8]

But not everyone enjoyed mealtime. Shortly after the ship left port, heavyweight boxer George Bird complained to team officials that he found it painful to chew solid food. An X-ray disclosed he had a slight fracture of the jaw. Fearing he might suffer permanent damage if he went into the Olympic ring with an injured jaw, Bird took himself out of competition. While Bird found it painful to eat anything solid, two of his fellow boxers found it all too easy. In spite of repeated warnings, the two ate so much that they ate themselves right out of their weight class. When the two boxers reached Berlin and failed to pass their weigh-ins, they were booted off the team and sent home.[9] Landing back in Canada, one of the two banished boxers, nineteen-year-old Irving Pease from Toronto, complained to the *Ottawa Citizen* that he was so upset by the way he had been treated by Canadian Olympic officials he would never again have anything to do with any Olympic Games. Pease was particularly incensed that COC chairman P.J. Mulqueen publicly ridiculed them for treating the Olympics as a "joy ride."

> "Yeh?" he countered, "That's what he says. Well they [the Canadian Olympic Committee] didn't do much to help me lose any weight. They wanted me to lose weight through their method – running around a track. Who could lose 17 pounds by running in two weeks? You might be able to lose it all right, but you wouldn't be ready for anything more than a bed when you get through."[10]

The lack of appropriate shipboard training facilities and the temptations of the dining aside, the COC's official report on the Olympics declared that, for most of the Canadian team, the "voyage was uneventful."

In Europe

On the morning of 25 July, the *Duchess of Bedford* docked in Le Havre where Canadian Pacific's Berlin representative responsible for coordinating the team's European travel arrangements met the team. As the team's luggage was being secured, he escorted the group through passport control and onto a dockside train to Paris en route to Berlin. During an afternoon layover in Paris the Canadian Pacific agent also arranged for buses to take the Olympians on a whirlwind sightseeing tour of the city followed that evening by a formal dinner. After dinner the team was bussed to the railway station for their overnight trip to Berlin.[11]

As chance would have it, that same day Sammy Luftspring and Baby Yack were also in Paris en route back to Toronto. Their trip to the People's Olympics had proven a casualty of the Spanish Civil War. A few days earlier, the Barcelona-bound Canadians, unaware that the Spanish political crisis had exploded into a shooting war, arrived in Paris at 5:30 in the morning. According to Luftspring, they received nothing resembling the escort service the Canadian Pacific laid on for the Berlin-bound Olympians:

> We looked around for a place to eat breakfast but nobody could understand what we wanted so we caught the 8:30 A.M. train for Toulouse France. This train took us right down the southern part of France with its streams and rivers and neat farmhouses. Our train was a very stuffy place with mostly peasant men and women with their children eating garlic. We were all pretty sick and tired when our train pulled into Toulouse at 8:30 P.M. The British Consul there informed us that it would be useless to go further as they didn't let anybody into Spain at the present as there was trouble in the country and also that the Games in Barcelona which we were headed for were cancelled, and if we did manage to get into the country it would be a long time before we would be able to get out. We took the first train we could get going back to Paris that was at 9:30 P.M.[12]

If Luftspring and Yack were disappointed that the Barcelona competitions were cancelled, there is no hint of it in Luftspring's diary. The two boxers seemed content just to be back in Paris where they were able to finally sit down to a good meal "because by this time we were making ourselves understood."[13]

By chance, Luftspring and Yack learned that the Canadian Olympic team was then in Paris and about to leave for Berlin. The two Canadian boxers "grabbed a bus and hurried to the [train] station to see them off." Luftspring noted in his diary that the Berlin-bound athletes, many of whom he and Yack knew well, were "surprised and glad to see us." Luftspring and Yack hung out with the team members until their train departed. The next morning the pair left Paris for London and, after a short layover, boarded a ship back to Canada.[14]

Henry Roxborough, who authored a number of books on Canadian sport and who accompanied the 1936 Canadian Olympic team to Germany as its "Special Press Correspondent," offered an erroneous and demeaning account of the chance Paris encounter between the Barcelona-bound athletes and the Canadian Olympic team. In a book about Canadian Olympic participation, Roxborough recalls the encounter but mistakenly claims that Luftspring and the others were then on their way to Barcelona rather than on their way back to Canada. But, more importantly, he claims that those who set out for Barcelona did so because they were not good enough "to be chosen for the national team." Certainly, Roxborough was wrong in the case of Eva Dawes, who was regarded as a sure medal prospect. He clearly forgot that the COC had reversed its decision to remove her amateur status and appointed her to the team, an offer she refused. He was also wrong in the case of Luftspring, who was a leading contender in his weight class.[15]

Roxborough also rewrote the historical record by claiming that the German-bound Canadian Olympians were negatively disposed to the Nazis and had a prescient sense of what Hitler and the Nazis were up to in hosting the Olympic Games: "It was apparent that Hitler was cunningly using sport as a propaganda weapon." Why then, in spite of this knowledge and in spite of the Canadian boycott campaign, did Canadian athletes participate in the games? According to Roxborough, the Canadian team went to defend the integrity of the Olympics and show all those who sought to corrupt the Games for their own narrow political gain – both "Jewish-inspired" protest groups and Nazis alike – that true Olympians would ensure that the "Olympic statutes were being observed in every way" and that the Olympics Games could not be co-opted for partisan ends.[16]

If Canadian Olympians and the Canadian Olympic officials who accompanied the team to Berlin imagined themselves defending the Olympic idea against Jewish and Nazi corruption, it was not a topic of discussion as the team boarded the overnight train to Berlin. Most of the

Canadian team members were seated in their own separate couchette compartments. In some instances, however, they shared compartments with members of the larger travelling public. One of those seated with non-team members was Irving "Toots" Meretsky, a member of the Ford V-8s, the Canadian Olympic basketball team, and the only Jewish athlete on the Canadian team. But that did not mean that Meretsky was uncaring of his Jewish roots. According to Meretsky family stories, on the train to Berlin the young Olympian sat across from a German businessman returning home from Paris. While others in the compartment slept, the two struck up a conversation. Perhaps picking up on the ballplayer's name, the traveller concluded Meretsky was Jewish. The German quietly and cautiously revealed he too was Jewish. The stranger then warned the nineteen-year-old Canadian to be very careful while in Berlin. Meretsky would be well advised not to let anyone know he was Jewish. If he did occasion out of the athletes' village, Meretsky had best not venture into Berlin alone or in the dark. Nazi Germany was just not safe for a Jew.[17]

Meretsky did not share with his travelling companion that he felt duty-bound to leave the athletes' village and to do so alone. He was carrying several letters from Jews in Windsor that he had promised to deliver to their families in Berlin. True to his word, the young athlete found his way to the Berlin addresses he was given and delivered the letters. He reportedly found Jews so frightened they were reluctant to open their doors to him. They finally did open their doors, but only wide enough for Meretsky to slip the letter into each waiting hand. Terrified that a neighbour might inform on them, the recipient only wanted Meretsky gone. On another occasion, Meretsky ventured into a Jewish commercial district looking to buy a camera for a friend in Windsor. He found dejected proprietors in shuttered stores with empty shelves. As he later recalled, "You could tell they were scared."[18]

If Meretsky was struck by the plight of Jews in Nazi Germany, he was the exception. Most of the Canadians were swept up in a friendly and agreeable environment that welcomed Olympic athletes. If anything, the cordiality of their German hosts overwhelmed the Canadian team. And there is no denying the Germans pulled out every stop to make their Olympic guests feel welcome. As the Canadians' train pulled into Berlin's Friedrichstrasse Station, a large military band began to play. Heads of the German Olympic Committee were also on the platform to greet the team and after a few formal words they escorted the team to waiting busses. A police escort led the bus caravan past cheering

crowds to an official city hall reception. Standing atop a grand stair-
case, the mayor of Berlin, speaking in German, officially welcomed the
team. The Canadian response was enthusiastic. "Not understanding a
word he said, but assuming from the kindly expression on his face that
he was metaphorically handing us the keys of the city, we [Canadians]
gave him three cheers and a tiger." The team was then led in a mass
singing of "'The Maple Leaf' and 'O Canada' with gestures that would
have done credit to the conductor of the world's greatest symphony
orchestra."

Presented with inscribed copies of a "handsomely bound and illustrated" book about Berlin, the team re-boarded the busses and drove
to the Olympic village. The Canadians disembarked and listened to
another series of welcoming speeches followed by a ceremonial raising
of the Canadian ensign. They were then escorted to their living quarters. The women went to Friesenhaus, described in the Canadian Olympic Committee official report on the Berlin Games as "commodious
living quarters" not far from the Olympic stadium.[19] While the official
German Olympic Committee's report described the women's quarters
as "suitable as any first-class hotel in the city," not all were so generous
in their assessment.[20] The youngest member of the Canadian women's
swim team recalled, "We were in *Friesen Haus* and we called it 'freez-
ing house.'"[21] Apparently with good reason; A German report on the
women's accommodations admitted that "it was impossible to satisfy
all those living in the house, despite our greatest efforts to fulfill every
wish. We heated the large building in August, so that girls who found
the temperature too low should not be cold."[22] Obviously some were.

Male Olympic athletes housed in the self-contained Olympic village found little to complain about. Dubbed by the German Olympic
Committee a "Village of Peace," the facilities were ironically built and
administered by the German military and would be converted into a
military compound as soon as the athletes went home. But the village
and its surrounding grounds did not look or feel garrison-like – far
from it. While security was tight, every effort was made to ensure the
Olympic village was not only utilitarian but also pleasing to the eye.
An American coach marvelled at the carefully manicured landscaping:

The Olympic Village itself was a grand sight to anyone who ever experienced the problem of housing a large number of people under somewhat
similar circumstances. The Germans had constructed a veritable international city at the edge of their nation's greatest city. It was a home of

champions designed entirely for their needs and desires, where thousands of athletes of different races, religions, and color resided, with opportunities to practice their particular specialties, enjoy the association of friendly visitors, and commune with people from most parts of the world. The entire Village was surrounded by fencing. Visitors gained entrance only through the administrative building where there was to be found Olympic Village officials as well as stores, shops, and several service agencies for the benefit of the Village inhabitants. Miles of driveways between houses or residence, areas of green grassy fields, trees, and shrubs aided in creating a beautiful landscape.[23]

Every national team was assigned its own military liaison officer ostensibly to see to the team's comfort and deal with any administrative issues that might arise. No doubt the liaison officer was also expected to monitor, as much as possible, the comings and goings of team members and guide them to a positive impression of the new Germany. In the Canadian case, the liaison officer was Lieutenant Werner Heinrichs. The associate coach of the Canadian men's swim team, Joe Griffiths, noted with pleasure that Heinrichs was fluent in English:

> He was in New York for some years, came back in 1933, joined Hitler's working battalion and finally gravitated to the army. He has got on well. At the present time, he is on the [Army's] general staff in Berlin. During the games, his job is to look after the Canadians and see that they are fixed up and get everything they want. He is an awfully nice fellow. I like him very much.[24]

Heinrichs stuck to the Canadians like glue. He kept such careful watch of the team that he even volunteered to accompany team members on their excursions into the heart of Berlin. But there was little for Heinrichs to worry about. The Canadians were compliant and grateful guests. Certainly they had little to complain about. Like all national teams, the Canadian men were given their own comfortable "cottages" and every effort was made to meet the team's needs. In the case of food, Germany might have then been suffering shortages, but not so the Olympic village. Not only were there no food shortages in the Olympic village but, as the Official Report of the 1936 Olympics explains, the Olympic village had forty separate and tastefully appointed team dining rooms and kitchens to assure the food offered each national team accorded with national culinary tastes.

The [Olympic village] reception building was balanced by the main household building with dining-rooms for each competing nation, this being situated at the top of the upper Village section. It was also in quadrant form and three storeys [*sic*] in height, these descending to the rear in order to harmonize with the terrace. This building was a utility construction, its ground plan being conditioned by the requirements drawn up by the Organizing Committee and North German Lloyd Company as the quarters responsible for the accommodation of the participants. The 40 dining-rooms of the nations were located on the outer ring facing the terraces, while the 40 kitchens regulated in size to correspond to the dining-rooms faced the inner ring. The cellar contained storage space and refrigeration rooms as well as washing and dressing rooms for the employees. Two large dining-rooms and kitchens each capable of accommodating 150 participants were located on the ground floor for the nations which had sent large teams, while two upper storeys [*sic*] provided the necessary space for the smaller teams.[25]

In addition to well-prepared meals, team members were likely to find any and all the goods or services they might need readily available inside the village compound. There was a post office, bank, theatre, shops that sold sporting goods, stationary, souvenirs, photographic supplies, fruit, and confectionary, a travel office, police station, and the most modern of medical facilities. Nor were the male athletes' carnal needs forgotten; according to Swiss Olympian Paul Martin, the Germans provided white athletes with a "love garden":

The Olympic athlete in Berlin was elevated to a godlike creature ... The Germans had even reserved a sort of heavenly forest for those gods. And there the prettiest handpicked maidens would offer themselves to the athletes – to the good Aryan types ...The maidens were usually sports teamers or members of Hitler's *Bund deutscher Mädel* [League of German Maidens] and they had special passes to enter the Village woods and mingle with the athletes. It was a lovely birch forest which had a pretty little lake, and the place was tightly ringed by Schupos [Berlin city police] so no one could disturb the sportive couples. It was interesting that before submitting to the Olympic god of her choice, the girl would request her partner's Olympic badge. In case of pregnancy, they give his information to the state or Red Cross maternities to prove the Olympic origin of her baby. Then the state would pay for the whole works.[26]

It is not known if or how many Canadian team members partook of "the love garden" but, for those who did not, other female companionship was not to be found in the Olympic village. The facility was gated and only authorized persons could enter the area of living quarters. No Canadian women Olympic team members were so authorized. Of course, male athletes were free to come and go from the village as they pleased, but it was "recommended" they always travel with a volunteer German companion who would, for those who needed it, serve as translator. Whether with or without a companion, an athlete's identification pass privileged the holder to free public transit, free entry to public attractions, and discounts at many Berlin shops and restaurants. As a result, most Olympic athletes, including Canadians, spent time wandering through tourist areas of Berlin and the surrounding vicinity.

Berlin Excursions

Among those who enjoyed Berlin was Canadian swim coach Joe Griffiths. One evening he and another Canadian swim team official headed into town:

> It was a 45 minute ride in the bus. I have never seen so many people together in my life. The streets were packed and every restaurant and show were filled to capacity. Berlin is noted for its night life. We went in to a couple of cabarets to see what they were like, but couldn't get a seat anywhere, so we had to get out and didn't see any of the dancing after all. I was disappointed because I really did want to see how they [the Germans] carry on. However, I might have another chance. I wouldn't like to come away without seeing how the Germans enjoy themselves at night.
>
> I like the streets in Berlin. They are much wider and cleaner than the streets of London and just now, with all the magnificent [Olympic] decorations and illuminations, they look their best.[27]

Griffiths was not alone. Visitors to Olympic Berlin found the city alive and festive day and night – more like a vacation resort than a Depression-wracked middle-European city. On the eve of the Olympics, *The Toronto Daily Star*'s European correspondent, Matthew Halton, no friend of the Nazi regime, was in Berlin to cover the spectacle. He was saddened but not surprised to find Olympic visitors so swept up in Olympic euphoria that they were blind to what lay behind all the

Olympic bunting. Berlin was on its best behaviour. Those who knew
Nazi Germany knew the iron fist had only temporarily slipped into a
velvet glove. But for most Olympic visitors, Berlin was a party:

> Tremendously beflagged, crowded and back-slapping, Berlin to-day holds
> the cream of athletic youth of more than 50 nations. You can't see the sky
> for flags and you can't see the flags for people and athletes loud in their
> praise of everything German ... There's noise, excitement and frantic zeal
> in the air as Nazi Germany goes to bat to show the world what an Olympic
> really is.[28]

The Nazis made no secret of their desire that Berlin – sans Roma and
Sinti – appear, at least on the surface, an open and welcoming city. Ber-
liners were admonished to be joyful, courteous, and hospitable – even
to non-whites. And for the moment at least, the police were told to look
the other way, especially where foreigners were concerned. And so as
not to appear excessively militaristic, when off duty, street clothes often
replaced police and military uniforms. Taking pride in this Nazi version
of a Potemkin village, one German newspaper boasted, "We are not
only going to show off the most beautiful sports arena, the fastest transportation and the cheapest currency: we are going to be more charming
than the Parisians, more lively than the Romans, more worldly than the
Londoners, and more efficient than the New Yorkers."[29]

The friendly face of Berlin was merely a facade. While the Nazis had
forcibly removed the Roma and Sinti from Berlin in advance of the
Olympics, they did not round up the Jews. But as Meretsky discovered,
Berlin Jews made themselves scarce during the Games and certainly
avoided public contact with Olympic visitors. And, not withstanding
Rabbi Eisendrath, visitors to Germany were discouraged from prying
into the plight of German Jews. According to the *New York Times*, any
Olympic visitor who inquired about the "Jewish question" was directed
to discuss the matter with the Gestapo. Those foolish enough to do so
were then kept under surveillance for the remainder of their German
stay.[30] The authorities might not be in uniform, but few doubted they
were alert as to where foreigners were going, what they were doing
and, above all, whom they were doing it with. And just as Germany's
Jews knew enough to stay away from Olympic guests, they also knew
better than to take heart from the Nazi's removal of all the "Jews Not
Welcome" signs, previously ubiquitous in Berlin hotels, restaurants,
and public places. Nazi storm troopers may have been cautioned to

refrain from any public actions against Berlin Jews during the Olympics, but every German Jew knew that just as night follows day, when the athletes and visitors went home, the Olympic pause would end and the Nazis would again roll out antisemitism full force.

With the exception of Meretsky, likely none of this was of much concern to members of the Canadian team. They were mostly young, enthusiastic, and came from Canada to compete in the Olympic Games, not probe German social conditions. At worst, all this talk of racial troubles was an internal German matter of no business of the Canadian team. What is more, everybody was just so friendly, and those wearing the distinctive crimson Canadian blazer were treated like visiting royalty. Wandering around Berlin with another Canadian team member, Griffiths noted that, "our red coats always drew a crowd of curious people. They were very kind to us and treated us very well."[31] Why court trouble?

Volkoff's Dancers

Not all those who enjoyed the celebrity treatment that came from wearing the crimson Canadian blazer were athletes, coaches, or administrators. Other Canadians in Germany came to participate in cultural events organized in conjunction with the Olympics. In September 1935, for example, the Canadian Olympic Committee was invited by its German counterpart to send a group of dancers to participate in what the COC understood would be an international artistic dance competition.[32] While the Canadians explained they followed the British lead in accepting the German Olympic invitation, the game of follow-the-British-leader did not extend to the dance event. The British declined the German invitation. In addition to the British, other "important dance nations" including France, Sweden, and, most significantly, the United States, decided to take a pass on the dance event. In the American case, Martha Graham pointedly rejected a personal invitation to attend:

> I would find it impossible to dance in Germany at the present time. So many artists whom I respect and admire have been persecuted, have been deprived of their right to work, and for such unsatisfactory and ridiculous reasons, that I should consider it impossible to identify myself, by accepting the invitation, with the regime that has made such things possible. In addition, some of my concert group would not be either welcome in Germany or willing to go.[33]

The Canadians showed no similar compunction. In late March 1936, only four months before the opening of the summer Olympics, the COC officially approached Boris Vladimirovich Volkoff, Toronto ballet master, teacher, and choreographer, to represent Canada. Unlike Graham, Volkoff was unperturbed at the idea of performing in Nazi Germany. According to historian John Ayre, Volkoff, a Russian defector, "had no great love of Communists, but no particular Fascist sympathies either. He simply saw Berlin as an opportunity to promote Canadian dance. He knew the best way to capture Canadian attention was to win international recognition."[34] Dancing in Berlin in the shadow of the Olympics was an opportunity too good to turn down. Volkoff and his ballet troupe prepared to present an original ballet based on Aboriginal legends *Mon-ka-ta* and *Mala*.[35] But dance was one thing – dollars were another. Without financial support from the COC, Volkoff had to reach into his own pocket and pass the hat at several Toronto benefit dance performances to ensure that he and fourteen of his dancers – most still in their teens – with their costumes, props, and what staging they could take with them, had sufficient funds to make the trip. The troupe sailed steerage class on the *Empress of Britain*. Onboard ship, partly as a rehearsal and partly to entertain passengers, the group performed excerpts from their planned repertoire.

When they arrived in Berlin the Volkoff dancers, decked out in their crimson Canadian Olympic blazers, were received with much the same fanfare as the Olympic athletes. One of the young dancers reported to her school *Bulletin*:

> From the moment of our arrival at the Friedrichstrasse station, where our country's flag and a military escort awaited us, Germany as a host made an unforgettable impression. Every day as we passed along the street on our way to the theatre or Government dance hall where we rehearsed, the small children greeted us with quaint curtseys.[36]

Another of the Volkoff dancers was equally captivated by the German welcome. In a letter home to her mother the young woman explained, "We got into Berlin about 5:30. There we were royally met and welcomed. There was a huge Canadian flag draped over the stairs. The soldiers saluted us. Then our pictures were taken and we were driven away in a private bus." Obviously young and impressionable, she also commented approvingly on another fact of Berlin life: "One nice thing about the place is that there are no Jews and all the people are so nice to each other. There is a great deal of discipline here."[37]

If there was one major glitch in Volkoff's planning it was that the Canadian troupe had wrongly been led to believe they would be participating in an amateur dance competition. When they arrived in Berlin they learned that the dance event was neither amateur nor competitive. It was instead a multi-national stage performance, and as a performance, "the amateur spirit of the Olympics" did not apply.[38] Much to Volkoff's shock, he learned the Canadians were the only amateur troupe among the fourteen participating national dance groups. Many of Volkoff's dancers regarded this an unexpected bonus. Just dancing alongside "the greatest professional dancers in the world to-day, watching them in their work and play, was a thrilling experience for Canada's enthusiastic amateurs."[39]

Perhaps so, but not wanting his amateur dancers upstaged by professionals, Volkoff set a blistering rehearsal schedule. As one Canadian newspaper reported, "they decided to 'work like mad' and at least try to make an intelligent showing on behalf of Canada."[40] They performed to a packed house in the Volksbühne ("People's Theatre") on Friday evening, 24 July, to mixed reviews. One highly respected German dance critic writing for an American journal commented of Volkoff that he seemed intent on developing "a new style [of dance] by combining existing ones." After viewing the Canadian effort, he declared, "I am sorry to say that such a combination of practices could not excite a deep and convincing impression."[41] The Nazi press was more fulsome in its praise of the Canadian effort, and the official COC Olympic report hailed the German press acclaim as just recognition of the Canadian dancers being reportedly ranked "among the best five by the judges at the close of the performances."[42]

However, press reports that the Canadian dancers placed fifth in competition were, at best, stretching the truth. In reality, there was no competition, no judges, no Olympic-like ranking of the national dance groups, and no Olympic medals. At a gathering marking the end of the dance event, all the participating dance troupes were given the same citation in recognition not of their ranking but of their participation. Where then did the story that the Canadians placed fifth out of fourteen dance groups come from? Apparently, at the closing gathering, one of the German dance organizers told Volkoff that if there had been a competition, in his estimation the Volkoff troupe would have taken fifth place. Volkoff, hoping for a positive publicity bounce from the German visit, promptly announced his group had placed fifth. The Canadian press happily congratulated the dancers for doing so well against such stiff competition and Volkoff in turn promised his troupe would place even higher at the 1940 Olympics in Japan.[43]

Other Invitees to Berlin: Teachers and Youths

In addition to the Volkoff dance troupe, two other crimson-blazered non-competing Canadian groups travelled to Berlin to participate in Olympic cultural events. One group was composed of twenty-eight Canadian professors, teachers, and directors of physical education, guests of the German Olympic Committee invited to Berlin to partici-pate in what the Germans billed as a Physical Education Congress. The Canadians joined more than 900 other male physical education experts from thirty-two countries including the United States and Great Britain. The Congress, homage to the cult-like Nazi obsession with the Aryan body, was staged in Berlin during the week preceding the opening of the Olympic Games. Participants were housed not in the Olympic vil-lage but in a tented International Sports Students' encampment on the grounds of the University Institute for Physical Culture, four miles from the centre of Berlin and one mile from the Olympic Stadium. Each national delegation was assigned its own separate large, white sleeping tent:

> The name and national flag of the respective countries were placed in front of the tents assigned to them. Six wash tents, each provided with three 10 metre long wash troughs and running water, were located behind the living quarters, and six large lavatory houses were erected at the edge of the encampment.

In addition a central circus-like dining tent large enough to accom-modate the entire camp at one sitting was erected at the centre of the encampment. Mealtime was a marvel of technical efficiency with elec-tric conveyers transporting full meals to the campers.[44]

Like Olympic athletes, each educator was presented with an Olym-pic identification card also valid for free transportation on the Berlin public transit system. The German hosts encouraged the educators to use their downtime at the Congress site, or to stay on after the Con-gress to enjoy the myriad other cultural events that coincided with the Games. During the weeklong Congress, participants were kept busy. The formal program included morning calisthenics, lectures on eugen-ics, race, and the "science" of sport, together with a series of site visits to Labour and Youth Camps, schools, and the Olympic facilities. Each national delegation was also encouraged to prepare a demonstration athletic or sporting routine for presentation to the Congress.

Also in Berlin for the Olympic festivities was a group of twenty-eight Canadian teenage boys between fifteen and eighteen accompanied by several adult male chaperones. They were also in Germany at the invitation of the German Olympic Committee to attend an International Youth Gathering. The Canadian Olympic Committee, "recognizing the educational value of such a trip," enthusiastically endorsed the German invitation and "appointed a special committee to take charge of the organization of this group."[45] Like the delegates at the Physical Education Congress, the Canadian teens "would be guests of the Reich from the time they crossed the German frontier, with free housing and meals, and [the chance] to witness the Olympics." Also like the educators, the boys were accommodated in a specially constructed tent encampment at walking distance to the Olympic Stadium:

> The plan provided that all the different nations should become one single unit. The spirit of unity which pervaded the entire group, constituted the best guarantee of success for the project. The foreign boys, who for the greater part were not yet familiar with camp life, should find a camp possessing all possible modern and technical equipment. It was to be a camp in which life would be pleasant to them during the three weeks of their stay without being luxurious. A tent was provided for each nation. These were erected in a circle symbolizing the world around the Olympic Flag. For the first time the youth of the world was to be brought together under this symbol. It was essential that the technical equipment should, as far as possible, be adapted to the plan of the camp. They must not deteriorate the fine aspect of the tent encampment, but nevertheless be able to stand the rush of about 1,000 inmates.[46]

Sixteen year-old John Derry from Toronto was among the teens from twenty-four countries – including Great Britain, but in this instance not including the United States – who assembled for the Youth Gathering two days before the official opening of the Olympics. Derry arrived not knowing what to expect. In fact, his attendance at the Youth Gathering was something of a fluke. He attended St. Paul's School for Boys in Toronto, a small private Anglican-affiliated high school run by Norval Waddington, one of the adults who accompanied the Canadian teens on their German trip. Derry's closest friend at St. Paul's was Peter Mavor Moore, son of Scottish-born Dora Mavor Moore, celebrated pioneer of Canadian theatre and a close friend of Derry's parents. Mavor Moore learned about the proposed Youth Gathering from Waddington and, then planning her own trip to Scotland and England with her three sons in July and August, thought it a good idea to send her son Peter to the Youth Gathering. Not only did she feel it would be a learning experience for him but, with one less son to watch over, it would also help free up her own schedule.

To placate her son, a little hesitant about attending the Berlin event, Mavor Moore convinced Derry's parents to allow their son to join her and her family in Britain and then to accompany the young Mavor Moore to the International Youth Gathering in Germany. It was an unexpected adventure for Derry. He travelled with the Moores by train from Toronto to Montreal then by ship to Glasgow, eventually on to London where he and his friend joined other Germany-bound Canadian teens, most from elite private schools or highly regarded public collegiates. Like Canadian Olympic athletes, each of the boys was smartly decked out in his red Canadian blazer, the official Canadian Olympic uniform. In a letter to Derry's mother, Mavor Moore assured her that "the blazers are stunning" and that her son "looks fine in his." Chaperoned by several teachers from a Winnipeg high school, the Canadian teens made their way to the Youth Gathering, first by boat across the Channel then by train to Berlin.[47] On 31 July the Canadian group was greeted at the Berlin train station by Youth Gathering organizers and then transported by military busses to the tent encampment where the official welcome for the foreign youth took place, including the "hoisting of the colours" of all the nations involved. A Canadian ensign was raised on a flagpole in front of the assigned Canadian tents. The visiting boys were then instructed to select a bunk bed, unpack and rest up and get ready for a full three weeks of activity.[48]

Derry's youthful memories of the International Youth Gathering remained vivid seventy-five years later. He recalled an orderly campground surrounded by a chain-link fence patrolled day and night by armed and uniformed guards. No one was supposed to enter or leave without permission. The camp facilities, constructed by the German military, were more basic than most of the Canadian teens were used to or prepared for. According to Derry, neither he nor his buddy brought along much by way of rough-and-tumble clothing. What clothing they did bring got a workout. Each day began with a pre-breakfast camp assembly that included raising the Olympic flag. The rest of the day was tightly programmed with sporting and scouting activities in the camp, site visits in Berlin and the surrounding area, and attending the Olympic Games. Evening programming included various forms of entertainment: campfires, nature activities, and musical events. Meals in camp took place in a huge tent in which each national group was assigned three tables over which was suspended their national flag. Two boys from each national group were assigned to serve at every meal. During what little spare time the boys had, they were encouraged to get to know boys from other countries, even though language was often a barrier. The encampment was also equipped with a large tent containing a television where Derry was witness to history as the Berlin Olympics became the first Games ever televised.[49] While he remembered being impressed by television, his most pronounced memory was of being endlessly marched around military style. Whether it was en route to an Olympic venue, through the streets of Berlin, or just to meals in the mess tent or to wash up, the organizers of the gathering seemed to regard casually strolling at a leisurely pace as a sign of languor to be discouraged. Even a visit to the washroom was to be executed as if participating in a close-order drill. According to Derry, some of the participating national groups seemed to take to military-like fashion better than others, as if they were born to it. This, he concluded, was particularly true of the Germans who took obvious pride in trooping about in straight lines while singing vigorous marching songs. By contrast, Derry chuckled that the Canadians teens were not very good at either marching or singing. Much as some might try – and some didn't – the Canadians often looked more like a disorderly rabble than a troop on parade. The German teens, Derry recalls, were always polite but obviously "disgusted" with the seeming Canadian indifference to military-style order.

The boys were allowed very little free time and spent most of it within the fenced-off campgrounds. The few times Derry left the encampment, he was always part of a supervised group and always in the company of a German "translator." Some of the boys chafed under the tight restrictions. Derry remembered one night when several boys slipped under the fence and headed off to "buy pop and candy." They were caught and punished by being restricted to their bunks for two days.[50]

Derry's memories of mindless marching and overprogramming do not square with the official Canadian record of the Youth Gathering. The Canadian Olympic Committee's report on the 1936 Olympics includes a short section which applauds the high standard of marching demonstrated by many of the national groups and how the Canadians matched the others stride for stride. The report was especially effusive in its praise of the crimson-blazered Canadian teens' stamina and marching ability during a mass parade of Olympians – athletes, officials, educators, and dancers – to the German Soldiers' Monument, the Memorial to the Fallen of the War, on the morning of 1 August, the opening day of the Olympic Games.

> Down through the packed streets and milling crowds they marched. Little groups of foreigners, cheered as they saw their own boys march past. "Hunk, Hunk, Hoir" – Hungarians acclaiming their group. "Sic hoic, Sic hoic" – Jugoslavia. And an occasional "Hip, hip, hurray." The Canadians rose to the occasion and marched with the best of them. They looked pretty fine in their red blazers and white flannels, and when they got tired of singing "O Canada" they sang "There is a tavern in our town'" and not many people knew the difference. To them it was just another national song.
>
> After they had all lined up in front of the War Memorial, the next part of the ceremony could be heard long before they saw it. Away up Unter den Linden, far out of sight, they could hear a muffled "thud, thud, thud." Closer and closer it came, until the source of the sound was in sight. Berlin's crack troops, goose-stepping – four miles of goose-stepping – legs swinging almost interlocked, almost waist high, feet down again with a resounding whack on the pavement, all in perfect rhythm.[51]

While the Canadian report showed reverence at the solemnity of the gathering and awe at German military bearing and precision, Derry's teen memories of the event remained decidedly less positive and certainly less respectful. At the end of the march he recalled being packed into the crowd "belly to bum," while Hitler and others on a raised podium "routed and shouted' in German for what seemed to Derry an eternity. The summer heat also took its toll: "Kids dropped like flies."[52]

Olympic Pageantry

When the speeches ended at exactly 12:45 p.m., the assembled marchers remained in place as a runner carrying the Olympic torch entered the square. The Olympic flame, originally lit by a concave mirror in Olympia, Greece, had been carried for twelve days and eleven nights by some 3,300 runners for more than 3,000 kilometres across Greece, Bulgaria, Czechoslovakia, and finally into Germany. Hitler hailed this first-ever Olympic Torch Relay as a symbolic link between his Reich and the mythical notion of ancient and Aryan Greece.[53] The Olympic

Torch Relay reached the outlying districts of Berlin earlier that morning and as trumpet blasts marked its progress through city streets, a crowd six-deep cheered as the torch made its way up Unter den Linden and finally into the square in front of the Soldiers' Monument. As the torch-bearer entered the square the Canadians joined the assembled Olympic community in observing two minutes of silence for the fallen. Then, at exactly 12:50 p.m., torch held high, the runner proceeded out of the square "amid the wild joy and excitement of the assembled youth" to finish at the Olympic opening several hours later.[54]

When the torch left the square, the crowd dispersed. The Canadian Olympic competitors and officials, accompanied by the Canadian dance troupe, were transported to an assembly point from which they would join the nation-by-nation parade into the Olympic Stadium for the official opening of the Nazi Olympic Games. The Canadian teens and physical fitness instructors were escorted to privileged seating in the stadium from which they could view the opening ceremonies. And the Olympic opening was, according to the Canadian Olympic Committee report, a flawlessly executed "pageant" that was, as one might expect of a German-organized event, carefully choreographed so as to "[unfold] itself in precise movements on time, without a single untoward incident to mar the great spectacle."[55]

Well, almost none. As the COC Olympic report makes clear, the opening pageant proved as much an act of veneration of the German Führer as it was a celebration of sport and athletics. "In fact homage to Hitler all through the ceremony stood out boldly against the setting of the Olympic opening ritual." Event organizers left nothing to chance. At exactly 3 p.m., as the competitors assembled in an open area adjacent to the stadium, Hitler, in a brown military uniform, and his entourage, began their drive to the Olympic Stadium. The Führer was driven in an open car accompanied by a military guard and protected by 40,000 storm troopers who lined the five-mile cavalcade route, jammed on both sides by a cheering five-deep crowd. He arrived outside the stadium to the sound of a thirty-trumpet fanfare. No sooner did he finish inspecting his honour guard than a 100-piece orchestra inside the stadium began playing a Hitler favourite, Wagner's "March of Allegiance." On cue, Hitler, flanked by representatives of the International and German Olympic Committees, entered the stadium on foot and made his way across the sports field towards a reserved stadium section dubbed the "Loges of Honour." All the while a capacity stadium crowd of more than 100,000 stood as one to cheer, many offering the

Führer the straight-armed Nazi salute. As Hitler and the official party took their places in the "Loges of Honour," "a tiny little girl in a blue frock stepped out of the crowd like a ladybird and in the vastness of the place, curtsied and presented the Führer with a lovely bouquet of flowers." The crowd roared its approval and then joined in song as the orchestra struck up "Deutschland über Alles" followed immediately by the "Horst Wessel Song."[56]

Next came the Parade of the Nations led by the Greeks and followed in alphabetical order by each participating country. Germany, the host country, entered last. As the athletes circled the stadium track, "each group presented a different picture in its uniforms and methods of saluting when it passed the Chancellor's station." The Americans, as was their custom, doffed their hats and placed them over their hearts but did not dip their flag. The Canadians, including Volkoff's dancers, all decked out in their crimson blazers, white pants or skirts, and white shoes, paraded in behind six-foot flag-bearer and hurdler Jim Worrall.

After the Winter Olympic confusion between the straight-armed Nazi salute and the almost-identical Olympic salute one might think the Canadians would have learned. They didn't. The British announced a week before the opening of the Games that they would not offer either of the salutes. Instead, according to a report in the New York Times, they would only turn eyes right as they paraded by the reviewing stand. Mulqueen later claimed that the Canadians would not have given the ambiguous salute had they known of the decision of the British team. Mulqueen clearly did not read the New York Times, which had reported the British decision a week before the Games began.[57] The Canadians, seemingly oblivious to the impression they were making, offered Hitler a straight-armed Olympic salute. According to Halton at the Toronto Daily Star, the Canadians were "given a riotous ovation as they marched past the official box saluting in Nazi fashion."[58]

Worrall, the Canadian flag-bearer in the Parade of the Nations, later claimed the Canadian team was taken aback by the kerfuffle their salute generated. "We took a lot of backlash criticism for that," Worrall explained. "But it was done, I think, well you might say, the kindest thing you might say is it was done in naivety." Another member of the Canadian Olympic track and field team, Ab Conway, had a different and more self-justifying take on the Canadian decision to offer a straight-armed Olympic salute. Rather than a product of "naivety," it was, he said, a calculated and proprietorial move designed to reclaim the Olympic salute from the Nazis. "Were (we) going to salute in the sort of army method, or were we going to give the Olympic salute? Not the Nazi salute, the Olympic salute. But the Nazis had taken it over. We decided that we were not going to let them do it, that the Olympic salute was the Olympic salute and we were going to give the Olympic salute."[59] Joan McLagan, at thirteen – the youngest member of the Canadian team – agrees with Conway. "People thought we were using the Hitler salute," McLagan later explained, "It wasn't, of course. It was the Olympic salute."[60]

Olympic salute or Nazi salute, as Halton noted, the stadium crowd, and many in Canada, failed to distinguish between the two. It was widely assumed that yet again Canada was paying homage to the Führer. The COC report on the Berlin Olympics discreetly avoided any direct reference to the Canadian salute debacle preferring, in the absence of comment on the Canadian salute, to point out instead that the French team gave not the Olympic salute, but an unambiguous Nazi salute and, as a result, received a tumultuous ovation from the stadium crowd in return.[61]

As the lengthy Parade of the Nations concluded, the nearly 5,000 Olympians filling the sports field listened as the foundational words of de Coubertin came booming out over the speaker system. "The important thing in the Olympic Games is not winning, but taking part. The essential thing in life is not conquering, but fighting well." Hitler, who had somewhat of a different notion of conquering, then stepped forward to officially declare the Games open. In quick succession, the white five-ring Olympic flag was raised, 30,000 white pigeons were released as a symbol of peace, and the orchestra began playing Richard Strauss' "Olympic Hymn" as a lone runner, a model of Aryan manhood, entered the stadium carrying aloft the Olympic torch. He ran past Hitler's box and up a set of stairs to an Olympic altar and ignited the Olympic flame contained in a large copper bowl. The Olympic flame now ablaze, a German weightlifter stepped forward. In the name of all the assembled Olympians, he swore the Olympic Oath to participate in the Games in "the true spirit of sportsmanship for the honor of our country and for the glory of sport." The Olympics now officially opened, the crowd cheered as the dignitaries left the "Loges of Honour" and the Olympic teams filed out of the stadium to Schiller's "Ode to Joy."

The Germans planned the opening to be an exhilaratingly awe-inspiring event and they succeeded. It was, according to one Canadian team member, a sight "never to be forgotten."[62] A Canadian dancer observed that "competitors of all nations experienced the same sensations in their throats and up and down their spines during the tense moments when the cheers from 100,000 throats were heard in the splendid arena." But thrilling though the opening ceremonies were, with the long Parade of the Nations, standing in the playing field all that time without a break was tiring. The same dancer recalled that "if it had not been for the nice Mexican boys who threw us packages of biscuits from their line next to ours, we wonder if we would have been able to sing the 'Maple Leaf' so cheerfully as we were leaving the Reichsportsfeld, overlooking so optimistically the stiffness in our knees which was the result of standing in the wet grass for five hours."[63] The COC Olympic report hailed the Olympic opening pageant as a "miracle of organization and synchronization, and very impressive."[64] Many in the stands would agree. Among them were Albertans Elizabeth Fairfield and her husband, who were in Germany to participate in an international agricultural congress. She declared the Olympic opening "more impressive than one could ever describe."[65]

Races and Racism

The next morning began two weeks of athletic and sports competitions spread across a number of sporting venues. But of the thousands of athletes at the Games, one athlete came to command crowd attention in the Olympic Stadium and dominate popular memory of the Nazi Olympics: American track and field star Jesse Owens. Owens, one of ten Blacks on the sixty-six-person American track and field team, participated in four track and field events and took home four gold medals (the 100-metre, the long jump, the 200-metre, and the 400-metre relay race). In the process, he also broke two Olympic records. But it was not just Owens's athletic achievements that made his name a household word. It was the symbolic meaning many attributed to his achievements. By winning four gold medals at the Nazi Olympics, Owens is often celebrated for delivering a crushing blow to Nazi hopes that their Games would validate their claims of Aryan racial superiority, and Owens did so as Hitler and his henchmen looked on. It has even been suggested that Owens's personal goal in going to the Olympics was to challenge Nazi claims to racial superiority. This popular narrative is repeated in the official website of the Jesse Owens Trust that today claims licensing rights to Owens's name and image:

Jesse entered the 1936 Olympics, which were held in Nazi Germany amidst the belief by Hitler that the Games would support his belief that the German "Aryan" people were the dominant race. Jesse had different plans, as he became the first American track & field athlete to win four gold medals in a single Olympiad. This remarkable achievement stood unequaled until the 1984 Olympic Games in Los Angeles, when American Carl Lewis matched Jesse's feat. Although others have gone on to win more gold medals than Jesse, he remains the best remembered Olympic athlete because he achieved what no Olympian before or since has accomplished. During a time of deep-rooted segregation, he not only discredited Hitler's master race theory, but also affirmed that individual excellence, rather than race or national origin, distinguishes one man from another.[66]

But as is often the case, there is a wide gulf between comforting myth and hard-nosed reality. There is no evidence that Owens set out to puncture Nazi racial dogma. What is more, a widely circulated and complementary story holds that Hitler was so appalled at seeing a Black man win the prestigious 100-metre race, Owens's first gold medal, that the Führer deliberately left "Loges of Honour" rather than have to personally congratulate Owens. This too is false. Whatever Hitler thought of Owens's medal win, after the first day of competition, the Führer was not about to publicly shake hands with Owens or any other medal winner, white or black, German or non-German. During the first day of competition Hitler had personally congratulated several medal winners, but that evening, the head of the IOC admonished Hitler that Olympic protocol demanded he treat all Olympic competitors equally. Either Hitler would congratulate each and every Olympic medal winner or none. Hitler chose to congratulate none. That included Owens, who won his first gold medal on the second day of the Games.[67]

What is more, Owens did not regard himself or other Black athletes as mistreated by Hitler or the German people. Rather, he claimed, Roosevelt and the American people mistreated him. In the years that followed the Nazi Olympics, Owens let it be known that he encountered no discrimination when riding public transportation or eating in restaurants in Berlin. The United States was something else again. He repeatedly complained about being subject to Jim Crow laws in the American South and often being denied service in northern hotels and restaurants. In its obituary for Owens, who died in Tucson, Arizona, on 1 April 1980, the *New York Times* observed that, for all the post-Olympic hoopla that followed Owens's four gold medals, including a ticker-tape parade up Broadway on his return, Owens knew that winning gold did not make him any less Black. "When I came back to my native country, after all the stories about Hitler and his snub," Owens noted, "I came

back to my native country and I couldn't ride in the front of the bus ...
I had to go to the back door. I couldn't live where I wanted." Just as he
was not invited to shake hands with Hitler, he was not invited to the
White House to shake hands with the president.[68]

Ironically, if Owens was victim of American racism, he was also
unwittingly party to what many regard an egregious antisemitic incident internal to the American Olympic track and field team. Owens,
who won his fourth gold medal in the 400-metre relay, was originally not scheduled to run that race. He was one of two last-minute
substitutions in the relay after two American-Jewish members of the
four-person relay crew, Marty Glickman and Sam Stoller, were unex-
pectedly dropped from the race the day before their event, even though
the Americans were odds-on favourites to take the gold. It has even
been argued by some that the two Jews were benched precisely because
they would win the gold. Glickman, for one, argued that he and Stoller
were shuffled aside because American Olympic officials, led by Avery
Brundage, were determined not to offend Hitler by having him witness
two American Jews stand on the Olympic podium and receive gold
medals, a charge Brundage dismissed as absurd.[69]

If Glickman was correct, one might wonder why Hitler would be any
more offended at Jews winning gold medals than he would be at Blacks
taking home still more gold medals. Perhaps it is because Nazis had a
racially acceptable explanation for why Black athletes could excel in
track and field and Jews not. Hitler and the Nazis regarded those of
African lineage as more biologically and intellectually primitive, closer
to the animals of the jungle than were whites and thereby, of necessity,
endowed with physical attributes adaptable to the demands of life in
the wild. Accordingly, like animals in the wild, it was natural to Nazis
that Blacks should be able to outrun and outjump whites. While many
in the American press hailed Owens's athletic achievements for both
the boost it gave the American medal count and the drubbing it gave
Nazi claims of Aryan racial superiority, the Nazi press dismissed the
American Olympic medal count as courtesy of the American team's
"black auxiliaries." Goebbels' newspaper, *Der Angriff*, grumbled that
"if the Americans had not enlisted their black auxiliary forces, it would
have been a poor outlook for them."[70] An official in the Nazi Foreign
Ministry reportedly went even further. He complained that Americans bringing "non-humans, like Owens and other Negro athletes," to
Berlin to compete against white athletes was tantamount to American
cheating.[71]

For Hitler and the Nazis, Jewish successes in track and field, unlike that of Blacks, were not so easily explained away. Jews prospered not through animal strength but through unbridled satanic cunning. Negating previous Jewish achievements in sport and athletics, Jews were commonly caricatured by the Nazi propaganda machine as physically weak and repulsive bogeymen – short, fat, beady-eyed, round-shouldered, and hook-nosed. They were hardly fit competition for the fraternity of strong white Olympic combatants. As a result, if Black athletic success validated Nazi racial theory, any comparable Jewish success served to undermine it.[72]

While Glickman and Stoller did not compete for an Olympic medal, the German Helene Mayer did. Mayer, a champion fencer born to a Jewish father and non-Jewish mother, was a *Mischling*, a person of mixed blood under the Nuremberg Laws and, therefore, stripped of her German citizenship. In 1936 Mayer was studying and training in California when German Olympic authorities "invited" her to compete with the German Olympic team. She was invited to join the German Olympic team precisely because of her lineage. Warned that their Aryan-only policy was fanning the Olympic boycott flames, the German Olympic Committee needed Mayer or someone like her on the German team to mollify mounting international, and particularly American, protests that German racial policy was applied in the selection of German Olympic athletes. Charles Sherrill of the American Olympic Committee quietly pleaded this point with Hitler. And it worked. Once Mayer, a non-Aryan, agreed to join the team, Sherrill and Brundage were quick to trumpet the German action as proof that selection of the German Olympic team was in accord with the Olympic rules and the spirit of the Olympic Creed. And Mayer played her part well. She won the silver in women's individual fencing. One of the most dramatic images from the Nazi Olympics shows Mayer standing on the Olympic medal podium, her arm extended in a straight-armed Nazi salute.[73]

Mayer's silver added to the German medal count – eighty-nine medals, thirty-three of them gold. The Americans stood next and took fifty-six medals, twenty-four of them gold. For Hitler the Olympics were a triumph, in no way undercut by any medals that Black athletes took home. That American Blacks took home medals was not, he believed, to the shame of Germany. It was to the shame of the United States. And so pleased was Hitler with the Olympic performance of German athletes that at a celebratory gathering "for the fatherland's athletes," the *Toronto Daily Star* reported that Hitler awarded every German Olympic athlete a half-year holiday paid for by major German industrial firms "solicited to sponsor and finance one entrant each."[74]

Canadian Athletes

Popular memory recalls the pageantry of the Nazi Olympic opening, Jesse Owens's four gold medals, the disappointment of Glickman and Stoller at being bumped from their event, and the image of Mayer on the Olympic podium, arm extended in the Nazi salute. But what of Canadian impressions of the Nazi Games? Was there public apprehension among Canadians of the larger propaganda context within which the Games were taking place? In the main, Canadian observers were positively taken with the new Germany. But there were exceptions. Halton at the *Toronto Daily Star* continued to regard the Berlin Olympics as well-staged theatre designed to draw the world's attention away from the coming Nazi main event. Behind a Nazi facade of sportsmanship, he claimed, Germany was a predatory state, "a nation on the march and actually seeking trouble."[75] But Canadian athletes, officials, and Olympic visitors were so blinded by Olympic glitter that they could not or would not see the veneer of Nazi civility for what is was – camouflage for a nation that pulsed with racism, aggressive nationalism, and a marshal spirit that would soon be tested. On Olympic opening day, as Canadian team members turned out smartly in their crimson blazers, Halton scorned the entire German Olympic enterprise as an exercise in ideological piety rather than any celebration of life:

> Though Berlin looks like one vast carnival, holiness prevails rather than gaiety. Something like religious ecstasy rather than gay, sporting enthusiasm, is the spirit abroad here to-day. It is impossible to get out of earshot of innumerable loudspeakers which pour hymns, marches and solemnly rapturous orations into our ears. The announcers all speak in that dramatic but holy clerical voice as if the Deity were hiding nearby in one of the clouds which threaten to rain on us any minute.

The Canadian Olympic team had reason to hope the deity might indeed be hovering about the Olympic Stadium. The team could use all the divine inspiration it could get. Much as the Canadians looked sharp in their Olympic uniforms, barring a miracle, the vast majority of the Canadian team was destined to end up in the "also ran" column. The Germans, Americans, and Japanese were touted to dominate the final medal count. Canadian Olympic Committee members quietly agreed. Writing about Canada's thin medal chances, a tongue-in-cheek Halton noted, "Canada's contenders are calm, smiling, hopeful as the curtain rings up on history's most ballyhooed Olympiad. 'I won't be surprised,' said P.J. Mulqueen, 'if we win something.' Nor will he be surprised if we don't. Nothing seems to surprise Mr. Mulqueen." Sammy Richardson, a member of Canada's Olympic relay team was a tad more optimistic than Mulqueen. "Sure we'll win something," said Richardson. "Now we're here and feeling so good, I know we'll win something. Maybe we'll win the aesthetic dancing. Maybe we'll even win the running broad jump." Canadian Olympic swimmer Phyllis Dewar, assessing the Canadian swim team's medal chances, suggested Canada's best hope was for the competitors not to show up. She told Halton, "We might win the women's swimming if there were no Americans or Dutch swimmers here."[76] Unfortunately for the Canadian Olympic team, the Americans and Dutch did not get lost on their way to the swimming pool.

Of course, there were notable Canadian performances that rescued Canada from a complete medal drought. Canoeing proved a Canadian highlight. A group of eight Canadian paddlers participated in the 1936 Olympic Games, the first time canoeing was listed as an official Olympic sport. And Canadians did well, winning three medals including a gold won by Frank Amyot in the single-man sprint C-1 1,000-metre race. Amyot, somewhat of a guardian angel to the other paddlers – taking care of the team's luggage, watching over meals, and organizing training sessions – paid his own way to the Berlin Games after being turned down for financial assistance by the COC, much to the later embarrassment of the Canadian Olympic organizers.[77] His gold medal, the only Canadian gold at the 1936 Games, occasioned a telegram of congratulations from Prime Minister Mackenzie King to which Amyot graciously replied "it has been a source of great satisfaction to me to have been able to bring in a first for Canada."[78] The paddlers also took home a silver and a bronze. Demonstrating some modesty at his team's medal wins, paddler Harvey Charters allowed that "considering the style of boats used, to which we were not accustomed, and the strong competition, we did remarkably well."[79]

Another exception to an otherwise disappointing Canadian medal count was the silver taken by Windsor's John Loaring. Loaring's Olympic achievement is a tale of personal victory against great physical challenges. As a teen Loaring was afflicted with rheumatic fever and his family doctor told him he would never again be strong enough to participate in sports. Defying his doctor's predictions, Loaring not only became an athlete, he became a champion runner and went to the Berlin Olympics as a "400-trippler," chosen to compete in three events – the 4x400-metre run, the 400-metre relay and the 400-metre hurdle. He made the finals in all three events. He had run only one previous 400-metre hurdle in his life, "but that run qualified him for the Olympic trip." The day after his twenty-first birthday Loaring stood on the Olympic podium after "he ran and jumped like a hare" and accepted a silver medal in the hurdles.[80] It has also been claimed that he would also have won a bronze in the 4x400-metre relay had Canadian Olympic officials lodged a formal protest against an obvious American fault during the race. The Canadians declined to protest and Canada was assigned a fourth-place finish. The Americans took home the bronze.[81]

Loaring's hometown of Windsor was also home to Canada's silver medal-winning basketball team, the Windsor V-8s. Unlike the European teams entered in the Olympic basketball tournament, the Canadians were accustomed to playing on a wooden indoor court. The Canadians arrived at the basketball venue to discover they were to play on a converted outdoor clay tennis court marked off with chalk lines. There were also several other surprises for the Canadian team. Unlike the Spalding basketballs the Canadians were used to playing with (two of which went into the Atlantic during the Canadian team's one-and-only shipboard practice game), the official ball of the 1936 Olympic Games was of German manufacture, a Berg. It looked like a soccer ball and wasn't much heavier than a volleyball. It tended to wobble when it was passed and, as players soon learned, it took odd and unpredictable bounces when dribbled.

The rules approved for this first-ever Olympic basketball tournament were also not what the Canadians were used to. For example, the twenty-three participating teams were only allowed to suit up seven players each per game. The American team, overwhelmingly favoured to win the gold, was composed of fourteen members: seven from a Hollywood, California, team – the Universal Pictures team – and six players from the McPherson Globe Refiners supplemented by an added collegian. Adhering to the "seven rule," the Americans decided to rotate game-to-game between the two squads. The Canadians played differently. They also brought fourteen players to Berlin, but decided to rotate only through ten players. As a result, four of the Canadians never got onto the court.

While the Canadian players were not entirely comfortable with the conditions of play, spectators were not all that comfortable watching the games. Although the Olympic Stadium could seat more than 100,000, the outdoor basketball court was not even supplied with bleachers. Instead the Germans erected several wooden platforms where spectators could stand if they were so inclined. Any spillover spectators were forced to stake out a spot to stand or sit on the grass. Some spectators began to cart their own chairs to games.

Canadians did well in the round-robin elimination tournament. The plucky Canadians went undefeated in games against Brazil, Latvia, Switzerland, Uruguay, and Poland. The much-favoured Americans had a free ride in their first scheduled game. Spain, suddenly engulfed in civil war, did not send a team to Berlin. The Americans then went on to win lopsided victories over Estonia, the Philippines, and Mexico. The final game would see the two undefeated North American teams face one another for the Olympic gold.

The American-Canadian game turned out to be memorable, not for the quality of play but for the weather. During the second week of the Olympic Games, the skies above Berlin turned grey and rainy. The gold medal basketball game was twice postponed because of rain. But with only two days left before the Olympic closing ceremony, German Olympic officials ruled there could be no more delays. The game had to be played rain or no rain. In the end it was rainy, windy, and unseasonably cold on 14 August when the two teams lined up for the opening jump. Many in the crowd of some 2,000 who gathered around the court to watch the game – including James Naismith, the "Father of Basketball" – wore heavy coats and huddled under umbrellas. One Canadian athlete brought a movie camera to the game, but there was not much to see except dark skies, a brief view of the scoreboard with its lopsided halftime score, and teams trying to stay warm and dry for their time on the court.[82] And what a court it was. The surface was awash with puddles that quickly got broader and deeper as the players churned up the clay. As the rain continued, the court eventually resembled nothing more than a muddy stew. Dribbling became impossible. Players, often ankle deep in the muck, could only pass forward to advance the ball up the court. The game soon had the feel of slapstick comedy: "On the opening play, an American player raced down the court, caught a pass as his feet went from under him and completed the last 15 or 20 feet to the basket sliding on the seat of his shorts, water spraying out from both sides."[83]

With control of the unpredictable German-made ball difficult at the best of times – and the drenched gold medal match was hardly the best of times – the score remained low. At half-time the American team, with the advantage of greater height on their side, still only managed to put fifteen points on the scoreboard while the Canadians managed to score four points. Things did not get any better in the second half. As the rain continued, the two teams, soaked to the skin and increasingly tired, barely managed to score another eight points between them. When the final whistle blew, the Americans had a 19–8 lead. An American player lamented over the gold medal game: "A comedy of errors and unfortunate circumstances had combined to make a sandlot affair of what should have been the greatest basketball tournament ever."[84]

The Americans took the gold but the Canadians took the ball. According to Jim Stewart, son of Ford V-8 team member Jimmy Stewart, at the final whistle, with the victorious Americans thumping one another on the back, Stewart discreetly scooped up the mud-covered game ball. He strolled over to his wife, sitting on the sidelines with a Hudson's Bay blanket across her knees to ward off the damp. "He shoved it under the blanket and said, 'Hold on to that.'" The game ball remains a family keepsake.[85] Stewart also stood on the Olympic platform to collect his Olympic silver medal. But not all the team members were so lucky; the German Olympic Committee only minted seven each of gold, silver, and bronze medals for basketball. As a result, Naismith, given the honour of awarding the medals, had only enough medals to hand to the seven players who suited up for the final game. The other team members were out of luck.[86]

The Canadians also took home bronze medals in five events. In addition to the one in canoeing, they won medals in the women's 4x100-metre relay, the women's 80-metre hurdle, men's freestyle welterweight wrestling, and the men's 800-metre race. The 800-metre bronze was taken by Phil Edwards, dubbed "The Man of Bronze" after winning a total of five bronze medals during three consecutive Olympic games, the last in Berlin. Edwards was born in Georgetown, British Guyana. His father, a wealthy magistrate, was his first running coach. In 1926 Edwards moved to the United States where he enrolled in New York University and continued to compete in amateur running events. As a non-American, Edwards was disqualified from trying out for the 1928 American Olympic team. But, in 1927, Canadian Bobby Robinson, a sports reporter for the *Hamilton Spectator* and manager of Canada's 1928 Olympic track and field team, approached Edwards and invited him to come to Canada where, although Black, as a British subject he could quickly gain Canadian status and join the Canadian Olympic track and field team. Edwards agreed and, armed with a degree from NYU, enrolled in medicine at McGill University where he was soon a mainstay of McGill's track and field team. Edwards went to Amsterdam as part of the 1928 Canadian Olympic team and brought home a bronze in the 4x400-metre relay, the first time a Black athlete had ever won an Olympic medal for Canada. Edwards returned to the Olympics as a member of the 1932 Canadian Olympic team. He participated in three events – the 800-metre, the 1500-metre, and 4x400-metre relay – and won a bronze in each.

In 1936, recently graduated in medicine from McGill, Edwards was again off to the Olympics. This time his teammates voted him captain of the Canadian track and field team. Edwards ran the 800-metre race and made it to the final where he initially held the lead, but in a see-saw battle, he eventually gave way to the gold medal winner, American John Woodruff, and, at the last second, allowed Italian Mario Lanzi to overtake and win the silver.

Much like Jesse Owens, Edwards stood out as a Black athlete competing in the Nazi Olympics. But for all the attention this brought Edwards, Owens, and the other Black athletes at the Games, Edwards, like Owens, claimed to have experienced no overt racial hostility directed at him during the Games. Ironically, it was after the Games while in London on the return leg of the Canadian team's visit that Edwards encountered racism. When the team checked in at their London hotel, several hotel patrons were said to have complained to hotel management that they were uncomfortable staying in the same hotel as a Black man. When Edwards was asked to give up his reservation, Canadian team officials, with full team backing, decided that if Edwards were forced to leave, the entire team would also pack up and leave. A female Canadian fencer, Cathleen Hughes-Hallett, is quoted as summing up the Canadian team response. "If this hotel is too good for Phil Edwards," she said, "it's too good for me."[87] Later that same year Edwards became the first-ever recipient of the Lou Marsh Trophy, awarded annually to the outstanding Canadian athlete of the year, amateur or professional.

A Canadian Cabinet Minister in Germany

While Canadian athletes were hustling for medals, a Canadian cabinet minister was doing a little hustling of his own. Coincidental with the summer Olympic Games, the Canadian minister of trade, William Daum Euler, accompanied by several members of his staff, visited Berlin for trade talks with the Germans. Euler, a child of German immigrants to Canada and a former German-speaking mayor of Kitchener, Ontario, hoped to put an end to Canada's negative trade deficit with Germany. In so doing he was certainly no friend of the call by the Jewish community and the left for a Canadian boycott of German goods and services. Rather than curtail trade, the minister came to lobby for an increase in German imports of Canadian "wheat flour, lumber, newsprint, smoked salmon and eels."[88] In return he dangled the possibility of an increase in Canadian imports of "German machinery and manufactured articles." According to both German and Canadian spokespersons, the bilateral trade talks got off to a good start. Negotiation of a formal trade agreement was a distinct possibly.

Hitler, mindful of the damage any international boycott of German goods would do to the German economy recovery, was pleased to lend support to the trade talks. Even though he was then up to the top of his jackboots in dignitaries visiting Berlin for the Olympics, Hitler honoured Euler with a private audience. Speaking to the *Toronto Daily Star* following his meeting with the German Führer, Euler seemed genuinely taken with Hitler's frankness:

> I talked to Reichsführer Hitler for more than half an hour ... Hitler allowed me to ask him numerous questions about the international situation. He answered for me very carefully and with reasoned argument. He expressed an earnest desire for peace and described his fear of bolshevism. He also spoke of the possibility of developing trade with Canada and of Germany's difficulties in regard to raw materials, having no colonies of her own.[89]

Euler came away from the meeting convinced that Hitler wore the face of the future. In a subsequent press interview the minister gushed that Hitler "impressed me with his sincerity and earnestness. He told me 'we must have peace; we can't afford to go to war.' I believe him ... I believe the Germans are behind Hitler almost to a man."[90] Of course, Euler was not in Germany for peace talks or even for the Olympics. He was there to talk trade. But even though Euler did not wear a crimson blazer, he knew full well the importance with which Hitler regarded these Olympic Games. Had Canada not sent a team to the Olympics, bilateral trade talks with Nazi Germany would have been a non-starter and the minister would not likely have been granted an audience with

Hitler. The Canadian government may have been at a distance from the workings of the Amateur Athletic Union of Canada and its Canadian Olympic Committee, but it was certainly pleased to ride on Canadian Olympic coat-tails straight into the Führer's office.

In this regard it has been suggested that Euler was more than just taken with the Nazi leader. According to noted author Pierre Berton, after returning to Canada from Germany, Euler flirted with the Nazi-controlled German Unity League in Kitchener.

> The German Unity League was a union of all the Nazi organizations, with branches in most provinces. It was formed for the purpose of arranging the annual German Days in order to gain control of other non-political organizations and disseminate Nazi propaganda [among those of German heritage in Canada]. In 1937 the league managed to secure the Minister or Trade and Commerce and M.P. for Waterloo North, the Hon. William Daum Euler, as guest speaker at the Nazi mass meeting during Kitchener's German Days. Euler agreed with other speakers who deprecated stories and articles critical of Germany, "which instead of healing sores (tend) to keep up hatreds." The minister declared that he sometimes thought that the publication of such propaganda should be made a criminal offence for newspapers. In a town whose citizens have strong German ties, Euler was a good catch for the League.[91]

But Berton's suggestion that Euler was soft on the Nazis would seem a gross overstatement. No doubt the German-Canadian Nazi sympathizers attempted to use German Days to drum up Canadian *Volksdeutsche* support in the Kitchener area, but historians also agree that Nazi appeals to German nationalist sentiment largely fell on deaf ears, especially in more urban and industrial eastern Canada, including the Kitchener-Waterloo area where ethnic Germans were generally "integrated or assimilated into the non-German society in which they lived." As a result, Euler's attendance at carnival-like German Day was likely more an opportunity at political glad-handing and baby-kissing, much as a local politician might today attend Oktoberfest, than it was any effort to tap into any constituent pro-Nazi sentiment.[92]

"Knightly Canadian Gesture"

Nonetheless, politicking does not preclude the conclusion that in voicing admiration for Hitler, Euler demonstrated great naivety about Hitler's vision for Germany. If it does, Euler was not alone. The same might also be said of the Canadian Olympic Committee in Berlin. Four days into Olympic competition a member of Euler's staff accompanied Mulqueen and several other Canadian and German Olympic dignitaries on what the 1936 report of the Canadian Olympic Committee described as a "Knightly Canadian Gesture." The ad hoc delegation, which also included J.G. Merrick, Canadian member of the International Olympic Committee, Werner Haag, Germany's Olympic representative in Canada, and Lieutenant Heinrich, German military attaché of the Canadian Olympic team, assembled at the Luftwaffe Headquarters in Berlin. With great ceremony, the delegation presented General Erhard Milch, deputy to Hermann Goering, Luftwaffe commander-in-chief, a rudder fragment from the airplane piloted by twenty-five year old Manfred von Richthofen, the Red Baron, shot down in combat on 21 April 1918.[93]

Exactly who shot down von Richthofen is still a matter of historical dispute. Just before he was hit by a single bullet and crashed, the German air ace, flying his legendary bright red Fokker, was in active combat against Canadian fliers' second lieutenant, Wilfred "Wop" May, and Captain Arthur R. Brown over the Somme River. Flying low, von Richthofen was also the subject of ground fire from Australian gunners who had been watching the dog fight in the sky above them. Whether the Canadian fliers downed the German pilot or, as is more likely, the Australian gunners on the ground hit him, it was Australian soldiers who first reached the downed plane and its mortally wounded pilot. When they realized the pilot was the legendary Red Baron, the Australians began cannibalizing the Fokker for souvenirs.[94]

But the Australians did not overlook the Canadian airmen who challenged the Red Baron. They sought out and presented a fragment of the Red Baron's rudder to Lieutenant May who took it back to Canada with him. As Mulqueen ceremoniously explained to General Milch, May delivered the fragment to the COC with the expressed wish "that on the occasion of the XIth Olympic Games in Berlin this fragment be handed over [to the Luftwaffe] as a sign of the good feeling, friendliness and esteem of the Canadian Olympic team and the Canadian people." Milch responded in kind. He spoke of the high regard with which the German Air Force regarded "the fair fighting methods of their Canadian opponents during the war," and accepted the rudder fragment as symbolic "proof of the friendly feeling on the part of the Canadian people." Milch also read aloud a cable sent in gratitude by General Goering to Wilfred May:

With the German Air Force and the whole German people I send you my sincere thanks for the fragment of Richthofen's aeroplane which was handed over here today by the President of the Canadian Olympic Committee. In the name of my flying comrade and all my compatriots, I reciprocate the friendly feelings which have been expressed, and greet you in comradeship.[95]

Ten days later, on 16 August, the Canadian athletes again marched into the Olympic Stadium, this time intermingling with teams from other countries rather than marching separate from other national teams. With great ceremony the Olympic flame was extinguished and the 1936 Olympics declared over. As the Germans celebrated their medal victory and many Americans cheered Owens's accomplishments, Canadian athletes consoled themselves with their nine medals, ranking Canada seventeenth among the Olympic teams. But there were two more medals taken back to Canada. "At the conclusion of the Games, Canadian Olympic Committee President Mulqueen and Canadian Chef de Mission S.R. Manson were honoured, along with Olympic officials from all other nations, by being invested with the German Order of Olympia-*Ehrenzeichen*, the first decoration to be created in Germany since the Republic." And if there were those who found fault with the quality of the Canadian performance, the COC sounded no sour note. Moreover, the COC's Olympic report heaped special praise on their German hosts even as it had words for "critics in Canada." As far as the Canadian Olympic Committee was concerned, it was "satisfied that the representative which [*sic*] Canada sent to Berlin worthily maintained the highest Olympic ideals and traditions, and their country's honour."[96] Three years later, in September 1939, that honour would be tested again as Canada declared war on its one-time Olympic host.

Chapter Seven

Conclusion

On 16 August, as night descended on Berlin, the 1936 Olympics officially ended. Looking back at the two-week-long event, the 148-page report of the Canadian Olympic Committee hailed the Berlin Olympics as far more than just games. Of course the 1936 Olympics were the world's premier athletic competition. But, most significantly, they were harbingers of international goodwill and harmony between nations:

> To most people present at the Games the day of the closing ceremony came only too soon. This ceremony – always most solemn and impressive – was in many respects a converse of the opening ceremony. The flags around the Stadium were drawn slowly down, the Olympic flame was slowly extinguished and the Olympic flag handed over by Mr. W.M. Garland, representing Los Angeles, to the Mayor of Berlin, for safe custody in that City until the next Olympiad. At the final parade the flags were carried by representatives of the different countries. These flags were crowned with laurel wreaths and the final anthems played, the Stadium gradually growing darker and darker until only the three flags of the "Victory flag poles" remained in light: in the centre the flag of Ancient Greece – home of the Olympic Games – on the left the flag of Germany – the host of the XIth Olympiad – and on the right the flag of Japan – where the next Games will be held. And so what was surely one of the greatest Sports Festivals of all times came to an end, having made its magnificent contribution toward a fitter youth and more peaceful international relationships.[1]

But while the COC heralded the Nazi Olympics as a portent of international fellowship, the Nazis were busy making a mockery of that claim. Rather than seeking peaceful relations with its neighbours, the Nazis were pushing ahead with an aggressive policy of rearmament and, on the home front, pressing ahead with legalized persecutions of minorities and political opponents. None of this was secret. Even as preparations for the 1936 Olympics were ongoing, the Canadian press reported on the darker side of the German state, including the impact of the Nuremberg Laws and the systematic exclusion of Jews from Nazi sport. How then could the COC sing the praises of the Olympic organizers? Were COC members so naively taken in by Nazi propaganda they could remain blind to what others saw so clearly? Or did COC members just not want to see, not want to believe ill of their hosts?

And what fine hosts they were. They accorded Canadian Olympic officials VIP status in Berlin and the Canadians revelled in it. Canada might not have been on the A-list of world powers or even Olympic gold-medal nations, but Canadian Olympic officials were made to feel like dignitaries and invited to hobnob with Olympic muckety-mucks from around the world. Some invitations had to be declined "through press of official duties," but prestige events demanded attendance. Black-suited Canadian officials felt honoured to rub shoulders with the rich and the royal at a German state dinner for the International Olympic Committee, presidents of national Olympic committees, "distinguished military and naval officers," and various other worthies. The COC also turned out for a dinner celebrating the 800 members of the international press covering the Olympics and yet again at a function hosted by the British ambassador for athletes and officials from British Empire teams. Of course, not to be forgotten, at the close of the Olympics there was the state reception and formal investiture of the Canadian Olympic *chef de mission* and COC chairman J.P. Mulqueen, alongside ranking officials from other Olympic participating countries, into the newly formed German Order of Olympia-*Ehrenzeichen*.[2]

The COC's public praise for their Nazi hosts stood in sharp contrast to the low regard with which opponents of Canada's Olympic participation – mostly Jews and those on the left – were held. As guardians of Canada's Olympic aspirations, the COC held itself out to be engaged in a nation-building exercise, inviting pride in Canada's athletic achievement at the highest level. In this regard, COC members had little time or sympathy for those Olympic naysayers who would undermine the committee's efforts for their own narrow parochial interests. Warnings by Olympic boycott advocates about racism in selecting the German Olympic team, or using the Olympics as a Nazi propaganda vehicle to further entrench the regime or boost its image abroad, made no difference. As holder of the Olympic franchise in Canada, the COC was hell-bent on Canada participating in the Olympics, no matter what. That was the COC's mandate. That is what the COC was determined to make happen. That is what COC members proclaimed was best for Canada.

If that meant the COC had to be wilfully blind to what was going on in Germany and remain deaf to all anti-Olympic protests, so be it. Certainly in elite Canadian circles of the mid-1930s there were no points to be lost in disregarding what the core constituency of anti-Olympic protest, the left and the Jews, wanted. They might protest loudly – although, at one point, Mulqueen publicly declared that no hint of anti-Olympic protest had reached his committee's ears – but they were marginal to mainstream political discourse. In any event, Canada's British connection – whether as an excuse or as a matter of conviction – certainly trumped Jewish and left-wing interests. Once Britain announced it was going to Germany, Canada was going, too. Mulqueen, who had previously pledged to welcome an open discussion of Canadian Olympic participation, promptly wrapped himself in the Canadian red ensign and declared that Canadians should take pride at seeing their athletes "march proudly to do battle with the rest of the world for the Maple Leaf." According to the COC, that is exactly what Canadian Olympians did.[3]

Other Olympic stakeholders also felt pride. As the curtain came down on two weeks of Olympic events, the International Olympic Committee looked back at Berlin with a mixture of satisfaction and relief. The IOC, ever defensive of the Olympic brand and the committee's exalted status as the international overlord of sport, had stared down the threatened Olympic boycott without ceding an inch to those who denounced Nazi racism and antisemitism in sport and condemned flagrant Nazi violations of the IOC's own rules on amateurism. What did it matter to the IOC that it had to feign ignorance of what the Nazis were up to? The Nazis put on a good show and the IOC came away from the Nazi Games with their control of the Olympics intact.

For the Nazis, the Olympic Games proved as great a propaganda success as their triumph in the medal count. On the international stage, the Games enabled the Nazis to polish their tarnished image and, temporarily at least, divert world attention from those aspects of Nazi domestic and foreign policy that might otherwise create alarm. It would seem that a world unready to challenge the Nazis – in spite of repeated Nazi provocations and treaty violations – was ready to take comfort in Nazi Olympic pledges of peace and cooperation. And perhaps, many hoped, the Nazis were sincere. Could a nation so open and welcoming to the world really be a racist and militarist threat to the peace of nations?

What of the German domestic front? If the Olympic pomp and pageantry provided the Nazi regime a veneer of international respectability, at least in the short term, then at home the success of the Games and the unprecedented German medal count provided proof positive that Hitler had indeed revived German greatness and helped firm up popular support for the Nazi regime and its policies. As a result of the Olympics, the popular German embrace of Hitler, according to Matthew Halton, was nothing short of a "semi-religious rapture."[4]

Ongoing Boosterism

The Games over, most of the Canadian Olympic team set off for home. In fact, some left Berlin before the Games ended. In order to "lessen our financial burden," the COC encouraged athletes to return to Canada as soon as their Olympic events were completed. Others, rather than returning directly to Canada, headed off to sporting meets in Europe or to "the British Empire vs. U.S.A. games, which were held in London prior to the largest groups [of athletes] sailing for home."[5]

A group of twelve athletes who left Berlin for Canada before the end of the Olympics arrived in Montreal aboard the *Duchess of York* on 21 August. Interviewed by reporters, the athletes griped a little about the quality of officiating at the Games but overall, they agreed that "everything was swell."[6] Ottawa cyclist George Turner, personally disappointed at his showing, was representative of many on the Canadian Olympic team. In his words, the Nazi Olympics were "the most thrilling spectacle I have ever seen."[7] And no doubt they were. Jews and the left might denounce National Socialism and challenge the morality of Germany hosting the Games, but Turner was indifferent to all that. He and his Olympic teammates had earned the right to represent Canada at the world's premier sporting event. That, in and of itself, was an honour. And once in Berlin, thousands of miles from home, they competed for Canada against the world's best and in front of tens of thousands of spectators, including not just Hitler and many in his inner circle, but also visiting dignitaries and sports enthusiasts from around the world. Yes, it was a thrill for Turner and the others who wore the crimson blazer. Yes, he was proud to have gone. No, Canadian athletes had nothing to apologize for. In that, Turner was right.

Turner and his teammates acknowledged that they had not done well in the medal count. For the most part, however, the Canadian press post-mortem on the team's Olympic performance was notably gentle, offering up every manner of excuse to explain away Canada's lacklustre showing or arguing that Canada did well punching above its weight class. A mid-Olympics *Toronto Globe* editorial entitled "Good Work! Olympics" cautioned readers to always judge Canadian results in the larger Olympic context. As the newspaper explained, many Olympic athletes came from countries with much larger populations than Canada "and some of them [countries] lay far greater stress on physical achievement and prowess in sport." But, the *Globe* argued, if population size were factored into the awarding of Olympic medals, Canada would come second only to Finland, "an amazing little country with only three and a half million people."[8]

At the close of the Games, Dunc MacDonald, sports columnist for the *Montreal Gazette*, rhetorically asked, "Was it worth sending a Canadian team to the Olympics?" His answer was "yes." To say otherwise, he protested, "is consistent neither with the aims of the Olympics nor the meaning of true sportsmanship." Winning, he urged, is less important than doing your best; being defeated by someone better is not a disgrace if you did your best. The Canadians did just that. "And it would be downright stupid not to remember that, after all, there can be only one winner in every race." And using that yardstick, Canadians, he contended, did not do so badly.[9] The *Globe* agreed. Canadians should be proud of their team: "We know they gave their best."

So did Germany. Its achievement in the medal count and its management of the Games were second to none. Remarkably, the *Globe* also offered sympathetic understanding of German press censorship during the Games:

> Nazi Germany can look back with justifiable pride at these Olympics, the largest and best organized meet of its kind ever held in the world. Germans showed themselves to be perfect hosts. Press copy came under close scrutiny because Germany spent money to advertise the "New Germany" through the medium of Olympic sports. They were just making sure that none of the things written were detrimental.[10]

The Other Side

Canadian press praise for Nazi Germany's organization of the Games did not resonate with the political left in Canada or the organized

Jewish community. The left and the Jewish community had each separately championed an Olympic boycott and came away empty. And in the wake of the Nazi Games they shared none of the enthusiasm for Canada's waving the flag in Berlin, nor did they take comfort in all the platitudes about the Olympics serving the cause of fraternity among peoples. The Olympic competition over, the Olympic athletes and visitors gone home, Jews and the left were convinced a renewed Nazi assault on those the Nazi labelled enemies of the new Germany was coming fast. Mindful of that reality, the obligation to continue to battle against fascism in Canada and abroad continued. Nor did those who had been outspoken in support of an Olympic boycott expend much energy wondering what, if anything, they might have done differently that could have changed history. That was a waste of time. Rather than beating themselves up over the defeat of the Olympic boycott campaign, most, whether on the Canadian left or in the organized Jewish community, quickly turned to other pressing issues. For the left, there was an almost seamless transition from the abortive Olympic boycott campaign to rallying popular support for the anti-fascist republican side in the Spanish Civil War, a war that erupted even as Olympic athletes from around the world were making their way to Berlin. Putting pacifism behind them, many on the left – more comfortable engaging in street-level activism than was the Jewish community – organized the Committee to Aid Spanish Democracy. The new group focused on raising funds to support the republican side in the Spanish Civil War, recruit Canadian volunteers to fight in Spain, and, after May 1937, to enlist in the newly organized Mackenzie-Papineau Battalion.[11]

No doubt most Canadian Jews hoped for a republican victory in Spain, especially as it would represent a humiliating reversal for Hitler. But, unlike the Canadian left, the organized Jewish community did not have the civil war in Spain anywhere near the top of its agenda. The Olympic battle lost, the mainstream Jewish community turned its attention to other concerns, such as the ongoing campaign for an economic boycott of Nazi Germany. On the day before the Olympic Games opened in Berlin, the *Canadian Jewish Review* made an impassioned plea to Canadians to join the economic boycott: "Let us smash Hitler with the collective buying power of the people of the civilized world. Let us show the German nation how Hitler has duped and dishonoured them. And let us show mankind that the moral consciousness of man is a realistic decisive power for justice and good."[12] This appeal, like others of its kind, was met with official silence in Ottawa. At the same time the organized Jewish community continued to implore Ottawa to open Canada's gates to Jewish immigrants and refugees suffering Nazi oppression. As was the case with the economic boycott campaign, appeals to conscience went unheard. Canada's immigration door remained locked to Jews.[13]

If these failed efforts brought home one truth for Jewish leaders, it was the political weakness of the organized Jewish community, a weakness already made abundantly clear by the presence of Canadian athletes in Germany. The Jewish community might be in Canada but, as far as those in positions of power in Canada were concerned, Jews were not really a part of Canada, at least not a part of Canada that those in power need be concerned with. And Jewish leaders were well aware of this. Politically and socially marginalized, Jews were made to feel that they were in Canada by sufferance rather than right. They believed themselves confined to those feeble political tactics – quiet diplomacy, reliance on the goodwill of non-Jewish sympathizers, cap-in-hand appeals to those with access who walked the corridors of power – that had failed to persuade government, the media and, most important of all, Canadian Olympic officials to decline participation in the Nazi Olympics. But if the organized Jewish community could not do more, it dared not do less. The crisis of European Jewry demanded it.

But with rare exception, few in Jewish leadership positions questioned these tactics or reflected on the failure of the Olympic boycott campaign. One of the exceptions was A.B. Bennett, a successful Toronto industrialist and mainstay of the Canadian Jewish Congress. In a post-mortem article on the Olympic Games in the *Jewish Standard*, Bennett, sidestepping the failure of the Jewish community to move the COC, was merciless in his condemnation of the COC and "their journalistic henchmen" as morally vacant. Regarding the Nazi-like salute given by Canadian athletes at the Olympic opening, Bennett found no fault with the young Canadian competitors. They were simply "athletic innocents abroad," doing the bidding of the overlords of the Canadian Olympic enterprise. It was Mulqueen and his "Old Boys" who should not be allowed to slough off responsibility for the ugly Canadian display: "The Canadian managers in their befuddlement seemed to forget that they were members of a liberty-loving democracy and permitted themselves to do gesticulatory service to a system that is abhorrent to the genius of their nation." And, according to Bennett, by choosing in the first instance to participate in the Nazi Games, Canadian Olympic officials proved themselves callously and morally indifferent to the suffering of millions.

Thus when the question of Canadian participation in the Olympics arose, our sporting fraternity shuddered at the suggestion of the possible invasion of their field by extraneous motives of a more or political character. Sportdom has its own laws, and principles of right and wrong, and it is not interested in what goes on in the rest of the world. Thus croaked the chorus of smug sports officials. And the sports writers chimed in with their approval ... Hitlerism, Nazism, concentration camps, the murder of and mutilation of thousands of liberals, labour leaders, Catholics – never mind the Jews – [and] the ravaging of all the decencies and amenities of civilized human society – these things have nothing to do with sport ... They live in their own petty little world. They wallow in its trivialities and picayune jealousies and politics. Beyond them there is that larger arena peopled by Canadians of a nobler stamp who are appreciative of the destiny of Canada as a nation devoted to the cause of humanity, and the pursuit of higher values in life.[14]

Rabbi Maurice Eisendrath was no less scathing. In his sermon on Yom Kippur, the most sacred day on the Jewish calendar that in 1936 fell just one month after the close of the Games in Berlin, the rabbi offered a vision of the future made bleak by the Christian world's unwillingness to deny the Nazis their moment of Olympic victory. This, Eisendrath lamented, proved to be a failure of Olympic proportions. It crushed what he regarded as the last best hope of undercutting the Nazi regime. As a result, Christendom had left the Nazis triumphant, while consigning German Jews to an unimaginable fate. By failing the test of humanity, Eisendrath proclaimed, Christendom had also relegated itself to moral darkness:

But behold the bitter, crushing disappointment. All the torture and terror, the madness and murder of Hitlerism was answered by well-nigh every Christian country going gaily and blithely to the Olympics, so that these master propagandists might sell their insidious ideas to hundreds of thousands of gullible and impressionable youth and maidens and thus spread their pagan and poisonous doctrines to the four corners of the earth with the inevitable consequence that havens of refuge which might have been mercifully opened to the harried and hunted Jew are now flung tightly closed, for as myriads of superficially tourists told me this past summer, after a few days visit to the Nazi Reich: "Now I understand why Germany had to rid herself of the Jews." And what is "destructive and deadly" to one land, must be likewise so in others. Such is the happy fruitage of the Olympic Games as we begin to recognize that what appeared three years ago to be but the darkest hour before the dawn was in reality but the first faint shadow of twilight presaging the deep, dark blackness of a seemingly endless night to come. Nay, the watchmen saw not deeply enough three years ago when calmly they announced the breaking of the day. Those faint glints of grey which they discerned upon the far distant horizon, and which they designated as the sure promise of the day, were but the last flickering rays of the setting sun fast sinking into the gaping sea leaving the world, the world of Israel especially cheerless and cold and lost beneath the glowing, starless sky.[15]

The Prime Minister

Prime Minister of Canada Mackenzie King did not share Eisendrath's apocalyptic vision. Following a 1937 Imperial Conference of Dominion Prime Ministers in London, coinciding with the coronation of George IV, Mackenzie King visited Germany at the invitation of Joachim von Ribbentrop, the German ambassador to Britain. In part, King hoped to build on the 1936 effort by his minister of trade and commerce, William Euler, to spark an increase in German-Canadian trade. King held informal trade talks with German air minister Hermann Goering before moving on to the Hindenburg Palace for a personal audience with Hitler.

King and Hitler seemingly got on well, or so King believed. Their conversation touched on a wide range of topics. When talk turned to German rearmament and German violations of the Treaty of Versailles, Hitler was reassuring of Germany's intentions. He explained to King that the Treaty, rather than warranting security in Europe, had proven a thorn in the side of peace. German abrogation of the Treaty was thus not a belligerent act. Rather, it paved the way to positive bilateral relations between Germany and its neighbours. Accordingly, Hitler insisted, "so far as war is concerned, you need have no fear of war at the instance of Germany. We have no desire for war; our people don't want war, and we don't want war."

If the Canadian prime minister had any qualms about Hitler's sincerity, there is no hint of it in his lengthy diary entry relating his meeting with the Führer. If anything, King seemed taken with Hitler, even commenting on his magnetic charisma. "My sizing up of the man as I sat and talked with him was that he is really one who truly loves his fellow-men, and his country, and would make any sacrifice for their good." King pronounced Hitler "a man of deep sincerity and a genuine patriot."[16]

King likely regarded his meeting with Hitler as the highlight of his Berlin visit, but he also allowed himself personal time to enjoy the capital of the new Germany. His German hosts arranged for him to visit youth camps, labour camps, and the Berlin Zoo – new home to several bison given by Canada. At the Olympic Stadium, he watched crowds of German sports enthusiasts enjoying the opening ceremonies of the All-German Sports Competition. King was especially honoured to view the event from the very seat that Hitler had occupied during the 1936 Olympic Games. Not far from where King sat, he could see the huge ceremonial metal bowl that had previously contained the Olympic flame. The Olympic flame that had burned for the entire two weeks of the Nazi Olympics was now extinguished, but in only a little more than two years following King's Berlin visit, the Nazis would set much of Europe ablaze.

And a Postscript

If most Canadians preferred not to contemplate the Nazi pre-war threat to peace, there were some clear-eyed Canadian observers who recoiled from what they saw in Germany during the Nazi Games. Shortly after personally witnessing vicious street-level Nazi barbarism against so-called enemies of the state, Halton warned his *Toronto Daily Star* readers, "You may not appreciate your democracy now, but some day you will. If you had been with me last week and seen fine men who had been completely broken on the Fascist wheel you would know whereof I speak."[17] Two weeks later, still repulsed by a Germany blind in its adoration of Hitler and Olympic visitors seemingly mesmerized by the Nazi spectacle, Halton cautioned Canadians to be watchful "for the first signs of Fascism in your own country."[18]

Matthew Halton's warnings notwithstanding, it is impossible to know whether, had the narrative been different, had Canada and other nations boycotted the 1936 Olympics, the march to war in Europe might have played out differently. History is not arithmetic. There are no certain answers, no absolute rights or wrongs. This was certainly the case with Canada's participation in the 1936 Nazi Olympics. Even those who felt certain of what was right in an earlier day, in light of subsequent events, might have had a change of heart.

So it was with Canadian Press correspondent Elmer Dulmage. He, like Halton, covered the Games; but Dulmage, unlike Halton, opposed a Canadian boycott. In 1980, as Canada debated participation in the upcoming summer Olympics in Moscow following the Soviet invasion of Afghanistan, Dulmage reflected on his experience of Berlin and his interaction with Halton. Dulmage remembered that Halton wasn't that interested in sports – "Halton didn't know a javelin from a boxing glove and didn't care" – but Halton was concerned about what was going on politically. Angered by what he saw in Berlin, Halton turned to Dulmage over dinner one evening and stated despondently, "Nothing can stop a war now. These Olympics depress me terribly. I see the razzle dazzle but I think of the thousands of Jews in this country who, as soon as the Games are over, will again be tormented and many of them killed. We should have boycotted these games. By coming here, we are encouraging Hitler." Several days later, Halton left a terse message for Dulmage: "Leaving for London at once. Kicked out. Good luck."

Writing some forty-four years later, Dulmage asked and answered the nagging question: "Should we have been in Berlin in 1936? I think Matt Halton was right. A boycott would have been better."[19]

Notes

Preface

1 *Olympic Charter: In Force as from 9 September 2013* (Lausanne: International Olympic Committee, 2013), 12.
2 John Hoberman, *The Olympic Crisis: Sport, Politics and the Moral Order* (New Rochelle, NY: Aristide D. Caratzas, 1986), 29.

1. Sport, Society, and Politics

1 For a primer on the Spanish economic and political crisis of the early 1930s, see Julián Casanova, *The Spanish Republic and Civil War* (Cambridge: Cambridge University Press, 2010), 9–36, and Stanley G. Payne, *Spain's First Democracy: The Second Republic, 1931–1936* (Madison: University of Wisconsin Press, 1993), 23–46.
2 International Olympic Committee, *The International Olympic Committee and the Modern Olympic Games* (Lausanne: IOC, 1931), 11.
3 William Murray, introduction to *The Nazi Olympics: Sport, Politics, and Appeasement in the 1930s*, ed. Arnd Krüger and William Murray (Urbana: University of Illinois Press, 2003), 5.
4 Jean-Loup Chappelet and Brenda Kübler-Mabbott, *The International Olympic Committee and the Olympic System: The Governance of World Sport* (London: Routledge, 2008), 19–27.
5 Garth A. Paton, "James G.B. Merrick (1871–1946): Sports Organizer, Negotiator, Canada's Second IOC Member," *Proceedings of the 8th International Symposium for Olympic Research* (London, ON: University of Western Ontario Centre for Olympic Studies, 2006), 264.

6 Robert K. Barney, Malcolm Scott, and Rachel Moore, "'Old Boys' at Work and Play: The International Olympic Committee and Canadian Co-option, 1928–1946," *Olympika* 8 (1999), 87.

7 Ibid.

8 While James Merrick was present at the 1931 meeting in Barcelona, he had failed to attend several consecutive meetings and was under pressure to give up his committee membership. Instead of resigning, Merrick attempted to explain away his repeated absences by claiming unavoidable business commitments. But, while he did not resign, Merrick's absenteeism proved another sore point between Merrick and key members of the COC. Paton, "James G.B. Merrick," 254–77.

9 Organisationskomitee für die Spiele der XI. Olympiade, *The XIth Olympic Games, Berlin, 1936: Official Report,* vol. 1 (Berlin: Wilhelm Limpert, 1937), 42.

10 *Official Bulletin of the International Olympic Committee* 6, no. 17 (March 1931), 11–5; *Toronto Globe,* 28 April 1931, 19.

11 *Ottawa Citizen,* 28 April 1931, 10.

12 James K. Pollock Jr., "The German Reichstag Elections of 1930," *The American Political Science Review* 24 (1930), 993.

13 Marion A. Kaplan, *Between Dignity and Despair: Jewish Life in Nazi Germany* (New York: Cambridge University Press, 1998), 5.

14 Robert Gellately, *Backing Hitler: Consent and Coercion in Nazi Germany* (New York: Oxford University Press, 2001), 25–9.

15 *Toronto Evening Telegram,* 28 March 1933, as quoted in Cyril H. Levitt and William Shaffir, *The Riot at Christie Pits* (Toronto: Lester and Orpen Dennys, 1987), 61. Levitt and Shaffir make extensive use of the Toronto mainstream and Yiddish press to document responses to the Nazis in the months following Hitler's assumption of power in Germany.

16 Gellately, *Backing Hitler,* 121–50.

17 *Yidisher zhurnal,* 2 April 1933, as quoted in Levitt and Shaffir, *Riot at Christie Pits,* 62.

18 *Toronto Daily Star,* 12 August 1933, as quoted in Levitt and Shaffir, *Riot at Christie Pits,* 205.

19 Anton Rippon, *Hitler's Olympics: The Story of the 1936 Nazi Games* (South Yorkshire: Pen and Sword, 2006), 19.

20 Richard D. Mandell, *The Nazi Olympics* (New York: Macmillan, 1971), 58–9.

21 Arnd Krüger, "Breading, Bearing and Preparing the Aryan Body: Creating Supermen the Nazi Way," in *Shaping the Superman: Fascist Body as Political Icon – Aryan Fascism,* ed. J.A. Mangon (London: Frank Cass, 1999), 42–68.

22 David B. Kanin, *A Political History of the Olympic Games* (Boulder: Westview Press, 1981), 52.

23 Hitler as quoted in Rippon, *Hitler's Olympics*, 33.

24 David Clay Large, *Nazi Games: The Olympics of 1936* (New York: W.W. Norton, 2007), 58–9.

25 Allen Guttmann, *The Olympics: A History of the Modern Games* (Urbana, IL: University of Illinois Press, 1992), 55.

26 James M. Pitsula, "The Nazi Olympics: A Reinterpretation," *Olympika* 13 (2004), 26.

27 Large, *Nazi Games*, 165–7.

28 International Olympic Committee, *The International Olympic Committee and the Modern Olympic Games* (Lausanne: IOC, 1933), 9.

29 Robb MacDonald, "The Battle of Port Arthur: The War of Words and Ideologies within the Canadian Olympic Committee," *Proceedings of the First International Symposium for Olympic Research* (London, ON: University of Western Ontario Centre for Olympic Studies, 1992), 135–8.

30 Bruce Kidd, "The First COA Presidents," *Olympika* 3 (1994), 109.

31 Bruce Kidd, *The Struggle for Canadian Sport* (Toronto: University of Toronto Press, 1997), 55–8.

32 Ibid., 69.

33 Ibid., 91; M. Ann Hall, *The Girl and the Game: A History of Women's Sports in Canada* (Toronto: Broadview Press, 2002), 47–53.

34 Paton, "James G.B. Merrick," 269–70.

35 *Toronto Daily Star*, 24 December 1946, 16.

36 Joseph Levy and Avi Hyman, "Fanny 'Bobbie' Rosenfeld: Canada's Woman Athlete of the Half Century," *Journal of Sport History* 26 (1999), 392–6. In 1950 Rosenfeld was named Canada's woman athlete of the half-century, edging out Barbara Anne Scott by one vote.

37 For a recent discussion of the English-French and Catholic-Protestant divide in 1930s Quebec, see Alan Gordon, "Lest We Forget: Two Solitudes in War and Memory," in *Canadas of the Mind: The Making and Unmaking of Canadian Nationalism in the Twentieth Century*, ed. Norman Hillmer and Adam Chapnick (Montreal: McGill-Queen's University Press, 2007), 159–73.

38 Bruce Kidd, *Tom Longboat* (Toronto: Fitzhenry and Whiteside, 1992); Charles Ballem, "Missing From the Canadian Sport Scene: Native Athletes," *Canadian Journal of History of Sport* 14 (1983), 33–9.

39 Kidd, *The Struggle for Canadian Sport*, 70–4; Katharine Moore, "'The Warmth of Comradeship': The First British Empire Games and Imperial Solidarity," *International Journal of the History of Sport* 6 (1989), 242–51.

40 As quoted in Florence A.E. McQuarrie, "The Struggle over Worker Leisure: An Analysis of the History of the Workers' Sports Association in Canada," *Canadian Journal of Administrative Sciences* 27 (2010), 395.

41 For a discussion of the political marginality of the Canadian Jewish community during the interwar years, see Gerald Tulchinsky, *Canada's Jews: A People's Journey* (Toronto: University of Toronto Press, 2008), 283–327.

42 Louis Rosenberg, *Canada's Jews: A Social and Economic Study of Jews in Canada in the 1930s* (Montreal: CJC Bureau of Social and Economic Research, 1939), 1–5.

43 Rosenberg, *Canada's Jews*, 12, 23.

44 Ibid., 30.

45 Joseph Kage, *With Faith and Thanksgiving* (Montreal: Eagle, 1962), 51–5.

46 Greg Kealey, "State Repression of Labour and the Left in Canada, 1914–20: The Impact of the First World War," *Canadian Historical Review* 73 (1992), 281–314.

47 Order-in-Council, P.C. 183, 31 January 1923; *Canada Gazette*, April–June 1923, 4106; P.C. 185, ibid., 4107.

48 *Canada Yearbook* (Ottawa, 1922–1923), 215.

49 Canada, Senate, *Proceedings of the Standing Committee on Immigration and Labour* (Ottawa, 1946), 171–5. For a complete airing of immigration regulations and procedures, see Canada, Agriculture and Colonization, *Select Standing Committee on Agriculture and Colonization Report 1928* (Ottawa, 1928).

50 Harold Troper, "Jews and Canadian Immigration Policy: 1900–1950," in *The Jews of North America*, ed. Moses Rischin (Detroit: Wayne State University Press, 1987), 44–61.

51 Barnett R. Brickner, as quoted in Kage, *With Faith and Thanksgiving*, 80.

52 Kage, *With Faith and Thanksgiving*, 51–5.

53 Tulchinsky, *Canada's Jews*, 190.

2. Press, Preparations, and Protests: January 1933–August 1935

1 L. Kempff to O.D. Skelton, records of the Department of External Affairs, 25 January 1934, file 187, RG 25, vol. 1697, Library and Archives Canada (LAC), Ottawa.

2 David Clay Large, *Nazi Games: The Olympics of 1936* (New York: Norton, 2007), 61–2.

3 Quoted in a letter summarizing the meeting in Large, *Nazi Games*, 63.

4 Large, *Nazi Games*, 64.

5 *Newsweek*, 22 April 1933, 13, cited in Deborah E. Lipstadt, *Beyond Belief: The American Press and the Coming of the Holocaust, 1933–1945* (New York: Free Press, 1986), 64.

6 Christopher Hilton, *Hitler's Olympics: The 1936 Berlin Olympic Games* (Stroud, UK: Sutton Publishing, 2008), 12.

7 Large, *Nazi Games*, 75.

8 *Toronto Daily Star*, 4 November 1933, 16.

9 Bruce Kidd, "Canadian Opposition to the Olympics in Germany," *Canadian Journal of the History of Sport* 9, no. 2 (December 1978), 21–2.

10 J. Crocker to O.D. Skelton, records of the Department of External Affairs, 13 February 1934, file 187, RG 25, vol. 1697, LAC, Ottawa.

11 J. Crocker to T. Lewald, 12 April 1934, 8076/25, Bundesarchiv (BA), Berlin.

12 Murray S. Donnelly, *Dafoe of the Free Press* (Toronto: Macmillan, 1968), 140–6; Dafoe's editorial is cited on 146.

13 Robert J. Young, "Hitler's Early Critics: Canadian Resistance at the *Winnipeg Free Press*," *Queen's Quarterly* 106, no. 4 (1999), 578–87. On the editor, John W. Dafoe, see also Ramsay Cook, *The Politics of John W. Dafoe and the Free Press* (Toronto: University of Toronto Press, 1963) and Donnelly, *Dafoe of the Free Press*.

14 Ross Harkness, *J.E. Atkinson of the Star* (Toronto: University of Toronto Press, 1963); for a recent survey of coverage of the Jewish plight in Nazi Germany in the *Star*, see Ulrich Frisse, "The 'Bystanders' Perspective': The 'Toronto Daily Star' and its Coverage of the Persecution of the Jews and the Holocaust in Canada, 1933–1945," *Yad Vashem Studies* 99 (2011), 213–43.

15 *Toronto Daily Star*, 27 March 1933, 1, 4.

16 Ibid.

17 *Toronto Daily Star*, 21 October 1933, 1.

18 *Toronto Daily Star*, 27 October 1933, 2.

19 *Toronto Globe*, 26 July 1933, 1.

20 Graeme Mount, *Canada's Enemies: Spies and Spying in the Peaceable Kingdom* (Toronto: Dundurn, 1993), 56–7; the quoted passage is on 57.

21 Cyril H. Levitt and William Shaffir, *The Riot at Christie Pits* (Toronto: Lester and Orpen Dennys, 1987), 228–49.

22 Ibid., 229.

23 Ibid., 250–1.

24 Robin Elise Studniberg, "'One Shudders to Think What Might Happen to German Jewry': Vancouver Newspapers and Canadian Attitudes towards Nazi Antisemitism" (master's thesis, University of British Columbia, 2011), 17.

25 *Montreal Gazette*, 15 September 1933, cited in David Rome, *Our Archival Record of 1933: Hitler's Year* (Montreal: National Archives of Canadian Jewish Congress, 1976), 82.

26 Mount, *Canada's Enemies*, 57–8.

27 Lita-Rose Betcherman, *The Swastika and the Maple Leaf: Fascist Movements in Canada in the 1930s* (Toronto: Fitzhenry and Whiteside, 1975); Martin Robin, *Shades of the Right: Nativist and Fascist Politics in Canada, 1920–1940* (Toronto: University of Toronto Press, 1992).

28 Jonathan F. Wagner, *Brothers Beyond the Sea: National Socialism in Canada* (Waterloo, ON: Wilfrid Laurier University Press, 1981), 68.

29 Ibid., 64–85. See also the description in the *Toronto Globe*, 2 September 1935, 3.

30 Wagner, *Brothers Beyond the Sea*, 119–20; A. Grenke, "From Dreams of the Worker State to Fighting Hitler: The German-Canadian Left from the Depression to the End of World War II," *Labour/Le travail* 35 (1995), 81–8.

31 Levitt and Shaffir, *Riot at Christie Pits*, 51–75.

32 Max Beer, "'What Else Could We Have Done?': The Montreal Jewish Community, the Canadian Jewish Congress, the Jewish Press and the Holocaust" (master's thesis, Concordia University, 2006), 41n35, citing the *Canadian Jewish Chronicle*, 31 March 1933, 3.

33 *Jewish Western Bulletin* (Vancouver), 3 August 1933, cited in Studniberg, "'One Shudders to Think,'" 25.

34 *Jewish Western Bulletin* (Vancouver), 8 February 1934, 2.

35 Maurice N. Eisendrath, "Hitler's Challenge," *Canadian Club Year Book* (1933), 3.

36 For Eisendrath's biography, see Avi M. Schulman, *Like a Raging Fire: A Biography of Maurice N. Eisendrath* (New York: UAHC Press, 1993); for his early skirmishes with Toronto Jewry, see Stephen A. Speisman, *The Jews of Toronto: A History to 1937* (Toronto: McClelland and Stewart, 1977), 242.

37 Other leaders included the Reform Rabbi Harry Joshua Stern, who had some remarkable encounters with the Catholic hierarchy in Montreal, as well as with Protestant leaders. In Winnipeg, Solomon Frank of the Congregation Shaarey Zedek took a leadership role in his region, as did one J.J. Eisen in Alberta, and Samuel Cass in Vancouver. They were the central figures in what was known as the "Lecture Department" in the anti-defamation work of the Canadian Jewish Congress, which kept long lists of these lectures, noting the subject, place, date, and whether the audience was Gentile or Jewish. See, for example, the list of lectures delivered between 1934 and 1936 by M.N. Eisendrath, H.J. Stern, and J.J. Eisen, "Anti-Defamation Work of the Canadian Jewish Congress (Lecture Department)," ZB Eisendrath box, Canadian Jewish Congress Charities Committee National Archives (CJCNA), Montreal.

38 Eisendrath Collection, file 3, MS 167, American Jewish Archives (AJA), Cincinnati; box 6 contains numerous clippings from the period.

39 Gerald Tulchinsky, "'Justice and Only Justice Thou Shalt Pursue': Considerations on the Social Voice of Canada's Reform Rabbis," in *Religion and Public Life in Canada: Historical and Comparative Perspectives,* ed. Margaret van Die (Toronto: University of Toronto Press, 2001), 313–28.

40 G.S. Russell to M.N. Eisendrath, 3 April 1933, MS 167, box 5, folder 6, Eisendrath Collection, AJA, Cincinnati.

41 Compare, for example, the talk summarized in the *Montreal Gazette,* 29 February 1931, to the talk quoted in the *Toronto Daily Star,* 20 March 1934.

42 L. Kempff to Berlin, 13 June 1933, AA R77315, BA, Berlin. Kempff also forwarded a letter from a deranged Toronto woman who had written to Kempff (1 June 1933) warning him that she had heard on the radio that Eisendrath was planning to go to Germany. For her, Eisendrath, along with journalist Pierre van Paassen, was making life unbearable for German Canadians.

43 *Toronto Daily Star,* 31 August 1933, 1, 2.

44 Maurice N. Eisendrath, "Why Are Jews Persecuted? Part One," *Holy Blossom Pulpit* 4, no. 1 (1933–4), 5.

45 *Toronto Daily Star,* 18 September 1933, 2.

46 Victor Lange, "Does Germany Want War?" *Canadian Comment* (November, 1933), 9, 13, 14, 42.

47 Maurice N. Eisendrath, "What, No Terror?" *Canadian Comment* (December, 1933), 11, 12, 31, 32.

48 Robert A. Wright, *A World Mission: Canadian Protestantism and the Quest for a New International Order, 1918–1939* (Montreal: McGill-Queen's University Press, 1991), 102–3. See also J.H. Rushbrooke, *Fifth World Congress, Berlin August 4–10, Official Report* (London: Baptist World Alliance, 1934), 234–5; for the resolution on "racialism," see page 17.

49 *Toronto Daily Star,* 9 October 1934, 21.

50 Letter to the editor, *Toronto Daily Star,* 11 October 1934, 9.

51 Maurice N. Eisendrath, "I Re-Visit Nazi Germany," *Holy Blossom Pulpit* 6, no. 3 (1935–6), 3. Although undated, this was printed in early December 1935, based on the information on page 14. What Eisendrath saw, and especially the conclusions that he drew from that trip, are discussed in the next chapter.

52 Toby Thacker, *Joseph Goebbels: Life and Death* (London: Palgrave Macmillan, 2009), 141.

53 Wolfgang Benz, *A Concise History of the Third Reich,* trans. Thomas Dunlap (Berkeley: University of California Press, 2007), 24–34.

54 John Manley, "Moscow Rules? 'Red' Unionism and 'Class against Class' in Britain, Canada, and the United States, 1928-1935," *Labour/Le travail* 56 (2005), 16–7.

55 Ruth A. Frager, *Sweatshop Strife: Class, Ethnicity and Gender in the Jewish Labour Movement of Toronto, 1900–1939* (Toronto: University of Toronto Press, 1992), 184–99; Mercedes Steedman, "The Promise: Communist Organizing in the Needle Trades, the Dressmakers' Campaign, 1928–1937," *Labour/Le travail* 34 (1994), 36–73; Jodi Giesbrecht, "Accommodating Resistance: Unionization, Gender and Ethnicity in Winnipeg's Garment District," *Urban History Review* 39, no. 4 (2010), 12–3.

56 Ivan Avakumovic, *The Communist Party in Canada: A History* (Toronto: McClelland and Stewart, 1975), 67–8; Ivan Avakumovic, *Socialism in Canada: A Study of the CCF-NDP in Federal and Provincial Politics* (Toronto: McClelland and Stewart, 1978), 40.

57 Stefan Epp, "'Fighting for the Everyday Interests of Winnipeg Workers': Jacob Penner, Martin Forkin and the Communist Party in Winnipeg Politics, 1930–1935," *Manitoba History* 63 (2010), 14–26.

58 Craig Heron, *The Canadian Labour Movement: A Short History*, 2nd ed. (Toronto: Lorimer, 1996), 63.

59 J. Petryshym, "Class Conflict and Civil Liberties: The Origins and Activities of the Canadian Labour Defense League, 1925–1940," *Labour/Le travail* 10 (1982), 39–63. On 56–57, the author also shows how the CCF, despite its antipathy to section 96 and the arrests, would not associate with the protests of the CLDL and expelled members who did want to support Smith.

60 Cited in John Manley, "'Communists Love Canada!': The Communist Party of Canada, the 'People' and the Popular Front, 1933–1939," *Journal of Canadian Studies* 36, no. 4 (2002), 60.

61 Larry Ceplair, *Under the Shadow of War: Fascism, Anti-Fascism and Marxists, 1918–1939* (New York: Columbia University Press, 1987), 78–90.

62 Nigel Copsey, "'Every time they made a Communist, they made a Fascist': The Labour Party and Popular Anti-Fascism in the 1930s," in *Varieties of Anti-Fascism: Britain in the Interwar Period*, ed. Nigel Copsey and Andrzej Olechnowicz (London: Palgrave Macmillan, 2010), 57.

63 Gregory S. Kealey and Reg Whitaker, eds., *RCMP Security Bulletins: The Depression Years, Part I, 1933–34* (St. John's, NL: Canadian Committee on Labour History, 1993), 47–8.

64 Peter Hunter, *Which Side Are You On, Boys? Canadian Life on the Left* (Toronto: Lugus, 1988), 34–5.

65 *RCMP Bulletins, 1933–1934*, 142.

66 Ibid., 201–2.

67 Hunter, *Which Side Are You On Boys*, 53.

68 *RCMP Bulletins, 1933–1934*, 203.

69 Ibid., 321.

70 *Report. First Canadian Congress against War and Fascism, October 6th and 7th, 1934, Toronto, Ontario* (Toronto, 1934), 2–3.

71 Ibid., 4.

72 Ibid., passim, but see especially 13–4.

73 *RCMP Bulletins, 1933–1934*, 332.

74 *Report. First Canadian Congress against War and Fascism*, 23.

75 Levitt and Shaffir, *The Riot at Christie Pits*, 207–217; the quote is from *Der yidisher zhurnal*, 3 April 1933, quoted on 217.

76 Rome, *Archival Record of 1933*, 77; Allan Levine, *Coming of Age: A History of the Jewish People of* Manitoba (Winnipeg: Heartland, 2009), 256.

77 Rome, *Archival Record of 1933*, 67a.

78 Gerald Tulchinsky, *Canada's Jews: A People's Journey* (Toronto: University of Toronto, 2008), 184–91.

79 For a detailed discussion of the impetus to and politics of the 1933 reorganization of the Canadian Jewish Congress, see Jack Lipinsky, *Imposing Their Will: An Organizational History of Jewish Toronto, 1933–1948* (Montreal: McGill-Queen's University Press, 2011), 35–58.

80 Rome, *Archival Record of 1933*, 67–9.

81 Ibid., 78.

82 Levitt and Shaffir, *The Riot at Christie Pits*, 221. In fact, CJC would adopt the economic boycott into its platform in early 1934. See CJC, *Canadian Jewish Congress: Constitution and Resolutions, Adopted at Second General Session January 27, 28 and 29 1934 Toronto, Ont.* (Montreal, 1934), 7–8.

83 Rome, *Archival Record of 1933*, 78.

84 Ibid., 84–5.

85 Ibid., 78.

86 David Rome, *The Congress Archival Record of 1934* (Montreal: National Archives of Canadian Jewish Congress, 1976), 2.

87 Rome, *Archival Record of 1933*, 83.

88 Ibid., 81.

89 A *shtadlan* is a person of prominence who serves the Jewish community as an intercessor with the authorities.

90 *Canadian Jewish Chronicle*, 22 December 1933, 3, cited in Beer, "'What Else Could We Have Done?'" 44.

91 *Toronto Daily Star*, 30 January 1934, 13.

92 *Dos yidishe vort* (Winnipeg), 14 May 1935.

93 *Jewish Standard* (Toronto), February 1937.

94 John Herd Thompson and Allen Seager, *Canada 1922–1939: Decades of Discord* (Toronto: McClelland and Stewart, 1985), 229–35.

95 Walter D. Young, *The Anatomy of a Party: The National CCF, 1932–1961* (Toronto: University of Toronto Press, 1969), 259.

96 See the "Resolution on a letter to be sent to the National Council of the CCF," in *Report. First Canadian Congress against War and Fascism*, 24.

97 *New Commonwealth* (Toronto), 18 August 1934, 4; 1 September 1934, 5.

98 *New Commonwealth* (Toronto), 1 December 1935, 4.

99 *New Commonwealth* (Toronto), 8 December 1934, 4.

100 Young, *Anatomy of a Party*, 261–2.

101 *New Commonwealth* (Toronto), 30 March 1935, 8; 11 May 1935, 5.

102 *Report. First Canadian Congress against War and Fascism*, 19.

103 *Will Canada Escape Fascism?* (Toronto: Canadian League against War and Fascism, n.d. [1934/5]), 32.

104 *Report. First Canadian Congress against War and Fascism*, 11. For a description of Ida Siegel's involvement in Jewish communal activities, see Michael Brown, "Ida Siegel, 1885–1982," *Jewish Women: A Comprehensive Historical Encyclopedia*, online edition, accessed 22 September 2012, http://jwa.org/encyclopedia/article/siegel-ida

105 These two letters from mid-October are summarized in Rome, *Archival Record of 1934*, 19–20, but we have not located the originals.

106 Reproduced in H.M. Caiserman to M.N. Eisendrath, 17 October 1935 [*sic*], file 42, Box 4, ZA 1935, CJC Collection Series, CJCNA, Montreal. Although this letter is dated 1935, from internal evidence it is clear that it should be 1934.

107 Ibid.

108 Maurice N. Eisendrath, "One Hell of a Business," *Action against War and Fascism* 1, no. 1 (May 1935), 12–3. It was based on a sermon on the armaments industry.

109 David Rome, *Jewish Archival Record of 1935* (Montreal: National Archives of Canadian Jewish Congress, 1976), 43.

110 J.A. Cherniack, Q.C., "Reminiscences of 40 Years of Jewish Community Life," *The Jewish Historical Society of Western Canada. Second Annual Publication. A Selection of Papers Presented in 1969–1970* (April, 1972), 85; Y16 (Yiddish section).

111 Rome, *Jewish Archival Record of 1935*, 63–4.

112 See the detailed and useful study by Serge M. Durflinger, "'Six Thousand Tons of Fighting Apparatus': Canadian Reactions to the Visit of the Cruiser *Karlsruhe* to Vancouver, March 1935," *The Northern Mariner* 16, no. 2 (2006), 1–13.

113 Gregory S. Kealey and Reg Whitaker, eds., *RCMP Security Bulletins: The Depression Years, Part III (1936)* (St. John's, NL: Canadian Committee on Labour History, 1996), 187–8, 191; AJC, *American Jewish Year Book* (1936–7), 244.

114 Kirk Niegarth, "'Fight for Life': Dave Kashtan's Memories of Depression-Era Communist Youth Work," *Labour/Le travail* 56 (2005), 233.

115 For a discussion of the Nazi boycott of Jewish-owned enterprises and the Jewish response in Britain, see Avraham Barkai, *From Boycott to Annihilation: The Economic Struggle of German Jews, 1933–1943* (Boston: Brandeis, 1990), and Sharon Gewirtz, "Anglo-Jewish Responses to Nazi Germany: The Anti-Nazi Boycott and the Board of Deputies of British Jews," *Journal of Contemporary History* 26 (1991), 255–76.

116 CJC, *Canadian Jewish Congress*, 7.

117 Rome, *Archival Record of 1935*, 89–90.

118 Patrick Opdenhövel, *Die kanadisch-deutschen Beziehungen in der Zwischenkriegszeit: Handels- und Aussenpolitik* (Frankfurt: Peter Lang, 1993), 293. For a recent account of CJC's boycott campaign throughout the 1930s, see James Walker, "Claiming Equality for Canadian Jewry: The Struggle for Inclusion, 1930–1945," in *Nazi Germany, Canadian Responses: Confronting Antisemitism in the Shadow of War,* ed. L. Ruth Klein (Montreal: McGill-Queen's University Press, 2012), 228–31.

119 *Toronto Globe*, 8 January 1934, 12.

120 Rome, *Congress Record of 1934*, 43.

121 Boycott report, file 11, box A11, Series A, Subseries 2, World Jewish Congress Collection, AJA, Cincinnati. The letter from the CJC was dated 16 July 1934. The report is a summary of CJC activity, mostly dealing with the economic boycott. The correspondence is summarized, except in one notable case where a letter is reproduced in full (below).

122 *Report. First Canadian Congress against War and Fascism, October 6th and 7th, 1934, Toronto, Ontario* (Toronto: 1934), 22.

123 *Dos yidishe vort*, 11 May 1934, 1.

124 *Toronto Globe*, 15 June 1934, 18; 21 November 1934, 12.

125 *Toronto Globe*, 14 August 1934, 9.

126 *Toronto Globe*, 18 May 1934, 12; 22 June 1934, 12; 14 September 1934, 13; 28 September 1934, 13.

127 *Toronto Globe*, 28 September 1934, 6.

128 W.G. Hardy to A.S. Lamb, 25 October 1935, file 7, MG 30 C164, vol. 20, Jack Davies Fonds, LAC, Ottawa.

129 Boycott report, letter of J. Hornstein to A.H.J. Zaitlin of the CJC, 31 December 1935, file 11, box A11, Series A, Subseries 2, World Jewish

Congress Collection, AJA, Cincinnati. The report reproduces the letter of J. Hornstein to A.H.J. Zaitlin of the CJC, where Hornstein reviews what happened at the meeting. Hornstein was appointed to the executive committee of the AAUC as the representative of the Quebec branch in 1935, and attended the COC meeting on 16 November.

130 Ibid.
131 If this is the report that Brundage delivered after his return from Germany in the fall of 1935, then Mulqueen's timeline is off as the COC meeting in the spring of 1934 agreed unanimously to go Germany for the Games.
132 Boycott report, letter of J. Horstein to A.H.J. Zaitlin, 1935, AJA, Cincinnati [RM].
133 Minutes of the Canadian Olympic Committee Meeting, Royal York Hotel, Toronto, Friday Morning, 16 November 1934, file 7, MG 30 C164, vol. 20, Jack Davies Fonds, LAC, Ottawa.
134 *Toronto Daily Star*, 16 November 1934, 17.
135 Minutes of the Canadian Olympic Committee Meeting, Royal York Hotel, Toronto, Friday Morning, 16 November 1934, file 7, MG 30 C164, vol. 20, Jack Davies Fonds, LAC, Ottawa.
136 Ibid.
137 J.H. Crocker [honorary secretary of COC], "to the Editors of the Canadian Newspapers," 6 February 1935, file 7, MG 30 C164, vol. 20, Jack Davies Fonds, LAC, Ottawa.
138 After Marsh's sudden and premature death in early 1936, Mulqueen was made an honourary pall-bearer and the *Star* made him the first chair of the Lou Marsh Award, to be bestowed on the top athlete in the country. See *Toronto Daily Star*, 23 December 1946, 13.
139 *Toronto Globe*, 21 September 1935, 1–2.
140 *Vancouver Sun*, 6 August 1936, 1.
141 Ibid., 6.
142 Large, *Nazi Games*, 81–2.
143 *Toronto Daily Star*, 8 August 1935, 16.
144 *Canadian Jewish Chronicle*, 2 August 1935, 7.
145 *Jewish Western Bulletin*, 22 August 1935, 1.
146 *Vancouver Sun*, 17 August 1935, 2.
147 *Toronto Globe*, 13 August 1935, 6.
148 *Toronto Globe*, 6 August 1935, 6.
149 Bruce Kidd, *The Struggle for Canadian Sport* (Toronto: University of Toronto Press, 1996), 153–4.

150 Ibid., 155.

151 *Young Worker*, 8 June 1935, 1. On the tour, see Kidd, *The Struggle for Canadian Sport*, 176.

152 Correspondence from P. Leslie, Correspondence of representative of Communist Party of Canada attached to Executive Committee of the Communist International ... with (Central Committee of the Communist Party of Canada) and individual members, on situation in Canada, work of party, personnel, etc., 16 June 1935, file 174, MG 10 K 3, Reel #21 [K-289],The Comintern Fonds (Communist International), LAC, Ottawa.

153 *Young Worker*, 3 August 1935, 4.

154 *Young Worker*, 31 August 1935, 9.

155 Minutes of Council Meeting, 14 August 1935, file 1, box 1, Canadian Youth Congress Fonds, William Ready Division of Archives and Research Collections, McMaster University Libraries, Hamilton.

156 *Toronto Daily Star*, 26 August 1935, 6; a clipping of the same letter to the editor (in an unknown newspaper), "Letters and Publications," 29 August 1935, file 10, box 7, Canadian Youth Congress Fonds, William Ready Division of Archives and Research Collections, McMaster University Libraries, Hamilton.

157 Minutes of the joint emergency meeting of the Dominion Executive of the Eastern Division of the Canadian Jewish Congress, 24 July 1935, file 5, vol. 300, Irma and Marvin Penn Archives of the Jewish Heritage Centre of Western Canada, Winnipeg.

158 CJC, Emergency Meeting Executive Committee, 29 July 1935, temp. box 13–5, Series BC-Minutes, Central Division, Executive, CJC Collection, CJCNA, Montreal.

159 Ibid.

160 Roger to H.M. Caiserman, 30 July 1935, file 16, box 2, Series ZA 1935, CJC Collection, CJCNA, Montreal.

161 Roger to H.M. Caiserman, 1 August 1935, file 16, box 2, Series ZA 1935, CJC Collection, CJCNA, Montreal.

162 Gathered from biographical information on Herschorn from several obituaries from 1962, as well as clippings in his file in the Jewish Canadiana Collection, Personalia (Community leaders), Jewish Public Library Archives, Montreal.

163 Louis Kraft, "The Y.M.H.A. and the Jewish Centre Movement," *Y.M.H.A. Beacon* 5, no. 14 (April 1920), 2. Kraft was, at the time, the JWB's director of Jewish community centre activities, and in 1938 he became the JWB's executive director.

164 Jack Rosenthal, "Canadian Jewish Youth Centres," *Y.M.H.A. Beacon* 10, no. 11 (May 1935), 11.

165 *Toronto Daily Star*, 19 April 1935, 10.

166 H.M. Caiserman to Brown, 7 August 1935, file 34, box 3, Series ZA 1935, CJC Collection, CJCNA, Montreal.

167 *St. Peter's Bote* (Münster, SK), 13 June 1935, 18.

3. "Moving Heaven and Earth"

1 Maurice N. Eisendrath, "I Re-Visit Nazi Germany," *Holy Blossom Pulpit* 6, no. 3 (1935–36), 3.

2 Ibid., 7–8, 9.

3 Ibid., 10.

4 Ibid., 13.

5 George S. Messersmith, as quoted in George Eisen, "The Voices of Sanity: American Diplomatic Reports from the 1936 Berlin Olympiad," *Journal of Sports History* 11 (1984), 68–9.

6 M.N. Eisendrath to H.M Caiserman, 9 September 1935, file 16, box 2, Series ZA 1935, CJC Collection, Canadian Jewish Congress Charities Committee Archives (CJCNA), Montreal.

7 H.M. Caiserman to M.N. Eisendrath, 11 September 1935, file 16, box 2, Series ZA 1935, CJC Collection, CJCNA, Montreal.

8 *New York Times*, 31 July 1935, 3.

9 George N. Shuster, "Gen. Sherrill and the Olympics," *The Commonweal*, 8 November 1935, 42.

10 Caiserman to Eisendrath 1935, CJCNA.

11 M.N. Eisendrath, to H.M. Caiserman, 9 October 1935, file 16, box 2, Series ZA 1935, CJC Collection, CJCNA, Montreal.

12 Bruce Kidd, *The Struggle for Canadian Sport* (Toronto: University of Toronto Press, 1996), 176.

13 Ibid.

14 Gregory S. Kealey and Reg Whitaker, eds., *RCMP Security Bulletins: The Depression Years, Part II, 1935* (St. John's, NL: Canadian Committee on Labour History, 1995), 449–50.

15 *The Young Worker*, 16 October 1935, 2.

16 For a full airing of issues related to Nazi race-science and its practical application, see Eric Ehrenreich, *The Nazi Ancestral Proof: Genealogy, Racial Science, and the Final Solution* (Bloomington: Indiana University Press, 2007).

17 Moshe Gottlieb, "The Berlin Riots of 1935 and Their Repercussions in America," *American Jewish Historical Quarterly* (March 1970), 302–28.

18 *New York Times*, 17 July 1935, 1, 4, editorial on 18; Deborah E. Lipstadt, *Beyond Belief: The American Press and the Coming of the Holocaust* (New York: The Free Press, 1986), 41. Berlin was not the only German city to witness anti-Jewish riots in the spring and early summer of 1935. Between March and May 1935, Munich, gateway city to Garmisch-Partenkirchen where the Winter Olympics would be held, had a series of well-orchestrated anti-Jewish actions as did many other smaller towns and cities. Saul Friedlander, *Nazi Germany and the Jews*, vol. 1, *The Years of Persecution 1933–1939* (New York: Harper Collins, 1997), 137–9.

19 Karl Schleunes, *The Twisted Road to Auschwitz: Nazi Policy Toward German Jews, 1933–1939* (Urbana: University of Illinois Press, 1970), 121.

20 Klaus P. Fischer, *Nazi Germany: A New History* (New York: Continuum, 1995), 208.

21 *Toronto Daily Star*, 13 September 1935, section 2, 1; *The Calgary Daily Herald*, 14 September 1935.

22 For a discussion of the pre-war introduction of Jewish property confiscation in Nazi Germany, see Martin Dean, *Robbing the Jews: The Confiscation of Jewish Property in the Holocaust, 1933–1945* (New York: Oxford University Press, 2008), 17–53.

23 Raul Hilberg, *The Destruction of the European Jews* (Chicago: Quadrangle Books, 1961), 43–53; Hermann Graml, *Antisemitism in the Third Reich* (Oxford: Blackwell, 1992), 116–25.

24 George Sherrill as quoted in David Clay Large, *Nazi Games: The Olympics of 1936* (New York: Norton, 2007), 85; also see Stephen R. Wenn, "A Tale of Two Diplomats: George S. Messersmith and Charles H. Sherrill on Proposed American Participation in the 1936 Olympics," *Journal of Sports History* 16 (1989), 37.

25 This discussion does not include the French-language press, not because French-Canadian media ignored the Nuremberg Laws or the fallout of the Laws, but because French Canada was largely absent from the Canadian Olympic Games debate.

26 See, for example, Robin Elise Studniberg, "'One Shudders to Think What Might Happen to German Jewry': Vancouver Newspapers and Canadian Attitudes towards Nazi Antisemitism, 1933–1935" (master's thesis, University of British Columbia, 2011).

27 *Calgary Daily Herald*, 16 September 1935, 1.

28 *Toronto Globe*, 16 September 1935, 1; Lipstadt, *Beyond Belief*, 58–9.

29 *Winnipeg Free Press*, 16 September 1935, 1.

30 *Toronto Daily Star*, 18 October 1935, 1, 29.

31 *Calgary Daily Herald*, 15 November, 1935, 1.

32 *Toronto Globe*, 16 November 1935, 2.

33 *Toronto Globe*, 19 November 1935, 4; *Toronto Globe*, 21 September 1935, 1, 2.

34 *Toronto Daily Star*, 28 September 1935, 35.

35 *Toronto Daily Star*, 12 October 1935, 12.

36 *Toronto Daily Star*, 23 October 1935, 21.

37 The anti-Jewish laws did, in fact, eventually fill a book. See Joseph Walk, ed., *Das Sonderrecht für die Juden im NS-Staat* (Heidelberg: Müller Juristischer Verlag, 1981).

38 *Toronto Daily Star*, 5 November 1935, 13, 37.

39 *Calgary Daily Herald*, 1 October 1935, 4.

40 Trades and Labour Congress, *Convention Proceedings, Halifax, 1935*, 182–183. Communication and copies of resolutions of the Trades and Labour Congress and its affiliates are found in file 41, box 2, DA 1, CJCNA, Montreal.

41 H.M. Caiserman, to M.N. Eisendrath, 27 October 1935, file 16, box 2, Series ZA 1935, CJC Collection, CJCNA, Montreal.

42 Elmer Ferguson as quoted in *Sports Magazine* (October–November 1935).

43 M.N. Eisendrath, to H.M Caiserman, 31 October 1935, file 16, box 2, Series ZA 1935, CJC Collection, CJCNA, Montreal.

44 One of Eisendrath's Sunday lectures was entitled "Freedom of Speech in British Tradition." In his talk Eisendrath described the "crowning glory of the British commonwealth." According to Eisendrath, it was to be found "not in the luster of her gold or the fortunes of her mines, not in the splendid cities or the mighty armada but in the freedom she has accorded to all who signal her gates." Eisendrath Toronto Manuscripts, Holy Blossom Temple Archives, Toronto.

45 "Strictly Confidential Report of Conversation with Mr. P.J. Mulqueen, Relative to Canada's Participation in the Olympic Games," n.d. [but certainly shortly after the 16 October 1935 meeting], file 16, box 2, Series ZA 1935, CJC Collection, CJCNA, Montreal.

46 H.M. Caiserman, to A.J. Freiman, 21 October 1935, file 16, box 2, Series ZA 1935, CJC Collection, CJCNA, Montreal; H.M. Caiserman, to W.N. Zimmerman, 21 October 1935, file 16, box 2, Series ZA 1935, CJC Collection, CJCNA, Montreal; H.M. Caiserman, to M.J. Finkelstein, 21 October 1935, file 16, box 2, Series ZA 1935, CJC Collection, CJCNA, Montreal.

47 M.I. Lieberman to H.M. Caiserman, 25 October 1935, file 16, box 2, Series ZA 1935, CJC Collection, CJCNA, Montreal.

48 H.M. Caiserman to S.W. Jacobs, 27 October 1935; S.W. Jacobs to O.D. Skelton, 11 November 1935; Laurent Beaudry to S.W. Jacobs, file 187, RG 25, vol. 1697, Records of the Department of External Affairs, Library and Archives Canada (LAC), Ottawa; Large, *Nazi Games*, 79.

49 M.J. Finkelstein to H.M. Caiserman, 4 November 1935, file 16, box 2, Series ZA 1935, CJC Collection, CJCNA, Montreal.

50 Ibid.

51 H.M. Caiserman to C.A. Gravenor, 26 October 1935, file 16, box 2, Series ZA 1935, CJC Collection, CJCNA, Montreal.

52 Cited in Bruce Kidd, "Canadian Opposition to the 1936 Olympics in Germany," *Sports History Review* 9, no. 2 (1978), 23.

53 Minutes of the Meeting of the Canadian Olympic Executive Committee, 2 November 1935, file 7, MG 30 C164, vol. 20, Jack Davies Fonds, LAC, Ottawa.

54 *Vancouver Sun*, 4 November 1935, 23

55 *Montreal Gazette*, 4 November 1935, 13.

56 Ibid.

57 Minutes of the Meeting of the Canadian Olympic Executive Committee, November 2, 1935, file 7, MG 30 C164, vol. 20, Jack Davies Fonds, LAC, Ottawa; *Gazette* (Montreal), 4 November 1935, 13.

58 A.S. Lamb to H.E. Herschorn, 30 November 1935, file 7, MG 30 C164, vol. 20, Jack Davies Fonds, LAC, Ottawa.

59 H.M. Caiserman to M. Eisendrath, 5 November 1935, file 16, box 2, Series, ZA 1935, CJC Collection, CJCNA, Montreal.

60 Minutes of the Meeting of the Canadian Olympic Executive Committee, 2 November 1935, file 7, MG 30 C164, vol. 20, Jack Davies Fonds, LAC, Ottawa.

61 H.M. Caiserman to M.N. Eisendrath, 5 November 1935, file 16, box 2, Series ZA 1935, CJC Collection, CJCNA, Montreal.

62 Kirzner to Sir, 6 November 1935, file 16a, box 2, Series ZA 1935, CJC Collection, CJCNA, Montreal.

63 Sam Cass to H.M. Caiserman, 7 November 1935, file 16, box 2, Series ZA 1935, CJC Collection, CJCNA, Montreal.

64 David Rome, *Jewish Archival Record of 1935* (Montreal: National Archives of Canadian Jewish Congress, 1976), 112.

65 *Toronto Evening Telegram*, 15 November 1935, 1.

66 *Winnipeg Free Press*, 7 November 1935, 1.

67 J.W. Buckley to H.M. Caiserman, 4 November 1935, file 41, box 2, DA 1, CJCNA, Montreal.

68 *Toronto Daily Star*, 4 November 1935, 14.

69 Clare Claus to local chapter of CYC, 4 November 1935, file f10, box 2, Canadian Youth Congress Fonds, William Ready Division of Archives and Research Collections, McMaster University Libraries, Hamilton.

70 L. Kempff to Canadian Youth Council, 9 November 1935, file f10, box 2, Canadian Youth Congress Fonds, William Ready Division of Archives and Research Collections, McMaster University Libraries, Hamilton.

71 H.H. Wrong to O.D. Skelton, 26 December 1935, file 187, RG 25, vol. 1697, Records of the Department of External Affairs, LAC, Ottawa. Wrong's letter summarizes details on Haag's arrival in Canada.

72 *Vancouver Sun*, 14 November 1935, 29.

73 Unity and Goodwill Association of Canada newsletter signed George Langsner, President, n.d., file 16, box 2, Series ZA 1935, CJC Collection, CJCNA, Montreal.

74 Diemut Majer, *"Non-Germans" Under the Third Reich*, trans. Peter Thomas Hill et al. (Baltimore: Johns Hopkins, 2003), 111–6.

75 S.W. Jacobs and H.M. Caiserman to The President, Amateur Athletic Union of Canada, 18 November 1935, file 16, box 2, Series ZA 1935, CJC Collection, CJCNA, Montreal.

76 A. Muroch Keith to P.J. Mulqueen, 20 November 1935, file 10, box 4, Canadian Youth Congress Fonds, William Ready Division of Archives and Research Collections, McMaster University Libraries, Hamilton.

77 P. Stuchen to H.M. Caiserman, 15 November 1935, file 16, box 2, Series ZA 1935, CJC Collection, CJCNA, Montreal.

78 Attached to a letter from Booth and Eisendrath to Ernest Best, general secretary of YMCA, 18 November 1935, file 12, MG 28 I 95, vol. 283, YMCA Fonds, LAC, Ottawa.

79 Meeting of 19 November 1935, Minute Book of Samuel Lodge, 1934–1935, B'Nai Brith Fonds, Jewish Historical Society of British Columbia, Vancouver.

80 Alan Davies and Marilyn F. Nefsky, *How Silent were the Churches? Canadian Protestantism and the Jewish Plight during the Nazi Era* (Waterloo: Wilfrid Laurier University Press, 1998), 119.

81 E. Best to G.R. Booth, 20 November 1935, file 12, MG 28 I 95, vol. 283, YMCA Fonds, LAC, Ottawa.

82 P. Stuchen to H.M. Caiserman, 15 November 1935, file 16, box 2, Series ZA 1935, CJC Collection, CJCNA, Montreal.

83 M.N. Eisendrath, "Hitler Invites the Youth of the World. Shall Canada Accept? Fictions and Fact Concerning the Olympics," Sermon, 17 November 1935, file 16, box 2, Series ZA 1935, CJC Collection, CJCNA, Montreal.

84 Amateur Athletic Association of Canada, *Minutes of the Forty-Eighth Annual Meeting 1935*, 59; *Toronto Mail and Empire*, 22 November 1935, 13.

85 *Winnipeg Free Press*, 22 November 1935, 17.

86 A.S. Lamb to H.E. Herschorn, 30 November 1935, file 7, MG 30 C164, vol. 20, Jack Davies Fonds, LAC, Ottawa. Although the letter, which was a copy for filing, does not have Lamb's signature, the Davies Fonds contains correspondence from the COC at the time, and the typewriter is the same as used in other letters that were definitely from Lamb.

4. "How Lonesome Our Position Is Becoming"

1 *Toronto Daily Star*, 22 November 1935, 14.
2 Quoted from *The Worker*, 23 November 1935, 5.
3 "Bulletin of the Unity and Goodwill Association," 29 November 1935, 4, file 16, box 2, series ZA 1935, CJC Collection, Canadian Jewish Congress Charities Committee National Archives (CJCNA), Montreal.
4 *Der kamf* (Toronto), 26 November 1935, 2.
5 *The Worker*, 25 November 1935.
6 *Montreal Gazette*, 10 December 1935, 9; L. Kempff to Berlin, 20 December 1935, R77315, Politisches Archiv des Auswärtigen Amts, Inland, Bundesarchiv (BA), Berlin.
7 *The Worker*, 23 November 1935, 1, 5.
8 Letter of A.D. Schatz to the editor, *Toronto Daily Star*, 28 November 1935, 7.
9 Clipping from the *Montreal Gazette*, 4 December 1935, YM-YWHA Fonds, Jewish Public Library Archives (JPLA), Montreal.
10 *Toronto Daily Star*, 22 November 1935, 14.
11 Merrick was indeed on the same page as Mulqueen. After the Austrians had decided to attend, Merrick told the *Toronto Daily Star* how pleased he was at the news. *Toronto Daily Star*, 12 December 1935, 14.
12 "Confidential memorandum from Mr. Herschorn, for record purposes, regarding the attitude of the Canadian delegates to the convention of the Amateur Athletic Union of the USA, which was held in New York on Dec. 6, 7 & 8," February 1936, YM-YWHA Fonds, JPLA, Montreal. Herschorn refers to himself in the third person throughout the memorandum. It is dated February 1936, without the day of the month. The *Montreal Gazette* only referred to the presence and non-votes of Mulqueen and Herschorn, but Merrick may have been seen by the paper as a member of the IOC and not included among the Canadians. *Montreal Gazette*, 9 December 1935, 15.
13 *Canadian Jewish Review* (Montreal, Toronto), 30 December 1935, 5.
14 Reinhard Rürup, ed., *1936: Die Olympischen Spiele und der Nationalsozialismus: eine Dokumentation* [1936: The Olympic Games and National Socialism: A documentation], 2nd ed. (Berlin: Argon, 1999), 90.

15 Olympic Games (11th: 1936: Berlin, Germany). Organisationskomitee für die Spiele der XI. Olympiade, *The XIth Olympic Games, Berlin, 1936: Official Report*, vol. 1 (Berlin: Wilhelm Limpert, 1937), 128.

16 David Clay Large, *Nazi Games: The Olympics of 1936* (New York: Norton, 2007), 115.

17 Large, *Nazi Games*, 117.

18 Large, *Nazi Games*, 117–9; Rürup, *Die Olympischen Spiele*, 91.

19 Large, *Nazi Games*, 120; Joseph Walk, ed., *Das Sonderrecht für die Juden im NS-Staat* (Heidelberg: Müller Juristischer Verlag, 1981), 143.

20 Rürup, *Die Olympischen Spiele*, 58.

21 Olympic Games (11th: 1936: Berlin, Germany). Organisationskomitee für die Spiele der XI. Olympiade, *The XIth Olympic Games: Official Report*, vol. 1, 148.

22 *Calgary Daily Herald*, 30 October 1935, 6.

23 H.H. Wrong to O.D. Skelton, 26 December 1935, file 187, RG 25, volume 1697, Records of the Department of External Affairs, Library and Archives Canada (LAC), Ottawa.

24 L. Kempff to Canadian Youth Council, 9 November 1935, file 10, box 4, Canadian Youth Congress Fonds, William Ready Division of Archives and Research Collections, McMaster University Libraries, Hamilton.

25 C. Gravenor to H.M. Caiserman, 25 November 1935, file 16, box 2, Series ZA 1935, CJC Collection, CJCNA, Montreal.

26 H.M. Caiserman to C. Gravenor, 28 November 1935, file 16, box 2, Series ZA 1935, CJC Collection, CJCNA, Montreal.

27 *Toronto Mail and Empire*, 2 December 1935, 1; M.N. Eisendrath to H.M. Caiserman, 4 December 1935, file 42, box 4, Series ZA 1935, CJC Collection, CJCNA, Montreal.

28 *The People versus War and Fascism: Proceedings Second National Congress against War and Fascism, Toronto, Ontario, December 6th, 7th, 8th, 1935* (Toronto: Canadian League against War and Fascism, 1935), 37.

29 German Work and Farm Association, Regina local, to Mackenzie King, 12 December 1935, file 187, RG 25, volume 1697, Records of the Department of External Affairs, LAC, Ottawa.

30 *Dos yidishe vort* (Winnipeg), 6 December 1935, 1; *Toronto Mail and Empire*, 2 December 1935, 1.

31 F.C. Blair to S.W. Jacobs, 7 December 1935, file 63, box 4, Series ZA 1935, CJC Collection, CJCNA, Montreal; F.C. Blair to S.W. Jacobs, 11 December 1935, file 63, box 4, Series ZA 1935, CJC Collection, CJCNA, Montreal.

32 O.D. Skelton to H.H. Wrong, 20 December 1935, file 187, RG 25, volume 1697, Records of the Department of External Affairs, LAC, Ottawa.

33 F.C. Blair to S.W. Jacobs, 11 December 1935, file 63, box 4, Series ZA 1935, CJC Collection, CJCNA, Montreal.

34 Minutes of meeting of COC, Royal York Hotel, Toronto, 10 March 1936, file 8, MG 130 C164, volume 20, Jack Davies Fonds, LAC, Ottawa.

35 David Rome, *Jewish Archival Record of 1935* (Montreal: National Archives of Canadian Jewish Congress, 1976), 35.

36 Gregory S. Kealey and Reg Whitaker, eds., *RCMP Security Bulletins: The Depression Years, Part II, 1935* (St. John's, NL: Canadian Committee on Labour History, 1995), 615–6.

37 Rome, *Jewish Archival Record of 1935*, 35–6.

38 Ibid., 36.

39 Henry Felix Srebrnik, *Jerusalem on the Amur: Birobidzhan and the Canadian Jewish Communist Movement, 1924–1951* (Montreal: McGill-Queen's University Press, 2008), passim, but especially 104 and 116 on the relationship with CLAWF.

40 *The People versus War and Fascism*, 41–2.

41 Ibid., 37, resolution (8).

42 Ibid., 36, 40–1.

43 H.M. Caiserman to M.N. Eisendrath, 28 November 1935, file 16, box 2, Series ZA 1935, CJC Collection, CJCNA, Montreal.

44 In a letter to Toronto's boycott committee, Caiserman explains how Gravenor came to assume such a high position in so short a time. H.M. Caiserman to Glass, 2 December 1935, file 16, box 2, Series ZA 1935, CJC Collection, CJCNA, Montreal.

45 P. Stuchen to H.M. Caiserman, 2 December 1935, file 16, box 2, Series ZA 1935, CJC Collection, CJCNA, Montreal.

46 M.N. Eisendrath to H.M. Caiserman, 12 December 1935, file 42, box 4, Series ZA 1935, CJC Collection, CJCNA, Montreal.

47 C.H. Moses to H.M. Caiserman, 18 January 1936, file 26, box 2, Series ZA 1936, CJC Collection, CJCNA, Montreal; on Orlick, see Bruce Kidd, *The Struggle for Canadian Sport* (Toronto: University of Toronto Press, 1996), 172.

48 H. Glucksman to H. Golden, [responding to Golden's letter of 24 December 1935 (not preserved)], 27 December 1935, YM-YWHA Fonds, JPLA, Montreal.

49 "Report submitted by Mr. Harvey Golden on the trip made to New York City and New Jersey for the purpose of investigating the policy of American YMHA's as to their attitude to the Olympics, which are scheduled to be held in Germany," 20 January 1936, YM-YWHA Fonds, JPLA, Montreal.

50 Athletic Board, Minutes for 14 January 1936, McGill University Minute

Book, 1935–1946, file 30, container 12, RG 46, McGill University Archives, Montreal. (The dates of the meeting and of the letter are odd, as the meeting is supposedly taking place before the letter went out. However, the invitation and the McGill discussion are about the same event.)

51 H. Golden to H. Bronfman, 15 February 1936, YM-YWHA Fonds, JPLA, Montreal. Golden summarizes the decision of the Board, but the actual minutes of the meeting have not, to date, been uncovered.

52 Minutes of the meeting of the Special Committee on Olympics, 30 January 1936, YM-YWHA Fonds, JPLA, Montreal.

53 The best description of that world is in Sammy Luftspring and Brian Swarbick, *Call Me Sammy* (Scarborough, ON: Prentice-Hall, 1975), 1–79.

54 *Toronto Daily Star*, 2 January 1936, 14. *Gut yontif* is Yiddish for "Happy Holiday," traditionally offered between Jews on religious holidays.

55 *Toronto Daily Star*, 26 December 1935, 14.

56 *Toronto Daily Star*, 2 January 1936, 14.

57 *Toronto Daily Star*, 22 January 1936, 11.

58 Minutes of the Canadian Olympic Committee meeting, Royal York Hotel, Toronto, 16 November 1934, file 7, MG 30, C164, Jack Davies Fonds, LAC, Ottawa.

59 H.M. Caiserman to Cass (Vancouver), 20 November 1935, file 16, box 2, Series ZA 1935, CJC Collection, CJCNA, Montreal; H.M. Caiserman to Bercovitch (Quebec), 20 November, 1935, file 16, box 2, Series ZA 1935, CJC Collection, CJCNA, Montreal; H.M. Caiserman to Finkelstein (Winnipeg), 21 November 1935, file 16, box 2, Series ZA 1935, CJC Collection, CJCNA, Montreal.

60 Editorial, *Dos yidishe vort* (Winnipeg), 26 November 1935, 2; M.A. Gray to H.M. Caiserman, 25 November 1935, file 16, box 2, Series ZA 1935, CJC Collection, CJCNA, Montreal.

61 *BC Worker*, 29 November 1935, cited in Kidd, *Struggle for Canadian Sport*, 32.

62 *The Worker*, 8 January 1936.

63 See below, page 128 (Winter) and page 156 (Summer).

64 National Labour Council to King, 27 November 1935, mfm C3679, 175933, Mackenzie King Papers, LAC, Ottawa.

65 G. Langsner to King, 4 December 1935, file 187, RG 25, volume 1697, Records of the Department of External affairs, LAC, Ottawa.

66 Minutes of the meeting of the Canadian Olympic Committee, Queen's Hotel, Montreal, 13 January 1936, file 8, MG 30 C164, volume 20, Jack Davies Fonds, LAC, Ottawa.

67 *Canadian Jewish Chronicle* (Montreal), 17 January 1936, 4.

68 Francis Mansbridge, *Hollyburn: The Mountain and the City* (Vancouver: Ronsdale Press, 2008), 87–88.

69 Clipping from the *Montreal Daily Star*, 13 January 1936, file 8, MG 30 C164, volume 20, Jack Davies Fonds, LAC, Ottawa.

70 Minutes of the meeting of the COC, 13 January 1936, LAC.

71 Ibid.

72 *Toronto Daily Star*, 17 January 1936, 10.

73 *The Worker*, 23 January 1936, 2.

74 "Olympia," *Canadian Ski Year Book* (1935), 76.

75 Lukin Robinson, interview with Harold Troper, Toronto, Ontario, 10 February 2010.

76 *Canadian Ski Year Book* (1935).

77 Lukin Robinson, interview.

78 The following description of the treatment of the Wolverines, and the implications, draws on the thorough study by Mark Savoie, "Broken Time and Broken Hearts: The Maritimes and the Selection of Canada's 1936 Olympic Hockey Team," *Sport History Review* 31 (2000): 120–8.

79 Stitt to Caiserman, 3 December 1935, cited in Rome, *Jewish Archival Record of 1935*, 36.

80 *Dos yidishe vort* (Winnipeg), 20 December 1935, 1; *Montreal Gazette*, 20 December 1935; *Dos yidishe vort* (Winnipeg), 26 December 1935, 1.

81 Bruce Kidd, "Canadian Opposition to the Olympics in Germany," *Canadian Journal of the History of Sport* 9, no. 2 (December 1978), 32, citing an article from *The Worker*, 23 January 1936.

82 *Toronto Globe*, 31 December 1935, 6.

83 The details on the Montreal protest come from a summary of Arnold Robertson's recollection of the protest, as told by his son, in "Chapter 19 – The Canadian League against War and Fascism/Berlin Olympics Protest," *have it your own stupid way* (blog), 28 February 2011, http://haveityourown stupidway.blogspot.ca/2011/02/chapter-19-league-against-war-and.html; as well as Gregory S. Kealey and Reg Whitaker, eds., *RCMP Security Bulletins: The Depression Years, Part III, 1936* (St. John's, NL: Canadian Committee on Labour History, 1995), 53; and L. Kempff to Berlin, 14 January 1936, R77315, Politisches Archiv des Auswärtigen Amts, Inland, BA, Berlin.

84 Cited in John Wong, "Sports Networks on Ice: The Canadian Experience at the 1936 Olympic Hockey Tournament," *Sport History Review* 34, no. 2 (November 2003), 196.

85 Minutes of the meeting of the COC, 13 January 1936, LAC.

86 Savoie, "Broken Time and Broken Hearts," 127–31.

87 *Toronto Daily Star*, 17 January 1936, 10.

88 *Montreal Gazette*, 3 January 1936, 12.

89 L. Kempff to Berlin, 14 January 1936, R77315, Politisches Archiv des Auswärtigen Amts, Inland, BA, Berlin.

90 *Montreal Gazette*, 14 January 1936, 12.

91 *Toronto Globe*, 28 January 1936, 6.

92 *Toronto Daily Star*, 3 January 1936, 1.

93 *Winnipeg Free Press*, 5 February 1936, 1; *Montreal Gazette*, 5 February 1936, 14. These press accounts refer to a thousand athletes; the Canadian Olympic Committee estimated 757 competitors from seventeen countries and historian David Large arrived at the number 688. See Canadian Olympic Committee, *Canada at eleventh Olympiad 1936 in Germany, Garmisch-Partenkirchen February 6th to 13th, Berlin August 1st to 16th: Official report of the Canadian Olympic Committee* (Dunnville, ON: W.A. Fry, n.d.), 93, and Large, *Nazi Games*, 127.

94 COC, *Canada at eleventh Olympiad 1936*, 93.

95 Large, *Nazi Games*, 123.

96 A.H. Pangman, "Canada's 1936 Olympic Ski Team," *Canadian Ski Year Book* (1936), 29.

97 Lois Butler, "Canada's 1936 Olympic Women's Ski Team," *Canadian Ski Year Book* (1936), 34–5.

98 Pangman, "Canada's 1936 Olympic Ski Team," 29–31.

99 For the Canadian angle on the controversy, but especially during the Summer Olympics, see James M. Pitsula, "Strange Salute," *The Beaver* 84, no. 4 (August–September 2004), 14–9. The quote is from that article as well.

100 Butler, "Canada's 1936 Olympic Women's Ski Team," 35. Kingsmill was born into a life of privilege and married an English aristocrat, but eventually divorced Gordon-Lennox, married the left-wing journalist and writer Jim Wright, and settled into a life in Saskatchewan where she edited a newspaper of the farmers' union and became a pioneer in the environmental movement.

101 Pangman, "Canada's 1936 Olympic Ski Team," 28–33.

102 Ralph St. Germain, "Olympic Fact and Friction," *Newsletter of the Phi Kappa Pi Almuni Society, McGill Chapter* (April 1936), 2–3. This forthright article, written within weeks of the return of the team to Canada, was by St. Germain but approved by four other members of the team. A copy of the newsletter is in file 8, MG 30 C164, volume 20, Jack Davies Fonds, LAC, Ottawa.

103 St. Germain, "Olympic Fact and Friction," 3.

104 Wong, "Sports Networks on Ice," 195–202. Most of our discussion on tensions between the CAHA and the international body comes from that detailed article.

105 Andrew Podnieks, *Canada's Olympic Hockey Teams: The Complete History* (Toronto: Doubleday, 1997).

106 Monique Berlioux, *Des jeux et des crimes. 1936. Le piège blanc olympique*, vol. 2 (Biarritz, France: Atlantica, 2007), 411–2. Berlioux seems to be relying on information from Bunny Ahearne, but unfortunately the book does not provide references for this and other important points.

107 Wong, "Sports Networks on Ice," 201–2.

108 *Montreal Gazette*, 14 February 1936, 14; *Die Tagebücher von Joseph Goebbels. Sämtliche Fragmente*, Part 1, ed. Elke Frölich, vol. 2 (Munich: Sauer, 1987), 573.

109 *Toronto Daily Star*, 17 February 1936, 1.

110 Wong, "Sports Networks," 203.

111 St. Germain, "Olympic Fact and Friction," 3.

112 J.P. Bond in Berlin to A.S. Lamb in Montreal, 1 March 1936, file 8, MG 30 C164, volume 20, Jack Davies Fonds, LAC, Ottawa. The question mark is in the original.

113 St. Germain, "Olympic Fact and Friction," 3.

114 J.P. Bond in Berlin to A.S. Lamb in Montreal, 1 March 1936, file 8, MG 30 C164, volume 20, Jack Davies Fonds, LAC, Ottawa. All the emphases (using underlining) are in the original.

115 *Montreal Gazette*, 17 February 1936, 7, cited in Wong, "Sports Networks on Ice," 204.

116 Wong, "Sports Networks on Ice," 204.

117 *Die Olympische Spiele 1936 in Berlin und Garmisch-Partenkirchen*, vol. 1. (Altona-Bahrenfeld: Cigaretten-Bilderdienst, 1936), 20.

118 Conversions mattered little in Nazi racial thinking, although they did have some impact on status as defined by the Nuremberg Laws.

119 The most detailed information on Ball is currently online. See, for example, Birger Nordmark and Patrick Houda, "Rudi Ball: 1910–1975," on the website for the Swedish Ice Hockey Historical and Statistical Society, accessed 3 May 2012, http://www.sihss.se/RudiBallbiography.htm

120 Berlioux, *Des jeux et des crimes*, vol. 2, 419.

121 *Toronto Daily Star*, 28 February 1936, 1, 7.

122 *Toronto Daily Star*, 29 February 1936, 1, 7.

123 *Toronto Daily Star*, 28 February 1936, 7.

124 *Die Olympische Spiele 1936 in Berlin und Garmisch-Partenkirchen*, vol. 1, 1.

125 St. Germain, "Olympic Fact and Friction," 3.

126 Len Rountree, "The Winter Olympics," *Canadian Olympic Trials Review* (Montreal: Perrault, 1936), 50, preserved in Charles Mayer Fonds,

127 *Globe*, 4 March 1936, 9.

128 *Montreal Gazette*, 14 February 1936, 14; *Die Tagebücher von Joseph Goebbels*, vol. 2, 574.

129 *Toronto Mail and Empire*, 12 February 1936. On Haag's authorship, see L. Kempff to Berlin, 28 February 1936, R8077-166, H-M, Politisches Archiv des Auswärtigen Amts, Inland, BA, Berlin.

5. Preparations and Protests: March–July 1936

1 Brundage, back in New York, quoted in the *Toronto Daily Star*, 26 February 1936, 10; also in the *Toronto Globe*, 26 February 1936, 6.

2 Wolfgang Benz, *A Concise History of the Third Reich*, trans. Thomas Dunlap (Berkeley: University of California Press, 2007), 159.

3 David Clay Large, *Nazi Games: The Olympics of 1936* (New York: Norton, 2007), 149–50; Fabrice Abgrall and François Thomazeau, *La France à l'épreuve des jeux Olympiques de Berlin* (Paris: Alvik, 2006), 126–7.

4 *Toronto Globe*, 11 March 1936, 6.

5 Daphné Bolz, *Les arènes totalitaires: Hitler, Mussolini et les jeux du stade* (Paris: CNRS Éditions, 2008), 202.

6 Susanne Dost, *Das Olympische Dorf 1936 im Wandel der Zeit* (Berlin: Verlag Bernd Neddermeyer, 2004), 12–4.

7 Ursula Breymayer and Bernd Ulrich, "Commemorating Heroes: The Conflict Surrounding the Commemoration of the Dead from the First World War," in *1909 Historic Site: 1936 The Olympic Grounds 2006*, ed. Rainer Rother (Berlin: Jovis Verlag, 2006), 22–37; see also, in the same volume, pp. 118–33.

8 *Historic Site, 1936*, 133.

9 Bolz, *Les arènes totalitaires*, 215.

10 Dost, *Das Olympische Dorf*, 33–4.

11 Large, *Nazi Games*, 184–5; Reinhard Rürup, ed., *1936: Die Olympischen Spiele und der Nationalsozialismus: eine Dokumentation* [1936: The Olympic Games and national socialism: A documentation], 2nd ed. (Berlin: Argon, 1999), 321.

12 Peter Longreich, *Holocaust: The Nazi Persecution and Murder of Jews* (Oxford: Oxford University Press, 2010), 49–50.

13 Longereich, *Holocaust*, 49.

14 Rürup, *Die Olympischen Spiele*, 140–1.

15 Guenter Lewy, *The Nazi Persecution of the Gypsies* (New York: Oxford University Press, 2000), 22–3.

16 W. Haag to A.S. Lamb, 18 January 1936, file 14, MG 130 C164, vol. 20, Jack Davies Fonds, Library and Archives Canada (LAC), Ottawa.

17 Jonathan F. Wagner, *Brothers Beyond the Sea: National Socialism in Canada* (Waterloo, ON: Wilfrid Laurier University Press, 1981), 55.

18 Wagner, *Brothers*, 58–60; 78–9.

19 L. Kempff to Berlin, 28 February 1936, R8077-166, Bundesarchiv (BA), Berlin.

20 Memorandum by L. Kempff on camps, file 187, RG 28, vol. 1697, Records of Department of External Affairs, LAC, Ottawa; O.D. Skelton to J.H. Crocker (COC), file 187, RG 28, vol. 1697, Records of Department of External Affairs, LAC, Ottawa.

21 L. Kempff to Berlin [including memorandum by Kempff on art exhibition], 28 February 1936, R8077-166, BA, Berlin.

22 Ibid.

23 O.D. Skelton to L. Kempff, 7 December 1935, file 187, RG 28, vol. 1697, Records of Department of External Affairs, LAC, Ottawa.

24 O.D. Skelton to J.H. Crocker (COC), 2 March 1936, file 187, RG 28, vol. 1697, Records of Department of External Affairs, LAC, Ottawa.

25 P.J. Mulqueen to "Organizing Committee for the XIth Olympiad Berlin," 16 March 1936, R8076/166, BA, Berlin.

26 O.D. Skelton to J.H. Crocker, 24 March 1936, file 187, RG 28, vol. 1697, Records of Department of External Affairs, LAC, Ottawa.

27 J.H. Crocker to O.D. Skelton, 29 March 1936, file 187, RG 28, vol. 1697, Records of Department of External Affairs, LAC, Ottawa.

28 R.T. McKenzie to A.W. Treadaway, 1 June 1936, R8076/166, BA, Berlin.

29 H.J. Crocker to O.D. Skelton, 19 March 1936, file 187, RG 28, vol. 1697, Records of Department of External Affairs, LAC, Ottawa.

30 E. Brown to O.D. Skelton, 24 March 1936, file 187, RG 28, vol. 1697, Records of Department of External Affairs, LAC, Ottawa.

31 E. Brown to O.D. Skelton, 30 March 1936, file 187, RG 28, vol. 1697, Records of Department of External Affairs, LAC, Ottawa.

32 Ibid.

33 L. Kempff to O.D. Skelton, 14 April 1936, file 187, RG 28, vol. 1697, Records of Department of External Affairs, LAC, Ottawa.

34 O.D. Skelton to L. Kempff, 2 May 1936, file 187, RG 28, vol. 1697, Records of Department of External Affairs, LAC, Ottawa.

35 *Montreal Gazette*, 12 February 1936, 15. See also the minutes of the meeting of the COC, Halifax, 22 November 1935, file 7, MG 30 C164, vol. 20, Jack Davies Fonds, LAC, Ottawa.

36 Meeting of Athletic Board, 14 January 1936, McGill University Minute Book 1935–1946, file 30, container 12, RG 46, McGill University Archives (McGUA), Montreal.

37 A.R. Robertson to A.S. Lamb, 16 January 1936, file 8, MG 30 C164, vol. 20, Jack Davies Fonds, LAC, Ottawa.

38 Minutes of the meeting of the Canadian Olympic Committee, Queen's Hotel, Montreal, 13 January 1936, file 8, MG 30 C164, vol. 20, Jack Davies Fonds, LAC, Ottawa.

39 Meeting of Athletic Board, 14 January 1936, McGUA. Curiously, the preserved letter is dated 16 January, but the minutes of the McGill meetings, where this letter was clearly discussed, is shown as 14 January.

40 Minutes of the meeting of the Canadian Olympic Committee executive, Royal York Hotel, Toronto, 20 March 1936, file 9, MG 30 C164, vol. 20, Jack Davies Fonds, LAC, Ottawa.

41 Ibid.

42 *Montreal Gazette*, 7 July 1936, 13; *Montreal Gazette*, 8 July 1936, 6.

43 Count Baillet-Latour, "The Eleventh Olympiad," in *Canadian Olympic Trials Review* (Montreal: Perrault, 1936), 5, preserved in file A, MG 30 C76, vol. 20, Charles Mayer Fonds, LAC, Ottawa.

44 A.S. Lamb, "The Olympiad," in *Canadian Olympic Trials Review* (Montreal: Perrault, 1936), 7, 9, 49.

45 *Montreal Gazette*, 7 July 1936, 13.

46 *Montreal Gazette*, 11 July 1936, 12.

47 *Montreal Gazette*, 8 July 1936, 14.

48 *Toronto Daily Star*, 16 March 1936, 11.

49 Resolution of Hamilton District Trades and Labor [*sic*], 15 March 1936, forwarded to Mackenzie King, microfilm, C-3649, pp. 19, 608–9, Mackenzie King Papers, LAC, Ottawa.

50 Gregory S. Kealey, "Stanley Brehaut Ryerson: Canadian Revolutionary Intellectual," *Studies in Political Economy: A Socialist Review* 9 (1982), 106.

51 Gregory S. Kealey and Reg Whitaker, eds., *RCMP Security Bulletins: The Depression Years, Part III, 1936* (St. John's, NL: Canadian Committee on Labour History, 1996), 138.

52 Program of symposium, 27 March 1936, YM-YWHA Fonds, Jewish Public Library Archives (JPLA), Montreal.

53 On the CCF-LSR meeting, held on the day after the Montreal symposium, see Walter D. Young, *The Anatomy of a Party: The National CCF, 1932–6* (Toronto: University of Toronto Press, 1969), 264.

54 "Memorandum of a meeting held in Mr. Golden's office, Sunday, March 22nd, 1936, 3 p.m.," YM-YWHA Fonds, JPLA, Montreal.

55 The "Horst Wessel Song" was commonly sung at Nazi Party functions alongside "Deutschland über Alles." The lyrics were originally written by S.A. member Horst Wessel, posthumously hailed as a Nazi martyr after his 1930 murder said by the Nazis to be at the hands of a communist. Before the Nazis assumed power, the "Horst Wessel Song" was widely used as a Nazi marching song and Nazi Party anthem. When Hitler became chancellor in 1933 the song was given official status alongside "Deutschland über Alles." It was also decreed that the right arm should be raised in salute when the first and fourth verses were sung. While Germans were accustomed to singing the "Horst Wessel Song" following "Deutschland über Alles," non-Germans attending the Olympic opening might well have been taken aback by the aggressive message contained in the lyrics:

> Flag high, ranks closed,
> the S.A. marches with silent solid steps.
> Comrades shot by the red front and reaction
> march in spirit with us in our ranks.
> The street free for the brown battalions,
> the street free for the Storm Troopers.
> Millions, full of hope, look up at the swastika;
> the day breaks for freedom and for bread.
> For the last time the call will now be blown;
> for the struggle now we all stand ready.
> Soon will fly Hitler-flags over every street;
> slavery will last only a short time longer.
> Flag high, ranks closed,
> the S.A. marches with silent solid steps.
> Comrades shot by the red front and reaction
> march in spirit with us in our ranks.

56 "Address by Mr. Harvey Golden, Friday, March 27, 1936, Symposium against Canadian participation in Olympic Games," YM-YWHA Fonds, JPLA, Montreal.

57 *Daily Clarion*, 15 May 1936, 2.

58 Michael Brown, "On Campus in the Thirties: Antipathy, Support and Indifference," in *Nazi German, Canadian Responses: Confronting Antisemitism in the Shadow of War,* ed. L. Ruth Klein (Montreal: McGill-Queen's University Press, 2012), 154–5, 166.

59 *Daily Clarion*, 15 May 1936, 4.

60 Alan Abrams, *Why Windsor? An Anecdotal History of the Jews of Windsor and Essex County* (Windsor: Black Moss Press, 1981), 99.

61 H.A. Minden (Hamilton) to H.M. Caiserman, 8 July 1936, file 16, box 2, CJC series, CJC series, ZA 1935 [*sic*], Canadian Jewish Congress Charities Committee National Archives (CJCNA), Montreal. Note: the [*sic*] is to indicate that the 1936 document has been miscatalogued with the 1935 material.

62 *Montreal Gazette*, 16 July 1936, 13.

63 McGeer quoted the telegram by Houde in the form letter used for fundraising found in files 6 and 7, Mayor's Olympic Fund, General Correspondence, loc. 33-C-5, series 483, Mayor's Office Fonds, City of Vancouver Archives (CVA), Vancouver.

64 *Montreal Standard*, 18 July 1936, a clipping preserved in files 6 and 7, Mayor's Olympic Fund, General Correspondence, loc. 33-C-5, series 483, Mayor's Office Fonds, CVA, Vancouver.

65 Files 6 and 7, Mayor's Olympic Fund, General Correspondence, loc. 33-C-5, series 483, Mayor's Office Fonds, CVA, Vancouver.

66 W.G. Swan to G. McGeer, 14 July 1936, file 6, Mayor's Olympic Fund, General Correspondence, loc. 33-C-5, series 483, Mayor's Office Fonds, CVA, Vancouver.

67 V.W. Odlum to G. McGeer, 14 July 1936, file 7, Mayor's Olympic Fund, General Correspondence, loc. 33-C-5, series 483, Mayor's Office Fonds, CVA, Vancouver.

68 Records of donations to Mayor's Olympic Fund, file 7, Mayor's Olympic Fund, General Correspondence, loc. 33-C-5, series 483, Mayor's Office Fonds, CVA, Vancouver.

69 These are all reported in the *Montreal Gazette*, 15 July 1936, 13, and 16 July 1936, 13.

70 *Winnipeg Free Press*, 21 July 1936, 15.

71 R.B. Bennett to P.J. Mulqueen, 27 July 1936, file 5A, box 5063, AFC 62, J. Howard Crocker Fonds, University of Western Ontario Archives (UWOA), London, ON; P.J. Mulqueen to R.B. Bennett, 22 September 1936, file 5A, box 5063, AFC 62, J. Howard Crocker Fonds, UWOA, London, ON.

72 Canadian Olympic Committee, financial statement, 1 May 1933–31 August 1937, file 1, box 5063, AFC 62, J. Howard Crocker Fonds, UWOA, London, ON.

73 Minutes of the meeting of the Special Committee on Olympics, held on Thurs. Jan. 30th, 1936, YM-YWHA Fonds, JPLA, Montreal.

74 H.M. Adelstein (business manager) to Lions Club, 7 July 1936, YM-YWHA Fonds, JPLA, Montreal.

75 Minutes of the meeting of the Special Committee on Olympics, 30 January1936, JPLA.

76 H.M. Caiserman to O.B. Roger, 6 July 1936, file 26, box 2, CJC Collection ZA 1936, CJCNA, Montreal.

77 Sid Tafler, *Us and Them: A Memoir of Tribes and Tribulations* (Victoria, BC: NETBC, 2006). Our thanks to Mr. Tafler for giving us a copy of this fascinating memoir of his father.

78 Description of the annual meeting of the CASwA, 24–25 April 1936, YM-YWHA Fonds, JPLA, Montreal.

79 Ibid., citing the *Montreal Daily Star*, 27 April 1936.

80 *The New Commonwealth*, 1 February 1936, 1 and 2.

81 "Minutes of the CCF Provincial Convention held in Vancouver, B.C., July 3, 4, 5, 6," p. 10, file 4, box 55, MacInnis Collection, University of British Columbia Library, University Archives (UBCLUA), Vancouver.

82 Ibid.

83 Xavier Pujadas and Carles Santacana, "The Popular Olympic Games, Barcelona, 1936: Olympians and Antifascists," *International Review for the Sociology of Sport* 27 (1992), 139–144. On Canada and the Barcelona Olympiad, see Bruce Kidd, "Canadian Opposition to the 1936 Olympics in Germany," *Canadian Journal of the History of Sport and Physical Education* 9 (1978), 33–6.

84 *Daily Clarion*, 19 May 1936, 1. At the beginning of May 1936, the *Daily Clarion* superseded *The Worker*.

85 *Daily Clarion*, 29 May 1936, 1.

86 Kealey and Whitaker, eds., *RCMP Security Bulletins (1936)*, 232.

87 *Daily Clarion*, 6 June 1936, 4.

88 *Daily Clarion*, 27 June 1936, 4.

89 Edward S. Shapiro, "The World Labor Athletic Carnival of 1936: An American Anti-Nazi Protest," *American Jewish History* 74 (1985), 260–1, 264–6.

90 Clipping from *Time Union* (Albany), scrapbooks of the Carnival, box 13, folder 6, series I, Records of the Jewish Labor Committee, New York University, Tamiment Library and Robert F. Wagner Labor Archives (NYU), New York. These scrapbooks are now only available on the microfilms made of the collection; we used microfilms at Concordia University Library (reel 29 has the scrapbooks).

91 Schedule of events preserved in scrapbooks of the Carnival, box 13, folder 6, series I, microfilm reel 29, Records of the Jewish Labor Committee, NYU, New York.

92 Clipping from *Ottawa Citizen*, 17 August 1936, in scrapbooks of the Carnival, box 13, folder 6, series I, microfilm reel 29, Records of the Jewish Labor Committee, NYU, New York.

93 Clipping from *Forverts*, 27 August 1936, scrapbooks of the Carnival, box 13, folder 6, series I, microfilm reel 29, Records of the Jewish Labor Committee, NYU, New York.

94 *Daily Clarion*, 17 June 1936, 4.

95 *Daily Clarion*, 6 July 1936, 1.

96 Kidd, "Canadian Opposition to the 1936 Olympics in Germany," 34.

97 Kidd, "Canadian Opposition to the 1936 Olympics in Germany," 23.

98 M. Ann Hall, *Globe and Mail*, 19 June 2009, section 11.

99 *Daily Clarion*, 4 July 1936, 1.

100 Sammy Luftspring with Brian Swarbrick, *Call Me Sammy* (Scarborough: Prentice-Hall, 1975), 33–4.

101 *Toronto Daily Star*, 4 June 1936, 14.

102 *Toronto Daily Star*, 4 June 1936, 14.

103 H. Golden to H.M. Caiserman, 22 June 1936, file 26, box 2, CJC Collection ZA 1936, CJCNA, Montreal.

104 Cohn to H. Golden, 19 June 1936, file 26, box 2, CJC Collection ZA 1936, CJCNA, Montreal.

105 Ibid.

106 *Globe*, 16 June 1936, 6.

107 Cohn to H. Golden, 19 June 1936, CJCNA.

108 Cohn to H. Golden, 24 June 1936 and 3 July 1936, YMHA Fonds, JPLA, Montreal.

109 The letter is dated Sunday, July 4th, but 4 July 1936 was a Saturday. Because the letter refers to a planned press conference the next day, which took place on Monday, it must have occurred on the Sunday and the written date must be inaccurate.

110 O.B. Roger to H.M. Caiserman, 6 July 1936, file 26, box 2, CJC Collection ZA 1936, CJCNA, Montreal.

111 *Der yidisher zhurnal*, 7 July 1936, 1.

112 *Toronto Globe*, 7 July 1936, 7.

113 H. Golden to Cohn, 8 July 1936, YMHA Fonds, JPLA, Montreal.

114 H.M. Caiserman to O.B. Roger, 6 July 1936, file 26, box 2, CJC s Collection ZA 1936, CJCNA, Montreal.

115 *Der yidisher zhurnal*, 7 July 1936, 4.

116 Luftspring with Swarbrick, *Call Me Sammy*, 87–8.

117 Invitation for stag on 9 July 1936, Luftspring scrapbook, Luftspring Papers, Fonds 61, Ontario Jewish Archives (OJA), Toronto.

118 "Trip to Barcelona and Return," 10 July 1936, Luftspring Papers, Fonds 61, OJA, Toronto.

119 *Toronto Daily Star*, 11 July 1936, 12.

120 *Toronto Daily Star*, 17 July 1936, 4.

6. Crimson Blazers

1 "Trip to Barcelona and Return," 10 July 1936, Luftspring Papers, Fonds 61, Ontario Jewish Archives (OJA), Toronto.
2 Jacqueline Hucker, "The Meaning and Significance of the Vimy Monument," in *Vimy Ridge: A Canadian Reassessment,* eds. Geoffrey Hayes et al. (Waterloo, ON: Wilfrid Laurier University Press, 2007), 279–90.
3 Passenger list, Duchess of Bedford, 17 July 1936, file 12, box 1, Vimy Ridge Pilgrimage Collection-1936, William Ready Division of Archives and Research Collections, McMaster University Libraries, Hamilton.
4 See Liverpool Ships at http://www.liverpoolships.org/empress_of_france_canadian_pacific.html, accessed 8 September 2012.
5 Ibid.
6 Alia Dharssi, "'A Patched Bathing Suit': Joan McLagan's Experience at the 1936 Olympics," *Zachor* (2010), 6.
7 Tony Techko and Carl Morgan, *The Olympians Among Us: Celebrating a Century of Excellence* (Tecumseh, ON: TravelLife Publishing Enterprises, 1995), 12.
8 Menu, Duchess of Bedford, Saturday July 18, box 1, F3, 1936, Vimy Pilgrimage Collection 1936, William Ready Division of Archives and Research Collection, McMaster University Libraries, Hamilton.
9 Canadian Olympic Committee, *Canada at Eleventh Olympiad 1936 in Germany, Garmisch-Partenkirchen February 6th to 13th, Berlin August 1st to 16th: Official report of the Canadian Olympic Committee* (Dunnville, ON: W.A. Fry, n.d.), 90.
10 *Ottawa Citizen,* 31 August 1936, 2.
11 COC, *Canada at Eleventh Olympiad 1936,* 12–3.
12 "Trip to Barcelona and Return," Tuesday, 21 July 1936, Luftspring Papers, Fonds 61, OJA, Toronto; *Globe,* 24 July 1936.
13 "Trip to Barcelona and Return," Wednesday, 22 July 1936, Luftspring Papers, Fonds 61, OJA, Toronto.
14 "Trip to Barcelona and Return," Saturday, 25 July 1936, Luftspring Papers, Fonds 61, OJA, Toronto.
15 Henry Roxborough, *Canada at the Olympics,* 3rd ed. (Toronto: McGraw-Hill Ryerson, 1975), 92–4.
16 Ibid.
17 Belle Weisman, interview by telephone to Boulder, Colorado, 25 March 2009, interviewed by Harold Troper; Warren Meretsky, interview by telephone to Ft. Lauderdale, Florida, 25 March 2009, interviewed by Harold Troper.
18 Tony Atherton, "Berlin Olympics a Breakthrough for Canadian Basketball," *Postmedia News,* 9 August 2011.

19 COC, *Canada at Eleventh Olympiad 1936*, 13.

20 Olympic Games (11th: 1936: Berlin, Germany). Organisationskomitee für die Spiele der XI. Olympiade, *The XIth Olympic Games, Berlin, 1936: Official Report*, vol. 1 (Berlin: Wilhelm Limpert, 1937), 225.

21 Dharssi, "'A Patched Bathing Suit,'" 7.

22 *The XIth Olympic Games Berlin, 1936*, vol. 1, 226.

23 Paul R. Washke, "The Eleventh Olympiad," *Journal of Health and Physical Education* 7 (1936), 540–1.

24 Joe Griffiths, "Diary of My Trip to Germany, 1936," 19, Joe Griffiths Papers, University of Saskatchewan Archives, (USaskA), Saskatoon.

25 *The XIth Olympic Games Berlin, 1936*, vol. 1, 177.

26 Quoted in David Clay Large, *Nazi Games: The Olympics of 1936* (New York: Norton, 2007), 182–3.

27 Griffiths, "Diary of My Trip to Germany, 1936," 29.

28 *Toronto Daily Star*, 31 July 1936, 2.

29 *Der Angriff* as quoted by Large, *Nazi Games*, 184.

30 *New York Times*, 25 July 1936, 10.

31 Griffiths, "Diary of My Trip to Germany, 1936," 27.

32 German Olympic Committee, 30 September 1935, R8077/184, Bundesarchiv (BA), Berlin. Among the other scheduled cultural events was the "World Leisure and Recreation Congress" in Hamburg, an "International Sports Medicine Congress," a "Chess Olympics" in Munich, music and arts festivals, and, with Canadian participation, an international Physical Education Congress and International Youth Gathering. Large, *Nazi Games*, 204–9.

33 *New York Times*, 13 March 1936, 6; Mark Franko, *Martha Graham in Love and War: The Life in the Work* (New York: Oxford University Press, 2012), 12.

34 John Ayre, "Berlin, 1936: Canadian Dancers at Hitler's Olympics," *The Beaver* 76 (February–March 1996), 37. For a background discussion of Canadian participation in the German dance competition, see Christine M. O'Bonsawin, "Spectacles, Policies and Social Memory: Images of Canadian Indians at World Fairs and Olympic Games," (PhD diss., University of Western Ontario, 2006), 256–86.

35 For a discussion of the mythical native content, see Christine M. O'Bonsawin, "'An Indian Atmosphere': Indian Policy and Canadian Participation in Berlin's Internationale Tanzwettspiele" (paper presented at the Cultural Relations Old and New: The Transitory Olympic Ethos, Seventh International Symposium for Olympic Research, Los Angeles, 2004), 105–14.

36 Bunny Lang, "Internationaler Tanz," *The Bulletin* (Winter 1936–7), 13.

37 Mary Wilder to her mother, 19 July 1936, 212.2012-1-1, Mary Wilder Collection, Dance Collection Danse Archives (DCDA), Toronto.

38 Ayre, "Berlin, 1936," 39.

39 Lang, "Internationaler Tanz," 13.

40 Press clipping, "Volkoff Dancers Score in Germany," scrapbook, Mary Wilder Collection, DCDA, Toronto.

41 Arthur Michel, "International Dance Festival, Berlin 1936," *Journal of Health and Physical Education* 7 (1936), 552.

42 COC, *Canada at Eleventh Olympiad1936*, 103.

43 O'Bonsawin, "Spectacles, Policies and Social Memory," 277–9.

44 Olympic Games (11th: 1936: Berlin, Germany). *The XIth Olympic Games Berlin, 1936: Official Report*, vol. 2, 1149–51.

45 COC, *Canada at Eleventh Olympiad 1936*, 110.

46 *The XIth Olympic Games Berlin, 1936: Official Report*, vol. 2, 1141.

47 Thomas Dora Mavor Moore to J.A. Derry, 5 July 1936, box 158:2, MC 207, Mavor Moore Collection, Thomas Fisher Rare Book Library, University of Toronto.

48 *The XIth Olympic Games Berlin, 1936: Official Report*, vol. 2, 1144.

49 Ibid., 1144–6.

50 John Derry, interview with Harold Troper, Thornhill, ON, 11 April 2011.

51 COC, *Canada at Eleventh Olympiad 1936*, 111.

52 Derry, interview.

53 James M. Pitsula, "The Nazi Olympics: A Reinterpretation," *Olympika* 13 (2004), 1–25.

54 Christian Carstensen, "Bearers of the Olympic Flame," *Journal of Health and Physical Fitness* 7 (1936), 479–80.

55 COC, *Canada at Eleventh Olympiad 1936*, 26.

56 COC, *Canada at Eleventh Olympiad 1936*, 26–7.

57 *New York Times*, 25 July 1936, 7.

58 *Toronto Daily Star*, 1 August 1936, 2.

59 McGill Athletics and Recreation, "Hall of Fame, accessed 8 September 2012, http://www.mcgillathletics.ca/hof.aspx?hof=12&path=&kiosk=

60 *Globe and Mail*, 19 July 2012, S1.

61 COC, *Canada at Eleventh Olympiad 1936*, 28. For a full overview of the salute controversy, see James M. Pitsula, "Strange Salute," *The Beaver* 84, no. 4 (2004), 14–9.

62 Griffiths, "Diary of My Trip to Germany, 1936," 23.

63 Lang, "Internationaler Tanz," 14.

64 COC, *Canada at Eleventh Olympiad 1936*, 30.

65 "Diary of trip to 1936 Olympics," p. 24, P19901046002, Fairfield Family Fonds, Sir Alexander Galt Museum and Archives, Lethbridge, AB.

66 "About Jesse Owens," Jesse Owens Trust, accessed 8 September 2012, http://www.jesseowens.com/about/

67 Susan D. Bachrach, *The Nazi Olympics: Berlin 1936* (Boston. Little Brown, 2000), 95–6.

68 Owens is quoted in *New York Times*, 1 April 1980, 1, D17.

69 Large, *Nazi Games*, 240–242; Peter Levine, *Ebbets Field: Sport and the American Jewish Experience* (New York: Oxford University Press, 1992), 232–3.

70 *Montreal Gazette*, 12 August 1936, 12.

71 Lewis A. Erenberg, *The Greatest Fight of Our Generation: Louis vs. Schmeling* (New York: Oxford, 2006), 105.

72 George Eisen, "Jews and Sport: A Century Retrospective," *Journal of Sport History* 26 (1999), 225–39.

73 Large, *Nazi Games*, 84–7.

74 *Toronto Daily Star*, 17 August 1936, 1.

75 *Toronto Daily Star*, 11 August 1936, 2.

76 *Toronto Daily Star*, 1 August 1936, 2.

77 *Montreal Gazette*, 10 September 1936, 13.

78 F. Amyot to W.L. Mackenzie King, n.d., 1936, microfilm C-3685, p. 183, 500, Mackenzie King Papers, Library and Archives Canada (LAC), Ottawa.

79 COC, *Canada at Eleventh Olympiad 1936*, 73.

80 COC, *Canada at Eleventh Olympiad 1936*, 52; *Toronto Daily Star*, 4 August 1936, 1.

81 Kevin Shea, "John 'Johnny' Loaring: Windsor Athlete Par Excellence" *Windsor Life Magazine* (May–June, 2009), 22–3.

82 "Berlin Olympics: Canadian Team Training, Travelling and Competing," film, V1987:14/001.02, James G. McKeachie Collection, Provincial Archives of British Columbia, Victoria, BC. This may be the only footage of the game.

83 Atherton, "Berlin Olympics a Breakthrough for Canadian Basketball."

84 *Ottawa Citizen*, 30 July 2011. For a history of the 1936 Olympic basketball tournament, and particularly the American team, see Richard Hughes, *Netting Out Basketball: The Remarkable Story of the McPherson Refiners, the First Team to Dunk, Zone Press, and Win the Olympic Gold Medal* (Victoria, BC: Friesen Press, 2011).

85 Quoted in Techko and Morgan, *The Olympians Among Us*, 10.

86 In 1999, following media comment that Meretsky had been short-changed his silver medal, the Meretsky family appealed to the IOC to award him a

medal. The IOC minted a silver medal from the original cast. It was presented to the Canadian player on his 70th birthday, 47 years following the end of the Berlin Olympics. Meretsky, interview.

87 McGill Athletics and Recreation, "Hall of Fame," accessed 8 September 2012, http://www.mcgillathletics.ca/hof.aspx?hof=12&path=&kiosk=

88 *Toronto Daily Star*, 4 August 1936, 2.

89 *Toronto Globe*, 7 August 1936, 1.

90 Euler, quoted in *Toronto Daily Star*, 29 August 1936, 3.

91 Pierre Berton, *The Great Depression: 1929–1939* (Toronto: Anchor, 1990), 464.

92 Jonathan F. Wagner, *Brothers Beyond the Sea: National Socialism in Canada* (Waterloo, ON: Wilfred Laurier University Press, 1981), 21; Bastian Bryan Lovasz, "Animosity, Ambivalence and Cooperation: Manifestations of Heterogeneous German Identities in the Kitchener-Waterloo Area During and After the Second World War" (master's thesis, University of Waterloo, 2008), 29–37.

93 Erhard Milch, who oversaw the development of the Luftwaffe as part of the re-armament of Germany and was tried and found guilty of war crimes following the Second World War, was also rumoured to be a Jew. Samuel W. Micham, Jr., *Eagles of the Third Reich: Men of the Luftwaffe in WWII* (Mechanicsberg, PA: Stackpole Books, 2007), 5–11; United Nations War Crimes Commission, *Law Reports of Trials of War Criminals* (London: His Majesty's Stationary Office, 1947), 27–66.

94 Richard Townshend Bickers, *Von Richthofen: The Legend Evaluated* (Annapolis: Naval Institute Press, 1996), 130–6.

95 COC, *Canada at Eleventh Olympiad 1936*, 100; *Toronto Globe*, 5 August 1936, 1–2.

96 COC, *Canada at Eleventh Olympiad 1936*, 10–11.

7. Conclusion

1 Canadian Olympic Committee, *Canada at Eleventh Olympiad 1936 in Germany, Garmisch-Partenkirchen February 6th to 13th, Berlin August 1st to 16th: Official Report of the Canadian Olympic Committee* (Dunnville, ON: W.A. Fry, n.d.), 140.

2 COC, *Canada at Eleventh Olympiad 1936*, 10.

3 Ibid.

4 *Toronto Daily Star*, 24 August 1936, 1.

5 COC, *Canada at Eleventh Olympiad 1936*, 32.

6 *Ottawa Citizen*, 21 August 1936, 2.

7 *Ottawa Citizen*, 22 August 1936, 11.

8 *Toronto Globe*, 10 August 1936, 4.

9 *Montreal Gazette*, 17 August 1936, 14.

10 *Toronto Globe*, 15 August 1936, 6.

11 William C. Beeching, *Canadian Volunteers: Spain 1936–1939* (Regina, SK: University of Regina Press, 1989); Michael Petrou, *Renegades: Canadians in the Spanish Civil War* (Vancouver: University of British Columbia Press, 2008); Mark Zuehlke, *The Gallant Cause: Canadian in the Spanish Civil War, 1936–1939* (Toronto: Wiley, 2007).

12 *Canadian Jewish Review* (Montreal, Toronto), 31 July 1936, 4.

13 Irving Abella and Harold Troper, *None Is Too Many: Canada and the Jews of Europe, 1933–1948* (Toronto: Lester, Orpen and Dennys, 1982), 1–66.

14 A.B. Bennett, "Athletes Abroad," *Jewish Standard* (Toronto), August 1936, 2, 15.

15 Maurice N. Eisendrath, "The Only Gate" (unpublished sermon), 26 September 1936, box 3, folder 2, Collection 167, Eisendrath Collection, American Jewish Archives (AJA), Cincinnati.

16 Diary entry, 29 June 1937, 542, MG26-J, series 13, Diaries of Prime Minister William Lyon Mackenzie King, Library and Archives Canada (LAC), Ottawa; C.P. Stacey, "The Divine Mission: Mackenzie King and Hitler," *Canadian Historical Review* 61, no. 4 (1980), 502–12.

17 *Toronto Daily Star*, 11 August 1936, 2.

18 *Toronto Daily Star*, 25 August 1936, 22.

19 *Vancouver Province*, 29 January 1980.

Bibliography

Archival Collections

American Jewish Archives (Cincinnati)
  Eisendrath Collection
  World Jewish Congress Collection
Bundesarchiv (Berlin)
  Politisches Archiv des Auswärtigen Amts
Canadian Jewish Congress Charities Committee Archives (Montreal)
  CJC Organizational Records Chronological Files
  CJC Organizational Records Personalia Files (ZB – Eisendrath Box)
  Caiserman Files (DA 1)
City of Vancouver Archives (Vancouver)
  Mayor's Office Fonds
Dance Collection Danse (Toronto)
  Mary Wilder Collection
Holy Blossom Temple Archives (Toronto)
  Maurice Eisendrath Papers
  Eisendrath Manuscripts
Jewish Historical Society of British Columbia (Vancouver)
  B'Nai Brith Fonds
Jewish Historical Society Western Canada (Winnipeg)
Jewish Pubic Library Achieves (Montreal)
  Jewish Canadiana Collection, Personalia
  YM-YWHA Fonds
Library and Archives Canada (Ottawa)
  Charles Mayer Fonds

Comintern Fonds
Diaries of Prime Minister William Lyon Mackenzie King
Jack Davies Fonds
Jewish Labour Committee Papers
Mackenzie King Papers
Records of the Department of External Affairs
YMCA Fonds
McGill University Archives (Montreal)
  McGill University Minute Book, 1935–1946
McMaster University Archives (Hamilton)
  Canadian Youth Congress Fonds
  Vimy Ridge Pilgrimage Collection-1936
New York University, Tamiment Library and Robert F. Wagner Labor Archives
  Records of the Jewish Labor Committee Microfilm copy at Concordia
  University, Montreal
Ontario Jewish Archives (Toronto)
  Luftspring Papers
Provincial Archives of British Columbia (Victoria)
  James G. McKeachie Collection
Sir Alexander Galt Museum and Archives (Lethbridge)
  Fairfield Family Fonds
Thomas Fisher Rare Book Library (Toronto)
  Mavor Moore Collection
University of British Columbia Archives (Vancouver)
  MacInnis Collection
University of Saskatchewan Archives (Saskatoon)
  Joe Griffiths Papers
University of Western Ontario Archives (London)
  J. Howard Crocker Fonds

Newspapers

Advance (superseded *The Young Worker*)
Calgary Daily Herald
Canadian Jewish Chronicle (Montreal)
Canadian Jewish Review (Montreal, Toronto)
Commonweal
Daily Clarion (superseded *The Worker*)
Victoria Daily Colonist
Toronto Evening Telegram

Forverts/Forward (New York)
Montreal Gazette
Toronto Globe
Globe and Mail
Der kamf (Toronto)
Der keneder adler (Montreal)
Jewish Post (Winnipeg)
Jewish Standard (Toronto)
Jewish Western Bulletin (Vancouver)
McGill News (Montreal)
Toronto Mail and Empire
Montreal Daily Star
New Commonwealth (Toronto)
New York Times
Ottawa Citizen
Montreal Standard
St. Peter's Bote (Muenster, SK)
Toronto Daily Star
Vancouver Province
Vancouver Sun
Winnipeg Free Press
Winnipeg Tribune
The Worker (superseded by *Daily Clarion*)
Dos yidishe vort (Winnipeg)
Der yidisher Zhurnal (Toronto)
The Young Worker (superseded by *Advance*)

Printed Primary Sources

Amateur Athletic Association of Canada, *Minutes of the Forty-eighth Annual Meeting 1935.* Halifax: Amateur Athletic Association of Canada, 1935.

American Jewish Year Book. Vol. 38 (1936–7). Philadelphia: Jewish Publication Society of America, 1936.

Canada Yearbook (Ottawa, 1922–1923).

Canada. Agriculture and Colonization. *Select Standing Committee on Agriculture and Colonization Report 1928.* Ottawa, 1928.

Canada. Senate. *Proceedings of the Standing Committee on Immigration and Labour.* Ottawa, 1946.

Canadian Ski Year Book (1935).

Canadian Jewish Congress. *Constitution and Resolutions, adopted at Second General Session, January 27, 28 and 29, 1934*. Montreal: Canadian Jewish Congress, 1934.

Canadian League against War and Fascism. *Report. First Canadian Congress against War and Fascism. October 6th and 7th, 1934, Toronto, Ontario*. Toronto: 1934.

Canadian League against War and Fascism. *The People versus War and Fascism: Proceedings Second National Congress against War and Fascism, Toronto, Ontario, December 6th, 7th, 8th, 1935*. Toronto: 1935.

Canadian Olympic Committee. *Canada at Eleventh Olympiad 1936 in Germany, Garmisch-Partenkirchen February 6th to 13th, Berlin August 1st to 16th: Official report of the Canadian Olympic Committee*. Dunnville, ON: W.A. Fry, n.d.

Carstensen, Christian. "Bearers of the Olympic Flame." *Journal of Health and Physical Fitness* 7 (1936).

Cherniack, J.A., Q.C. "Reminiscences of 40 Years of Jewish Community Life." *The Jewish Historical Society of Western Canada. Second Annual Publication. A Selection of Papers Presented in 1969–1970* (April 1972).

Eisendrath, Maurice N. "Hitler's Challenge." *Canadian Club Year Book* (1933).

— "What, No Terror?" *Canadian Comment* (December 1933).

— "Why Are Jews Persecuted? Part One." *Holy Blossom Pulpit* 4, no. 1 (1933–4).

— "One Hell of a Business." *Action against War and Fascism* 1, no. 1 (May 1935).

— "I Re-Visit Nazi Germany." *Holy Blossom Pulpit* 6, no. 3 (1935–6).

Frölich, Elke, ed. *Die Tagebücher von Joseph Goebels: sämtliche Fragmente .Bd. 3:2. März 1936–Februar 1937*. 2nd ed. Munich: K.G. Saur, 1998.

Hunter, Peter. *Which Side Are You On, Boys? Canadian Life on the Left*. Toronto: Lugus, 1988.

International Olympic Committee. *The International Olympic Committee and the Modern Olympic Games*. [Report.] Lausanne: IOC, 1931.

International Olympic Committee. *The International Olympic Committee and the Modern Olympic Games*. [Report.] Lausanne: IOC, 1933.

Kealey, Gregory S., and Reg Whitaker, eds. *RCMP Security Bulletins: The Depression Years, Part I 1933–34*. St. John's, NL: Canadian Committee on Labour History, 1993.

— eds. *RCMP Security Bulletins: The Depression Years, Part II, 1935*. St. John's, NL: Canadian Committee on Labour History, 1995.

— eds. *RCMP Security Bulletins: The Depression Years, Part III, 1936*. St. John's, NL: Canadian Committee on Labour History, 1996.

Kraft, Louis. "The Y.M.H.A. and the Jewish Centre Movement." *Y.M.H.A. Beacon* 5, no. 14 (April 1920).

Lang, Bunny. "Internationaler Tanz." *The Bulletin* (Winter 1936–7).

Lange, Victor. "Does Germany Want War?" *Canadian Comment* (November 1933).

Michel, Arthur. "International Dance Festival, Berlin, 1936." *Physical Education* 7 (1936).

Olympic Games (11th: 1936: Berlin, Germany). Organisationskomitee für die Spiele der XI. Olympiade. *The XIth Olympic Games, Berlin, 1936: Official Report.* Vol. 1. Berlin: Wilhelm Limpert, 1937.

Olympic Games (11th: 1936: Berlin, Germany). Organisationskomitee für die Spiele der XI. Olympiade. *The XIth Olympic Games, Berlin, 1936: Official Report.* Vol. 2. Berlin: Wilhelm Limpert, 1936.

Pollock, James K., Jr. "The German Reichstag Elections of 1930." *The American Political Science Review* 24 (1930).

Rosenthal, Jack. "Canadian Jewish Youth Centres." *Y.M.H.A. Beacon* 10, no. 11 (May 1935).

Rushbrooke, J.H. *Fifth World Congress, Berlin August 4–10. Official Report.* London; Baptist World Alliance, 1934.

St Germain, Ralph. "Olympic Fact and Friction." *Newsletter for the Phi Kappa Alumna Society, McGill Chapter* (April, 1936).

United Nations War Crimes Commission, *Law Reports of Trials of War Criminals.* London: His Majesty's Stationary Office, 1947.

Walk, Joseph, ed. *Das Sonderrecht für die Juden im NS-Staat.* Heidelberg: Müller Juristischer Verlag, 1981.

Washke, Paul R. "The Eleventh Olympiad." *Journal of Health and Physical Education* 7 (1936).

Secondary Sources

Abella, Irving, and Harold Troper. *None Is Too Many: Canada and the Jews of Europe, 1933–1948.* Toronto: Lester, Orpen and Dennys, 1982.

Abgrall, Fabrice, and François Thomazeau. *La France à l'épreuve des jeux Olympiques de Berlin.* Paris: Alvik, 2006.

Abrams, Alan. *Why Windsor? An Anecdotal History of the Jews of Windsor and Essex County.* Windsor, ON: Black Moss Press, 1981.

Avakumovic, Ivan. *The Communist Party in Canada: A History.* Toronto: McClelland and Stewart, 1975.

— *Socialism in Canada: A Study of the CCF-NDP in Federal and Provincial Politics.* Toronto: McClelland and Stewart, 1978.

Ayre, John. "Berlin, 1936: Canadian Dancers at Hitler's Olympics." *The Beaver* 76 (February–March, 1996).

Bachrach, Susan D. *The Nazi Olympics: Berlin 1936.* Boston: Little Brown, 2000.

Ballem, Charles. "Missing From the Canadian Sport Scene: Native Athletes." *Canadian Journal of History of Sport* 14 (1983).

Barkai, Avraham. *From Boycott to Annihilation: The Economic Struggle of German Jews, 1933–1943.* Boston: Brandeis, 1990.

Barney, Robert K, Malcolm Scott, and Rachel Moore, "'Old Boys' at Work and Play': The International Olympic Committee and Canadian Co-option, 1928–1926." *Olympika* 8 (1999).

Beeching, William C. *Canadian Volunteers: Spain 1936–1939*. Regina, SK: University of Regina Press, 1989.

Beer, Max. "'What Else Could We Have Done?': The Montreal Jewish Community, the Canadian Jewish Congress, the Jewish Press and the Holocaust." Master's thesis, Concordia University, 2006.

Benz, Wolfgang. *A Concise History of the Third Reich*. Translated by Thomas Dunlap. Berkeley: University of California Press, 2007.

Berlioux, Monique. *Des jeux et des crimes. 1936. Le piège blanc olympique*. 2 vols. Biarritz: Atlantica, 2007.

Berton, Pierre. *The Great Depression: 1929–1939*. Toronto: Anchor, 1990.

Betcherman, Lita-Rose. *The Swastika and the Maple Leaf: Fascist Movements in Canada in the 1930s*. Toronto: Fitzhenry and Whiteside, 1975.

Bickers, Richard Townshend. *Von Richthofen: The Legend Evaluated*. Annapolis: Naval Institute Press, 1996.

Bolz, Daphné. *Les arènes totalitaires: Hitler, Mussolini et les jeux du stade*. Paris: CNRS Éditions, 2008.

Breymayer, Ursula, and Bernd Ulrich. "Commemorating Heroes: The Conflict Surrounding the Commemoration of the Dead from the First World War." In *1909 Historic Site: 1936 The Olympic Grounds 2006*, edited by Rainer Rother. Berlin: Jovis Verlag, 2006.

Brown, Michael. "Ida Siegel, 1885–1982." *Jewish Women: A Comprehensive Historical Encyclopedia*. Accessed 22 September 2012. http://jwa.org/encyclopedia/article/siegel-ida.

— "On Campus in the Thirties: Antipathy, Support and Indifference." In *Nazi German, Canadian Responses: Confronting Antisemitism in the Shadow of War*, edited by L. Ruth Klein. Montreal: McGill-Queen's University Press, 2012.

Carstensen, Christian. "Bearers of the Olympic Flame." *Journal of Health and Physical Fitness* 7 (1936).

Casanova, Julián. *The Spanish Republic and Civil War*. Cambridge: Cambridge University Press, 2010.

Ceplair, Larry. *Under the Shadow of War: Fascism, Anti-Fascism and Marxists, 1918–1939*. New York: Columbia University Press, 1987.

Chappelet, Jean-Loup, and Brenda Kübler-Mabbott. *The International Olympic Committee and the Olympic System: The Governance of World Sport*. London: Routledge, 2008.

Cook, Ramsay. *The Politics of John W. Dafoe and the Free Press*. Toronto: University of Toronto Press, 1963.

Copsey, Nigel, and Andrzej Olechnowicz, eds. *Varieties of Anti-Fascism: Britain in the Interwar Period*. London: Palgrave Macmillan, 2010.

Copsey, Nigel "'Every Time They Made a Communist, They Made a Fascist': The Labour Party and Popular Anti-Fascism in the 1930s." In *Varieties of Anti-Fascism: Britain in the Interwar Period*, edited by Nigel Copsey and Andrzej Olechnowicz. London: Palgrave Macmillan, 2010.

Davies, Alan, and Marilyn F. Nefsky. *How Silent Were the Churches? Canadian Protestantism and the Jewish Plight during the Nazi Era*. Waterloo, ON: Wilfrid Laurier University Press, 1998.

Dean, Martin. *Robbing the Jews: The Confiscation of Jewish Property in the Holocaust, 1933–1945*. New York: Oxford University Press, 2008.

Dharssi, Alta. "'A Patched Bathing Suit': Joan McLagan's Experience at the 1936 Olympics." *Zachor* (2010).

Donnelly, Murray S. *Dafoe of the Free Press*. Toronto: Macmillan, 1968.

Dost, Susanne. *Das Olympische Dorf 1936 im Wandel der Zeit*. Berlin: Verlag Bernd Neddermeyer, 2004.

Durflinger, Serge M. "'Six Thousand Tons of Fighting Apparatus': Canadian Reactions to the Visit of the Cruiser *Karlsruhe* to Vancouver, March 1935." *The Northern Mariner* 16, no. 2 (2006).

Ehrenreich, Eric. *The Nazi Ancestral Proof: Genealogy, Racial Science, and the Final Solution*. Bloomington: Indiana University Press, 2007.

Eisen, George. "The Voices of Sanity: American Diplomatic Reports from the 1936 Berlin Olympiad." *Journal of Sports History* 11 (1984).

— "Jews and Sport: A Century Retrospective." *Journal of Sport History* 26 (1999).

Epp, Stefan. "'Fighting for the Everyday Interests of Winnipeg Workers': Jacob Penner, Martin Forkin and the Communist Party in Winnipeg Politics, 1930–1935." *Manitoba History* 63 (2010).

Erenberg, Lewis A. *The Greatest Fight of Our Generation: Louis vs. Schmeling*. New York: Oxford, 2006.

Fischer, Klaus P. *Nazi Germany: A New History*. New York: Continuum, 1995.

Frager, Ruth A. *Sweatshop Strife: Class, Ethnicity and Gender in the Jewish Labour Movement of Toronto, 1900–1939*. Toronto: University of Toronto Press, 1992.

Franko, Mark. *Martha Graham in Love and War: The Life in the Work*. New York: Oxford University Press, 2012.

Friedlander, Saul. *Nazi Germany and the Jews, Volume I: The Years of Persecution 1933–1939*. New York: HarperCollins, 1997.

Frisse, Ulrich. "The 'Bystanders' Perspective: The 'Toronto Daily Star' and the Coverage of the Persecution of the Jews and the Holocaust in Canada, 1933–1945." *Yad Vashem Studies* 99 (2011).

Gellately, Robert. *Backing Hitler: Consent and Coercion in Nazi Germany*. New York: Oxford University Press, 2001.

Gewirtz, Sharon. "Anglo-Jewish Responses to Nazi Germany: The Anti-Nazi Boycott and the Board of Deputies of British Jews." *Journal of Contemporary History* 26 (1991).

Giesbrecht, Jodi. "Accommodating Resistance: Unionization, Gender and Ethnicity in Winnipeg's Garment District." *Urban History Review* 39, no. 4 (2010).

Gordon, Alan. "Lest We Forget: Two Solitudes in War and Memory." In *Canadas of the Mind: the Making and Unmaking of Canadian Nationalism in the 20th Century*, edited by Norman Hillmer and Adam Chapnick. Montreal: McGill-Queen's University Press, 2007.

Gottlieb, Moshe. "The Berlin Riots of 1935 and their Repercussions in America." *American Jewish Historical Quarterly* (1970).

Graml, Hermann. *Antisemitism in the Third Reich*. Oxford: Blackwell, 1992.

Grenke, A. "From Dreams of the Worker State to Fighting Hitler: The German-Canadian Left from the Depression to the End of World War II." *Labour/Le travail* (1995).

Guttmann, Allen. *The Olympics: A History of the Modern Games*. Urbana: University of Illinois Press, 1992.

Hall, M. Ann. *The Girl and the Game: A History of Women's Sports in Canada*. Toronto: Broadview Press, 2002.

Harkness, Ross. *J.E. Atkinson of the Star*. Toronto: University of Toronto Press, 1963.

Hayes, Geoffrey, Andrew Iarocci, and Mike Bechthold, eds. *Vimy Ridge: A Canadian Reassessment*. Waterloo, ON: Wilfrid Laurier University Press, 2007.

Heron, Craig. *The Canadian Labour Movement: A Short History*. 2nd ed. Toronto: Lorimer, 1996.

Hilberg, Raul. *The Destruction of the European Jews*. Chicago: Quadrangle Books, 1961.

Hilton, Christopher. *Hitler's Olympics: The 1936 Berlin Olympic Games*. Stroud, UK: Sutton Publishing, 2008.

Hoberman, John M. *The Olympic Crisis: Sport, Politics and the Moral Order*. New Rochelle, NY: Aristide D. Caratzas, 1986.

Hughes, Richard. *Netting Out Basketball: The Remarkable Story of the McPherson Refiners, the First Team to Dunk, Zone Press, and Win the Olympic Gold Medal*. Victoria, BC: Friesen Press, 2011.

Kage, Joseph. *With Faith and Thanksgiving*. Montreal: Eagle, 1962.

Kanin, David B. *A Political History of the Olympic Games*. Boulder: Westview Press, 1981.

Kaplan, Marion A. *Between Dignity and Despair: Jewish Life in Nazi Germany*. New York: Cambridge University Press, 1998.

Kealey, Gregory S. "Stanley Brehaut Ryerson: Canadian Revolutionary Intellectual." *Studies in Political Economy: A Socialist Review* 9 (1982).

— "State Repression of Labour and the Left in Canada, 1914–20: The Impact of the First World War." *Canadian Historical Review* 73 (1992).

Kidd, Bruce. "Canadian Opposition to the Olympics in Germany." *Canadian Journal of the History of Sport* 9, no. 2 (1978).

— *Tom Longboat*. Toronto: Fitzhenry and Whiteside, 1992.

— "The First COA Presidents." *Olympika* 3 (1994).

— *The Struggle for Canadian Sport*. Toronto: University of Toronto Press, 1997.

Kiein, L. Ruth, ed. *Nazi Germany, Canadian Responses: Confronting Antisemitism in the Shadow of War*. Montreal: McGill-Queen's University Press, 2012.

Krüger, Arnd. "Breeding, Bearing and Preparing the Aryan Body: creating Supermen the Nazi Way." In *Shaping the Superman: Fascist Body as Political Icon – Aryan Fascism*, edited by J.A. Mangon. London: Frank Cass, 1999.

Krüger, Arnd, and William Murray, eds. *The Nazi Olympics: Sport, Politics, and Appeasement in the 1930s*. Urbana: University of Illinois Press, 2003.

Large, David Clay. *Nazi Games: The Olympics of 1936*. New York: W.W. Norton, 2007.

Levine, Allan. *Coming of Age: A History of the Jewish People of Manitoba*. Winnipeg: Heartland, 2009.

Levine, Peter. *Ebbets Field: Sport and the American Jewish Experience*. New York: Oxford University Press, 1992.

Levitt, Cyril H., and William Shaffir. *The Riot at Christie Pits*. Toronto: Lester and Orpen Dennys, 1987.

Levy, Joseph, and Avi Hyman. "Fanny 'Bobbie' Rosenfeld: Canada's Woman Athlete of the Half Century." *Journal of Sport History* 26 (1999).

Lewy, Guenter. *The Nazi Persecution of the Gypsies*. New York: Oxford University Press, 2000.

Lipinsky, Jack. *Imposing Their Will: An Organizational History of Jewish Toronto, 1933–1948*. Montreal: McGill-Queen's University Press, 2011.

Lipstadt, Deborah E. *Beyond Belief: The American Press and the Coming of the Holocaust, 1933–1945*. New York: Free Press, 1986.

Longreich, Peter. *Holocaust: The Nazi Persecution and Murder of Jews*. Oxford: Oxford University Press, 2010.

Lovasz, Bastian Bryan. "Animosity, Ambivalence and Cooperation: Manifestations of Heterogeneous German Identities in the Kitchener-Waterloo Area During and After the Second World War." Master's thesis, University of Waterloo, 2008.

Luftspring, Sammy, with Brian Swarbrick. *Call Me Sammy*. Scarborough, ON: Prentice Hall of Canada, 1975.

MacDonald, Robb. "The Battle of Port Arthur: The War of Words and Ideologies within the Canadian Olympic Committee." In *Proceedings of the First*

International Symposium for Olympic Research. London, ON: University of Western Ontario Centre for Olympic Studies, 1992.

Majer, Diemut. *"Non-Germans" Under the Third Reich*. Translated by Peter Thomas Hill, Edward Vance Humphrey, and Brian Levin. Baltimore: Johns Hopkins University Press, 2003.

Mandell, Richard D. *The Nazi Olympics*. New York: Macmillan, 1971.

Manley, John. "'Communists Love Canada!': The Communist Party of Canada, the "People" and the Popular Front, 1933–1939." *Journal of Canadian Studies* 36, no. 4 (2002).

— "Moscow Rules? 'Red' Unionism and 'Class against Class' in Britain, Canada, and the United States, 1928–1935." *Labour/Le travail* 56 (2005).

McQuarrie, Florence A.E. "The Struggle over Worker Leisure: An Analysis of the History of the Workers' Sports Association in Canada." *Canadian Journal of Administrative Sciences* 27 (2010).

Micham, Samuel W., Jr. *Eagles of the Third Reich: Men of the Luftwaffe in WWII*. Mechanicsberg, PA: Stackpole Books, 2007.

Moore, Katharine. "'The Warmth of Comradeship': The First British Empire Games and Imperial Solidarity." *International Journal of the History of Sport* 6 (1989).

Mount, Graeme S. *Canada's Enemies: Spies and Spying in the Peaceable Kingdom*. Toronto: Dundurn, 1993.

Niegarth, Kirk. "'Fight for Life': Dave Kashtan's Memories of Depression-Era Communist Youth Work." *Labour/Le Travail* 56 (2005).

O'Bonsawin, Christine M. "'An Indian Atmosphere': Indian Policy and Canadian Participation in Berlin's Internationale Tanzwettspiele." Paper presented at Cultural Relations Old and New: The Transitory Olympic Ethos, Seventh International Symposium for Olympic Research, Los Angeles, 2004.

— "Spectacles, Policies and Social Memory: Images of Canadian Indians at World Fairs and Olympic Games." PhD diss., University of Western Ontario, 2006.

Opdenhövel, Patrick. *Die kanadisch-deutschen Beziehungen in der Zwischenkriegszeit: Handels- und Aussenpolitik*. Frankfurt: Peter Lang, 1993.

Paton, Garth A. "James G.B. Merrick (1871–1946): Sports Organizer, Negotiator, Canada's Second IOC Member." In *Proceedings of the 8th International Symposium for Olympic Research*. London, ON: University of Western Ontario Center for Olympic Studies, 2006.

Payne, Stanley G. *Spain's First Democracy: The Second Republic, 1931–1936*. Madison: University of Wisconsin Press, 1993.

Petrou. Michael. *Renegades: Canadians in the Spanish Civil War*. Vancouver: University of British Columbia Press, 2008.

Petryshym, J. "Class Conflict and Civil Liberties: The Origins and Activities of the Canadian Labour Defense League, 1925–1940." *Labour/Le travail* 10 (1982).

Pitsula, James M. "The Nazi Olympics: A Reinterpretation." *Olympika* 13 (2004).
— "Strange Salute." *The Beaver* 84, no. 4 (August–September 2004).
Pujadas, Xavier, and Carles Santacana. "The Popular Olympic Games, Barcelona, 1936: Olympians and Antifascists." *International Review for the Sociology of Sport* 27 (1992).
Rippon, Anton. *Hitler's Olympics: The Story of the 1936 Nazi Games.* South Yorkshire: Pen and Sword, 2006.
Robin, Martin. *Shades of the Right: Nativist and Fascist Politics in Canada, 1920–1940.* Toronto: University of Toronto Press, 1992.
Rome, David. *Our Archival Record of 1933: Hitler's Year.* Montreal: National Archives of Canadian Jewish Congress, 1976.
— *The Congress Archival Record of 1934.* Montreal: National Archives of Canadian Jewish Congress, 1976.
— *Jewish Archival Record of 1935.* Montreal: National Archives of Canadian Jewish Congress, 1976.
— *The Jewish Congress Archival Records of 1936.* Montreal: National Archives of Canadian Jewish Congress, 1978.
Rosenberg, Louis. *Canada's Jews: A Social and Economic Study of Jews in Canada in the 1930s.* Montreal: CJC Bureau of Social and Economic Research, 1939.
Roxborough, Henry. *Canada at the Olympics.* 3rd ed. Toronto: McGraw-Hill Ryerson, 1975.
Rürup, Reinhard, ed. *1936: Die Olympischen Spiele und der Nationalsozialismus: eine Dokumentation* (1936: The Olympic Games and national socialism: A documentation), 2nd ed. Berlin: Argon, 1999.
Schleunes, Karl. *The Twisted Road to Auschwitz: Nazi Policy Toward German Jews, 1933–1939.* Urbana: University of Illinois Press, 1970.
Schulman, Avi M. *Like a Raging Fire: A Biography of Maurice N. Eisendrath.* New York: UAHC Press, 1993.
Shapiro, Edward S. "The World Labor Athletic Carnival of 1936: An American Anti-Nazi Protest." *American Jewish History* 74 (1985).
Shea, Kevin. "John 'Johnny' Loaring: Windsor Athlete Par Excellence." *Windsor Life Magazine* (May/June, 2009).
Speisman, Stephen A. *The Jews of Toronto: A History to 1937.* Toronto: McClelland and Stewart, 1977.
Steedman, Mercedes. "The Promise: Communist Organizing in the Needle Trades, the Dressmakers' Campaign, 1928–1937." *Labour/Le travail* 34 (1994).
Studniberg, Robin Elise. "'One Shudders to Think What Might Happen to German Jewry': Vancouver Newspapers and Canadian Attitudes towards Nazi Antisemitism." Master's thesis, University of British Columbia, 2011.
Tafler, Sid. *Us and Them: A Memoir of Tribes and Tribulations.* Victoria, BC: NETBC, 2006.

Techko, Tony, and Carl Morgan. *The Olympians Among Us: Celebrating a Century of Excellence*. Tecumseh, ON: TravelLife Publishing Enterprises, 1995.

Thacker, Toby. *Joseph Goebbels: Life and Death*. London: Palgrave Macmillan, 2009.

Thompson, John Herd, and Allen Seager. *Canada 1922–1939: Decades of Discord*. Toronto: McClelland and Stewart, 1985.

Troper, Harold. "Jews and Canadian Immigration Policy: 1900–1950." In *The Jews of North America*, edited by Moses Rischin. Detroit: Wayne State University Press, 1987.

Tulchinsky, Gerald. "'Justice and Only Justice Thou Shalt Pursue': Considerations on the Social Voice of Canada's Reform Rabbis." In *Religion and Public Life in Canada: Historical and Comparative Perspectives*, edited by Margaret van Die. Toronto: University of Toronto Press, 2001.

— *Canada's Jews: A People's Journey*. Toronto: University of Toronto Press, 2008.

Wagner, Jonathan F. *Brothers Beyond the Sea: National Socialism in Canada*. Waterloo, ON: Wilfrid Laurier University Press, 1981.

Walker, James. "Claiming Equality for Canadian Jewry: The Struggle for Inclusion, 1930–1945." In *Nazi Germany, Canadian Responses: Confronting Antisemitism in the Shadow of War*, edited by L. Ruth Klein. Montreal: McGill-Queen's University Press, 2012.

Wenn, Stephen R. "A Tale of Two Diplomats: George S. Messersmith and Charles H. Sherrill on Proposed American Participation in the 1936 Olympics." *Journal of Sports History* 16 (1989).

Wong, John. "Sports Networks on Ice: The Canadian Experience at the 1936 Olympic Hockey Tournament." *Sport History Review* 34, no. 2 (2003).

Worrall, James. *My Olympic Journey: Sixty Years with Canadian Sport and the Olympic Games*. Toronto: Canadian Olympic Committee, 2000.

Wright, Robert A. *A World Mission: Canadian Protestantism and the Quest for a New International Order, 1918–1939*. Montreal: McGill-Queen's University Press, 1991.

Young, Robert J. "Hitler's Early Critics: Canadian resistance at the 'Winnipeg Free Press.'" *Queen's Quarterly* 106, no. 4 (1999).

Young, Walter D. *The Anatomy of a Party: The National CCF, 1932–6*. Toronto: University of Toronto Press, 1969.

Zuehlke, Mark. *The Gallant Cause: Canadian in the Spanish Civil War, 1936–1939*. Toronto: Wiley, 2007.

Index

Aberdare, Lord (British Olympic Committee), 56

Aboriginal participation in Canadian amateur sport, 22, 25–6

Action against War and Fascism (CLAWF journal), 53

Ahearne, Bunny (British hockey team), 132

All-German Sports Competition (Berlin 1937), 215

Amateur Athletic Union (US), 33, 56, 62, 74, 108, 109–10, 161–3

Amateur Athletic Union of Canada (AAUC), 6, 21, 23, 24, 26, 27, 63, 117, 167; Alberta resolution, 58–60; boycott of Nazi Games, 33–4, 58–9, 67, 68–9, 74, 75, 87–8, 90–1, 95, 100, 105, 203; decision to go to 1936 Olympics, 87–91, 94, 95, 96–106, 107, 109; funding issues, 127; issues of amateur status, 106, 135; Ontario branch (OAAU), 121, 165; ruling on athlete delegation to the Soviet Union, 76, 98; Winnipeg, 90. *See also* Canadian Olympic Committee (COC).

Amateur Code, 21

amateur sport in Canada, 24–7, 68–9, 89, 117, 158

amateur status of Olympic athletes, 69, 19, 21, 106, 127–8, 135

American athletes, and Olympic participation, 117–21

American Jewish athletes, 56

American Jewish Committee, 118

American Jewish Congress, 56, 62, 118

American Jewish organizations, 118–20

American Jews, opposition to Nazi Olympics, 32–3, 55, 56, 58, 62

American League against War and Fascism, 46, 118

American Olympic Committee (AOC), 139; antisemitism in Berlin, 194; boycott of Moscow Summer Games (1980), xii; and Nazi Olympic boycott campaign, 33, 56, 58, 59, 161, 195. *See also* United States.

Amsterdam Summer Games (1928), 25

Amsterdam World Congress against (Imperialist) War (1932), 44

Amyot, Frank (Canadian canoeist), 197

anti-apartheid protests, xi